ANXIETY MUTED

Anxiety Muted

AMERICAN FILM MUSIC IN A SUBURBAN AGE

Edited by Stanley C. Pelkey II
and Anthony Bushard

OXFORD
UNIVERSITY PRESS

OXFORD

UNIVERSITY PRESS

Oxford University Press is a department of the University of Oxford.
It furthers the University's objective of excellence in research, scholarship,
and education by publishing worldwide.

Oxford   New York
Auckland   Cape Town   Dar es Salaam   Hong Kong   Karachi
Kuala Lumpur   Madrid   Melbourne   Mexico City   Nairobi
New Delhi   Shanghai   Taipei   Toronto

With offices in
Argentina   Austria   Brazil   Chile   Czech Republic   France   Greece
Guatemala   Hungary   Italy   Japan   Poland   Portugal   Singapore
South Korea   Switzerland   Thailand   Turkey   Ukraine   Vietnam

Oxford is a registered trademark of Oxford University Press
in the UK and certain other countries.

Published in the United States of America by
Oxford University Press
198 Madison Avenue, New York, NY 10016

Library of Congress Cataloging-in-Publication Data
Anxiety muted : American film music in a suburban age / edited by Stanley C. Pelkey II
and Anthony Bushard.
pages cm
Includes bibliographical references and index. ISBN 978–0–19–993615–1 (hardcover :
alk. paper) — ISBN 978–0–19–993617–5 (pbk. : alk. paper)
1. Motion picture music—United States—History and criticism.
2. Television music—United States—History and criticism.   3. Suburban life in popular culture—United
States.   I. Pelkey, Stanley C., editor of compilation.   II. Bushard, Anthony, 1974– editor of compilation.
ML2075.A595 2014
781.5'420973—dc23

9 8 7 6 5 4 3 2 1
Printed in the United States of America
on acid-free paper

Contents

Figures, Tables, and Musical Examples

TABLES

MUSICAL EXAMPLES

Acknowledgments

THIS PROJECT HAS been taking shape since we first met while giving papers at the Great Lakes/Great Plains Super Regional Conference of the College Music Society at Illinois State University (Normal, Illinois) in March 2008. The process has taken longer than we had originally anticipated, but we share a sense of mutual gratitude for the work that each has put into preparing this collection and for the tenacity to see it to completion.

We also owe much gratitude to our contributors, who have partnered with us, answered our many questions, and worked with us at every stage of the collection's development, all with patience and fortitude. On their behalf, we also thank the librarians and staff at the various libraries and collections that we and our contributors depended upon while researching our topics. Hearty thanks, too, to the colleagues at all of our academic institutions who have read and commented on sections of the book, to the anonymous readers who provided timely and helpful responses to the initial draft of the project while it was under consideration by Oxford University Press, and to Norman Hirschy, our editor at Oxford, who believed in this collection from early on, waited patiently as we wrote and edited, and never failed to provide advice and guidance when needed.

Finally, and most importantly, we thank our families for giving us the time and support to bring this project to fruition.

Stanley C. Pelkey II
Rochester, New York

Anthony Bushard
Lincoln, Nebraska

With gratitude to Boosey & Hawkes for permission to quote from published compositions by Aaron Copland; to Hal Leonard Corporation for permission to reprint musical excerpts from *High Noon* and *The Fly*; and to WB Music Corp. for permission to reprint musical excerpts from *The Bad Seed*:

Quiet City by Aaron Copland
© Copyright 1941 by The Aaron Copland Fund for Music, Inc. Copyright Renewed.
Boosey & Hawkes, Inc. Sole Licensee. Reprinted by permission.

Concerto for Piano and Orchestra by Aaron Copland
© Copyright 1929 by The Aaron Copland Fund for Music, Inc. Copyright Renewed.
Boosey & Hawkes, Inc. Sole Licensee. Reprinted by permission.

Piano Variations by Aaron Copland
© Copyright 1932 by The Aaron Copland Fund for Music, Inc. Copyright Renewed.
Boosey & Hawkes, Inc. Sole Licensee. Reprinted by permission.

Piano Sonata by Aaron Copland
© Copyright 1942 by The Aaron Copland Fund for Music, Inc. Copyright Renewed.
Boosey & Hawkes, Inc. Sole Licensee. Reprinted by permission.

Piano Fantasy by Aaron Copland
© Copyright 1957 by The Aaron Copland Fund for Music, Inc. Copyright Renewed.
Boosey & Hawkes, Inc. Sole Licensee. Reprinted by permission.

High Noon (score)
Music by Dimitri Tiomkin
Copyright © 1952 Volta Music Corp. Copyright renewed
All Rights Controlled and Administered by Universal Music Corp.
All Rights Reserved. Used by Permission
Reprinted by Permission of Hal Leonard Corporation.

The Fly. Words and Music by Howard Shore.
Copyright © 1986 Brooksfilms Music.
All Rights Reserved. Used by Permission.
Reprinted with Permission of Hal Leonard Corporation.

The Bad Seed
By Alex North
© 1956 (Renewed) WB Music Corp. (ASCAP)
All Rights Reserved.

Contributors

The Editors

Stanley C. Pelkey II completed his MA and PhD degrees in Musicology and his MA in History at the University of Rochester. Dean of the School of Liberal Arts and Sciences at Roberts Wesleyan College (Rochester, New York), he was previously an Associate Professor at Western Michigan University (2005–2012) where he taught undergraduate and graduate courses on music history and theory, film music, and non-Western music.

Co-editor of *Music and History: Bridging the Disciplines* (University Press of Mississippi, 2005), Pelkey has also published articles in *The New Grove Dictionary of Music and Musicians*, *The New Catholic Encyclopedia 2011 Supplement*, and *The Early Keyboard Journal*, as well as reviews in *The American Historical Review*, *Music Reference Services Quarterly*, and *Choice: Current Reviews for Academic Libraries*. His work on film and television music has appeared in *Buffy, Ballads, and Bad Guys Who Sing: Music in the Worlds of Joss Whedon* (Scarecrow Press, 2010) and *Movies in American History: An Encyclopedia* (ABC-CLIO, 2011).

Anthony Bushard earned MM and PhD degrees in Musicology from the University of Kansas. He is currently an Associate Professor of Music History at the University of Nebraska, Lincoln, where he teaches courses in film music history/analysis, jazz history, American music, world music, and an introduction to undergraduate studies for first-year students.

His work on film music and sociopolitical undercurrents of the 1950s has been featured in *The Journal of Film Music*, *Studies in Musical Theatre*, and the *College Music Symposium*, and he has published a monograph for the Scarecrow Film Score

Guide Series on Leonard Bernstein's score for *On the Waterfront* (2013). He also contributed the chapter on "Film Music" to Craig Wright's *Listening to Music*, 6th–7th ed., and has published reviews in *Notes*, the *Journal of Music History Pedagogy*, the *Journal of the Society for American Music*, and *American Music*.

Contributors

Christina Gier completed her PhD in Musicology from Duke University and is currently an Assistant Professor of Musicology at the University of Alberta. She researches gender and music through the lens of identity and subjectivity and focuses on different aspects of European and American early twentieth-century music, including film music. She is currently working on a book about the musical practices of American civilians and soldiers during World War I and how songs shaped ideas of identity, gender, and race. She has also published articles on the modernist aesthetics of Alban Berg.

Samantha London is a graduate student in the Arts Journalism program at the University of Southern California and a recipient of the University's Annenberg Fellowship. Prior to beginning her studies at USC, she completed her BM in Piano Performance from the University of Michigan and her MM at Western Michigan University. In her current work, London examines classical music from a writer's perspective, assessing how it functions today and seeking paths it might pursue in the future.

Joshua Neumann is a PhD candidate in Musicology and a College of Fine Arts Humanities Teaching Fellow at the University of Florida. Neumann's research focuses on the evolution of operatic performance practice. His dissertation analyzes the evolution of these traditions in Puccini's *Turandot* at the Metropolitan Opera. In addition to performance studies, he is interested in the interface of operatic and film music, society, and politics and has presented papers at international and regional conferences. He has taught high school music and has worked in opera administration and as a conductor since completing his MM in Music History from the University of Nebraska, Lincoln.

Jesse Schlotterbeck is an Assistant Professor of Cinema at Denison University. He received his PhD in Film Studies from the University of Iowa, where he wrote a dissertation that surveys the musical biopic from the 1960s to the present. In addition to work on the American cinema and film genre, he studies documentaries and the relationship between film and other media. His work has been published in *Scope: An Online Journal of Film and Television Studies*, *M/C—A Journal of Media and Culture*, and *The Journal of Popular Film and Television*.

Linda K. Schubert writes about film scores, particularly those for history films made in Hollywood. Working frequently with archival material, she studies the original contexts of these scores, the circumstances under which they were composed, and the shifting layers of meaning they accrue over time. Her articles have appeared in German, Canadian, and U.S. publications; she is a member of the editorial board for *The Journal of Film Music* and a former editor for *The Polish Music Journal*. She holds a PhD in Musicology from the University of Michigan; a former lecturer at the University of Southern California, she currently teaches in the University of Wisconsin system and for Anderson University (Indiana).

Meghan Schrader completed her MA in Music at the University of New Hampshire. She has presented papers at annual conferences of The Society for Disability Studies, as well as at the 2011 Mid-Atlantic American and Popular Culture Association Conference and the 2012 Society for American Music Conference. Her research explores the intersection of music, cultural representations and attitudes toward disability, particularly in film, and social justice.

Joanna Smolko has taught at Athens Technical College (Athens, Georgia) and the University of Georgia. She completed her PhD in Musicology at the University of Pittsburgh, where she worked in the Center for American Music. She was co-editor of *Stephen Collins Foster: Sixty Favorite Songs* (Mel Bay, 2009), and she has served as a contributing editor for the *New Grove Dictionary of American Music*, 2nd ed. (Oxford University Press, 2013).

Tim Smolko completed his MLS at the University of Pittsburgh and his MA in Musicology from the University of Georgia, and he currently works as a Monographs Original Cataloger in the Main Library at the University of Georgia. He is the author of *Jethro Tull's Thick as a Brick and A Passion Play* (Indiana University Press, 2013).

Christopher D. Stone received his PhD from Indiana University and is currently an Assistant Professor of History at the University of Wisconsin-Manitowoc. He has published essays and reviews in *Film & History*, *OAH Magazine of History*, *Indiana Magazine of History*, and the *Southwest Historical Quarterly*. He is currently writing on representations of the Sixties in American cinema.

Mariana Whitmer directs special projects at the Center for American Music at the University of Pittsburgh, where she also teaches a course on music and film, and she is Executive Director of the Society for American Music. Whitmer completed a Scarecrow Film Score Guide on Jerome Moross's score for *The Big Country* (2012) and contributed an essay to *Music in the Western* (Routledge, 2010). She co-edited a special issue of *American Music* on Stephen Foster, including her article "Josiah Kirby Lilly and the Foster Hall Collection," and she is currently working on a monograph about the classic Hollywood Western film score.

Reba Wissner completed her MFA and PhD degrees in Musicology at Brandeis University, where she wrote a dissertation on Francesco Cavalli's opera *Elena*. She is the author of several articles, has presented papers at conferences throughout the United States and Europe, and was the recipient of a dissertation research grant from the Andrew W. Mellon Foundation. Her book, *A Dimension of Sound: Music in The Twilight Zone* (2013), was recently published by Pendragon Press.

ANXIETY MUTED

1 A Survey of History, Themes, and Trends

STANLEY C. PELKEY II

Time and Place

THIS COLLECTION PROCEEDS from the shared perspective that film music (like film) provides "evidence of the discourses, attitudes and values" in society[1] and captures the "mood and tone" of an era.[2] While others have addressed film, its music, and history within particular genres or the work of certain directors or composers, our contributors focus on motion picture culture (including film and television) in the United States from 1950 to 1970, as well as in more recent audiovisual texts that recreate or reflect upon the Fifties and Sixties.[3]

Public and private life in the United States was transformed during the 1950s and 1960s, as were the themes, surfaces, and stories of film, television, and music. The baby boom, rapid growth of suburbs, expanding economy, and rise of service industries, commercial television, and modern approaches to advertising are some of the factors that changed America. Furthermore, the start of the Cold War (1945–1991), the hearings of the House Committee on Un-American Activities (HUAC, 1938–1975) into Hollywood (beginning in 1947), and the Hollywood Antitrust Case of 1948 (the "Paramount Decree")[4] marked a new era of motion picture culture, as we discuss further in chapters 2, 3, and 4. It concluded as the increasingly realistic treatment of sexuality and violence resulted in the modern ratings system replacing the Motion Picture Production Code.[5] Motion picture culture of the 1970s bears witness to the "hollowing out" of American civic life, the result of "sustained decline" in community involvement that began in that decade.[6] Additionally, hybridization of genres and audiovisual styles, evident by the 1980s, narrowcasting,[7] and increased viewer control over scheduling and content—first through cable and VCRs,[8] then computers, the Internet, and mobile devices—suggest we inhabit a period of motion picture culture several steps removed from that of the 1950s and 1960s.

Our contributors explore music in film and television to uncover how audiovisual media from, or related to, the 1950s and 1960s have treated anxieties about suburbanization, conformity, the family, and gender. Anxiety (muted or otherwise) and the suburban age are not the only meaningful ways to understand motion picture culture, but they provide useful critical lenses. Likewise, we recognize that music plays many roles in film and television. It represents times, places, situations, and characters; expresses emotion; narrates, interprets, contradicts, and illustrates action and relationships. It can be an object in the action, a structuring device, or a signifier of innocence, guilt, marginalization, loyalty, redemption, youth, or maturity (for example). Music can even become an "*actor* within the drama" (chapter 8), a character, or "persona" (chapter 3). Its impact on the viewer is also complex. Music becomes caught up in personal histories, identities, and perceptions, so music in film and television may draw us in, confront us, even prod us to reassess the world. Given these many roles and powers, we employ diverse critical methods and perspectives.

Limitations on time, place, and theme do not guarantee a straightforward endeavor. Film's polysemic nature undermines definitive interpretations and reception histories,[9] as does the instability of contemporary understanding of the 1950s and 1960s. Responses to social, political, and cultural changes and events were not uniform in those decades: Beat and hippie cultures countered explosive consumerism; feminism and conservatism jostled in the public square; feelings of alienation were widespread, while a chorus of critics alarmed by mass conformity created a counterpoint with those advocating all manner of liberation. Responses to the 1950s and 1960s remain contested because of such divergent values and impulses, but it may be appropriate to craft multivalent perspectives on a past more complex than we often acknowledge.[10] Indeed, during the 1950s and 1960s, American intellectuals Lewis Mumford and Norbert Wiener referred to the era as one of "shocking contradictions and tragic paradoxes" and "opposite, even contradictory trends."[11]

Differences between the 1950s/1960s (decades) and "the Fifties"/"the Sixties" (eras or concepts) reflect this multivalence and complexity. In chapter 11, Christopher Stone explains these differences more fully, noting, for example, that as an era, the Sixties is a contested site of memory consisting of "a complex mixture of fact, myth, and simplification" that can be deployed for social and political purposes. We see this whenever the political Left or Right invoke events and memories of the 1950s and 1960s, celebrating or condemning competing social forces embodied in or unleashed during those years. For example, the Right tends to view the Fifties as an era of "consensus worthy of celebration"; for the Left, it was "a low point for oppositional politics."[12]

Our chapters on film music from the 1950s and 1960s contribute to the history of those decades while becoming part of Fifties and Sixties reception history due to our own exposure to those contested sites of memory. Engagement with (and participation in) the history of the Fifties and Sixties (as eras or concepts) is even more apparent in our chapters on recent films and television programs. These began life as Fifties and Sixties audiovisual texts, but not simply because they are set in the past. To borrow Jesse Schlotterbeck's language from chapter 10, they also provide "retrospective account[s]" of past cultural practices that are themselves contested or illustrate "the compromises necessary to make . . . shameful or threatening aspects of history palatable to contemporary consumption." And Stone, exploring music in late 1980s "Sixties Postscript" films, engages the history of the Sixties because of the subject matter of those films, their employment of music from the 1960s, and the conflicted response several harbor toward that music.[13]

The lack of consensus regarding the qualities of these decades—as historical moments and cultural tropes—and all this multivalence (or ambiguity) precludes construction of definitive historical contexts that could contain or frame films, their music, and their meanings, especially in relation to broader social themes. When films are retrospective, inviting us to explore the employment of the past in contemporary storytelling,[14] we risk piling complicated reception histories onto contested interpretations of the past. Not surprisingly, we reach varied conclusions about audiovisual meanings, and our collection becomes a part of contested histories.

Exhaustive treatment of the history and meaning of 1950s and 1960s film and television music would require encyclopedic proportions. Furthermore, signs can accumulate additional signifying functions. We cannot hope, therefore, to trace all influences and echoes of 1950s and 1960s motion picture culture and its music, nor easily define the limits of Fifties and Sixties culture. The soundtrack to *WALL-E* (2008), for example, features "Put on Your Sunday Clothes" from *Hello, Dolly!* (musical, 1964; film, 1969), which emphasizes the eponymous character's longing. It also incorporates *The Blue Danube Waltz*. Alone, the waltz does not point to the 1960s, but combined with the appearance and behavior of the film's red-eyed computer "Auto," reminiscent of HAL from *2001: A Space Odyssey* (1968), it arguably echoes that film more than nineteenth-century Vienna. The potentially limitless impact of older signs and symbols and sheer volume of films and television shows from the 1950s and 1960s mean we can only open channels of inquiry with our essays. Nevertheless, as this chapter introduces those channels, it provides a wider-angle survey of history, themes, and trends.

Edith Sings: Commodifying Nostalgia

Malcolm X (1992), *Pleasantville* (1998), *Far From Heaven* (2002), *Walk the Line* (2005), *Mad Men* (2007–), *Cadillac Records* (2008), *Revolutionary Road* (2008), and *Hitchcock* (2012) markedly differ from each other yet demonstrate that signs, ideas, public figures, sounds, and music from the 1950s and 1960s saturate our audiovisual experience. What prompts this recycling? Nostalgia plays a significant role, but "rarely innocent,"[15] it requires further explanation. Two possible meanings are useful: nostalgia is the "subjective experience of an emotional state of consciousness of longing for one's own past," but twentieth-century mass media also generates "commodified nostalgia," enabling fashions and events to become "ever more widely shared experiences" and nostalgically packaging an "ever-more-recent past." As a result, film and popular music, particularly rock 'n' roll, link nostalgia and "generational solidarity," whether or not one "literally remembers the songs." All that is needed is the impression of the past brought to life.[16]

Television is a significant agent in the commodification of nostalgia and the generation of shared, but not necessarily lived, experience.[17] From almost the beginning of its broadcast history, television has recycled audiovisual texts.[18] These reruns and old films are not merely relics of a "dormant past." They form "a dynamic television heritage," anchoring the past—real and imagined—in the public mind.[19] They also reinforce knowledge of the musical past, which TV composers and producers use to communicate in a narrative form shorter than film but played within a larger broadcast "flow."[20] Rerun cable channels in the United States and Britain, such as AMC (1984–), Nick at Night (1985–), UK Gold (1992–), TCM (1994–), and TV Land (1996–), attest to the popularity of our motion picture heritage and "the dense signification of retro." Having become a "dominant cultural form," retro "recirculates the past as an array of mediated sounds and images, consumer artifacts that . . . bear the full weight of their original eras."[21] As a result, old programs may come to represent "a form of 'knowledge' about life" in the past.[22]

In this light, *Pleasantville* appropriates signs from the 1950s, but it does not gaze back on a real 1950s society. Like *Back to the Future* (1985), it constructs a model of a presumed repressive Fifties. Unlike *Back to the Future*, however, *Pleasantville* features a contemporary character enthralled by a (fictitious) 1950s television program who enters that fictional world. Thus the film self-reflexively represents the ongoing presence of 1950s motion picture culture in our lives today and identifies television—and related technological mediation, such as DVDs and streaming video—as one of the most potent agents by which nostalgia has been commodified and the Fifties has become a "site of memory."[23]

Nostalgia may drive the rebroadcasting/re-watching of 1950s and 1960s audio-visual texts, but other phenomena are also at work. Older media still provide pleasure, and their lighter treatment of sexuality and violence may also be appealing. Nevertheless, as older media helps generate collective sites of memory, it can distort perceptions of past and present. Family life in the 1950s was more complex than was represented in 1950s media, yet these simplified representations continue to be viewed. This sustains the myth of Fifties family life, the "memory" of which shapes policy debates in the United States.[24]

At the same time, contemporary recreations are not necessarily value neutral. In chapter 10, Schlotterbeck notes that our fascination with past culture often plays out through the representation of both "dystopic and utopic moments," which both "provoke and allay" our anxieties about the past. Thus in the "bizpic" *Cadillac Records*, which Schlotterbeck considers, anxieties about the "pathos" of minority experience may be muted by enjoyment of recreations of "the more transcendent achievements of their cultural production."[25] "Dystopic/utopic" recollections also occur when contemporary characters are projected into reanimations of the Fifties and Sixties through time travel (e.g., *Back to the Future*, and *Doctor Who*'s "Remembrance of the Daleks" [1988] and "The Idiot's Lantern" [2006]), technologically induced flashbacks (e.g., *Smallville*'s "Relic" [2003]), or trans-dimensional travel to a world where the Fifties never ended (e.g., *Slider*'s "Gillian of the Spirits" [1996]).

Whether offering what Stone calls a "revisit" or a "revision," biopics, bizpics, science fiction films and television episodes, and other retrospective audiovisual storytelling perform manifold work. Nostalgic romps, they may also provide a sense of self-satisfaction at "how far we've come," hold up a mirror to reveal our societal failings, or make the case that the values of the past remain "living options." Because of this last possibility, Stone contrasts filmic moments that simply look back longingly and those that foreground work still to be accomplished.

Indeed, Stone's chapter demonstrates that the representation of the Fifties and Sixties in film and television is not merely a cultural phenomenon. It is also personal and generational: real and fictional communities continue to wrestle with the ramifications of social and political change. The final moments of *The Hours* (2002), when characters from two of the narrative's temporal zones converge in the present, as well as the whole of *Julie & Julia* (2009), stress the ongoing influence of the 1950s and 1960s on personal lives today. The former film portrays intergenerational dysfunction as a significant outcome of the 1950s and 1960s, a trope evident earlier in *Pleasantville*, *Back to the Future*, and several of the films Stone considers, including *Pump Up the Volume* (1990). In that film, generational conflict between youth from the 1960s and their children in the 1980s is not limited to differing social or political values. The main character, Mark Hunter, "is both repulsed and attracted to the Sixties" and its music. Stone shows that conflict over the meaning of the Sixties even spills into recent popular music, as some lyrics suggest similar attraction to and alienation from 1960s music.

The Red Scare, McCarthyism, HUAC, and the Hollywood Blacklist touched the lives of Fred Zinnemann, Carl Foreman, Miklós Rózsa, and Elmer Bernstein, among many others. In chapters 3 and 4, Anthony Bushard and Linda Schubert, respectively, explain how structural changes in the entertainment industry and political anxieties influenced choice of stories, production and casting decisions, and even musical style in *High Noon* (1952) and *Quo Vadis* (1951). Schubert also shows Rózsa's care and attention to historical detail and the personal artistic challenge he embraced while composing *Quo Vadis*'s music. In chapter 13, Mariana Whitmer considers Bernstein's music for *Far From Heaven*; with Schubert, Whitmer highlights ways the personal can drive the recycling of past culture as creative careers take unexpected turns or return to previously tilled soil during a more welcoming age.

Before exploring the changing structures and sounds of motion picture culture in the 1950s and 1960s, let's consider nostalgia once more. Nostalgia was already a media trope before 1950s reruns became a staple of cable television or 1950s music became a signifier of rebellious youth. Ward Cleaver (Hugh Beaumont), whom I address in chapter 6, exhibited conflicted attitudes about his youth (ca. 1920s) even as he expressed positive feelings of nostalgia felt by Fifties parents through his introductory narration in early episodes of *Leave It to Beaver* (1957). Longing for and attempting to recapture one's past is also the premise, at least on the surface, of *Sunset Boulevard* (1950), the subject of Christina Gier's chapter.[26]

The performance of "Those Were the Days," the theme song to *All in the Family* (1971–1979), is one of the most memorable moments of motion picture nostalgia. First broadcast at the end of our period, the series became one of the most popular in television history. Jean Stapleton's humorous and unforgettable performance style as she sings as Edith Bunker can easily distract attention from the song's lyrics, muting their impact (Figure 1.1a). Yet the lyrics, like the series, foregrounds nostalgia and anxiety over change. Archie (Carroll O'Connor) and Edith Bunker represent the past: he, all that was wrong; she, all that was wholesome. In those other moments when Edith sings (e.g., "Edith Writes a Song" [1971]; Figure 1.1b; "Archie Sees a Mugging" [1972]), we hear her out-of-date cultural preferences, but we also witness her old-fashioned moral earnestness, regularly "shushed" by Archie, who frets about a world from which he is becoming increasingly estranged. The Bunkers inhabit a world of anxiety—muted and otherwise.

FIGURE 1.1A Edith (Jean Stapleton) and Archie (Carroll O'Connor) Bunker sing "Those Were the Days."

FIGURE 1.1B Edith's moral earnestness shines through in "Edith Writes a Song."

Changing Motion Picture Structures and Sounds

Our contributors' interest in recurring topics in motion picture culture from the 1950s and 1960s and audiovisual texts about the Fifties and Sixties is not meant to suggest that film and television have been static. Differences in subject matter and tone between just the 1950s and 1960s belie this. Indeed, with its "increased reliance on graphic visual and sound effects" and faster pacing, 1960s film culture can be understood as a "cinema of sensation" in contrast to 1950s "cinema of sentiment."[27] Narrative strategies, production styles, and production and consumption technologies continue to evolve, while the popularity of the Western, science fiction, and the musical, for example, have fluctuated.[28]

Several overarching conditions nevertheless separate motion picture culture in the suburban age from film culture of the 1930s and 1940s. The studio system's demise was one of the most significant. The Paramount Decree of 1948 forced studios to sell their theater chains. Revenues fell, a situation made worse by surging independent production and a new audiovisual mass medium.[29] Chapters 2, 3, and 4 address the impact evident in particular films.

Television's continuous availability since 1948 has transformed society, provided a baseline of cultural experience for all living in the suburban age, and been among the most decisive conditions separating the 1950s/1960s from the 1930s/1940s. The relationship between film and television was among the "fiercest cultural rivalry of the 1950s";[30] indeed the sharp decline in movie theater attendance has been blamed on the new medium.[31] Eventually, television and film drew more closely together: TV became an outlet for film libraries,[32] and Hollywood came to dominate television production.[33] Gier argues in chapter 2 that the "real life legal and economic battles" Hollywood faced were so potent *Sunset Boulevard*'s Norma Desmond (Gloria Swanson) can be read as embodying Hollywood's anxieties about aging stars, the loss of financial stability, the "dampened hopes" of its personnel, and the allure of youth in an age of advertising.

Television's influence on social life in the United States has not been limited to its impact on the film industry. While its quality as a whole and the merits of particular programs were debated, 1950s television reshaped domestic space, inspiring new home designs, furniture, mobile appliances, foods,[34] table manners, and forms of entertaining, such as the stand-up cocktail party and patio barbeque.[35] Its early programming and schedules, designed to revolve around housewives' chores,[36] reinforced prevailing attitudes about gender roles. And it has seduced generations to stay home: after simple generational change—the replacing of the highly engaged WWII generation by increasingly disengaged generations—television is the second most significant cause of the postwar collapse of civic engagement in the United States.[37]

Television also reconfigured American culture's tone. *I Love Lucy* (1951–1957), the most highly rated program at midcentury, embodied the shift from vaudeville to situation comedy then taking place.[38] The Mertzes' defunct vaudeville careers, the increasing importance of television and film for Ricky's career, particularly in season 4, and fewer performances by Desi Arnaz in later episodes mirrored the shifting cultural landscape. Television in the 1950s also provided a venue for performances of rock 'n' roll as it burst into American cultural life.[39]

Rock 'n' roll generated new vocal and instrumental performance styles while marginalizing classical, jazz, and older forms of popular music.[40] Music supervisors and composers were already expanding their palette of soundtrack sounds and styles in the 1950s. Otto Preminger's *The Man with the Golden Arm* (1955, music by Elmer Bernstein) and *Anatomy of a Murder* (1959, music by Duke Ellington) are well-known films that included jazz-inspired nondiegetic music.[41] Concurrently, Alex North, Leonard Rosenman, Bernard Herrmann, and Jerry Goldsmith, among others, incorporated modernist idioms into their scores.[42] Yet the future was with the new popular sounds,[43] and during the 1960s, rock increasingly made its way into film and television soundtracks, while its musicians joined the film industry as actors and composers.

Youth culture and advertising geared toward the youth market emerged with rock 'n' roll.[44] Gier argues in chapter 2 that youth was distinguished from age through the use of popular music as opposed to classical scoring in *Sunset Boulevard*, but Hollywood was generally slow to address emerging youth culture during the 1950s.[45] This changed in the 1960s as a global market for both television and film developed,[46] which linked popular music, social problems, and youth culture,[47] and leisure pursuits were marketed to adolescents and young adults in industrial countries.[48]

Hollywood's financial problems in the 1950s contributed to these musical (and marketing) transformations. Film and television composers faced the expectation that their music would generate revenue, especially after the commercial success of Dimitri Tiomkin and Ned Washington's "The Ballad of High Noon" from *High Noon*, which Bushard discusses in chapter 3. Studios also started record companies and publishing houses to maximize potential profits from their film music.[49] Prendergast argues that the "aesthetic effect on film music was immediate and devastating."[50] Others may not share his judgment, but it is indisputable that by the late 1960s, music supervisors were using many kinds of music for diegetic and nondiegetic purposes. The relatively tame *With Six You Get Eggroll* (1968), for example, included rock, club music, light jazz, and orchestral cues with drum set accompaniment; quotations of Handel's "Hallelujah Chorus" sanctify the film's resolution as man and woman marry, uniting their families in a new (and larger) suburban home.

Several of our chapters address the expanding use of popular music in motion picture culture. In chapter 8, Joanna Smolko and Tim Smolko consider how American popular music was purposefully employed in episodes of *The Prisoner* (1967–1968) because it represented "both individual freedom and youth." Against the backdrop of the Cold War, Vietnam, and civil rights, such music was an appropriate soundtrack as "Number Six," a British secret agent, tried to retain his individuality while imprisoned. The relatively staid *Leave It to Beaver* (chapter 6) was not immune to the pull of the popular; its final season featured a jazzed-up version of its theme song, twist and bossa nova instrumental excerpts, and more adult themes focusing on Wally (Tony Dow). In retrospect, "The Twist" is a perfect accompaniment to *Mad Men*'s depiction of "extended adolescents" navigating the "changing tides between the Fifties and Sixties," as Samantha London addresses in chapter 12. In concert with the series' visuals, it captures their angst, but also their newfound economic power, the decisive influence of their taste, and their sexual liberation.

Representations and interpretations of the past are mediated in no small part by musical soundtracks. London, Schlotterbeck, and Stone remind us that the Sixties and the music of the 1960s are inextricably linked in the collective imagination. Thus the use of that music today does much more than conjure up a particular time. Freighted with symbols and ideas, it has, as Stone notes, "immense cultural capital," which can be problematic depending on how it is employed.

Age of Anxiety: Cold War, Technology, and Politics

Alfred Hitchcock's *North by Northwest* (1959) features a memorable Saul Bass title sequence in which a skyscraper gradually takes form before viewers are drawn to street level to witness New York's nameless, jostling crowds dash to and fro (Figures 1.2a–b). The nervous, kinetic rhythms and chromatic rising neighbor tones of Bernard Herrmann's music match the movement embodied in the visuals, yet the pounding timpani, rattling tambourine, shrill flutes, and mock heroic fanfares sound rhetorically overblown. This cue makes more sense when reprised during chase sequences, but the mere directionality of the crowds in the opening does not match the dire purposefulness of characters in those chases.

Herrmann may have intended this "kaleidoscopic orchestral fandango" to evoke the "crazy dance about to take place between Cary Grant and the world,"[51] but Herrmann and Hitchcock also sonically and visually captured one of Lewis Mumford's anxiety-laden concerns regarding society and spirit in the 1950s: "The automaton and the id, the uncontrolled machine and the unconditional brute, have captured the normal sphere of the personality."[52] Order, routine, and predictability might save humankind from war and "anxiety for the future" or curse the individual to "the external, the quantitative, the measurable." Highly regulated factory life suggested the latter was the likely outcome.[53] Lyman Bryson and Norbert Wiener also fretted about factory, office, and department store workers endlessly repeating the same gesture without exercising judgment.[54] The midcentury reorganization of workers and citizens by and into machines promised security, comfort, and material success. Yet Bryson reminded readers, these "are not forever satisfactory as the end of life or of civilization";[55] even if they were, the obsession with machines threatened

FIGURES 1.2A–B *North by Northwest*: jostling crowds or the id running rampant?

to destroy the individual's "balance and wholeness," lead to passivity and isolation, overwhelm culture with images of despair, and replace democracy with mechanized fascism.[56]

Anxieties concerning technology, mechanization, and consumption persisted in the waning years of our period.[57] Jay Martin, writing in *America Now* (1968), warned that "transpersonal time systems" dictated when to eat, travel, work, and make love.[58] Martin saw this reflected in the "lonely, gray-suited, status-seeking organization man" of the Fifties,[59] an image found in *The Man in the Gray Flannel Suit* (novel, 1955; film, 1956). But Hitchcock's visuals as *North by Northwest* begins also reflect the negative repercussions of transpersonal time: the brute, the id, the mindless rushing to achieve meaningless, routinized ends, a society becoming a spirit-crushing machine rather than an association of free individuals. When the title sequence is viewed this way, Herrmann's music sounds like an anxious dance of death.

References to anxiety and alienation fill the pages of *America Now*. John G. Kirk noted Americans commonly felt that "ours is peculiarly an age of anxiety, of complex, ambiguous challenges and of dissolving certainties" as fears, insecurities, and "gnawing doubts" traumatized the national spirit.[60] While Richard Rovere (journalist, *The New Yorker*) and T. George Harris (senior editor, *Look*) identified the political and economic roots of such widespread feelings, Benjamin DeMott (professor of English, Amherst College) emphasized a misguided glorification of rugged independence in American literature and films (including better-quality Westerns). Eric Mann, representing Students for a Democratic Society, stated universities failed to prepare students for meaningful, socially beneficial employment, which fueled students' alienation, but William Jovonovich (president, Harcourt, Brace & World), contrasting collegiate dissent in the 1930s with that of the 1960s, argued alienation was a cliché, a form of nostalgia among those who felt they had been cheated out of something they believed had once existed.[61]

All this anxiety occurred during a period of economic growth,[62] yet the expansion could not dispel Cold War tensions or the existential terror nuclear weaponry inspired. It may be reductive to read Cold War anxiety into all of 1950s culture,[63] and in chapter 7, Reba Wissner notes other anxieties of the time, such as fear over the erosion of traditional social values. Nevertheless, the gloomy shadows cast by the Cold War, Communism, political paranoia, and the Bomb over American life in the 1950s and 1960s are not difficult to discern, especially when nuclear weapons were often blamed.[64] Jordan Lyman (Fredric March), the aging and unpopular President in *Seven Days in May* (1964), described the Enemy as "an age. A nuclear age. It happens to have killed man's faith in his ability to influence what happens to him."[65]

Hollywood responded to the beginning of the Cold War and conflict in Korea with several dozen anti-Communist films, but the treatment of "distrust, hatred, anxiety" infiltrated other genres,[66] as did paranoia regarding surveillance.[67] Science fiction films provide numerous examples: fears of annihilation and Communist takeover merged "in the form of invasion from outside forces," as in *The Thing* (1951).[68] In chapter 3, Bushard notes similar concerns in *High Noon* in which the repeatedly seen railway suggests danger accompanies more modern technological means.

Even when invasion was not foregrounded, anxiety about science gone wrong,[69] fallout, and the end of the world abounded. Viewers may have mentally linked these to the Cold War anyway, as Wiener suggests: "To defend ourselves against the phantom, we must look to new scientific measures, each more terrible than the last. There is no end to this vast apocalyptic spiral."[70] Thus the giant ants from *Them!* (1954), victims of home-grown accidents, such as Andre Delambre from *The Fly*

(1958), whom Meghan Schrader addresses in chapter 9, the malfunctioning computers of *Fail-Safe* (1964), and Dr. Strangelove, the "personification of scientific reason
gone amuck,"[71] are just some of the scientific/nuclear nightmares of the 1950s and
1960s, while *When Worlds Collide* (1951), its "ticking" music counting down the
hour, reflects world-ending anxieties. Cosmic chance destroys Earth, yet the movie
still depicts self-serving brutality and the collapse of community. The id running
rampant, machine anxieties, and the Cold War—they are the same nightmare. This
conjoining is poignantly seen and heard in *On the Beach* (1959), with its set pieces
that revolve around machines and technology as the world-ending repercussions
of a distant nuclear war unfold. From the movie's midpoint, random and frantic
notes on the piano and other pitched percussion create dissonant, machine-like
timbres. These join harrowing brass fanfares to intrude with increasing frequency
on the sentimental settings of "Waltzing Matilda" that otherwise fill Ernest Gold's
award-winning soundtrack. In one unaccompanied scene, the scientific horrors
leave nuclear scientist Julian Osborne (Fred Astaire) speechless: "The world went . . .
crazy . . . . And . . . And—"[72] (Figure 1.3).

Cold War paranoia touched the lives of Lucille Ball and Desi Arnaz,[73] but not *I
Love Lucy*'s plots. Ward Cleaver was a Seabee during World War II, yet he remained
mute regarding the Cold War. (Ironically *Leave It to Beaver* briefly appears on screen
during *Mad Men*'s "Meditations in an Emergency" [2008], which concerns the
Cuban Missile Crisis.) Television programming generally remained immune to the
Cold War and nuclear fears until the 1960s. Then, as the Smolkos note in chapter 8,
spy dramas, like *The Prisoner*, became increasingly popular, and Rod Serling began
to explore current political and social anxieties in *The Twilight Zone* (1959–1964), as
Wissner traces in chapter 7. Likewise, *Star Trek* (1966–1969) addressed Cold War
political tensions and nuclear fears in "A Taste of Armageddon" (1967), "The City on

FIGURE 1.3 Modern nuclear
and scientific horrors leave
Julian Osborne (Fred Astaire)
speechless.

the Edge of Forever" (1967), and "The Doomsday Machine" (1967), as did the BBC's *Doctor Who* (1963–1989) in "The Daleks" (1963–1964), "Day of the Daleks" (1972), and "Genesis of the Daleks" (1975). Despite these Cold War legacies, nuclear anxiety is less pronounced in the revived *Doctor Who* (2005–) and later *Star Trek* series.

The fear engendered by the Cold War, Communism, and the belief that American society and its institutions had been infiltrated by enemy agents plagued American society, distorted its political discourse, and shattered lives in Hollywood. Though contemporaneous with Senator Joseph McCarthy's activities, the October and November 1947 investigations into Communism in Hollywood by HUAC were a distinct response to concerns about Communist infiltration. However, the Hollywood studios created the blacklist, placed directors, actors, screenwriters, musicians, and others on it, and enforced it until the mid 1950s.[74] Lives and careers were damaged or destroyed, as Gier, Bushard, Schubert, and Whitmer address in their chapters, where additional summaries of the Red Scare, McCarthyism, and HUAC are provided.

Not surprisingly, serious social commentary in film was dampened during the 1950s.[75] When it occurred, it was often masked in the trappings of science fiction, as Wissner discusses in relation to *The Twilight Zone* in chapter 7, or displaced into America's "mythic past"[76] through Westerns, such as *High Noon* or *The Searchers* (1956). Thus, as the Smolkos address in chapter 8, *The Prisoner*'s episode "Living in Harmony" incorporated themes from *High Noon* to propel its commentary on conformity while also implicitly criticizing American military violence. The rise of biblical spectaculars, such as *Quo Vadis*, which Schubert discusses in chapter 4, *The Robe* (1953), *The Ten Commandments* (1956), and *Ben-Hur* (1959), may also be read in this context of dampened social commentary. Hollywood needed big spectacles to draw audiences back to movie theaters, and it needed safe content in an era of political conservatism.[77] Such movies have been dismissed as "cartoons of religious piety,"[78] but Schubert sees a "double-edge" to *Quo Vadis*: "It focused on a very specific group of innocent people who are accused, hunted down, and punished for a terrible crime against the state.... The makers of *Quo Vadis* were walking a fine line between support and critique of current politics."[79]

By the 1960s, the national political discourse was changing; Hollywood responded with films such as *Advise and Consent* (1962), *The Ugly American* (1963), *The Best Man* (1964), *Fail-Safe*, and *Seven Days in May*. Still gloomy and anxious, they nevertheless critiqued society and prevailing political attitudes. Several rebuked fear-mongering, McCarthy-like figures, as in the climactic confrontation between President Lyman and General Scott (Burt Lancaster) in *Seven Days*, and in the conversation about political methods in *The Best Man* between former President Hockstader (Lee Tracy) and the popular, self-serving, anti-Communist Senator Joe Cantwell (Cliff Robertson).

Of course, the surfaces of these political dramas mask other pernicious social attitudes; some suggest homosexuality is as terrifying as an impending nuclear apocalypse.[80] But we should take aspects of the political commentary and the openness to divergent opinion at face value, given the increasingly common representations of moral complication and corruption within supposedly friendly governments and their agencies in Anglosphere audiovisual texts since 1960. Differences, for example, between the 1958 and 2002 film adaptations of Graham Greene's *The Quiet American*, representations of governments in earlier versus later *Star Trek* series, increasingly negative portrayals of Time Lord civilization on *Doctor Who* during the 1970s and 1980s (its period of popularity on PBS channels), and changing musical styles and characterizations of police, their personal lives, violence, and attitudes regarding civil authority in American television police dramas between the 1950s and the 1990s[81] are all telling.

A Suburban Age: Anxiety and Conformity

Americans today live in a suburban age. Between 1950 and 1996, the number of those residing in small towns and rural areas fell from 44 percent to 20 percent of the nation's population; those in suburbs rose from 23 percent to 49 percent.[82] While many relocated from older northeastern and midwestern industrial cities to newer southern and western communities, total numbers in the central cities of the country's metropolitan areas only slumped slightly.[83]

Suburbs existed before the 1950s, but modern suburbia was something new.[84] The product of postwar social and economic forces, it transformed the spatial organization of the United States.[85] Servicemen returning from World War II married and established families as quickly as possible. The subsequent baby boom increased the need for affordable housing, already scarce before the war, which led to rapid construction of tract housing.[86] Governmental policy fueled these developments through the GI Bill and support for suburban infrastructure and transportation.[87] Businesses relocated to suburban shopping malls as more affluent populations concentrated in the suburbs and consumer tastes changed,[88] and drive-ins (and later multiplexes) began to replace downtown theaters.[89]

American culture in the 1950s and 1960s captured the new reality. Sloan Wilson's *The Man in the Gray Flannel Suit*, Max Shulman's *Rally Round the Flag, Boys!* (1957), and John Updike's *Rabbit, Run* (1960) differ in tone and substance, yet each depends upon the increasing significance of the suburbs. Early television sitcoms were often situated in suburbs, and the lure of the West was also strong.[90] During 1954–1955, Lucy and Ricky Ricardo moved to California to pursue their

Hollywood dreams; *Leave It to Beaver's* Mayfield vacillated between eastern (or midwestern) small town and West Coast suburb in later seasons; and the popular *Beverly Hillbillies* (1962–1971) was permanently situated there. More significantly, television programs' surface details provide visual evidence supporting the contention that suburbia contributed to social and civic disengagement due to increased travel and segregation.[91] Social card playing among couples or socializing women,[92] regularly featured in *I Love Lucy* and *Leave It to Beaver*, has vanished from contemporary sitcoms. So have church attendance and family dining,[93] though the latter was prominent in *I Love Lucy*, *Leave It to Beaver*, *Gilligan's Island* (1964–1967), and *All in the Family*, among other comedies.

Consensus regarding suburbia's merits, meanings, and impact on society, politics, the economy, culture, and gender remains elusive.[94] Likewise, the portrayal of suburbia in American motion picture culture has been unstable. Strongly tied to the Fifties in the "collective cultural imagination,"[95] suburbia is treated as "a self-sufficient space of the 'good life' and an alienating 'noplace,'"[96] a site for exploring "an idealized image of middle-class life and specific cultural anxieties about the very elements of society that threaten this image," though television in the 1950s and early 1960s willfully ignored "contentious social issues."[97] More recent audio-visual texts may be no more accurate, however. *Pleasantville*, *Far from Heaven*, *The Hours*, *Revolutionary Road*, *Julie & Julia*, and *The Iron Lady* (2011),[98] as well as *Mad Men*, have explored the Fifties and Sixties with a mixture of nostalgia and criticism regarding the experiences of women. But pop criticism regularly fails to represent the complexity of experiences of women (and men) trying to balance personal, interpersonal, and public demands.[99]

Nevertheless, many were critical of suburbia's influence on the American character during the 1950s and 1960s, fearing that suburbia amplified the trend toward conformity. This can be seen in films from those decades. For example, in *A Period of Adjustment* (1962), George Haverstick (Jim Hutton) compares the relative merits of a "pastoral" ranching life in West Texas with suburban existence and calls his old war chum Ralph Baitz (Anthony Franciosa) a "TV-watching, canned-beer drinking Spanish-suburban type jerk" and a "square."[100] In chapter 3, Bushard sees musical features of *High Noon* echoing underlying themes of fear, anxiety, and ambiguity, while the film as a whole puts the dangers of conformity on display and ultimately chides suburban America for its "lack of social awareness." Likewise, in chapter 9, Schrader considers suburban conformity as she investigates the relationship between "normalcy" and the monstrous in horror films, a theme also taken up in *The Twilight Zone's* "The Eye of the Beholder" and discussed by Wissner in chapter 7.[101]

Bryson acknowledged conformity existed in "many trivial details of living, in merchandise, in entertainment," yet he maintained there was still "wide choice open to any individual."[102] David Potter was more pessimistic. Abundance had determined American culture and character.[103] As new economic structures emerged, new behavioral codes and competitive systems, including "rivalry in consumption,"[104] developed, altering personality and inspiring increased conformity.[105] Borrowing David Riesman's language, Potter noted that in earlier eras, the "inner-directed" man worked for himself, subduing the environment. But in the modern era, when most work for others and "organizing and manipulating" people lead to greater wealth than would "further raids upon nature," the "'other-directed' has forged to the front."[106]

Modern advertising bore much of the blame for social change, and abundance (plus conformist consumption) was thoroughly on display on television, itself a consumer product and "an audio-visual showroom for advertisers' consumer goods."[107] Historically, churches, schools, colleges, and businesses encouraged conformity; nevertheless, Potter argued, they had "tried to improve man and to develop in him qualities of social value."[108] Advertising, contrarily, lacked "institutional responsibility," only encouraged "conformity to material values," and exploited "emulative anxieties."[109] Heavily subsidized by advertising, television programs were inducements to accept commercials, while commercials were inducements to buy products.[110] In such a system, "controversial or esoteric" aspects of life are suppressed, messages are simplified, and a "stereotype of society" is created with "all questions of social significance . . . carefully screened out."[111]

These charges persist regarding Fifties culture, yet our contemporary media fantasies may similarly project little more than a "stereotype of society." We suffer our own muted anxieties. Consider the debate regarding the nature of the economic, political, and cultural interaction between cities and suburbs. For some critics, urban spaces have become "relics from a past economy";[112] while abandoned buildings house the "worst fantasies of suburban whites," "others sit, mute and decaying."[113] It remains to be seen whether urban farming, retrofitting older (and decaying) inner suburbs, and other renewal efforts will stem the tide of decline, if not reinvent cities. In the meantime, America's urban landscape may be symptomatic of persistent, muted concern for economic and social justice.

Gender and Sexuality

Suburbia's transformation of society and the anxieties it inspired drew out other fears. During the Cold War, the family became the "'front line' of defense against treason,"[114] yet it harbored insecurities, particularly a crisis of masculinity, with negative implications for national well being.

Immediately after World War II, many fretted about the problems that service-men faced in returning to civilian life.[115] Some worried veterans would hold too high an opinion of the marketplace value of their wartime skills; others that former officers would be unable to adjust to nonleadership roles in work and society. There were also sexual questions: had life in the armed forces led to increased homosexual conduct?[116]

William Wyler's award-winning *The Best Years of Our Lives* (1946) focused on civil-ian readjustment.[117] While recognizing the film's artistic and technical achievements, Leonard Quart and Albert Auster claim it "obfuscate[d] social issues," particularly "class as a factor in American life."[118] Chopra-Gant, however, emphasizes how the film engages in "performative masculinity" or the "highly self-conscious performance of gender,"[119] thus drawing attention to the postwar crisis of masculinity. Ward Cleaver was among the returning servicemen facing an uncertain future; although his read-justment went smoothly, the post-war "performance of gender" associated with mili-tary service touched two episodes of *Leave It to Beaver*. In "Boarding School" (1958), Wally briefly considers attending a military school after Johnny, an older pupil, visits in full military dress uniform. Brassy nondiegetic quotations of "You're in the Army Now" accompany Johnny's precise movements, while a humorous woodwind version mocks Wally's attempts to emulate them. More poignantly, in "Beaver's Hero" (1959), Wally and Beaver (Jerry Mathers) are dismayed when Ward's service trunk reveals their father's wartime experience was not very "macho."

The absence of the macho and decline of manliness haunted 1950s and 1960s motion picture culture. Treated with dark humor in *Dr. Strangelove* (1964), it was no laughing matter in Hitchcock's *Strangers on a Train* (1951). Anti-Communism and concerns about homosexuality are not primary themes in *Strangers on a Train*, "but it uses these elements to help create the background of anxiety so characteristic of film noir and of Hitchcock's films in general."[120] *Rear Window* (1954), *Vertigo* (1958), *North by Northwest*, and *Psycho* (1960) also feature men caught up in the crisis of masculinity.[121] So does *Sunset Boulevard*, with Norma's "overly devoted first husband-turned-butler Max," whom Gier says "epitomizes emasculation," and Joe (William Holden), whose masculinity "suffers blows at every turn."

Early Cold War political discourse was preoccupied with and anxious about mas-culinity, fused anti-Communist, antimodernist, anti-conformist, and antihomo-sexual attitudes, and linked concerns about mass culture with fears regarding the victimization of men.[122] All may have been motivated in part by increasing female self-assertiveness and homosexual visibility.[123] Efforts at "remasculinization" in film (e.g., bare-chested Charlton Heston, Yul Brynner, William Holden, and Rock Hudson) and television (the boom in 1950s TV Westerns) are evident,[124] yet doubts remained.

At the same time, civil rights and other reform movements of the 1960s altered Americans' attitudes toward race, gender, and sexuality.[125] *Mad Men* has retrospectively captured some of these issues, especially the expanding role of women, as London discusses in chapter 12. Women's place in society was already being addressed in some 1950s films. In chapter 5, Joshua Neumann explores this in Hitchcock's *The Man Who Knew Too Much* (1956), which starred Doris Day. An actress who regularly played independent working women, Day's significance may rest more in the unusual "drive, ambition, and spunkiness" of her characters than in their sexual innocence.[126] But it was 1960s motion picture culture that began to thoroughly consider the changing moral and social landscape.[127] The youth-oriented "beach party" movies,[128] the mini-skirted, multiracial cast of *Star Trek*, the tradition-defying attitudes in films such as *The Defiant Ones* (1958), *Hud* (1963), and *Cool Hand Luke* (1967), and *All in the Family*'s unrelenting engagement with politically charged issues (e.g., blockbusting and redlining)[129] are all examples, as is William Wyler's *The Children's Hour* (1961), which placed both the challenge of women balancing family and career and lesbianism on center stage.

Nevertheless, cynicism, muted despair, and the lingering need for lasting social change are also evident in the 1960s and long after. *Cadillac Records*' retrospective exploration of how Leonard Chess, his masculinity, as Schlotterbeck explains in chapter 10, "equated with his relative success or failure as a businessman," "solidifies his status as a *man*" through his interaction with his bluesmen, and the similarities and differences between Douglas Sirk's *All That Heaven Allows* (1955) and Todd Haynes's *Far From Heaven*, which Whitmer addresses in chapter 13, suggest that the renegotiation of gender and sexuality in American society is not yet complete. Neither is the reformation of racial relations, as the treatment of race on television in recent decades attests. Dramatic representations of the City featuring "brown and black characters galore" continue to emphasize the "urban jungle," while comedic representations highlight white characters engaged in "cozy consumption."[130] These patterns are readily identifiable when contrasting *NYPD Blue* (1993–2005) or *Law & Order* (1990–2010) with *Seinfeld* (1989–1998), *Friends* (1994–2004), and even *The Big Bang Theory* (2007–). They may influence future generations' perceptions of our present and their past. Now, however, they imply that we, too, are adept at muting social anxieties in our contemporary motion picture culture.[131]

Anxiety Muted?

Discussion of music in film and television studies is, understandably, often muted: authors and intended audiences may not possess the requisite technical language to consider both music's affective and material qualities; and motion picture music itself is often muted as it is rarely designed to be the center of attention. This collection helps to ameliorate the former. Beyond that, however, our contributors are interested in how films and television programs implicitly and explicitly broadcast anxieties through music, or the ways they may attempt to emotionally mute those anxieties by covering them over with reassuringly familiar musical gestures.

For example, in chapter 14, Bushard considers the dissonant (anxiety-) muting qualities of Aaron Copland's "elegiac aesthetic," then compares these to elements in Thomas Newman's scores. Newman employs drones to create dreamy, "amplified silence," against which images of "suburban discontent" in *American Beauty* (1999) are brought into sharp relief.

Ironically, although motion picture music rarely takes the center of attention, film "mutedness" and music regularly go hand-in-hand because music has been repeatedly employed to convey things that cannot be said. The Smolkos state that "music begins where words leave off," while Gier notes that music can help "tell the story," particularly in the gaps between "speech and silence." For Norma Desmond, *Sunset Boulevard*'s aging silent film star, gesture is important as a means of acting and control. In such a filmic context, music emphasizes dramatic tension and reveals more than words say. Likewise, as Bushard shows, Tiomkin's ballad in *High Noon* anticipates action and implies much that is left unsaid. In the final chase scene on Mount Rushmore in *North by Northwest*, affective music takes on full narrating force as dialogue is suspended for several minutes. Similarly, in *The Children's Hour*, a minute-long cue, gentle but emotionally ambiguous, the first nondiegetic music since the credits, replaces dialogue and conveys multiple layers of sexual tension among teachers Martha Dobie (Shirley MacLaine) and Karen Wright (Audrey Hepburn) and the latter's boyfriend, Doctor Cardin (James Garner).

During the 1960s, sexuality continued to occupy the gap between speech and silence in American films. Directors and producers avoided censors' attention with artistic integrity by creating visual-sonic moments in which image and music communicated meaning in the absence of "damning" dialogue. Thus in *The Children's Hour*, the malicious bully Mary (Karen Balkin), her leitmotif snippets of "Skip to My Lou," tells her grandmother Amelia Tilford (Fay Bainter) that her teachers, Karen and Martha, are "unnatural." As the content of her lie becomes more intense, Mary stops speaking and whispers directly into Amelia's ear. Alex North's increasingly loud and dissonant cue mirrors Amelia's mortified expression as the meaning of the (unheard) words sinks in. Soon after, parents begin pulling their daughters from the all-girls boarding school. Stunned by the sudden exodus and unable to discover what has happened (everyone is tight-lipped), Martha finally demands that one father explain the situation. He is unwilling to speak of such things in the foyer, yet he willingly tells Karen everything when she follows him outside. Body language and gesture convey that accusations have been made, but viewers do not hear a word. Likewise, in *The Best Man*, once the opening musical and visual "processional" of presidents concludes, the musical soundtrack remains "mute" for some time. But when Joe Cantwell is left speechless after learning a former army companion claims they had a sexual relationship, it is the sudden intrusion of music that broadcasts anxiety about what former President Hockstader labels the "degenerate."

Many films had little music during the 1960s and early 1970s, and what was included often eschewed the sentimental, just as the topics addressed did. Jerry Goldsmith's score for *Seven Days in May*, for example, sparingly employs timpani, snare drum, and percussive piano. *The Boston Strangler* (1968) and *10 Rillington Place* (1971), both directed by Richard Fleischer and based on the stories of real serial killers, incorporate little music or reassuring sentiment. In the former, a split-screen technique rather than music provides the "gesture that says more than words," sometimes simultaneously providing viewers with information that characters both can and cannot yet see. The visual field's fracturing mimics the shattered psyche of Albert DeSalvo (Tony Curtis), the strangler, left mute and unable to answer as Detective Bottomly (Henry Fonda) calls his name at the film's conclusion.

Music (and sentimentality) are also absent as *The Heart is a Lonely Hunter* (1968) begins. Spiros Antonapoulos (Chuck McCann), arrested after breaking into a bakery, is deaf and mute, as is his friend, caregiver, and possibly lover, the ironically named John Singer (Alan Arkin). The film's lengthy cold start establishes that Spiros will be sent to a mental hospital; John will live nearby, waiting to hear if he will be made Spiros's custodian. The introduction concludes as Spiros's bus pulls away, while John, hurrying along beside, signs frantically. But no one is listening (or seeing). The camera zooms in on Singer's frantic hands; physical gesture takes the place of sound, but all is ineffectual (Figures 1.4a–b).

Music finally starts as the opening credits roll. Lyrical strains, almost Mozartian, on something like a harpsichord are interrupted by dissonant interludes, as if the title sequence anticipates both Mick Kelly's fascination with Mozart's music and the film's underlying societal angst. Mick (Sondra Locke) is coming of age with a disabled and unemployed father (e.g., the postwar masculinity crisis) and a mother who demolishes Mick's dreams. When Mick, a surrogate for all 1960s youth, confesses she wants to be more than ordinary, her mother replies, "We all have that feeling when we're young. It will pass."[132]

Ultimately, no one listens to the despair of any character, mute or otherwise. The film presents society's impassivity, untempered by musical utterance. Instead, music functions as a diegetic object, further highlighting the contrast between

FIGURES 1.4A–B John Singer (Alan Arkin) signs frantically but is unheard.

despair and passivity. Mick is seen sitting outside on a fire escape listening to an orchestra play Mozart's Symphony No. 41 in C Major; John cannot hear the music at all. Yet music briefly draws them together: as Mick helps John "hear" through her music-inspired physical gestures, she realizes she is not alone (Figure 1.5). Still, when it really matters, Singer has no one with whom to share his grief; the consequences are staggeringly painful (Figure 1.6). At the film's conclusion, we alone hear Mick confess her love for John Singer beside his grave, just before the opening credit music is reprised.

In chapter 3, Bushard suggests *High Noon* can be understood as something more than an allegory about Hollywood and the blacklist. It may also represent Zinnemann's "frustration with the small-mindedness of the United States

FIGURE 1.5 Mick Kelly (Sondra Locke) conducts music for John so that he can experience what she feels.

FIGURE 1.6 John is profoundly alone.

toward the rest of the world." This sentiment, perhaps uncommon in the 1950s and 1960s, was not unique as it also runs through Eugene Burdick and William Lederer's *The Ugly American* (1958). George Englund's 1963 film version peculiarly misconstrues other significant ideas in the novel, such as the power of

FIGURE 1.7 A suburban voter tunes out Ambassador MacWhite (Marlon Brando) midsentence. No one is listening . . .

support for small, local development projects rather than large-scale ones, but it retains the concern over American small-mindedness. Indeed, the closing scene is particularly pointed. As Ambassador MacWhite (Marlon Brando) makes a televised speech calling for greater efforts by the United States to combat ignorance, hunger, and disease, a viewer walks across the TV room of his suburban home, reaches for the dial, and turns off MacWhite, mid-sentence (Figure 1.7). Once again, no one is listening.

Conclusion

In our age of smartphones, tablets, and texting, it is easy to imagine that we uniquely face technologically induced social isolation. Our media, music, and digitized social and cultural mediation may be muting our awareness and willingness to respond to social need and to each other. But fear of the machine was present from the start of the suburban age. Marshall McLuhan, writing in 1970, noted that as panic over illegal drug use erupted in the United States, many believed television was leading to "stoned" viewers.[133] Yet while record numbers of viewers tuned in, the music they heard often touched upon silent anxieties that were difficult to tune out, as the chapters that follow demonstrate.

Despite ongoing changes in the production, content, and consumption of motion picture culture, Americans continue to work out concerns about security, conformity, individuality, and gender in film and television, using music to temper anxieties. This collection teases out aspects of this history during and in relation to the early decades of the suburban age.

NOTES

1. Mike Chopra-Gant, *Cinema and History: The Telling of Stories* (London: Wallflower, 2008), 2.

2. Leonard Quart and Albert Auster, *American Film and Society Since 1945*, 3rd ed. (Westport, CT: Praeger, 2002), 1–2.

3. Recent film music histories include Mervyn Cooke, *A History of Film Music* (Cambridge, UK: Cambridge University Press, 2008); James Wierzbicki, *Film Music: A History* (New York: Routledge, 2009); and Kathryn Kalinak, *Film Music: A Very Short Introduction* (Oxford: Oxford University Press, 2010). For studies on individual film composers or music in the work of particular directors, see Steven Smith, *A Heart at Fire's Center: The Life and Music of Bernard Herrmann* (Berkeley: University of California Press, 1991); Jack Sullivan, *Hitchcock's Music* (New Haven, CT: Yale University Press, 2006); Kathryn Kalinak, *How the West Was Sung: Music in the Westerns of John Ford* (Berkeley: University of California Press, 2007); and Kendra Leonard Preston, ed., *Buffy, Ballads, and Bad Guys Who Sing: Music in The Worlds of Joss Whedon* (Lanham, MD: Scarecrow Press, 2010). Genre- or media-based collections include Ron Rodman, *Tuning In: American Narrative Television Music* (New York: Oxford University Press, 2010); Janet K. Halfyard, ed., *The Music of Fantasy Cinema* (Sheffield, UK: Equinox, 2012); Neil Lerner, ed., *Music in the Horror Film: Listening to Fear* (New York: Routledge, 2010); James Deaville, ed., *Music in Television: Channels of Listening* (New York: Routledge, 2011); Kathryn Kalinak, ed., *Music in the Western: Notes from the Frontier* (New York: Routledge, 2012); and Robert Miklitsch, *Siren City: Sound and Source Music in Classic American Noir* (New Brunswick, NJ: Rutgers University Press, 2011).

4. Mike Chopra-Gant, *Hollywood Genres and Postwar America: Masculinity, Family, and Nation in Popular Movies and Film Noir* (London: I. B Tauris, 2006), 17.

5. Peter Lev, *The Fifties: Transforming the Screen, 1950–1959*, vol. 7, *History of the American Cinema* (New York: Charles Scribner's Sons, 2003), 87, 93; Paul Monaco, *The Sixties, 1960–1969*, vol. 8, *History of the American Cinema* (New York: Charles Scribner's Sons, 2001), 56–65.

6. Robert D. Putnam, *Bowling Alone: The Collapse and Revival of American Community* (New York: Simon & Schuster, 2000), 55, 72.

7. Rodman, 246–247, 258–262.

8. Hal Himmelstein, *Television Myth and the American Mind*, 2nd ed. (Westport, CT: Praeger, 1994), xi.

9. Chopra-Gant, *Cinema and History*, 21.

10. A number of scholars have noted the tensions, contradictions, and lack of consensus in these decades, which was reflected in their cultures. See, for example, Martin Halliwell, *American Culture in the 1950s* (Edinburgh: Edinburgh University Press, 2007), 3, 4, 49, 229; Chopra-Gant, *Hollywood Genres*, 5; Janet Thumin, ed., *Small Screens Big Ideas: Television in the 1950s* (London: I. B. Tauris, 2002), 6; Robert Beuka, *SuburbiaNation: Reading Suburban Landscape in Twentieth-Century American Fiction and Film* (New York: Palgrave MacMillan, 2004), 7, 235; and Miklitsch, xiv.

11. Lewis Mumford, *Art and Technics* (New York: Columbia University Press, 2000), 3; Norbert Wiener, *The Human Use of Human Beings: Cybernetics and Society* (New York: Da Capo Press, 1954), 112.

12. Halliwell, 3, 232. For additional discussion of the manner in which "the Sixties" (as well as "the Seventies" and "the Eighties") evoke complex (and contested) "political, social, and cultural associations," see Bruce J. Schulman, *The Seventies: The Great Shift in American Culture, Society, and Politics* (Cambridge, MA: Da Capo Press, 2002), xii, xvii, 1–8. Indeed, Schulman's dating of the beginning of the Seventies to 1968 (1) contrasts with those conceptions of the Sixties that extend that era into the early 1970s (see chapter 11 in this collection).

13. For related discussion of representing the past on television, nostalgia, and notions of television programs as both archives of material history and performative texts, all in connection to *Mad Men*, see Lauren M. E. Goodlad, Lilya Kaganovsky, and Robert A. Rushing, "Introduction" (1–3), and Mabel Rosenheck, "Swing Skirts and Swinging Singles: *Mad Men*, Fashion, and Cultural Memory" (161, 162, 179) in *Mad Men, Mad World: Sex, Politics, Style & the 1960s*, ed. Lauren M. E. Goodlad, Lilya Kaganovsky, and Robert A. Rushing (Durham, NC: Duke University Press, 2013).

14. Chopra-Gant, *Cinema and History*, 2.

15. Halliwell, 234.

16. David R. Shumway, "Rock 'n' Roll Sound Tracks and the Production of Nostalgia," *Cinema Journal* 38, no. 2 (1999): 36–51; 39–40.

17. Lynn Spigel, *Make Room for TV: Television and the Family Ideal in Postwar America* (Chicago: University of Chicago Press, 1992), 100.

18. See William Boddy, *Fifties Television: The Industry and Its Critics* (Chicago: University of Illinois Press, 1990), 138.

19. Derek Kompare, "I've Seen This One Before: The Construction of 'Classic TV' on Cable Television," in Thumin, *Small Screens*, 20. See also Himmelstein, xiv.

20. Rodman, 22, 33, 38–39, 52–53, 107.

21. Kompare, 19.

22. Thumin, 1.

23. Beuka also notes *Pleasantville*'s self-reflexive character but states that its use of flawed Fifties models undermines its criticism of suburbia by having us view suburbia through the "reassuring lens of hyperbolic fantasy." Beuka, 14.

24. Stephanie Coontz, *The Way We Never Were: American Families and the Nostalgia Trap* (New York: Basic Books, 2000), x, 8, 14, 23, 175. See also Joanne Meyerowitz, ed., *Not June Cleaver: Women and Gender in Postwar America, 1945–1960* (Philadelphia: Temple University Press, 1994), 1; and chapter 6 in this collection.

25. For a different reading of the appropriation of African American musical traditions, see chapter 12.

26. See also Spigel, 34.

27. Monaco, 2. Monaco and Quart and Astor (74) view *Psycho* as a cultural watershed.

28. Boddy, 72; Lev, 5.

29. Lev, 2; Monaco, 15–20; and Roy M. Prendergast, *Film Music, A Neglected Art: A Critical Study of Music in Films*, 2nd ed. (New York: Norton, 1992), 98–102.

30. Halliwell, 147.

31. See Lev, 7; Monaco, 40–41; Prendergast, 98; Spigel, 1; and Halliwell, 148–149.

32. Lev, 211.

33. Janet Wasko, "Hollywood and Television in the 1950s: The Roots of Diversification," in Lev, *The Fifties*, 137.

34. Karal Ann Marling, *As Seen on TV: The Visual Culture in Everyday Life in the 1950s* (Cambridge, MA: Harvard University Press, 1994), 188–189, 217–218, 226, 266–267. See also Spigel, 37–39, 89–91.

35. Marling, 191. The former is featured in *With Six You Get Eggroll* (1968), the latter several times in *Leave It to Beaver*.

36. Boddy, 20; Spigel, 75–78.

37. Putnam, 223, 228, 231, 237.

38. Halliwell, 155.

39. Marling, 179.

40. New popular music of the 1950s "legitimated certain sounds and marginalized others" while creating "an ever-widening middle space between 'traditional' music (taking in folk, country, vaudeville, and Broadway) and 'serious' composition . . ." Halliwell, 121–122. Many traditional forms still appeared on television in the 1950s, as *I Love Lucy* demonstrates. Such diversity is less apparent, however, on prime time television today.

41. Both films also challenged accepted norms of decency in 1950s American media.

42. Prendergast, 105, 108, 119; Cooke, 194–201.

43. Royal S. Brown, *Overtones and Undertones: Reading Film Music* (Berkeley: University of California Press, 1994), 65–66.

44. Coontz, 38, 171.

45. Lev, 63.

46. Monaco, 10.

47. Cooke, 398.

48. Monaco, 1; Marling, 51–52.

49. Monaco, 32.

50. Prendergast, 103.

51. Smith, *A Heart at Fire's Center*, 227, 392; see also Cooke, 211.

52. Mumford, 150.

53. Ibid., 9–10.

54. Lyman Bryson, *The Next America: Prophecy and Faith* (New York: Harper & Brothers, 1952), 17, 48; Wiener, 51.

55. Bryson, 17.

56. Bryson, 17; Mumford, 7; Wiener, 51.

57. Humanity's need to rebalance its relationship with machines was central to emerging environmentalism in the late 1960s and early 1970s as pollution came to be seen as another consequence of the "machine-worshipping" of Americans. Roderick Nash, "Machines and Americans," in *The Study of American Culture: Contemporary Conflicts*, ed. Luther S. Luedtke (DeLand, FL: Everett and Edwards, 1977), 115.

58. Jay Martin, "American Culture: The Intersection of Past and Present," in *America Now*, ed. John G. Kirk (New York: Antheneum, 1968), 192.

59. Ibid., 194.

60. John G. Kirk, "Introduction," in Kirk, *America Now*, xii.

61. Eric M. Mann, "Students and Their Universities" (245–256); William Jovanovich, "America Revisited: Radicalism and Alienation" (257–275); Richard Rovere, "Alienation and the Future of Democracy" (279–292); T. George Harris, "From Rugged-Individualism to Helpless-Individualism" (315–324); and Benjamin DeMott, "America the Unimagining" (325–337), in

Kirk, *America Now*. Alienation and anxiety, prominent themes in David Riesman's *The Lonely Crowd* (1950), still concerned contributors to *Culture and Social Character: The Work of David Riesman Reviewed*, ed. Seymour Martin Lipset and Leo Lowenthal (New York: The Free Press of Glencoe, 1961), in which loneliness, anxiety, and alienation were understood as indices of changing social values (43, 49). Christopher Lasch also addressed the societal impact of lingering and widespread feelings of anxiety and alienation during the 1970s and 1980s in *The Culture of Narcissism: American Life in An Age of Diminishing Expectations* (New York: W. W. Norton, 1979) and *The Minimal Self: Psychic Survival in Troubled Times* (New York: W. W. Norton, 1984).

62. Robert H. Bremner and Gary W. Reichard, eds., *Reshaping America: Society and Institutions, 1945–1960* (Columbus: Ohio University Press, 1982), x–xi; Coontz, 24; Halliwell, 2; Monaco, 5.

63. Halliwell, 2–3.

64. See Bremner and Reichard, xi; and Kirk, "Introduction," xii. According to Lasch, "In the nuclear age, survival has become an issue of overriding importance." *The Minimal Self*, 17. Having lost their faith in the future due to the threat of nuclear war and the increasing fear that they inhabited an "implacable and unmanageable environment" (58), Americans increasingly embraced a "survival mentality," which altered the character of their society and culture (60–69).

65. *Seven Days in May*, DVD, directed by John Frankenheimer (1963; Burbank, CA: Warner Home Video, 2010), 1:35:28ff.

66. Lev, 33, 51.

67. On surveillance and suburbia, see Beuka, 77–81; and Marling, 5, 14.

68. Victoria O'Donnell, "Science Fiction Films and Cold War Anxiety," in Lev, *The Fifties*, 173. For more on 1950s science fiction movies and anti-Communism, see Cooke, 186.

69. Nash, "Machines and Americans," 110–112.

70. Wiener, 128.

71. Quart and Auster, 78.

72. *On the Beach*, DVD, directed by Stanley Kramer (1959; Santa Monica, CA: MGM Home Entertainment, 2005), 1:28:15ff.

73. Susan M. Carini, "Love's Labors Almost Lost: Managing Crisis During the Reign of 'I Love Lucy,'" *Cinema Journal* 43, no. 1 (2003): 44–62; 54–58.

74. Brian Neve, "HUAC, the Blacklist, and the Decline of Social Cinema" in Lev, *The Fifties*, 65, 67, 85.

75. Neve, 67.

76. Ibid., 77.

77. Prendergast, 125.

78. Quart and Auster, 51.

79. Even today, social problems are often addressed retrospectively. See chapter 10.

80. Quart and Auster, 75–77.

81. Rodman, 231–253.

82. Putnam, 206–207.

83. For statistics, see Ray Suarez, *The Old Neighborhood: What We Lost in the Great Suburban Migration: 1966–1999* (New York: The Free Press), 3, 5–8; Bremner and Reichard, x–xi; and Mark I. Gelfand, "Cities, Suburbs, and Government Policy" in Bremner and Reichard, *Reshaping America*, 266–267.

84. Bremner and Reichard, xii; Gelfand, 261.

85. Suarez, 2–14.

86. Robert H. Bremner, "Families, Children, and the State" in Bremner and Reichard, *Reshaping America*, 3, 16–17; Bremner and Reichard, ix; Gelfand, 262–264; Coontz, 26, 76; Halliwell, 148–149; and Beuka, 1.

87. Coontz, 77; Bremner, 16–17; Gelfand, 262–264, 274–275.

88. Suarez, 102.

89. Lev, 7, 212; Monaco, 46, 48.

90. Marling, 129.

91. Putnam, 214–215.

92. Ibid., 103.

93. Ibid., 69–75, 100–101.

94. For additional details, see chapters 6 and 14 in this collection.

95. Beuka, 4.

96. Ibid., 27.

97. Beuka, 7, 10; see also Spigel, 10.

98. Like *The Hours* and *Julie & Julia*, *The Iron Lady* is another postwar retrospective (it has several flashbacks that occur in those years) with a nonlinear narrative that crosses multiple temporal zones. These nonlinear narratives enable viewers to witness women negotiating love, family, career, and societal expectations across decades. Meryl Streep's "intertextual presence" in each film seems to strengthen their critique of Fifties attitudes toward gender.

99. Meyerowitz, 2–5; and Susan M. Hartman, "Women's Employment and the Domestic Ideal in the Early Cold War Years," in Meyerowitz, *Not June Cleaver*, 84–87.

100. *A Period of Adjustment*, DVD, directed by George Roy Hill (1962; Burbank, CA: Warner Home Video, 2012), chapter 24.

101. For more on suburban conformity, see Halliwell, 24; and Quart and Auster, 50–51, particularly their discussion of paranoia and mass conformity in *Invasion of the Body Snatchers* (1956). Regarding suburbia as a "purified" communal space, see Spigel, 110.

102. Bryson, 116–117.

103. David M. Potter, *People of Plenty: Economic Abundance and the American Character* (Chicago: The University of Chicago Press, 1954), 68–70, 72, 84.

104. Ibid., 56. Films of the 1950s often glorified the U.S. consumer economy; see Lev, 218.

105. Potter, 47.

106. Ibid., 59. Riesman defined the inner-directed as "internalization of adult authority" and the other-directed as "the product of his peers" (v). Yet, he seems to recognize social character always helps "insure or permit conformity" (6). David Riesman, *The Lonely Crowd: A Study of the Changing American Character* (New Haven, CT: Yale University Press, 1950).

107. Boddy, 20; see also Marling.

108. Potter, 176, 188.

109. Ibid., 177, 188.

110. Ibid., 67, 181, 182.

111. Ibid., 182–186. See Halliwell, 151–152, regarding the creation of a national public for advertisers.

112. Suarez, 86.

113. Ibid., 87.

114. Coontz, 33.

115. Chopra-Gant, *Hollywood Genres*, 95.

116. Ibid., 28–33, 95.

117. Ibid., 33–37, 98–107.

118. Quart and Auster, 20.

119. Chopra-Gant, *Hollywood Genres*, 97, 99.

120. Lev, 53–54.

121. Chopra-Gant, *Cinema and History*, 33–48; Halliwell, 40.

122. K. A. Cuordileone, "'Politics in the Age of Anxiety': Cold War Political Culture and the Crisis in American Masculinity, 1949–1960," *The Journal of American History* 87, no. 2 (2000): 515–545; 516, 522.

123. Ibid., 527.

124. Halliwell, 155.

125. Putnam, 152, 194; Monaco, 4, 5–7.

126. Quart and Auster, 55.

127. Monaco, 8.

128. Ibid., 7. See chapter 10 for a different reading of beach party movies.

129. Regarding the "harsh realities of urban working-class existence" in *All in the Family*, see Himmelstein, 165. For a summary of the economic issues driving "white flight," see Suarez, 17, 74.

130. Suarez, 127.

131. See also Himmelstein, 123–124.

132. *The Heart Is a Lonely Hunter*, DVD, directed by Robert Ellis Miller (1968; Burbank, CA: Warner Home Video, 2008), 1:40:17ff.

133. Marshall McLuhan, "Further Thoughts on Icons," in *Icons of Popular Culture*, ed. Marshall Fishwick and Ray B. Browne (Bowling Green, OH: Bowling Green University Press, 1970), 38.

2   Music and Mimicry in *Sunset Boulevard* (1950)

CHRISTINA GIER

THIS CHAPTER EXAMINES Franz Waxman's score to Billy Wilder's film *Sunset Boulevard* (1950) and explores how it works with the filmic narrative to heighten the portrayal of the film's core idea of mimicry. The narrative figuratively slows time down and represents the workings of a forgotten commodity fetish. For Norma Desmond (Gloria Swanson), age is a change that she, as former megastar, struggles against, and the story tells of how she attempts to stop time in the opulence of her home on Sunset Boulevard. She wants to return to the gaze of the cameras. For this task, she enlists the help of the young writer Joe Gillis (William Holden), who has stumbled into her home as he escapes creditors, and who soon finds himself spiraling ever more deeply into the recesses of her world.

The film presents a narrative about their relationship, which navigates the gaps between present and past, speech and silence, voice and body; because of these gaps, it often delegates storytelling to the musical score. As the film presents the ultimate incongruity of the aforementioned pairs through the demise of the writer and the irrationality of the effete star, the music interweaves their respective tales. As such, the score works to emphasize the film's dramatic tensions of youth versus age, excess versus poverty, and man versus woman. In this way, this film, written and produced in the last two years of the 1940s, is an inward-looking psychological critique of Hollywood that underscores its deepest betrayals and troubles with its seductive powers at a time when the industry was reeling from real life legal and economic battles. While Joe's voice-over narration guides us through his story, the filmic focus is on Norma, whose hopes and pains drive the narrative and much of the score. In fact, the entire score can be heard as the musical voice of Joe and Norma's battling personal dramas: Joe's troubles over his failing career and Norma's ruthless attempt to return to her youth. Unlike the narration of the voice, which is limited to Joe's perspective, the music insinuates itself into every corner of the metanarrative and reveals more than Joe's words can say. In this chapter I show how the fates of Joe and Norma become so intertwined that only the music can convey their essential relationship: a battling mimicry that Norma musically "wins" as she walks toward the camera in the final scenes.[1]

The film's backdrop is Hollywood of the late 1940s, revealed diegetically in its stark portrayal of the disparity between Hollywood's enormous success and obscene wealth in the 1920s and 1930s and the industry's downturn in the late 1940s due to various economic and legal factors. In an era filled with conspiracy and mistrust, government investigations bore down on the filmmaking industry: some studios succumbed to the Supreme Court's ruling in the Hollywood Antitrust Case of 1948 (the "Paramount Decree"), and many in the Hollywood community underwent investigations by the House Committee on Un-American Activities (1947–1953). Furthermore, these investigations were occurring as television went mainstream. By 1950 millions of houses received broadcast television, and more families were staying home for their entertainment instead of going to the cinema. In this changing environment, Charles Brackett and Billy Wilder wrote a screenplay that captured the sense of worry and gloom about Hollywood's status; it is a film noir that highlights the industry's emotional fears and, as J. P. Telotte writes, "literalizes the activity of a psychodrama."[2]

The Narrative as Psychodrama

Joe characterizes the gloom even as he works to succeed: he is a man foiled consistently and downtrodden by both societal expectations and his own incompetence. In the end, he is weakened and then eliminated by Norma's more powerful desires, fears, and madness. Betty Schaefer (Nancy Olson), Joe's apparent love interest, tries unsuccessfully to break the spell of Norma's grandeur and acts as the alternate force to Norma's instability and power; but Betty's goodness is thwarted, not by Norma, but rather by Joe's own devotion to and seduction by his life on Sunset Boulevard. Joe sets out on a trajectory toward ruin, and the score illustrates this downward path as his jazzy theme undergoes dramatic alterations. As I will discuss thoroughly in the next section, Waxman's score works at its own narrative level, sometimes in sync with the action, sometimes pushing narrative time in different directions, sometimes imparting information not stated in words, and sometimes foreshadowing narrative events. The score appears to follow the actions of Joe and seems to be guided by his narration

FIGURE 2.1 Norma (Gloria Swanson) surrounded by pictures of herself as a young star (29:38).

but actually supports Norma's tale and boosts her power as an enduring exotic. Her slippery theme turns around in our ears like the snaky gold cord she wears around her neck as she greets Joe on the second day he is in her house (Figure 2.1). In seeking her comeback, or "her return" as she prefers to call it, Norma relies on Joe's youth and modernity, who, after she hires him to edit her movie script for *Salome*, eventually becomes her lover. Both Joe and Norma, as different as they may seem initially, work through painful hardships from either end of the Hollywood spectrum.

Joe's struggles as a writer seem to mirror those of the Hollywood institution, which can be heard through the nature of his voice-over. The status of his narrator voice is ambivalent: the relation between body and voice is unstable, dislocated, never inhabiting the same present. Because of this, the narration, which often appears to carry the power of unity and truth, warrants questioning. Its workings can be compared to Jacques Derrida's articulation of the relation between the sign and signifier in writing. As Andrew Gibson writes, "Voice in film is no more a part of an immediate representation of a living world there before expression than writing is."[3] Joe's voice presents a false immediacy, not only because he is speaking out of time and after death, but because the voice's humanness conveys a sense of veracity; it hides any uncanniness in the dead man's voice. His voice speaks in a writerly style and is literally disembodied after the first shot of Joe's corpse in the pool. The voice-over functions as a dispassionate narrator as it matter-of-factly tells (at first in the third person) the tale of a writer's death (his own), and in the end the voice outlives the screen persona we come to know as Joe. Unlike Michel Chion's definition of the *acousmêtre*, Joe the narrator does not have a godlike perspective; instead he appears to be as uninformed as he was the "first time"—a writerly conceit on the part of Brackett and Wilder, necessary for telling a stylistically coherent Hollywood story.[4]

Norma refuses to decline and is intent on reviving her stalled career. She is assisted by her overly devoted first-husband-turned-butler Max (Erich von Stroheim), who epitomizes emasculation and facilitates the continuing dream of her commodity status. As he tells Joe, "She was the greatest of them all." As an actual actress from the 1910s and 1920s, whose real photos and films are in the film's narrative, Gloria Swanson as Norma presents a "resonant multiplicity of references" to the history of women in cinema.[5] She is, in the words of Jodi Brooks, "the site on which the various 'faces' of the commodity are brought into tension"—that is, both the fetish's growth and the fossil's decay are at work in Norma's world.[6] As Brooks suggests, effete female film characters like Norma from this period mimic youth so as to "practice a form of remembering as a means of refusing their status as the discarded." Norma fills her "dead time" with her gestures and her eyes, the unspoken magic in her performances from her glory days.[7] Her world is imbued with signifiers of the gothic that seem to reverse time, as the house and people in it present the living tensions of an outdated fetish in the modern Hollywood of 1950.

The narrative turns on Joe and Norma's mutual mimicry: each wants something that the other has, but which neither can attain. Joe wants to be a great success, a Hollywood hit, and obtain a star's wealth; Norma desires Joe's youth, his possibility, and she wants to inhabit a young body like his. Gender stereotypes support the film's trajectory and broader symbolism. While Norma acts as a *femme fatale* who consumes Joe's promise (for what it was), she also appears tender, fragile like a sweet girl (or *femme gentile*) caught in an aging body. Joe's voice is that of a confident young man, but his masculinity suffers blows at every turn—the lack of work and the loss of his apartment, his independence, and, most humiliatingly, his car. The film invites the viewer to feel compassion for both the hapless screenwriter and the aging star; however, it seems to contradict itself because it follows Joe's voice-over narration, when in fact Norma becomes the focus of the camera lens and musical score. She is a star—the most important character in the film around which all the male characters revolve; and notably, the score often speaks for her. In addition she could be called the most sympathetic character of the film, a representative of old Hollywood, with her Chaplin rendition for Joe and the bridge games with the "waxworks," as Joe calls her friends. While he considers her passé—"you used to be big," as he says when they first meet—he does not consider her a "waxwork," because his attraction to her lifestyle and the promise of payment morph into a mix of greed, disgust, pity, and fascination.

FIGURE 2.2 Joe (William Holden) enters Norma's grounds (14:05).

As Joe narrates, "the whole place was stricken with a kind of creeping paralysis." Age and decrepitude are painted starkly in the *mise-en-scène* of Norma's mansion with dead trees and an abandoned pool (Figure 2.2). This sense of "age" is perhaps most compellingly conveyed visually, but the film's diegetic music contributes to this aspect of the film's narrative, particularly through the stark juxtaposition between the music at Norma's house (the organ, the Charlie Chaplin routine, the tango at her New Year's Eve party-for-two) and the contemporary band music at Artie's bash, where Joe goes to escape the world of the past. As Noël Carroll argues, "form follows function," and the organ in Norma's house functions to tell us that "stardom breeds monstrosity."[8] Notably, the organ is also the sonic, musical reality that disturbs Joe's sleep on the first night, and it portends to dark days ahead. As an integral part of this form, the diegetic music operates as an incisive narrator of the story's key underlying points. However, while the stars of Hollywood, around whom the public wraps their dreams, can be monstrous, this single judgment is too simple for the complexity of Norma's character and for the film's symbolic and musical commentary on older female stars in Hollywood around 1950.

A Musical Psychodrama: Joe and Norma's Struggles in the Score

The music embodies Norma's persona with lush, string sounds that appear to reinvigorate and empower her, imparting a youth that is unreal and unstable.[9] The music that enters with Joe's narration also enlivens Joe's voice and traces his story from the grave. Music's role in this play between body and voice operates in unique ways, and the slippage of meaning works here as well. As narrative voice, the music is dense and full of thematic variations, in keeping with the standard 1940s Hollywood score style. While music does not carry the signifying capacity of language and does not lend itself directly to deconstruction, with the Hollywood style of thematic writing and dramatic association derived from Richard Wagner's idea of leitmotif, music is given an entry into a type of signification. Yet this is a particularly unstable sort of signification, as even Wagner recognized and as we hear in this film.[10] We first hear Joe's musical theme played by low brass as he introduces his floating corpse. He then invites us to hear the "facts" of a murder involving "one of the biggest" stars. The music mirrors the narration here and acts like a suture to draw the dead body and living voice together. Later, when we watch Joe confidently speeding away from the creditors in the film's only car chase sequence, we hear the chromatic low wind and brass "chase" theme from the opening, and we encounter Norma's decrepit home through his eyes. His confidence continues when he meets Norma and agrees to help edit her screenplay. Given his infectious hubris and the lack of another perspective to adopt, the audience initially has little reason to doubt his confident narration. As he starts to scheme and calculate the ways he can use her wealth and apparent generosity for his own gain, we begin to distance ourselves from him, aided partly by the musical score.

In classical Hollywood fashion, Waxman's score guides the filmic narrative, though the music does even more than is typical to shape the particular richness of this film's narrative. His score links themes with characters and narrates the story through sometimes subtle and sometimes overt variations of these themes. His themes and their associations mutate over the course of the film, however, in a way that belies any simple interpretation of musical meaning. As Waxman commented about the leitmotif, "motifs should be characteristically brief, with sharp profiles."[11] He is less concerned with the variation of the melodic profiles; while this does occur, he writes that "I believe the first and foremost principle of good scoring is the *color of orchestration* [sic]. The melody is only secondary. Looking at a scene I may use a horn, or I may see massed violins."[12] Some of the development occurs in pitch content but more importantly in the modes of orchestration, which can be quite diverse. Such variation on a relatively stable basic set of melodic materials has potent effects in the filmic narrative of *Sunset Boulevard*.

The melodic construction of themes associated with both Joe and Norma is quite important, however, because they present the two characters as dramatically different and highlight their opposite personalities. Joe's theme sounds contemporary and modern, while Norma's theme curls around the Phrygian mode, seeming remote and exotic. As mentioned, we first hear Joe's theme as we see his corpse floating in

Norma's pool. Split between solo low brass and high violin, the theme's discomfiting timbral combination sets the stage for his equally unsettling story. The camera focuses on the corpse's face, and high violin trills help segue the action as the images blur, and Joe the narrator takes us back to the beginning. Then we hear a livelier version of his theme outlined in the piano as the camera refocuses on a view of Franklin and Ivar Streets in Los Angeles and pans up through his apartment window. With its swinging eighth notes, the minor theme coincides with the narrator's first use of "I" and identifies Joe's space with a jazzy feel (Example 2.1).

This theme acts as our aural representation of his persona, as well as that of the enthusiasm of Hollywood's younger class of writers and dreamers, while the minor mode carries a sense of their anxieties and dampened hopes. As he toils at his work and speaks through the theme's various incarnations, the theme and voice share the same low reverberation. In the first third of the film, the orchestra acts as constant companion to Gillis; but his theme's musical truncation tells the tale. The musical world of Norma's palazzo marks a stark contrast to the modern jazzy sound of Joe's world. As Norma peers out through the bamboo blinds at Joe wandering her grounds, her sunglasses reflect the light, presenting her as masked and inhuman. At this same moment, her twisting theme announces her exoticism and her potential danger (Example 2.2). From this point onward, the orchestra starts to facilitate Norma's character, and because she exerts a godlike power within her house, the new musical arabesques slowly bend the narrative to her will.

Waxman does not mention in his essay his deployment of numerous important points of musical action, that is Mickey Mousing and stingers, to highlight the plot and conjoin the narrative. These techniques have greater and lesser narrative impact

EXAMPLE 2.1 Franz Waxman, *Sunset Boulevard*, Joe's Theme, with a light swing (02:56). (Transcribed by C. Gier.)

EXAMPLE 2.2 Franz Waxman, *Sunset Boulevard*, Norma's Theme in flute (14:33). (Transcribed by C. Gier.)

but tend to become more significant as the film progresses. When Joe first enters the house, he pleads to be understood by Max (who believes, like Norma, that Joe is the undertaker for the dead pet chimp), but at Norma's call he soon moves up the stairs in quick steps. The notable rising string line that accompanies this motion appears to be a standard musical gimmick until one inspects the narrative more closely. He glides up with ease on an orchestral line of stacked minor thirds set against a dissonant pedal, now in string timbres that are new to his actions (Example 2.3). It is her orchestral palette and tonality that draws him up the stairs, figuratively leading him into the web of her world.

Musical simultaneity had been used right before this scene to show Joe's career beginning to fall apart when we musically "hear" his agent's ball go down the hole on the golf course. After his agent offers no help ("the finest things in this world are written on an empty stomach"), a frustrated Joe marches off, and the repeated half-step motif from his theme and from the opening music signals the problems to come. The music in these two scenes foreshadows his entanglement before the narrator Joe appears aware of it. When the music synchronizes with Joe as he ascends the steps in Norma's house, it possesses narrative force: oblivious to any signs of trouble at Norma's, Joe has already begun to lose control.

EXAMPLE 2.3 Franz Waxman, *Sunset Boulevard*, Joe going up the stairs in Norma's house, accompanied by flute, clarinet, and violin (15:20). (Transcribed by C. Gier.)

Norma dominates the visual and auditory fields. When she removes her sunglasses as Joe enters her room, her eyes and expression introduce the power of gesture over speech in her world. With the saxophone now playing her theme, the gestures and the music are linked. In this introduction to her character, she fits well into the mold of a classic *femme fatale*; initially portrayed as inhuman by the shot of her through the blinds, in her house she is beautiful, glamorous, and strong, and intent on using the men cowed by her majesty. She fits into a dangerous older woman role that several aging actresses in the 1950s and 1960s performed for Hollywood. These included Bette Davis in *All About Eve* (1950) and Joan Crawford in *Torch Song* (1953). Both actresses were in their late forties when these films were made. After Gloria Swanson played Norma in *Sunset Boulevard* at the age of 50, it seems that Hollywood didn't know what else to do with aging female stars. As Lucy Fischer writes, "the aging actress tends to violate the cherished cultural myths concerning both Hollywood and woman."[13] However, the fact that several formerly beloved female actresses were turned toward such roles in the 1950s perhaps says something more about Hollywood itself. It reflects, at least, a need to connect with its gilded past and to hold the aging female star up as an example of its pain at the changed landscape of entertainment. One could even see it as a type of punishment of the great women for aging, for being real after all. Brooks focuses on *What Ever Happened to Baby Jane?* (1962) with Davis and Crawford as two old sisters who are former stars, and she argues that what fascinates the viewer is the "audacity of the performance, the ever-presence of performance as display."[14] This type of audacity is part of Norma's persona—she is always in the spotlight and wants recognition for it.

Norma is a silent screen star, and she has no voice-over and so no real verbal power in this film; her presence comes through her gestures, her shrill commands, and her music in the score. In their first meeting, she calls to Joe before he leaves, "You're a writer, you say!"—more as a pronouncement than a real question. This moment turns the plot and reorients the man; she needs a man to enable her words. When she establishes him as the editor for her script, he appears to take control of the situation: "The name is Gillis," but musically this is underscored by Norma's theme in a violin. As he sits down to read her *Salome* script, he says he doesn't need a light: "I've got 20/20 vision"; the orchestra underscores the irony of this line with her theme played against his words. He is, in fact, struck with blindness in her grand house as the greed of an unemployed scriptwriter clouds his judgment, and the music announces that Norma's control has been established. We can easily read Norma's character as a classic *femme fatale* in scenes like this, and perhaps this is what Brackett and Wilder wanted to convey, especially in her expressed attachment to her *Salome* script. However, Norma presents more complexity as the film progresses, particularly due to Swanson's convincing and sensitive portrayal of her character.

Mark Jankovich asserts that Norma is not the "independent woman," which the *femme fatale* characterizes, but rather someone who is a "wealthy, egotistical relic" (as he quotes from one 1950 review).[15] However, I would argue that the discomfort of the story comes from the fact that Norma, while a relic and egotistical, is also likeable, even though she rails at her butler Max, who maintains her self-fantasy, and ensnares and ultimately kills Joe. Her strength is accompanied by the charm of a star and her childlike eagerness, and with this complexity of contradictions, she becomes the film's most compelling character.

At the end of Joe's first day in Norma's world, he is ushered to his guest room above the garage by Max. This action is accompanied by Joe's theme, which, after one statement by the pizzicato double bass, is joined by an eerie and pianissimo chromatic descent in the violins in tremolo, a timbral link to Norma's music that had just played. We see his nighttime view from the guest room of the chimp's funeral, and his disgust at his surroundings is evident. In a musical bookend to the minor thirds described above that guided his character up the stairs when his misadventure in her home began, now a descending chromatic string line, muted but present, draws him to the window. This subtle descent soon infects his dream world and cements the symbolic conclusion of which Joe is unaware: he has replaced Norma's chimp. His nightmare of a masked organ grinder playing for a dancing chimp conveys what Julian Wolfreys characterizes as "one of the film's frequent grand guignol moments."[16] Joe's space is diegetically overwhelmed by Max's organ playing of the dark opening to Johann Sebastian Bach's Toccata in D Minor. This dramatic music marks the triumph of doom, and Joe's voice has no power to silence it. Like a voice from the past, the organ sounds as an old musical workhorse from the silent era because early silent film organists frequently employed the Toccata.[17] This is a striking musical metaphor for the pressure old Hollywood's successes exerted on the new troubled Hollywood of the late 1940s and early 1950s.

After this moment, Joe enters Norma's collection of trinkets, and she begins to groom him to become her next husband. Pointed incarnations of his theme mark crucial moments of his entrapment. Her musical persona even begins to invade the space of Joe's narrator voice, and this duel is first illustrated by a clear juxtaposition of themes. In the scene when Joe takes on the task of editing her unwieldy manuscript, his theme pushes forward as he confidently types away. His narrator voice now illuminates his thoughts of Norma: "she was still sleepwalking along the giddy heights of her lost career." In this scene, he sees himself as her benevolent caretaker, someone to protect her from falling from those heights and to prop up the celluloid images that plaster the rooms. This is not unlike how husband-turned-butler Max sees himself, though Joe does not immediately make this connection. Then in a stark juxtaposition to his thoughts of care and with a swift shift in musical theme, she asserts control by

retrieving the discarded passages of script from the waste, literally rescuing her gestures for the screen. His voice-over reveals his feelings of pity for her, while the orchestration immediately changes to her theme in strings to paint her force. He does not
win their argument of words versus gestures, and the strength of her move (sharply
underscored by a final string *sforzando*) concludes the exchange. Yet we know that Joe
has already fallen for her, so to speak, through the acknowledgment of his pity.

Joe's voice is still in control of the narration. However, after this exchange, the
diminution of Joe's theme and increasing dominance of Norma's theme, in addition
to changes in the orchestral palette, foretells the literal separation of voice and body
witnessed in the opening scene. Gradually, in the various stages of his emasculation,
musical phrases of his theme are reduced and altered: At the appearance of the repo
men at Norma's garage when his car is finally towed, the arpeggio phrase of Joe's
theme is repeated several times and then fades; next, Norma rejects his chewing
gum on their first ride in her 1929 Isotta-Fraschini, and here his theme is suppressed
and resolutely replaced by hers; and then the notable stinger at the purchase of the
vicuna coat. The salesman suggests the vicuna over the camel's hair, and a bitingly
altered piccolo version of the second motif from Joe's theme inverts the playful
eighth notes and turns it into a strident articulation of his weakness in the face of
her alluring life of wealth (Example 2.4).

The line then descends as the scene fades to rain, and the segue to the next scene
sets the mood for Joe's move into the former husbands' bedroom next to Norma's.
Rain often works in films to convey emotion and here functions in telling opposition to Joe's apparent feeling of success, while Waxman's attention to orchestration conveys his posh upgrade. His theme's opening arpeggio now sounds through
thick lush strings as he enters the room. He walks toward the window pointing, "I
guess that's the one you can see Catalina from . . . only this isn't the day." To underscore this moment Waxman tones the orchestral template down. Rising out of the
orchestra, a deep-toned solo cello arches into a line that turns around, descends,
and seems to sweep Joe across the room with its mournful minor third figurations
(Example 2.5). This line is derivative of the intervallic language of Joe's theme.

EXAMPLE 2.4 Franz Waxman, *Sunset Boulevard*, Vicuna coat stinger in piccolo (38:20). (Transcribed
by C. Gier.)

EXAMPLE 2.5 Franz Waxman, *Sunset Boulevard*, Excerpt of cello solo when Joe moves into the house (39:00). (Transcribed by C. Gier.)

The use of the solo cello to represent leading men in love relationships with the main female lead was already well established in Hollywood (e.g., Jerry's theme in Max Steiner's score for *Now, Voyager* [1942]); but here the love relationship is disturbingly altered. Joe's verbal and physical gesture toward the gray, rainy view from the window draws the downpour into his own perception, which we understand is also clouded. At this moment, his love of luxury overwhelms his judgment and spurs his nonchalant attitude toward the strong symbolism of this action. When he notices there are no locks on the doors, the visual shots of each empty lock ring with a harp flourish, as though to signal something important. Though Max explains the reason for the absent locks to Joe, the symbolism of these flourishes is not immediately apparent; particularly unanswered is the question of why so much filmic time is spent going from door to door with the same flourish. The music and shots act like a type of punctuation highlighting Norma's past and prefiguring her coming instability. The still shots with the music slow the narrative time in order to articulate a larger meaning: his doom.

The Music of Two Worlds

These changes in Joe's theme, from the first shot of his apartment to the scene in his new bedroom, illustrate just how much Joe has managed to mimic Norma and remove himself from his old life. Norma's world contrasts sharply to the "real" Hollywood in which Joe's friends (Artie and Betty) exist, and it is dominated by the steamroller of her star persona, which perpetuates her vision of herself. Like her oil wells that are, as Norma describes with the flick of her hand, "pumping, pumping, pumping," her world continues to involve the onlooker (us) and Joe, who is seduced by the constant wealth of her Hollywood lifestyle. He soon moves beyond his initial pity and personal poverty as his reasons for staying to an active fetishizing of her world as commodity. She becomes the definition of value to him, and he appears to take care of her as he immerses himself in her cocoon of luxury.

There are two scenes when Joe briefly emerges from this cocoon, and both involve Betty. The first time occurs on New Year's Eve and the second when he starts writing with Betty at the studio. On New Year's Eve, he flees Norma's stultifying tango-drenched party-for-two and lands at Artie's bash. The orchestral score, nearly omnipresent since the beginning, is absent from the youthful Hollywood party; instead a piano in the room plays contemporary popular tunes and gives it a sense of vitality. Joe and Betty spin out playfully stilted writerly lines in their flirtation with one another, and their crafted talk and gestures from movie clichés contrast sharply to the realness of their setting. The diegetic piano, which supports their dialogue, creates part of the clamor they escape by going into a side room to discuss *Dark Windows*. This is Joe's story that Betty finds good because, as she says, "it's real." Its sense of reality comes from it being something Joe experienced with a teacher once, and the irony is that Joe's control of his reality, whether in reference to a past teacher or his present employer, is questionable. This fact about Joe finds immediate proof. The spell of their heightened dialogue is broken when, at an urgent call from Max that Norma has slit her wrists, Joe returns immediately to the house. For a second time, the stairs in Norma's house become an important element of the *mise-en-scène* as we see Joe ascend, but this time he (and the viewer) no longer needs musical accompaniment to draw him up. He wants to go directly to her bedroom in a scene in which his initial pity turns into anger and serious concern, and then to affection. When his escape fails, he returns to her arms.

However, Joe lives like someone with two personalities. He begins to leave the house on the sly to work regularly on the script for *Dark Windows* with Betty at Paramount Studios at night. The symbolism of the script's title is apparent given Joe's circumstances; he is psychologically surrounded by darkness, but at the studios his world is brighter. Joe and Betty take a walk during one of their breaks; they stroll among the fabricated studio sets, and Joe's theme sounds light and carefree, now in the major mode for the first time and at a comfortable *andante* pace (Example 2.6).

Nevertheless, like the false sets and Betty's artificially straight nose, the theme is buoyantly disconnected from Joe's reality; and like the Old West sets they pass, Joe and Betty's relationship will never be real (Figure 2.3). Truth and certainty are under question as many small details in their relationship continue to confirm, from their writerly conversations to their location for writing.

As a counterpoint to Norma, Betty is the presentation of a "normal" figure of a woman. In fact, she functions symbolically as the Mary to Norma's Eve, in the way that Hollywood films from this time frequently portrayed both female stereotypes in some capacity in order to highlight each other and frame the male lead. She is representative of the Hollywood on the opposite side of the industry from Norma—behind the Hollywood screen. She is a script reader whose character is pretty, young, and ambitious, but she has no theme in the score. This appears to be the case until one examines her relationship to Joe. While she carries no distinct theme, she arguably enacts a powerful transformation on Joe's theme that only lasts for the times when they are together. When his theme sounds in major, as mentioned above, Joe hears about Betty's nose, a story that draws him closer to her. The music conveys this with a rising eager cello line emerging out of the orchestra and

EXAMPLE 2.6 Franz Waxman, *Sunset Boulevard*, Walking with Betty (1:21:24). (Transcribed by C. Gier.).

FIGURE 2.3 Joe and Betty (Nancy Olson) walk among the Old West sets (1:21:15).

a slow muted trumpet with higher flute descents. These flute descents are present when the scene at the studios begins, and they return in the violins in Betty's final scene when she comes to Norma's house and unsuccessfully tries to take Joe away. In this respect, the flute line could be understood as a sign for Betty, and it is a notable change of musical world for Joe's character, away from the dense string orchestration of Norma's scenes. During their continuing conversation at the studios, we hear a flute and violin duo, with a motif of alternating thirds played twice, first in the second measure and then in the seventh and eighth measures of the example. The violin plays a relaxed quarter-note line with alternating thirds as the instruments exchange gestures (Example 2.7). This third motif, derived from the first phrase of Joe's theme, returns later when Joe has returned to Norma's house and Betty visits unannounced. Notably, when he ends their relationship in this scene, he switches on the light in the pool—a haunting view of the scene of his destiny.

Joe's brief escape to Paramount Studios with Betty is subverted by the stark fact underscored by all the musical details up until now: even though we follow Joe's narrator voice willingly and worry about his travails and share his relief while strolling with Betty, the narrative is Norma's and is focused on her mimicry of youth and her resolute insistence on performing Salome, a desire she in the end takes to the extreme. A centerpiece of the narrative is her actual attempt to reverse the traces of time from her body in a montage that depicts Norma's grueling professional makeover. Stripped of her glamorous housecoats and snaky necklace, she is childlike as her hair is pinched and her eye magnified. We see her skin give way as a faceless technician pokes at her wrinkles and her eye peers out, frightened and defenseless. In this scene she becomes the vulnerable victim of Hollywood: the woman star who is old. As the makeover montage begins we hear Norma's theme in the strings, and the urgent orchestral "chase music" of the title leads to a restless solo violin passage

EXAMPLE 2.7 Franz Waxman, *Sunset Boulevard*, Joe and Betty talking at the studios (1:22:21). (Transcribed by C. Gier.)

that is agitated and uncontrolled. The fast violin line could be said to be like gypsy music (or similar to the version captured in Brahms's Hungarian Dances), such that it highlights the urgency, even franticness, of her attempt to reverse time. The scene finally resolves down to her preparing her nighttime attire. She is fragile here, wanting Joe's approval in a moment that foreshadows her final lack of control and act of desperation in response to her desires. Norma's audacity in thinking she can return to the cameras engenders the screen time given to her makeover montage. No other character gets a montage, and perhaps the writers saw this sequence as a way to elaborate on the "old woman star" topic, what here could almost be said to be a mockery of her age, but which also draws compassionate attention to Norma's personal travails and metaphorically those of old Hollywood.

The last time the camera follows Joe up the stairs we hear his movements Mickey Moused remarkably overtly. After bidding a final farewell to Betty, he turns to find Norma at the banister. We see her behind Joe, framed by the window; as he now ascends the stairs we hear a scalar *pizzicato*—which appears to grossly paint his diligence to her. Yet the music, as we discover in the next frames, has deceived us, and in retrospect the musical sound of diligence characterizes not his obedience but his determination to leave her life and break their bond. His voice-over reveals that his peccadilloes with Norma (from her tube rose perfume to her self-infatuation) have finally added up, and Betty's reaction of horror at his reality seems to have compelled him to do what the audience thinks he should have done long before: throw down the gold cuff links and leave. At this insult to her control, she becomes irrational and shoots him with the gun she had intended for herself.

In the final scene, the morning after, she leaves the world of language, so to speak, preparing to return to the unreality of the screen. Completely besotted by her own reflection in the mirror, she is Narcissus, doomed to destroy herself with love. Fischer characterizes this moment and Norma's plethora of self-images around the house in Lacanian terms: "like the Lacanian infant, [she] stands 'jubilant' in the 'assumption' of her image."[18] As she descends the steps in a "scene" orchestrated by Max, a version of Norma's music blasts bombastically in the brass, in a grand demented style like the Ravel *Valse*. She reaches the ground floor, and her *jouissance* is tenfold the pleasure of the viewers: to be expressive, to be viewed, is her joy. Joe's voice-over returns once more to tell us that Norma has won: her dreams have enveloped her. Then she explains, over a slow version of Joe's theme played by saxophone, "You see this is my life and always will be." This moment breaks the traditional thematic association with character as she takes possession of *his* musical theme. Like his voice-over, the theme we have associated with Joe appears to have survived the character's death. One reading of this moment could be to say that the *femme fatale* Norma has consumed Joe. However, this moment underlines just how slippery signs like musical themes are: their meanings do not stick. The theme was always about something more than just Joe; it was connected to him because of what his character represented, namely ambition. In the end, however, Norma possessed that in greater quantity than any other character. The crux of their relationship, the mimicry of each other's best qualities, is the ultimate downfall of both. The underlying moral of the film is revealed for the audience in the musical theme's transplantation.

Norma functions as a symbol of both Hollywood's glamour and its troubles; her over-anxious ambition parallels Joe's trajectory. The film suggests that her punishment for the murder of Joe will come as policemen wait to arrest her. It depicts, however, a more tragic end for her. Even more debilitating for the character is that she, as the woman who symbolizes Hollywood's extravagance, is condemned to madness. We could say that the musical score appears to save her in the end, but her perception of the real escapes her, just as the films of Hollywood play with the dreams of would-be actors and writers and with the fascination of the viewer. They envelop all concerned, if only temporarily, in a new sense of reality.

After Joe entered Norma's driveway, his sense of reality became skewed and was always thereafter off. He thought he was in control; both men in her life want to use her for their own gain: Joe for money and Max for the vestiges of the glory they once shared. The trajectory of this tragedy, which reflected the suffering in the movie industry around it, becomes obvious: Joe's downfall is caused by Woman (an archetypal symbol encapsulating all troubles). Woman is a force embodied by Norma; however, despite her charms, Hollywood needs to assert that she is ruined: the old way of doing things is over. Yet musically the saxophone line is a powerful force, and Norma walks toward the camera almost as if she would meld herself with that elusive, intoxicating medium, the image on the screen. Norma reaches out as if to touch it and merge herself with its splendor. But it is the music that welcomes her into its world as it underscores her gestures and her mastery of the world beyond language. In the end it is left unclear what happens next: she either blends into the attraction of the screen, which ensnares all, or she succumbs to the rule of law, waiting to claim her.

NOTES

1. For an introduction to the musical landscape of *Sunset Boulevard* (1950), see William Darby and Jack Dubois, *American Film Music: Major Composers, Techniques, and Trends* (Jefferson, NC: McFarland, 1990), 137–141.

2. J. P. Telotte, "Voices from the Deep: Film Noir as Psychodrama," in *Film Noir Reader 4: The Crucial Films and Themes*, ed. Alain Silver and James Ursini (New York: Limelight Editions, 2004), 150. This film also can be understood as an early horror film: reviews from the time complained that having the dead body in the opening scenes be the narrator was "ugly and sensationalist." See Mark Jancovich, "Realistic Horror: Film Noir and the 1940s Horror Cycle," in *Billy Wilder, Movie-Maker*, ed. Karen McNally (Jefferson, NC: McFarland, 2011), 67.

3. Andrew Gibson, "'And the Wind Wheezing Though That Organ Once in a While': Voice, Narrative, and Film," *New Literary History* 32 (Summer 2001): 648.

4. Michel Chion, *Audio-Vision: Sound on Screen*, trans. Claudia Gorbman (New York: Columbia University Press, 1994).

5. Lucy Fischer, "*Sunset Boulevard*: Fading Stars," in *Women and Film*, ed. Janet Todd (New York: Holmes and Meier, 1988), 99.

6. Jodi Brooks, "Fascination and the Grotesque: *What Ever Happened to Baby Jane?*" *Australian Journal of Media and Culture* 5, no. 2 (1990): 2.

7. Ibid., 4.

8. Noël Carroll, "Film Form: An Argument for a Functi onal Theory of Style in the Individual Film," *Style* 32, no. 3 (1998): 12.

9. The common characterization of the femme fatale in opera is well documented. See, for example, Catherine Clement, *Opera, or, the Undoing of Women* (Minneapolis: University of Minnesota Press, 1988); and Susan McClary, *Feminine Endings: Music, Gender, and Sexuality* (Minneapolis: University of Minnesota Press, 2002).

10. Thomas Grey, "' . . . Wie Ein Rother Faden: On the Origins of 'Leitmotif' as a Critical Construct and Musical Practice," in *Music Theory in the Age of Romanticism*, ed. Ian Bent (New York: Cambridge University Press, 1996).

11. Tony Thomas, ed., *Film Score: A View from the Podium* (New York: A. S. Barnes and Company, 1979), 58.

12. Ibid., 55.

13. Fischer, 100.

14. Brooks, 4.

15. Jancovich, 66.

16. Julian Wolfreys, "Hollywood Gothic/Gothic Hollywood: The Example of Billy Wilder's *Sunset Boulevard*," in *Gothic Modernisms*, ed. Andrew Smith and Jeff Wallace (New York: Palgrave, 2001), 215.

17. Rick Altman, *Silent Film Sound* (New York: Columbia University Press, 2004), 337. Bach's piece would never have been played in full. Altman notes "contemporary arbiters of theater organ music insisted that organists abandon ecclesiastical performance traditions."

18. Fischer, 109.

3 Who's Who in Hadleyville?

The Civic Voice in High Noon *(1952)*

ANTHONY BUSHARD

THE IMAGE OF Will Kane (Gary Cooper) walking down a dusty street under a hot, noonday sun to face his enemies in *High Noon* (1952), Carl Foreman's allegory of the Hollywood Blacklist directed by Fred Zinnemann, has left a permanent imprint in the minds of many moviegoers.[1] Yet, among the main characters, one of the most important did not even appear on screen. The ballad, "Do Not Forsake Me," by Dimitri Tiomkin and Ned Washington and sung by Tex Ritter, comments on the action and reminds the audience of the events yet to come. In fact, Tiomkin employed themes from the ballad in virtually every cue found in the score.

Many have reported the ballad's role in promoting the film, as well as its presence in the opening credits rather than the more standard orchestral fanfare.[2] I argue that one of the more intriguing features of the ballad is its ability, as a voice in the film's narrative as well as in Tiomkin's background scoring, to assume different "personas." As suggested by Mary Nichols in Jeremy Byman's *Showdown at High Noon*, "The song pleads, 'Do not forsake me, O my darling.' Who, we ask is doing the forsaking? Amy? Will? The town? Like the film, the seemingly simple ballad implies far more than it says."[3] Or as Neil Lerner posits, "The *High Noon* score also complicates, or at least calls into question, the Hollywood convention identified as 'inaudibility' by Claudia Gorbman as the song and score frequently compete with the images for the spectator's attention . . . in ways that simply do not permit us to ignore them."[4] In this chapter I demonstrate that the ballad's capacity to emanate from multiple characters, which enriches its role in the film's narrative and enhances the film's references to issues facing the United States in the 1950s, derives from the ballad's placement at key points, as well as Tiomkin's incorporation of the song's thematic elements into the score.

High Noon opens in the nineteenth century upon an arid landscape somewhere in the western United States. To set the mood and introduce the story to the audience, Tiomkin composed a song that would recur throughout the film at predetermined times. Throughout his score, Tiomkin also employs themes from the ballad, in A A'BA' form, for his primary musical material (Examples 3.1–3.2).[5]

In addition to frequently aligning the ballad's text with narrative events, there exists a striking contrast between the song's A and B sections. An important characteristic of the A theme is its melodic contour: mainly stepwise motion and in most phrases it forms an arc within a fairly narrow range, thus making it very singable. Whenever Tiomkin employs the theme in the score, he usually presents it in its familiar form and sometimes alters it melodically. While the B theme might lack the melodic interest of the A theme, it makes up for it with its driving rhythm, specifically the repeated figure comprised of two eighth notes followed by three quarter notes (Example 3.2, m. 1). In addition to being more rhythmically interesting, the B theme is also more motivic in nature and is therefore subject to more varied modification than the A theme. How Tiomkin further differentiates between the two will become apparent below.[6]

The opening sequence, which displays the ballad for the first time, provides good evidence of unity between the music and action on screen even in the opening

EXAMPLE 3.1 Dimitri Tiomkin, *High Noon*, The A melody from "Do Not Forsake Me," mm. 1–3. (Transcribed by A. Bushard.)

EXAMPLE 3.2 Dimitri Tiomkin, *High Noon*, The B melody from "Do Not Forsake Me," mm. 38–41. (Transcribed by A. Bushard.)

credits. As one hears the first lines (Example 3.1), the viewer connects the "me" from the ballad with a lone cowboy standing underneath a tree. Is this man being forsaken and by whom? As the text moves from the first A to the A' section, the title *High Noon* appears on the screen. The title's placement at this moment in the opening sequence is fascinating. Textually, the next ballad phrase is "The noon day train will bring Frank Miller," so there is a connection in that respect. More importantly, however, the lyrics introduce the concept of time, and noon specifically, as a threat to characters both good and bad. In addition, as the title fades, a man rides a black horse toward the camera at great speed, and the background passes by with greater and greater velocity. Not only does this racing rider foreshadow the impending arrival of Frank Miller (stated in the lyrics), but also suggests that time seems to flow faster and faster the closer one gets to noon.

Throughout this opening sequence and as indicated in the opening credits, Tex Ritter's voice guides us through the forthcoming narrative's dramatic essence, even drawing attention to the film's eventual showdown between Frank Miller (Ian MacDonald) and Will Kane. Because Capitol Records released a version of Ritter singing "Do Not Forsake Me" almost six weeks before *High Noon* opened in the United States, many audiences were familiar with the story through his voice.[7] It is interesting, then, that we see the villains assembling rather than Kane to whom the ballad's lyrics supposedly refer. In part because of this unprecedented familiarity with Ritter's voice *before* the film's release, the ballad occupies a nebulous position both inside and outside the film's narrative and its "musical score operates at the edge of those boundaries."[8] Through the camera's lens we view the present and through the ballad's lyrics better understand the past and future.

As the gang members proceed down the road, the audience receives a reminder of another visual threat used throughout the movie. Whenever Zinnemann sought to remind the audience of the danger to come in the form of Frank Miller, he used two visual devices: the clock and the railroad tracks. The symbol of the tracks is further explained by Zinnemann, "I visualized the threat as a static piece of film showing nothing but the railroad tracks running all the way to the horizon."[9] The road foreshadows this device by showing that danger comes to Hadleyville both by road and by train; increasingly modernized travel brings ever-greater danger.

As the Miller gang enters Hadleyville, gazed upon in fear by several townspeople, the ballad migrates to Tiomkin's background scoring as he uses a modified version of the B theme stated in the trombone and second horn and answered in the trumpet and oboe (Example 3.3). The dotted rhythm used here in conjunction with the B theme mirrors the same dotted rhythm of the church bell announcing the worship service, and combined with the slow tempo suggests a drum accompanying a funeral procession.[10]

EXAMPLE 3.3 Dimitri Tiomkin, *High Noon*, Statement of the B theme in Reel 1/Part 2, mm. 1–2.

As the camera cuts to a woman who reacts to the gang's arrival by making the sign of the cross, Zinnemann seems to highlight not only her fear, but also echoes what might have been a typical reaction in 1952 by an average American citizen in a similar situation. For instance, one could view it as a disruption of seeming normalcy by an outside presence in the form of Communists. Conversely, and maybe more appropriately, Foreman sought to bolster his political allegory by referring to the beginnings of HUAC's investigation into Hollywood and the subsequent reaction by the liberal community.[11]

Appropriately, Tiomkin highlights this sequence with increasingly dissonant music as opposed to the opening ballad's more pleasing strains. Beginning in m. 3 of this cue, Tiomkin preserves the dotted rhythm of the opening on beat 1, but alters the melody and employs straight eighth notes on subsequent beats (Example 3.4). Instead of maintaining the dotted rhythm on G-sharp, he changes the interval to a descending minor second between sixth and fifth scale degrees (in F-sharp minor, given the presence of the E-sharp in the bass), D-natural and C-sharp, found in the horns. However, because of the prominence of C-sharp in the altered B theme and the lack of any resolution on F-sharp, one could argue the immediate tonal center was C-sharp in this excerpt, and the tension between D-natural and C-sharp closer to that between flat-2 and 1. The dissonance receives further prominence in both its placement on beats 1 and 3 of mm. 3–4 and the increase in dynamic level from *piano* to *forte*.

Tiomkin's alteration of the B theme through the descending minor second on beats 1 and 3 in mm. 3–4 is important. As the woman enters the screen space, the audience gathers from her silent symbol of fear that the gang's presence should be taken seriously. Therefore, it is interesting that Tiomkin chose to set this variation of the B theme, characterized by the descending minor second in the aforementioned harmonic, rhythmic, and dynamic contexts, to enhance her dread. Throughout this score, Tiomkin's use of and emphasis on the second, especially the minor second often between flat-2 and 1, in a variety of musical contexts is one of the chief ways by which the composer creates melodic and harmonic instability, thus helping to echo a sense of fear, anxiety, and/or ambiguity inherent in the drama.[12] This relationship between flat-2 and 1 destabilizes the opening whole tone common to Western diatonic modes and suggests a completely different affect than similar relationships between scale degrees 7 and 1 or 4 and 3. Opening a scale with a minor second more closely approximates Phrygian or Locrian modes and contains an innate unnaturalness when viewed in terms of Western classical tonality. The use of this specific minor second is also rather convincing in this scene as the Miller gang, the foreign—and therefore *unnatural*—element,

EXAMPLE 3.4 Dimitri Tiomkin, *High Noon*, Altered B theme in Reel 1/Part 2, mm. 3–4.

descends upon the unsuspecting Hadleyville residents. Moreover, the flat-2 to 1 semitone appears throughout this and other scores in conjunction with specific agents of fear.

As the old woman crosses herself after the evil has passed, Tiomkin "resolves" mm. 3–4 inconclusively on a flatted II[7] with an added C-sharp—emphasizing music's long-prized signifier of fear, the tritone—through the chord's voicing in the piano.[13] Clearly the woman's gesture and the ashen demeanors of those residents who encounter the Miller gang point to the serious impact the gang will have on Hadleyville. Through the more dissonant, altered B theme, Tiomkin marries Kane's fate, as described in the ballad, with Hadleyville, its residents, and its future.

Eventually, word reaches Kane shortly after his marriage to Amy Fowler (Grace Kelly) that the Miller gang is in Hadleyville waiting for Frank Miller to arrive on the noon train. Urged by their friends (and the ominous strokes of the clock), Amy and Will decide to leave town to avoid any danger. Kane's friends load the two on their wagon and hurry them away. To accompany this "Wagon Flight,"[14] Tiomkin wrote a small orchestral interlude that reprises the ballad's A theme replete with "galloping" sixteenth-note passages.

"Wagon Flight" allows the audience to digest what has happened thus far, so employing the main ballad theme lends some symmetry to what has transpired and invites speculation on what is yet to come. However, the ballad theme works on several other musico-dramatic levels as well. When considering the ballad's relevance to a particular scene, it is crucial to consider not only the music, but also the lyrics. As Will and Amy leave town, the main theme recalls the lyrics, "Do not forsake me, O my darlin' on this our wedding day" heard in the accordion and strings. The reference to their wedding day is certainly appropriate, but they are still together, so who exactly has been forsaken? Kane's friends and colleagues encouraged them to leave and gave them their blessing, so it is not they who have been forsaken. In this instance, Tiomkin might be suggesting that the town of Hadleyville has become a character through these lyrics. As Kane and Amy leave, they both abandon the town to save themselves.

The music here acts almost as a siren song,[15] calling Kane back to Hadleyville to protect his town and honor the oath he swore to protect it. It would almost appear that Kane actually "hears" the ballad—as Louis Giannetti points out, "As the buckboard careens out of town, the hero's face is a study in confusion, anxiety, and panic"[16]—and might be reconsidering his decision to leave. After all "Hadleyville is *his* arena . . . he's the town's hero,"[17] as Giannetti reminds us, and it would appear Kane also recognizes that duty. Moreover, the theme here allows the audience to more fully share Kane's agony later when the town—in the form of its citizens—abandons Kane for the purpose of self-preservation.

Kane resolves to return to town and defend himself and his friends. This upsets Amy because she is a Quaker and therefore against any sort of violence. Kane tells Amy that he has never run away from anything before in his life and he is only doing so now because he was forced to flee by his friends. They return and while back at Kane's office, Amy tells him that she will not stay and watch him get killed. She adds that if he does not leave with her now, there is no hope for their marriage. Tiomkin captures the mood effectively as everything seems to be darkened—the lighting is dim, the expressions on the couple's faces seem ashen, and the room itself is drab with little light—and demonstrates again his capacity to develop the ballad.

As Kane goes on to tell Amy that the politicians up north commuted Miller's sentence to life, Tiomkin uses an altered version of the B theme to remind us of the vow Miller made while in prison (Example 3.5). Later, Kane tells Amy the reasons for coming back and the ramifications of staying, yet she continues to plead with him to go away with her as they had planned. Amy finally tells Kane that he "shouldn't try to be a hero" (even though Kane did not infer that his actions could be construed as "heroic"). At that moment, one hears the B theme; thus, Tiomkin ties heroism in with the B section of the ballad, which refers to Kane's fate. Kane tries to convince Amy that he will not be alone in this battle, but she disregards his empty promises by saying, "You know there'll be trouble," during which the audience hears the B theme in augmented note values, further emphasizing its prominence (Example 3.6).

Tiomkin's final incorporation of the ballad in this musical cue occurs toward the end of the excerpt. Kane continues to reassure Amy that there is nothing to worry about and asks her to wait at the hotel for him. However, Amy is not the typical Western heroine. She stands up to her man and exclaims, "You're asking me to wait

EXAMPLE 3.5 Dimitri Tiomkin, *High Noon*, Altered B theme, Reel 2/Part 5, mm. 3–4.

EXAMPLE 3.6 Dimitri Tiomkin, *High Noon*, The B theme foreshadowing violence to occur at high noon, Reel 2/Part 5, mm. 26–27.

an hour to find out if I'm going to be a wife or a widow. . . . I won't do it." As she defies Kane, we hear the A theme altered (Example 3.7).

Musically, Amy reminds Kane not to forsake her, while the altered A theme perhaps helps to comment on the breakdown of their relationship. And, because the A theme is usually quite consonant, the minor second (Example 3.7, m. 39, beat 1) Tiomkin uses to conclude the passage—instead of the expected major second— proves to be particularly disconcerting. Also, by changing this interval, Tiomkin alters the scale degree relationship between the opening and final notes of the phrase—scale degrees 5–1 (see Example 3.1)—to a tritone between 5 and raised-1. Moreover, the final semitone becomes 2 to raised-1, rather than 2–1. The combination between the tritone and semitone, both involving an altered tonic and thus

EXAMPLE 3.7 Dimitri Tiomkin, *High Noon*, The A theme modified to emphasize the ramifications of forsaking one another, Reel 2/Part 5, mm. 38–39.

undercutting our aural expectations, creates a dissonant musical passage that comments effectively upon a conflict of duty: Kane's duty to his town and its people and more importantly from Amy's perspective, Kane's duty to his wife.

Throughout this cue—from the tender, melancholy solo in the cello to the various reconsiderations of the A and B themes accompanied by dissonant chromatic lines—it is clear that Tiomkin seeks to emphasize the tension between Kane and Amy as they both make crucial decisions about the difficult situation and the future of their relationship. Given the screenplay's political implications, the conflict between the couple perhaps resonates on a much broader level as this scene alludes to minority political views during the 1950s. As Gwendolyn Foster suggests, Amy represents not gender, but a different set of ethics and therefore she embodies the "repressed anger of the other in American postwar society."[18]

It is, perhaps, significant that Foreman made Amy a Quaker because the group was not only known for its nonviolent stance, but was also one of the few groups that spoke out against the nuclear proliferation of the 1950s, and they were often the subject of derision in the media. As Amy fails to understand any of Kane's justifications for what he must do, Foster proposes that the filmmakers are alluding to the peace movement in the United States that cannot "understand" the potential for another world war: "The comment may be taken as stereotypically female, as a woman who cannot understand a man's world, but within the metanarrative of the repressed, it is calculatedly a rupture of the discourse of warmongering and blind patriotism."[19] When viewed in this perspective, the way Tiomkin highlights the struggle between Kane and Amy—and thus the conflicting ideologies—through the development of the ballad's themes and their corresponding dissonant accompaniment adds to the effectiveness of the entire passage and demonstrates the ballad's flexible point of view.

Kane then embarks on a search for people to aid him in facing the Miller gang. Running out of places to find deputies, he turns up the street with renewed vigor accompanied by Tex Ritter's haunting voice, to enlist another friend of his, Sam Fuller (Harry Morgan). Meanwhile, Fuller, who is at home, sees Kane coming and

EXAMPLE 3.8 "Battle Hymn of the Republic," mm. 1–3. (Transcribed by A. Bushard.)

Mine eyes have seen the glo-ry of the com-ing of the Lord.

EXAMPLE 3.9 Dimitri Tiomkin, *High Noon*, Modified version of "Battle Hymn of the Republic," Reel 5/Part 4, Accordion, mm. 1–4.

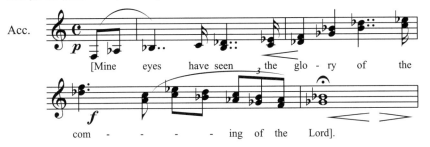

[Mine eyes have seen the glo - ry of the com - - - - ing of the Lord].

has other ideas. As Kane confronts Mrs. Fuller (Eve McVeagh), Tiomkin calls further attention to the Fullers' cowardice through a modified version of "The Battle Hymn of the Republic," heard earlier in the interior church scene wherein a choir was singing the hymn. A comparison of the original hymn text and tune (Example 3.8) and its superimposition upon the melody is represented in Example 3.9 by the accordion part heard during the scene. Tiomkin's modified version parallels the ascending contour of the original melody while exaggerating the dotted rhythms with double-dotted figures.

The dramatic connection is multifaceted. Tiomkin appears to connect the decision made by the Fullers with God's final judgment. The last lyric heard in the aforementioned church scene, "he is sifting out the hearts of men before his judgment seat," would be especially appropriate here where cowardice, or weakness of heart (demonstrated later in the film by the same congregation), is "sifted out" in favor of a heart that stands up for its convictions—like Kane's heart. Furthermore, Tiomkin with Foreman and Zinnemann seem to be chiding suburban America in this scene. As Kane leaves the Fuller house, the viewer notices the quaint home surrounded by a white picket fence—classic features of the 1950s suburban dwelling. Indeed, the Fullers, comfortable in their surroundings, seem to represent the sort of complacency and lack of social awareness that was a part of the 1950s suburban experience. In addition, as the Fullers use religion as an excuse for their cowardice, they parody and trivialize that which they do every Sunday. Similarly, Tiomkin parodies the theme accordingly to emphasize this hypocrisy. In so doing, he confers upon music the ability to tease out aurally competing moral dilemmas: stand firm in one's convictions despite certain danger (congregation singing the "Battle Hymn"), or recoil in fear when true crisis threatens one's community (Tiomkin's parodied version).

After Kane leaves, the Fullers reflect upon the situation. While this goes on, one notices an instrumental version of the ballad's A' theme suggesting the dual lyrics, "You made that promise when we wed . . ." and "If I'm a man I must be brave. . . ." Conceivably, the fear that drove Fuller to cower inside his house is similar to the terror that caused his wife to lie for her husband in order to save him. Their marriage and obligation to self-preservation was presumably greater than their devotion to Kane and Hadleyville. The use of the ballad here to suggest varying degrees of commitment demonstrates once again the song's ability to refer to different characters.

On a broader level, the filmmakers once again situate a tune's "voice" with the town. Throughout the film, the "High Noon" ballad has been used mainly as a transitional device following Kane from one rejection to another. So on one level, the recurrence of the ballad could be considered Kane's inner thoughts as he attempts to gather a posse of friends and townspeople, a reading agreed upon by most scholars. Deborah Allison points out that the "lyrics are in the first person and seemingly derive from Kane."[20] Neil Lerner refers to Phillip Drummond's book *High Noon* when observing that "Fortifying the claims towards the score's subjectivity, Drummond praises the music for its ability to convey Will Kane's inner emotions."[21] Finally, Ildar Khannanov comments: "Often [in the openings of Westerns] one hears a full orchestra with solo harmonica, but never a song with lyrics that reveal the thoughts of a protagonist."[22]

Yet, this particular interpretation appears problematic when Allison and Lerner (in addition to Mary Nichols's earlier reference to the ballad's multifaceted perspective) also admit that "the song, at first glance, seems very simple in both structure and message. A slightly closer look exposes a work of considerable complexity,"[23] or "[t]his film insists that it be read at multiple levels; the insistence comes, in part, from the music, which offers numerous clues that this film is more than just an escapist story and may be interpreted as such."[24]

So far we have considered both Kane and Amy as potential "subjects" in this ballad. On the other hand, the town and townspeople appear to give "voice" to the ballad through the background scoring as they watch the Miller gang ride into town. Moreover, since Kane is usually seen walking through Hadleyville's dusty streets while the ballad is heard, one could argue that the town *itself* is asking Kane not to forsake it. As Lerner continues:

At several points Tiomkin's score . . . shifts between the nondiegetic—the music supposedly heard only by the audience—and the diegetic: the music that appears to emanate from the story world, the music of which the characters in the story, along with the audience, are themselves aware. In *High Noon*, the boundaries between the diegetic and nondiegetic are continually collapsing.[25]

The voice one hears throughout the narrative (Tex Ritter's) does not derive from any of the film's characters. Yet as spectators—and evidenced in the aforementioned scholarly opinions—we are asked to believe the ballad and its lyrics derive from Kane. Clearly there is much tension in considering the multivalent subject of this ballad, but the town? The ballad in Tiomkin's hands even calls to mind Chion's acousmatic being, "[the *acousmêtre*'s] powers are four: the ability to be everywhere, to see all, to know all, and to have complete power."[26] From the beginning of the film the ballad informs us about the past, present, and future, and follows Kane wherever he goes. It is the relationship between Kane and Hadleyville that lies at the narrative's heart as well as the ballad's; several instances bear this out quite well.

Kane eventually goes to one of the last bastions of support in Hadleyville—the town church. Soon, chaos erupts in the congregation between those who want to help Kane and those who desire to discuss the matter more rationally. Finally, Mayor Henderson (Thomas Mitchell) steps in and states his beliefs.

> HENDERSON: [*Shot of Kane and Henderson*] Now, people up north are think-ing about this town, thinking mighty hard, thinking about sending money down here to put up stores and to build factories. It would mean a *lot* to this town, an *awful* lot. But if they're going to read about shooting and killing in the streets, what are they going to think then? I'll tell you. They're going to think this is just another wide-open town and everything we've worked for will be wiped out [*camera pans to congregation*]! In one day this town will be set back five years [*pause*] and I don't think we can let that happen [*camera pans back to Henderson only*]. . . . Tomorrow we'll have a new marshal and if we can all agree here to offer him our services I think we can handle anything that comes along [*camera moves back to include Kane and Henderson*]. To me that makes sense. To me that's the only way out of this. [*Pause*] Will, I think you better go while there's still time. It's better for you and it's better for us [*enter musical cue; camera moves to Kane, who is visibly disappointed*].[27]

In other words, Henderson desired for Hadleyville to be modernized. Ironically, a symbol of modernity throughout the film thus far has been the use of the train tracks going to the distance. Hadleyville is still a horse-and-buggy town, but the prominence of the railroad would mean unlimited urban development. As Stephen Prince notes:

Within the film, the tracks go north, to the land of business and banks, to the investment capital that entrepreneurs in development-hungry Hadleyville are anxious to secure for themselves, and, therefore, within the genre's logic, the tracks go toward the future, as embodied by an expanding industrial and capital-based economy.[28]

While those tracks may mean progress to some, they also represent the evil that is yet to come in the form of Frank Miller. This irony seems to suggest that those who desire progress must deal with the inevitable evils that come with that sort of development. Furthermore, Henderson believed that if Kane left immediately there would not be any trouble once the entire Miller gang arrived. As Henderson "sacrifice[d] him on the altar of capitalism"[29] and stated that this seemed to him the only choice, he pulled out a rag, apparently washing his hands of this treasonous display toward his friend, and with that, virtually the entire town forsakes Kane. Although there were several who were willing to defend Kane, the mayor spoke to their fears, disguised as good judgment, and was able to conform them to the town's will.

As Kane leaves the church, the audience sees children engaged in a "tug of war" similar to the verbal struggle that transpired between their elders in the sanctuary. One hears the A' theme in a grand orchestral presentation stating without lyrics, "You made that promise when we wed. Do not forsake me, O my darlin'." In the same way that Washington's words call to mind Kane and Amy's marriage that day, they also bind Kane to the town with the image of the church. Even though the mayor, speaking for the townspeople, has just dismissed Kane's request, it would seem that the town itself wants Kane to stay and fulfill his contract to the town and realize his destiny, referred to in the other lyrics associated with the A' melody, "If I'm a man I must be brave. And I must face that deadly killer."

The next image the audience sees is the haunting figure of the railroad tracks disappearing into infinity accompanied by the B theme, realized diegetically on harmonica by a Miller gang member. The dramatic progression from aisle to church steps to track is effective because it juxtaposes progressive modes of movement. In addition, the shot of the tracks reminds the audience not only of the means by which Miller comes to town, but also of the reason(s) Kane was betrayed at the church— the vast potential of economic expansion for Hadleyville.

Finally, the camera's point of view in this sequence invites speculation about the identity of the spectator following the track's path to the horizon. As the ballad enters the diegetic space through Jack Colby's (Lee Van Cleef) harmonica underneath the camera's distant gaze, thus dissolving the barrier between reality and fiction, the filmmakers seem to place the audience in league with the rest of Hadleyville's residents. Like the character of Sam Fuller peering fearfully from behind closed curtains, American society during and since *High Noon*'s premiere has become increasingly aware of external threats (both real and perceived), yet all too often has sought refuge in the safety and security of home when those threats manifest themselves. Zinnemann alluded to this phenomenon in his autobiography when he lamented, "In America [following World War II] there was no clear awareness of what had happened to countless humans in the rest of the world.... We were as on an island of stagnation and claustrophobia in the midst of a rapidly changing world."[30] The track represents the only way on or off the "island" of Hadleyville, and the ballad's existence in both diegetic and nondiegetic worlds implies that both encompass each other in the same Hadleyville.

In a later cue, known in many sources as the "clock montage," Tiomkin composed a sort of musical tableau that presumably matches the visual sequence envisioned by Zinnemann and Foreman. Tiomkin wrote approximately one measure of music to accompany each frame of the montage. Dramatically and musically, the suspense created here rivals that of any excerpt in the film. Since Zinnemann uses time to intensify the entire passage, Tiomkin brings back the clock ostinato heard earlier and builds to a climax whose tension is cut by the blast of the noon train's whistle. The juxtaposition of clocks and characters' expressions culminating in a collective glance at the clock upon high noon is also quite effective, thanks in no small part to Zinnemann's intentions in his script as realized by film editor Elmo Williams.

The scene begins with Kane writing his last will and testament, accompanied by a chromatic passage in the winds and emphasized by glissandos in the xylophone. Next the Miller gang prepares themselves for Frank Miller's arrival on the noon train, represented visually by yet another shot of the open railroad track. Here, Tiomkin employs the B theme in conjunction with these villains, replete with dissonant chords in the piano and bass, reinforcing in our ears the sense of visual unease associated with the gang. The montage then moves to the church where parishioners appear as if they are waiting for some approaching storm to pass. To bolster the sacred venue's importance, Tiomkin adds chimes as well as chorale-like voicing in the brass and woodwinds. As we witness Kane again, Tiomkin adds a quasi-fanfare in the trumpets, echoed later in Zinnemann's shot of the town square, suggesting once again that the town's fate rests with Kane. In the montage's closing moments, the clock returns one last time and the B theme sounds throughout the orchestra, signaling again the imminent threat represented by Miller's arrival.

From the clock's opening strokes to the howling of the train's whistle during which we witness all the townspeople encountered thus far, Zinnemann and Williams emphasize, in 3.2-second segments, that the train bearing Frank Miller will impact not only Kane but also an entire community. In a further testament to the importance of Tiomkin's ballad to this scene (as well as refuting conventional claims that the music was composed *after* filming), Elmo Williams indicates in his memoir that he recut the scene to fit Tiomkin's montage music.[31] Just as the ballad opened the film by providing a microcosm of the ensuing drama, the montage, with the ballad's help via background scoring, now summarizes the action thus far from the town's perspective whose "voice" highlights the impending conflict.

Later, just after Frank Miller's arrival on the noon train and in one of the most enduring images from the film, Kane finds himself alone on the street as a rising crane shot makes the marshal appear increasingly isolated. Kane is the only one left standing in what now appears to be a ghost town. Amidst a musical "halo" in the violas playing harmonics, Tiomkin features the ballad prominently, but in a much more ambiguous harmonic context. In addition, the vibraphones, chimes, and ascending chords in the piano contribute to a convincing realization of one of the more ethereal shots in the film. The ballad fades away and the audience hears several unresolved chords before a faint reprise of the B theme. It is still not clear what Kane will do; thus the fading away of the ballad throughout the cue. What is clear as Kane stands alone is the scope of what he has sworn to protect and to whom he is loyal—the town itself.

Throughout the cue Kane looks around him in what appears to be a final effort to see if anyone has come to his aid. As we hear the ballad's increasingly haunting strains, it is almost as if Kane is searching frantically for the source of the ballad that he now hears with us. Ironically this point is further evidenced by the inadvertent inclusion of telephone wires and buildings of distant Burbank and Hollywood— that other town in the west whose name begins with "H" and which Carl Foreman had in mind while writing the screenplay.[32]

The climactic scene takes place as Frank Miller takes Amy hostage and brings her out of Kane's office, hoping he will surrender. Miller's cowardly act draws Kane from his shelter, and one surmises that Miller has won this battle. In a flourish, Amy pushes Miller, distracting him enough so that Kane can kill him with two shots accompanied by two *fortissimo* chords heard throughout the orchestra. Though climactic, the one thing this scene and these chords do not provide is a sense of resolution. Yes, the Miller gang has been defeated, Kane has saved his marriage and the town he served for many years, but the ambiguity suggested by the climactic chords proposes that there are more questions than answers. As Prince reflects, Kane returned not only out of a sense of personal pride or a sense of duty, but also in an attempt to reestablish his place within a community. For most of the film, Kane's fellow citizens treated him as an outsider. Even when news of Miller first arrived, they did not ask the best marshal in Hadleyville's history to stay around. Rather, they whisked Kane and Amy out of the area so they would not get in the way. Through his return to town, Kane designated the community of Hadleyville as the site for his story to be fulfilled, rather than be alone in the countryside to battle his demons. As Prince summarizes, "He chooses fraternity over isolation, and it is the narrative irony which entails that the community will not honor the choice he has made."[33] Kane desires to be part of the group, but unfortunately for him, his inner-direction does not serve the will of the other-directed residents of Hadleyville.[34]

As Kane and Amy ride away, they leave to the ballad's lyrics, "Wait along," uttered repeatedly (though more distant-sounding because of the microphone's increased reverb): perhaps Hadleyville's last attempt to keep its "darlin'." In the same way that the townspeople had forsaken Kane, the symbolic gesture of tossing his badge to the ground demonstrates Kane's refusal to conform to the town's will. Returning to Chion, he also has this to say about the *acousmêtre*:

> Of course, the acousmêtre has only to show itself—for the person speaking to inscribe his or her body inside the frame, in the visual field—for it to lose its power, omniscience, and (obviously) ubiquity. I call this phenomenon de-acousmatization. *Embodying the voice* is a sort of symbolic act, dooming the fate of ordinary mortals.[35]

Interestingly, there is no "unmasking" in *High Noon*, and the identity of this *acousmêtre* is open for speculation. This ambiguity is ultimately realized as the ballad resolves incompletely on the fifth scale degree.

Foreman's allegory of his experiences battling the Hollywood Blacklist is well documented and provides an interesting way in which to view the film. However, Zinnemann's broader political perspective offers another avenue of interpretation. As Prince suggests, Kane's struggle within a larger community also represents Zinnemann and his frustration with the small-mindedness of the United States toward the rest of the world. On a more local level, Zinnemann often questioned the power of the studios in the days of the "studio system" and in 1950, he sided with his blacklisted screenwriter by refusing an attempt by the right-wing membership of the Screen Directors' Guild to establish an anti-Communist loyalty oath.[36]

Zinnemann stated that Foreman's political beliefs had no bearing on his decision to direct the picture. Zinnemann may have disagreed with Foreman's narrow interpretation of the film, but he shared with the writer his own concerns about postwar America as well. Prince maintains that *High Noon* was consistent with, "the anxieties [Zinnemann] felt about events on the national and world stages and, especially, about the political complacency of American culture."[37] Zinnemann witnessed the same phenomenon in his homeland of Austria in the years leading up to World War II. He also saw this "complacency" in Hollywood, where he was shocked to find a gross lack of knowledge concerning the effects of World War II on the rest of the world.

> Almost immediately after the end of World War Two, European film-makers [*sic*] began to deal with the shattering changes in their people's lives. Powerful movies, full of almost unbearable emotion, appeared in America from abroad. . . . In Hollywood studios there was a blissful ignorance; the average "product" continued unchanged, full of bland escapism and a sticky, unreal sentimentality. It was sickening to think of working on that type of material.[38]

Kane is the only one who appears to recognize the dangers, both real and abstract, that could arrive on those tracks from beyond and is willing to respond appropriately. Similarly, Zinnemann desired that America would cease inventing strife at home and instead be prepared to solve real problems throughout the world. Likewise, Tiomkin and Washington employ this ballad—part history, part destiny—to ask us, the residents of Hadleyville, not to forsake our communities and the world around us.

NOTES

1. Earlier versions of this chapter were presented at the "Two Greats" Super Regional Conference of the Great Lakes and Plains Chapters, College Music Society, Normal, IL (2008), and Music and the Moving Image, New York (2008).

2. See, for example, Deborah Allison, "Do Not Forsake Me: The Ballad of High Noon and the Rise of the Movie Theme Song," *Senses of Cinema* 28 (September–October 2003), http://sensesofcinema.com/2003/28/ballad_of_high_noon/; Kathryn Kalinak, *Settling the Score: Music and the Classical Hollywood Film* (Madison: University of Wisconsin Press, 1992), 185–186; Christopher Palmer, *The Composer in Hollywood* (London: Marion Boyars, 1990), 142–143; Roy M. Prendergast, *Film Music: A Neglected Art*, 2nd ed. (New York: W.W. Norton, 1992), 102–104; and Jeff Smith, *The Sounds of Commerce: Marketing Popular Film Music* (New York: Columbia University Press, 1998), 59–60.

3. Mary Nichols, "Law and the American Western: The Case of *High Noon*," *The Legal Studies Forum* 22, no. 4 (Summer 1998), 603, as quoted in Jeremy Byman, *Showdown at High Noon: Witch-Hunts, Critics, and the End of the Western* (Lanham, MD: Scarecrow Press, 2004), 261.

4. Neil Lerner, "Look at that Big Hand Move Along: Clocks, Containment, and Music in *High Noon*," *South Atlantic Quarterly* 104, no. 1 (Winter 2005): 153–173; see especially 153–154.

5. Examples 3.1–3.2 and 3.8 were transcribed by the author. All other examples have been transcribed from Dimitri Tiomkin's original manuscript score to *High Noon* (1952; Dimitri Tiomkin Papers, Cinema/TV Collection, Doheny Memorial Library, University of Southern California) and reprinted with permission.

6. William Darby and Jack Du Bois, *American Film Music: Major Composers, Techniques, Trends, 1915–1990* (Jefferson, NC: McFarland, 1990), 246–247.

7. Lerner, 152.

8. Ibid., 153.

9. Rudy Behlmer, *America's Favorite Movies: Behind the Scenes* (New York: Frederick Ungar, 1982), 278.

10. Neither Tiomkin nor his orchestrators provided cue titles, instead organizing by reel and part numbers.

11. As Foreman stated, "There are scenes in the film that are taken from life. The scene in the church is a distillation of meetings I had. . . . I became the Gary Cooper character" (Behlmer, 276). See also Stephen J. Whitfield, *The Culture of the Cold War* (Baltimore, MD: The Johns Hopkins University Press, 1991), 146.

12. Bernard Herrmann's *The Day the Earth Stood Still* (1951) and Leonard Bernstein's *On the Waterfront* (1954) for instance. See Anthony J. Bushard, "Fear and Loathing in Hollywood: Representations of Fear, Paranoia, and Individuality vs Conformity in Selected Film Music of the 1950s" (PhD dissertation, University of Kansas, 2006).

13. Like many other film composers, Tiomkin employed the tritone to help the filmmakers convey a sense of dramatic instability and/or ambiguity (marked by fear, apprehension, or ambivalence) to an audience. The tritone's tonally ambiguous nature derives from the fact that not only is the key unclear, so is the specific interval. Jay Rahn points out that the tritone is the only interval in which the chromatic size does not identify a specific diatonic size. Rahn calls this phenomenon an "ambiguity." See Jay Rahn, "Coordination of Interval Sizes in Seven-Tone Collections," *Journal of Music Theory* 35, nos. 1–2 (1991): 36.

14. On the first page of this cue, orchestrated by Herb Taylor, is the title "Wagon Flight." It is the only musical cue in the collection that bears a title.

15. Michel Chion, "The Siren's Song," *The Voice in Cinema*, ed. and trans. Claudia Gorbman (New York: Columbia University Press, 1999), 109–122.

16. Louis Giannetti, "Fred Zinnemann's *High Noon*," *Film Criticism* 1, no. 3 (Winter 1976): 6.

17. Giannetti, 6.

18. Gwendolyn Foster, "The Women in *High Noon* (1952): A Metanarrative of Difference," in *The Films of Fred Zinnemann: Critical Perspectives*, ed. Arthur Nolletti, Jr., (Albany: State University Press of New York, 1999), 96. See also Joanna E. Rapf, "Myth, Ideology, and Feminism in *High Noon*," *Journal of Popular Culture* 23, no. 4 (Spring 1990): 75–80.

19. Foster, 96.

20. Allison, "Do Not Forsake Me."

21. Phillip Drummond, *High Noon* (London: British Film Institute, 1997), 40, quoted in Lerner, 162.

22. Ildar Khannanov, "*High Noon*: Dimitri Tiomkin's Oscar-Winning Ballad and Its Russian Sources," *Journal of Film Music* 2, nos. 2–4 (Winter 2009): 226.

23. Allison, "Do Not Forsake Me."

24. Lerner, 156.

25. Ibid.

26. Chion, 24.

27. *High Noon*, DVD, directed by Fred Zinnemann (Los Angeles: Republic Entertainment, 2002), 49:18–50:40. (*Italics mine.*)

28. Stephen Prince, "Historical Perspective and the Realist Aesthetic in *High Noon* (1952)," in Nolletti, *The Films of Fred Zinnemann*, 86.

29. Ibid., 88.

30. Fred Zinnemann, *A Life in the Movies: An Autobiography* (New York: Charles Scribner's Sons, 1992), 55.

31. Elmo Williams, *Elmo Williams: A Hollywood Memoir* (Jefferson, NC: McFarland, 2006), 83, 86. For further consideration of this montage and its ambiguous interpretation of time, see Bushard, 192–193.

32. See Zinnemann, 96.

33. Prince, 86–87.

34. Inner-directed individuals tend to display a sense of individualism apart from tradition or any other social customs. Other-directed societies conform to the demands and choices of others. See David Riesman, *The Lonely Crowd: A Study of the Changing American Character* (New Haven, CT: Yale University Press, 1950), 9–15.

35. Chion, 27–28.

36. Zinnemann, 250–252.

37. Prince, 82.

38. Zinnemann, 55.

4   Anxieties of Accuracy

Miklós Rózsa's Score for Quo Vadis *(1951)*

LINDA K. SCHUBERT

METRO-GOLDWYN-MAYER (MGM) did not do things by halves when making the religious epic *Quo Vadis* (1951). The studio was determined to make the film both spectacular and historically accurate—and to make sure audiences knew it. One advertisement proclaimed it would be "the most genuinely colossal movie you are likely to see for the rest of your lives," while a promotional booklet provided an extensive list of "authentic" items and animals obtained for the film, including 32,000 costumes, 15,000 sandals, 450 horses, and two cheetahs. *Quo Vadis* was indeed "colossal" at the box office, and its success helped trigger the surge of epic films in the 1950s that included *The Robe* (1953) and *The Ten Commandments* (1956).[1]

The music, too, was intended to be equally as accurate, and several critics commented favorably on Miklós Rózsa's score: "Woven from painstaking research," said *The Hollywood Reporter*, it is "brilliant."[2] In this, his first score for a religious epic, Rózsa challenged himself to find early music from the time portrayed and to make it appealing and meaningful for general audiences. In the process he developed a style that evoked the past for many viewers, one he continued to polish in later films, including his Academy Award-winning score for *Ben-Hur* (1959).[3]

In this chapter I will consider why and for what purposes Rózsa started this musical excavation work, as well as what he did with it. To this end, I will focus on two particular aspects of the rich context from which *Quo Vadis* emerged: one was Hollywood's dire financial and political situation in the late 1940s that led to the increased production of religious epics; the other was the impact—according to Rózsa—that musicology exerted on this score, a claim I take seriously. Over the years some writers have focused on the originally composed background music ("incidental music," in Rózsa's words) of *Quo Vadis*; most at least mention the use of ancient melodies.[4] I, too, will discuss these tunes, but this is not simply an exercise in "spot the antiquities." These melodies made excellent grist for MGM's publicity mill, but they also represented a conscious effort by Rózsa to use the "new" repertory of early music in unique ways and even to bridge the gap between the worlds of film and the concert hall. Perhaps he also hoped they would help legitimize his work among classical musicians, many of whom had scant respect for film music at the time.

Rózsa originally wanted to present these melodies "authentically" (or, more currently, in a "historically informed" manner), but the practical requirements of writing for film—scene timings, budgets, and deadlines—overrode this intention. Rózsa quickly realized he had to write more familiar-sounding, accessible cues that would help audiences connect emotionally with the film, something ancient melodies alone might not do. Starting as a vehicle for historically informed performances, the score expanded into what might be described as more broadly imagined acts of composition based on those texts.[5] Rózsa's original vision for this music and the ultimate result offer insight into how some of the issues and aspects of historically informed performance can play out in a Hollywood film score.

To begin, I describe *Quo Vadis*'s history from novel to films and discuss Hollywood's problems in the late 1940s. I then discuss MGM's production, musicology's impact on Rózsa's score, the ancient pieces he chose, and their use. I conclude with some thoughts regarding the composer's view of the score as an important scholarly contribution.

Political Anxieties from Novel to Film

Polish author Henryk Sienkiewicz's original novel *Quo Vadis?* (Where are you going?) of 1896 became his most celebrated work, and its success led to Sienkiewicz being awarded the Nobel Prize in Literature in 1905. Internationally acclaimed, it was translated into more than fifty languages, and Jeremiah Curtin's English translation was hugely popular.[6] In the story, Marcus Vinicius, a young Roman soldier, is inspired by the woman he loves, Lygia, to convert to Christianity during the reign of Emperor Nero. The burning of Rome leads to the bloody persecution of the Christians there, but the couple manages to escape. The title refers to the words St. Peter speaks to a vision of Christ as the apostle flees Rome.

From the beginning, the novel *Quo Vadis?* combined religious and political themes, for many Poles identified their Catholic faith with their country's struggle to survive partition by Russia, Prussia, and Austria. For the Poles "analogies were drawn between the martyrdom of Christ and the dismemberment of Poland," while the resurrection of Christ foreshadowed the nation's resurrection.[7] The novel's portrayal of the oppression, survival, and (by implication) ultimate rise to power of the early Christians would have had these meanings for its earliest readers.

Outside Poland, readers also found meaning in the story, and as the popularity of *Quo Vadis?* grew, it acquired new shapes and forms of narration,[8] including at least eleven stage plays, two operas, an oratorio, and a "panoramic painting."[9] Stage performances, however, could not adequately depict the story, which featured such spectacular events as the burning of Rome. The new medium of film, on the other hand, could persuasively show these events no matter the setting, and music could be added to heighten the drama. The first moving picture of *Quo Vadis?* had appeared by 1901, and at least five subsequent versions were made during the silent era. The first sound film version was made by MGM in 1951; others have followed since, including made-for-television films in 1985 (Italian) and 1993 (German), and a feature film in 2001 (Poland).

The completed film of 1951 was a popular success and was nominated for eight Academy Awards, including Best Score. MGM had been planning a production of *Quo Vadis* (the question mark was dropped to make the punctuation historically accurate) since at least the mid-1930s.[10] Getting it made, however, was an unexpectedly lengthy process for several reasons, including the film industry's financial problems, in-house fighting among MGM's studio heads, and the national political climate.

In the late 1940s the film industry's income plummeted when studios were forced to give up control of the theaters they owned, following a long court battle that found them in violation of antitrust laws. Those theaters had provided a guaranteed venue for film distribution, and their loss slashed the budgets that had allowed the studio system to flourish.

To make matters worse, this ruling occurred just as studios were reluctantly admitting television might be more than a passing fad. People were staying home in droves to watch it, and film attendance dropped alarmingly. Desperate studios sought gimmicks and new technologies (such as 3-D) to pull viewers back and concentrated on making the kinds of films that could not be replicated on television, such as big-budget epics in color, sometimes featuring wide-screen technology (e.g., *The Robe*'s "CinemaScope") or stereo sound (*Julius Caesar*, 1953).

In this troubled economic environment MGM began work on *Quo Vadis*, a spectacular the studio hoped would be as popular and financially successful as Cecil

B. DeMille's *Samson and Delilah* had been in 1949.[11] Casting and crew decisions fluctuated continually, and tensions between Louis B. Mayer (vice president and general manager of MGM) and Dory Schary (MGM's chief of production) may have stalled the film. Schary wanted it to be a serious "message" picture with social and political implications referring to the recent horrors of World War II; he wanted a film that would "parallel Nero's persecution of the Christians with Hitler's persecution of the Jews."[12] Mayer, on the other hand, wanted a DeMille-style spectacle whose primary purpose was box office success; for him, a film that could compete with television was more important than communicating a message. Mayer finally won the fight and work stopped until a new cast and crew were assembled.[13] The director became Mervyn LeRoy, with Sam Zimbalist as producer, and Robert Taylor and Deborah Kerr—instead of Gregory Peck and Elizabeth Taylor—in the lead roles.

By this time, decisions about cast and crew had to take politics as well as money and aesthetics into account. In 1947 and 1951, the House Committee on Un-American Activities (HUAC) held hearings to investigate charges of Communist infiltration of, or influence on, the Hollywood film industry. This led to the blacklisting of some of the most talented people in the business, screenwriters (such as the "Hollywood Ten") in particular, but also directors, actors, and musicians. Studio heads like Mayer were keenly aware of the situation as they steered their productions; for instance MGM decided to cast Robert Taylor, a well-known conservative actor and "friendly witness" to HUAC, as the lead in *Quo Vadis* (though it should be remembered he had been a candidate for the role of Marcus since the late 1930s).[14]

Film subjects were also politicized. Stories based on or inspired by the Jewish Bible and the Christian New Testament took on patriotic significance, and some Americans viewed them as assertions of faith opposing the Soviet Union's "godless Communism." Maria Wyke has discussed how religious epics supported American Cold War ideology of the time, and though at first glance *Quo Vadis* looked like another such film, she notes that counter-elements could also be found there.[15] The film had, in fact, a double-edge in that it focused on a very specific group of innocent people who are accused, hunted down, and punished for a terrible crime against the state, a crime actually committed by those governing. Parallels between the unjustly persecuted Christians and those accused of Communism lay just below the surface.[16] The makers of *Quo Vadis* were walking a fine line between support and critique of current politics.

Musicians, like the more frequently discussed directors and writers, were also subject to accusations of Communism, and many inside and outside the film industry came under suspicion. Hanns Eisler and Paul Robeson, for example, were blacklisted, and Aaron Copland was questioned by Senator Joseph McCarthy's

Senate Permanent Subcommittee on Investigations. In 1950, the publication *Red Channels: The Report of Communist Influence in Radio and Television* listed the names of 151 people suspected of being Communist sympathizers, including Leonard Bernstein, Marc Blitzstein, Artie Shaw, Alan Lomax, and Pete Seeger.

Film composers were pulled into the fray to varying degrees. Film and television composer Jerry Fielding was blacklisted but found employment in Las Vegas directing the music for stage shows. David Raksin had been interested in left-wing causes and belonged briefly to the Communist Party in the late 1930s. Called to testify before HUAC and under intense pressure, he finally made the decision to name eleven names—a decision he regretted the rest of his life—and was not blacklisted.[17] Elmer Bernstein had also been sympathetic to left-wing causes and was "graylisted": though able to find work, he was relegated temporarily to composing for low-budget science fiction films. Alex North not only had left-wing sympathies, he had studied in the Soviet Union and was a member of the Union of Soviet Composers as well as the American-Soviet Music Society; his wife reported that early in his life he had been a member of the Communist Party. North had every reason to believe he would have to testify before HUAC, but in the end he did not and was never blacklisted.[18]

Quo Vadis: The Composer and the Production

During this tumultuous period, *Quo Vadis*'s composer Miklós Rózsa managed to avoid political attention. Rózsa was originally from Hungary (a Soviet-controlled country by 1949), and his father was a wealthy landowner who had once run for parliament as a socialist; both were good reasons to lie low.[19] No doubt it was an advantage that by 1949 he was working at MGM, the studio steered by the savvy and politically conservative Mayer. It probably also helped that by 1951 Rózsa was working on *Quo Vadis*, a film about Christianity set two thousand years before the existence of the atheist Soviet Union and which did not, at first glance, seem to be about current politics.

When Rózsa first heard about *Quo Vadis* he wanted the assignment—but he received it only after Managing Director L. K. Sidney had considered a list of other European composers (supposedly cheaper to hire) that included William Walton.[20] With Rózsa, Sidney had hired a composer with established credentials in both classical music and films. He had received his formal musical training in Leipzig studying musicology and composition, the latter with Hermann Grabner. He also attended choral performances directed by Karl Straube at the Thomaskirche in Leipzig. Straube, whose predecessors in the post included Johann Sebastian Bach, was active in German early music studies as an organist and conductor, and he helped spark Rózsa's interest in this field.[21] Rózsa wrote his first film score for Alexander Korda's *Knight Without Armour* (1937) and went on to polish his reputation in a variety of film genres.

Rózsa tried to incorporate historically accurate music into his film scores whenever possible, beginning with *Knight Without Armour*. Later, inspired by the book of historical information (compiled by classical scholar and friend Hugh Gray) used to guide the *Quo Vadis* production, Rózsa argued such accuracy should also extend to the music. Producers Arthur Hornblow, Jr. and later Sam Zimbalist agreed.[22] Early music would surely intensify the aura of authenticity MGM hoped would sell tickets at the box office, and though no one actually said so, they probably felt that using something so apparently esoteric might help discourage suspicions of incorrect politics. It couldn't hurt, at any rate.

Rózsa always saw himself as a classical composer who was fortunate enough to make a living as a film composer, and his writings, thoughts, and opinions are often phrased in the voice of one or the other. In an article he wrote about *Quo Vadis* for *Film Music Notes*, however, Rózsa acquired yet another—occasionally pompous—voice as "musicologist." In this voice Rózsa explained, "When *Quo Vadis* was assigned to me I decided to be stylistically, absolutely correct."[23] In his autobiography too, the composer spoke of the score as a kind of musicological project whose accuracy, he hoped, would make a contribution to the field: "I was sure that the music of *Quo Vadis* was going to be interesting not only to the audience but also to musicologists, on account of its authenticity."[24]

To keep costs down MGM moved the cast and crew, including Rózsa, to Cinecittà Studios in Rome, where production work took place from May 22, 1950, to November 1, 1950.[25] A few cues had already been composed and recorded in Los Angeles by the time the composer arrived in Rome, but once there he had to oversee an array of other tasks as well, including finding performers, hiring a choreographer for dance scenes, making recording decisions, and seeing to the construction of early instrument replicas for use on-screen (they made no sound). However, he was allowed over two years to work on the music in various capacities, instead of the more usual six weeks or less.[26]

In the midst of production in Rome, Rózsa was sent back to Los Angeles, where he continued working on the music. After the cast and crew returned home the final score was recorded in London in April 1951 with the Royal Philharmonic Orchestra (playing modern instruments) and the BBC Chorus (100+ singers) performing the choral sections. Small revisions were recorded on August 15 in Los Angeles (the music for the Christian hymns and Nero's march had to be recorded outside to obtain the right acoustic effect). Postproduction work took six weeks, during which time extra effects—such as lions roaring in the arena—were added to the soundtrack.

In the end, after all that time and effort, Rózsa was disappointed with the final result: he felt his friend Sam Zimbalist had let him down by allowing the music to be set at too low a volume and burying it under sound effects. But *Quo Vadis*'s success at the box office did firmly establish Rózsa as a composer in yet another genre of film, and as he noted, "I became, apparently, a specialist in historical pictures, much to my delight."[27]

Early Music and Sources of Information

Rózsa was not alone in his desire to work with early music.[28] In the years immediately following World War II, studies in that field had quickly expanded, capturing the interest and imagination of both European and American classical musicians. The situation was different in film scores: there, early music had occasionally been heard, but its use was still relatively rare. For Rózsa, a composer whose "double life" encompassed both worlds, *Quo Vadis* may have seemed a chance to win acceptance for his film work in the eyes of those classical musicians who had dismissed such scores as hack work.

By 1949 there existed considerable literature about ancient Greek music to consult from several disciplines. This music had long been a subject of classical studies, where scholars contributed—as they do today—their expertise in specialized skills not normally part of a musicologist's education, including anthropological field training, knowledge of ancient languages, and facility in deciphering inscriptions. By the early 1950s, however, musicologists such as Curt Sachs (now considered a forerunner of the discipline of ethnomusicology) had also embraced the study of ancient Greek works. In fact, music scholars were publishing new studies and transcriptions of many repertories of early music—challenging long-held beliefs and interpretations in the process—while new anthologies and performance editions were appearing, making more music available to more people.[29]

By 1950, the bicentennial year of Johann Sebastian Bach's death and the year *Quo Vadis* was filmed, early music had triggered vexed questions among musicians: What was—or should be—the nature of the relationship between music of the past and composers, performers, and listeners of the present? Should early music be performed in as historically accurate a way as possible, or can/should other interpretations apply? Bach was considered a composer of early music, and in the course of the commemorations for him extreme views were expressed. Paul Hindemith, for example, advocated "the wholesale restoration of the instruments and performing practices of Bach's own age," while Theodor Adorno "pour[ed] scorn on historical reconstruction."[30] As the classical world debated these issues, Rózsa constructed his own model for presenting early music within the context of a film: the score for *Quo Vadis.*

In his article for *Film Music Notes,* published soon after the release of the picture, Rózsa claimed—incorrectly—that all previous period films had ignored stylistically accurate music, fuming that studios worked hard to achieve historical accuracy in practically every area—script, art, costumes, hair, sets—except the music: "Why is it then that when we come to music . . . no one seems to care much about the genuineness of this most important factor of picture making?"[31] Rózsa announced that his score for *Quo Vadis* would change all that.

By the time he wrote this article, however, Rózsa had already learned why films set in ancient Rome did not use historically accurate music: there wasn't any. To find and select pieces Rózsa depended upon the invaluable help of MGM's highly experienced librarian, George Schneider.[32] Together they discovered that though many references to music exist in Greek and Roman literature, only a few notated examples actually survived from ancient Greece and none from Rome. (Even today, only around forty-five notated fragments have been found; fewer were known in 1949.)[33]

The references in ancient literature were helpful, however. We do not know the specific sources Rózsa and Schneider consulted, but translations of many primary sources were available, as were analytical secondary sources.[34] Roman literature, particularly Suetonius's *The Lives of the Twelve Caesars,* provided insight into the role music played in Emperor Nero's life (Figure 4.1).[35] The composer also learned that the impact of Greek culture on the arts in Rome had been considerable, and that the Romans had modeled their music directly on Greek practices, borrowing modes, genres, and performance styles. Armed with this information, Rózsa concluded he could use Greek melodies in the score and still claim historical accuracy.

The Score: Early Music for Romans and Christians

Rózsa explained in *Film Music Notes* that the score for *Quo Vadis* uses ancient pieces particularly as source music, and a few also appear in the incidental music.[36] Although one can regard source music as a kind of sound effect that also supplies "local color," Rózsa made it clear that here source music provides commentary and represents characters in ways comparable to the incidental score.

Rózsa noted that the source pieces are associated with three groups: the (pagan) Romans, the Christians, and those he identified as "slaves," "the Roman Empire," or more specifically, "Babylonians, Syrians, Egyptians, Persians and other conquered nations of oriental origin."[37] Ancient Greek melodies are usually associated with the Romans, while Christians are associated with melodies from a variety of sources. Rózsa said little about the music for the third group, except that it included "fragments of the oldest melodies found in Sicily . . . with Arabian influence, and others found in Cairo."[38] Because of this lack of information, the following outline focuses exclusively on the early music used as source music for the Romans and Christians. (The originally composed incidental music also falls outside the scope of this study.)[39]

Among the scenes of Roman entertainment (see Table 4.1)[40] is a dance performed at a banquet, the "Bacchanale," featuring music inspired by "fragments from an anonymous composer . . . which probably were written for a cithara school." Rózsa does not name a specific source, but they may have been the "Anonymous fragments" published by Friederich Bellerman in 1841, which originally may have been instrumental exercises.[41] In other scenes, individuals—the Emperor Nero (Peter Ustinov) and the slave woman Eunice (Marina Berti)—sing and accompany themselves on instruments. Nero's first song, with lyrics by Hugh Gray, describes an "epic spectacle" of the past, the burning of Troy. The melody is the most famous of the surviving Greek works, the first century CE "Epitaph of Seikilos," from a tombstone found in 1883.[42] More intimately, Eunice expresses her love for Petronius (Leo Genn) to a melody once attributed to the Greek lyric poet Pindar, supposedly discovered in Sicily in the seventeenth century. Rózsa used it because it was "hauntingly beautiful."[43]

FIGURE 4.1 Nero (Peter Ustinov) accompanies himself as he sings to the court.

TABLE 4.1.

MUSIC OF THE ROMANS

Association/Type of Music in Film	Source of Melody
1. Nero: "The Burning of Troy" (source)	Greek: "The Epitaph of Seikilos," first century CE
2. Eunice: Love song (source)	Greek: "First Ode of Pindar" (not accepted as authentic)
3. Banquet dancers: "Bacchanale" (source)	Greek: Based on Anonymous, second-century fragments for kithara (possibly Bellerman 97–104)
4. Nero: "The Burning of Rome" (source)	Plainchant: "Omnes sitientes venite ad aquas"
5. Rome: The city burns (incidental music)	Greek: "Hymn to the Sun" by Mesomedes, second century CE

A famous scene in *Quo Vadis* features Nero singing while Rome burns—a fire he ordered set to provide a suitable epic subject for his performance. The incidental music uses a quotation from Mesomedes's "Hymn to the Sun," but the source music is particularly striking. Nero does not play the proverbial fiddle but accompanies himself on a lyre as he sings of "The Burning of Rome" to a Christian plainchant melody, "Omnes sitientes venite ad aquas" (All you that thirst come to the waters). This is a curious—perhaps ironic—choice, not only because Rome burns as Nero sings a tune associated with water, but because it is Christian plainchant put into the mouth of that religion's most notorious persecutor. (Rózsa argued, unpersuasively, the melody was probably Roman in origin, surviving for centuries to later become chant.)[44] Rózsa balanced this odd assignment by giving the Christians something just as peculiar to sing, the melody of a Greek hymn to the goddess Nemesis (see further discussion below).

Christians sing for the first time in the film during a secret service of baptism (see Table 4.2). After this the members continue to sing in community and in that way seem to resemble a contemporary Protestant Christian congregation. The melody from the beginning of the baptism service, however, originates in Roman Catholic practice and is a setting of the "Kyrie," a Greek text from the Ordinary of the Mass. Rózsa used it to make a musical connection between the Christians and the Jewish faith of which they were originally a part, arguing that Christian music had roots partially within Jewish music of the first century. The composer described this particular Kyrie as originally a "Babylonian Jewish liturgical melody," a view that may have come from the work of German Jewish ethnomusicologist A. Z. Idelsohn, whom he cited as a source in his research. Based on this understanding of the music, Rózsa engaged a Jewish cantor to sing it for the recording. [45]

Rózsa also used other chants: Christians sing the Ambrosian "Aeterna rerum conditor" (Eternal maker of all things) as they burn to death on crosses,[46] and the opening titles music has a melodic line modeled on the Gregorian "Libera me, Domine" (Deliver

TABLE 4.2.

MUSIC OF THE CHRISTIANS

Association/Type of Music in Film	Source of Melody
1. Christians: Service of baptism (source)	Roman Catholic liturgy: Kyrie (also Jewish?)

2. Christians:
  a. Service of baptism (source)
  b. In arena with lions (source)
  c. End titles (incidental)
	Greek: "Hymn to Nemesis," Mesomodes, second century CE

3. Christians: On burning crosses (source)	Plainchant (Ambrosian): "Aeterna rerum conditor"
4. Christians: Opening titles (incidental)	Modeled on plainchant: "Libera me, Domine" (Gregorian) and a Kyrie
5. Lygia; Taken hostage (incidental)	Greek: "Second Delphic Hymn" (by Limenios?), second century CE

me, O Lord). Rózsa was well aware that plainchant was not historically accurate for the first-century setting of the film: he recalled that during an audience with Pope Pius XII in Rome, the Pope "asked me whether I was going to use Gregorian or Ambrosian chants in my music. I had to tell him that both were some centuries too late for that period." (This may have been a memory slip, since Rózsa had decided to record "Omnes sitientes venite ad aquas" even before he had arrived in Rome.[47])

Rózsa also used Greek melodies for the Christians but felt a need to justify this decision, explaining that later Christian music had roots not only in Roman and Jewish but also Greek music, since early Christians were "partly Jews and partly Greeks." In the score this meant Christians could now be plausibly associated with Greek music, when, for example, we hear the "Second Delphic Hymn" in the incidental music when Lygia (Deborah Kerr), a Christian, is taken hostage. Another particularly startling example occurs when the Christians sing a Greek hymn to the goddess Nemesis—with new words—as they die in the arena (music also heard at the end of the baptism service and during the end titles). Rózsa chose the melody for aesthetic reasons ("its beauty and fervor"), but it was also one of the few almost historically accurate pieces available at the time: a second century CE piece credited to Mesomedes and first published by Vincenzo Galilei in 1581.[48]

After choosing his melodies Rózsa had to decide how to present them, which meant reconciling contradictory goals. Whereas Rózsa the musicologist wanted listeners to know they were hearing early music, Rózsa the film composer wanted to make sure the melodies sounded familiar enough to keep audiences emotionally connected to the story. In particular, he had to decide how far to go in attempting to reconstruct the original sound of the music. It is unclear whether Rózsa believed literal replication was possible, but the studio's promotional material certainly raised hopes of it—one booklet confidently stated, "Although there is no record of exactly what kind of music the ancient Romans enjoyed, the tunes used in the production are believed to be as nearly authentic as possible."[49] In the end, the film composer's desire to enhance the drama correctly overrode his ambition to highlight the research.

Still, Rózsa did try to signal the presence of ancient melodies, for instance by imitating the timbre of early instruments while using the modern ones actually performing the score: a small Scottish harp, for example, was used for Nero's lyre and Eunice's harp.[50] Harmony could also signal "oldness." Since other scholars have discussed this at length, particularly with regard to the influence Hungarian folk music may have had on Rózsa's harmonic language,[51] my own comments here will focus on Rózsa's concern with historicism.

The original Greek tunes were notated without harmony, and supporting intervals in performance probably consisted of unisons, octaves, fifths, and fourths—rudimentary, though fundamental, intervals in Western music. Understandably, Rózsa did not want to limit his harmonic palette to those few, basic, and potentially uninteresting intervals, since once early music began to bore listeners it became a liability: "One had to avoid the pitfall of producing only musicological oddities instead of music with a universal, emotional appeal."[52] Rózsa recognized that simple intervals used circumspectly could sound "old" to audiences, and in the incidental score he featured them within a complex harmonic framework using parallel movement, "open" chords, and modal writing. In the source music, though, he aimed for a more historically informed sound based on what was known at the time. The melodies the Christians sing, for example, are presented in a straightforward, uncomplicated way: "It goes without saying that all these hymns are performed . . . in unison (or octaves) unharmonized, as they were sung," the composer adds confidently, "two thousand years ago."[53]

Though Rózsa did not discuss it, there are distinctions between how voices and instruments are distributed in the film. The source music for the pagan Romans always involves instruments, whether for Nero or Eunice singing, or public entertainments and ceremonies—in the main titles there is even a "musical duel" between brass instruments (the Romans) and voices (the Christians). Throughout the film, in fact, Christians are represented by singing: as mentioned earlier, this evoked contemporary Protestant practices and may have encouraged Christian viewers to identify more closely with the Christian characters (Figure 4.2). Rózsa may have been thinking also of an ancient view that elevated vocal above instrumental music,[54] which also brings to mind Calvinist (i.e., Protestant) injunctions made centuries later against the use of musical instruments during worship. Regardless, showing Christians singing together *a cappella* was heavily coded with meanings, signaling

FIGURE 4.2　The Christians sing in the arena.

the cohesion and spirituality of the community, "apartness" from society (since there are no instruments), and a similarity to the worship practices of some viewers.

Concluding Thoughts

The reader will note that while I have emphasized Rózsa's concern with musicology in *Quo Vadis*, I do not argue he was a musicologist or that creating this score constituted a musicological task: good library research to find materials to use in a composition does not make one a musicologist—it makes one a well-prepared composer.

Nevertheless, Rózsa felt he *was* doing musicological work: apart from actually referring to musicology, his frequent references to "reconstruction" and "authenticity" and the construction of involved arguments to justify the use of melodies seem to signal this. However, even if the composer primarily conceived of musicology as "collecting facts and tunes" rather than finding and critically interpreting evidence, simply pulling together a set of melodies specialists already knew existed hardly seemed to merit the scholarly attention he had hoped for. Why did he think this score was a scholarly contribution?

At the risk of sounding obvious, what set the early music in *Quo Vadis* apart from contemporary concert presentations was its use in a film. At a time when film composing was ignored by many in classical music, identifying this score as a musicological project may have been a bid for recognition. But in the end Rózsa seemed to feel the score deserved attention less for its musicological method than for its authenticity—a term implying not only historical accuracy, but also a kind of faithfulness to the spirit of the time and the original performers. Rózsa had persuaded MGM to allow him to use this music on the grounds that it would make the film more accurate and consequently more believable (therefore more marketable and perhaps even more politically safe). But he also hoped to persuade music scholars that the melodies were in some way more "authentic" because of their film context. He apparently felt that all the historically accurate elements of the film, taken together, reenacted—possibly literally—a performance of the music from the time portrayed, something that should have made both MGM and music scholars happy (though it seems no scholars paid any attention at the time).[55]

Today it may be tempting to accuse Rózsa of being too careful in his approach to early music in *Quo Vadis*, but considering the genre in which he worked, he was adventurous for the time. As Rózsa's musicologist alter ego fantasized about authentic performances, Rózsa the actual film composer created an original score with ancient melodies at its heart spiraling outward into new conceptions. Thus, *Quo Vadis* raises the question, "How far can a presentation of early music go before it becomes something else?" For the entire score included not only little-adorned early melodies, but also imitations of old tunes, exploratory fantasies based on ancient music, and originally composed cues. Ultimately it may be more helpful not to think of this score as a presentation of early music, even if Rózsa did. It was, in fact, something at least as rich in affects and implications: a composition *about* early music rather than a performance *of* it.

There are many reasons to study this score further, not least because it reminds us of how views of early music have shifted over the years, and because it prods us to ask what the score for a historical film can and should be doing. It also reminds us that supposedly specialized endeavors such as working with early music can be rooted in very practical financial, political, and ideological concerns. The more we study these issues, the more they become (to reverse Rózsa's own phrase) interesting not only to musicologists but to audiences as well.

NOTES

1. The "Quo Vadis" folder containing this advertisement, plus the promotional booklet *The Story Behind Quo Vadis*, MGM: n.d. (probably ca. 1951), are in the collection of the Margaret Herrick Library, Academy of Motion Picture Arts and Sciences, Beverly Hills, California (hereafter Herrick Library).

2. See David Hanna, "MGM's 'Quo Vadis' Colossal," *The Hollywood Reporter*, n.d. and "'Quo Vadis' Colossal in its New York Premier," *San Francisco Examiner*, n.a. (November 21, 1951), Herrick Library. Reproductions of the manuscript score for *Quo Vadis* are in the "Miklos Rozsa Papers," held by the Special Collections Research Center (formerly the George Arents Research Library) of Syracuse University. My thanks to the Center for copies of cues.

3. See especially Roger Hickman, *Miklós Rózsa's Ben-Hur: A Film Score Guide* (Lanham, MD: Scarecrow Press, 2011).

4. The score's earliest (and most authoritative) discussion is Miklós Rózsa, "The Music in QUO VADIS," *Film Music Notes* 11 (Nov.–Dec. 1951): 4–10; among the most recent is Hickman, *Miklós Rózsa's Ben-Hur.*

5. My language is influenced by Richard Taruskin, *Text & Act: Essays on Music and Performance* (New York: Oxford University Press, 1995). Solomon speaks of Rózsa's "synthesis" of "ancient musical fragments, theory and instrumentation with melodic lines, harmonies, and orchestrations suitable to modern ears and able to evoke familiar emotional responses from modern audiences," Jon Solomon, "The Sounds of Cinematic Antiquity," in *Classics and Cinema*, ed. Martin M. Winkler (Lewisburg, PA: Bucknell University Press, 1991), 269–270.

6. Curtin's translation sold 800,000 copies in one year alone. Josef Schmidt and Edyta Laszczewska, "Henryk Sienkiewicz, 'Quo Vadis?'," *Encyclopedia of Catholic Literature*, vol. 2, ed. Mary R. Reichardt (Westport, CT: Greenwood Press, 2004), 641.

7. "The term 'Polish messianism' was coined to express the belief that the political humiliations, reversals, and defections served a higher purpose." Schmidt and Laszczewska, 639.

8. Ibid., 647.

9. See Schmidt and Laszczewska; Maria Wyke, *Projecting the Past: Ancient Rome, Cinema and History* (New York: Routledge, 1997); Derek Elley, *The Epic Film: Myth and History* (Boston: Routledge & Kegan Paul, 1984), 192; and "Quo Vadis," The Internet Movie Database, accessed April 9, 2010, http://www.imdb.net.

10. See "Notes to 'Quo Vadis'," AFI Catalog: Feature Films, American Film Institute, accessed May 4, 2010, http://www.afi.com/members/catalog/DetailView.aspx?s=&Movie=50257. See also Wyke, 138; Ronald Bowers, "Quo Vadis," in *Magill's Survey of Cinema: English Language Films*, First Series: Vol. 3 (Englewood Cliffs, NJ: Salem Press, 1980), 1412; and "In the Beginning: *Quo Vadis* and the Genesis of the Biblical Epic," featurette in *Quo Vadis*, Special Edition DVD, directed by Mervyn LeRoy (1951; Burbank, CA: Warner Home Video, 2008).

11. *Samson and Delilah* was a box office and critical hit, grossing $11,500,000 in the United States and receiving Academy Awards for Best Art Direction/Set Decoration (color) and Costume Design (color). See "Notes to 'Samson and Delilah'," AFI Catalog: Feature Films, American Film Institute, accessed August 27, 2012, http://www.afi.com/members/catalog/DetailView.aspx?s=&Movie=26090; see also "Samson and Delilah: Box Office/Business for," The Internet Movie Database, accessed August 31, 2012.

12. Gary A. Smith, "Quo Vadis," in *Epic Films: Casts, Credits, and Commentary on Over 250 Historical Spectacle Movies* (Jefferson, NC: McFarland, 1991), 175.

13. Smith, 175. Mayer, however, was ousted from power in 1951. "Mayer, Louis B." in Ephraim Katz, *The Film Encyclopedia*, 2nd ed. (New York: HarperPerennial, 1994).

14. Taylor belonged to the conservative Motion Picture Alliance for the Preservation of American Ideals and testified before HUAC in 1947 as a friendly witness. For the history of the cast and crew, see AFI, "'Quo Vadis' Notes."

15. Wyke, 143–144.

16. Elley views Petronius's farewell letter to Nero in *Quo Vadis* as "a great anti-McCarthy speech for fifties America." See Elley, 125.

17. See Victor S. Navasky, *Naming Names* (New York: Penguin Books, 1981), 249–252.

18. Heathcliff Blair, "Biography for Jerry Fielding," The Internet Movie Database, accessed September 21, 2010; and Jon Burlingame, "Biography for Elmer Bernstein," Elmer Bernstein, the Official Site, accessed September 21, 2010, http://www.elmerbernstein.com/bio/biography.html. North's biographer explains that he managed to avoid the Committee mostly by traveling constantly between Los Angeles and his home in Connecticut. See Sanya Shoilevska Henderson, *Alex North, Film Composer* (Jefferson, NC: McFarland, 2003), 49–50. For additional discussion of blacklisting of composers in the early 1950s, see chapter 13 in this collection.

19. See Andrea Weever, "Miklós Rózsa," *American National Biography*, Supplement 1 (New York: Oxford University Press 2002), 532.

20. See "Rozsa Relates His Memories Composing *Quo Vadis* (1970s)," courtesy of Alan Hamer in "Interviews," The Miklós Rózsa Society Website, accessed May 14, 2010, http://www.miklosrozsa.org. See also Miklós Rózsa, *A Double Life* (New York: Wynwood Press, 1989), 163.

21. Rózsa, *Double Life*, 32. For information about Straube, see Harry Haskell, *The Early Music Revival: A History* (London: Thames and Hudson, 1988), 56, 57, 77, 82, 116, 121.

22. Interview, "Rózsa Relates Memories"; Rózsa, *Double Life*, 163; and " 'Quo Vadis' Will Aim at Authenticity," *Los Angeles Times*, May 22, 1949. For more about Gray, see article (no title or author) in *The New Yorker*, October 7, 1950, "Quo Vadis" folder, Herrick Library.

23. Rózsa, "Music in QUO VADIS," 4. Article reprinted in Frank K. DeWald, *Quo Vadis*, liner notes for MGM E103 (October, 1951), reissued in Miklós Rózsa, *Treasury: 1959–1968 Film Score Monthly*, FSM 04, CD set and published in *Film Score Monthly*, "FSM Online Liner Notes," accessed May 3, 2010, http://www.filmscoremonthly.com/notes/quo_vadis2.html.

24. Rózsa, *Double Life*, 170. The word "authenticity" is now avoided in early music, since without recordings it is impossible to know what a completely authentic performance would sound like (notation alone cannot provide this information). Unfortunately, the term is often still used in the film industry and film criticism.

25. For the following production description I depend particularly on Rózsa, *Double Life*, 164–171; see also Rózsa, "Music in QUO VADIS," and DeWald, *Quo Vadis*, liner notes.

26. One cue, for example, was a revision dated April 22, 1949, while final work recording the score took place on August 15, 1951 (in Culver City). See cue, "Jesu Lord," #4544/19678 Rev. in Rózsa, ms. *Quo Vadis*; for dates, see DeWald, *Quo Vadis*, liner notes.

27. Rózsa, *Double Life*, 171.

28. For a discussion of Rózsa's—and Hollywood's—interest in modernism, see Hickman, 15–21.

29. Easily accessible collections from the time include Archibald T. Davison and Willi Apel, *Historical Anthology of Music: Oriental, Medieval and Renaissance Music*, rev. ed. (Cambridge, MA: Harvard University Press, 1946 and 1949); and Carl Parrish and John F. Ohl, *Masterpieces of Music Before 1750* (New York: W. W. Norton, 1951).

30. Hindemith stated his view in a 1950 speech given for the Bach commemoration in Hamburg, Germany; cited in John Butt, *Playing with History: The Historical Approach to Musical Performance* (New York: Cambridge University Press, 2002), 3–4. For Adorno's statement, see "Bach Defended Against his Devotees" (1951) in *Prisms*, trans. Samuel and Shierry Weber (Cambridge, MA: Harvard University Press, 1981), 140.

31. Rózsa, "Music in QUO VADIS," 4. While it is true that many historical films did not use historically accurate music, there were important exceptions, including William Walton's score for *Henry V* (1944) and Herbert Stothart's for *Romeo and Juliet* (1936). Rózsa probably knew of both: the former was quite famous, and the latter was written by one of MGM's top

composers who was aided in his work by George Schneider, who later assisted Rózsa. See Linda K. Schubert, ' "A Brilliant New Symphonic Effect': The 'New' Early Music in Stothart's Score for *Romeo and Juliet* (MGM, 1936)," *The Journal of Film Music* 4, no. 1 (2011): 27–43.

32. Rózsa, "Music in QUO VADIS," 4. Schneider was the administrator of the vast MGM music library. He specialized in this work, having been originally hired to seek out and acquire copyrights for preexistent pieces used in films. See Danette Cook Adamson and Mimi Tashiro, "Servants, Scholars, and Sleuths: Early Leaders in California Music Librarianship," *Music Library Association Notes* (March 1992): 806–819; and Fred Stanley, "Film Tune Sleuths," *New York Times*, part II (August 17, 1947): 4.

33. For discussions of surviving ancient Greek and Roman music, see *New Grove Dictionary of Music and Musicians*, 2nd edition, ed. Stanley Sadie (London: Macmillan, 2001), s.v. "Greece, §I, 2 and §I, 8" by Thomas J. Mathiesen; and Thomas J. Mathiesen, *Apollo's Lyre: Greek Music and Music Theory in Antiquity and the Middle Ages* (Lincoln: University of Nebraska Press, 1999), 12.

34. References to music could be found in the works of Aristoxenus, Cleonides, and Athenaeus, translations of which appeared in Oliver Strunk's *Source Readings in Music History*, first published in 1950. Other sources included collections and transcriptions, such as Theodore Reinach, *La musique grecque* (Paris: Payot, 1926; repr. Paris: Editions d'Aujourd'hui, 1975); and studies of instruments, such as Curt Sachs, *The History of Musical Instruments* (New York: W. W. Norton, 1940).

35. See especially John G. Landels, *Music in Ancient Greece and Rome* (New York: Routledge, 2001). Rózsa also cites Seneca as a source in Rózsa, "Music in QUO VADIS," 5.

36. In his autobiography, Rózsa uses the term "incidental music" to refer to background music. I use that term here to avoid controversies regarding the terms "background music" and "underscore" (both used by film composers) and "nondiegetic music" (used by some film music scholars).

37. Rózsa, "Music in QUO VADIS," 5, 7.

38. Ibid., 7.

39. For incidental music, see Hickman.

40. The cues in Tables 4.1 and 4.2 are arranged according to Rózsa's discussion in *Film Music Notes* and employ his plainchant spellings. A print version of the composer's handwritten examples can be found online at DeWald, *Quo Vadis*, liner notes. See also transcriptions in Reinach, *La Musique Grecque*. The standard edition of ancient Greek works and fragments is Egert Pöhlmann, *Denkmäler altgriechischer Musik* (Nuremberg, 1970), though additional fragments have since been found since then.

41. Rózsa, "Music in QUO VADIS," 6. Johann Friedrich Bellermann, *Anonymi scriptio de musica* (Berlin: Foerstner, 1841), nos. 97–104.

42. Rózsa and Schneider may have found this piece and others in Reinach.

43. Rózsa, "Music in QUO VADIS," 6. Solomon identifies this as "Athanasius Kircher's recreation of the music to Pindar's *First Pythian Ode*" but associates it with a court dance rather than Eunice's song. See Solomon, 328–329.

44. Rózsa, "Music in QUO VADIS," 5.

45. Rózsa, "Music in QUO VADIS," 6; and Rózsa, *Double Life*, 164. Abraham Zvi Idelsohn was a scholar of Jewish music who collected examples from a range of Jewish communities, including Babylonian and Yemeni groups, in the process discovering "relationships between ancient Hebrew (mainly Yemenite) and early Christian . . . chant that had hitherto remained

undetected." See Edith Gerson-Kiwi and Israel J. Katz, "Idelsohn, Abraham Zvi," in Grove Music Online. Oxford Music Online, accessed May 21, 2014, http://www.oxfordmusiconline. com/subscriber/article/grove/music/13702. Publications of the time, doubtless acquiring their information from Rózsa, frequently mentioned the use of "Babylonian and Yemeni" music in *Quo Vadis*.

46. Rózsa, "Music in QUO VADIS," 7. The spelling is Rózsa's; the manuscript adds the word "Rerum." See "Evensong," #20413 in Rózsa, ms. score for *Quo Vadis*.

47. Rózsa, *Double Life*, 165; DeWald, *Quo Vadis*, liner notes.

48. Rózsa, "Music in QUO VADIS," 67; Reinach, 199201.

49. "The Music," in *The Story Behind Quo Vadis*.

50. For the complete list of modern instruments played and those imitated, see Rózsa, "Music in QUO VADIS," 7–8.

51. See especially Christopher Palmer, *The Composer in Hollywood* (New York: Marion Boyars, 1990), 213; Roy M. Prendergast, *Film Music: A Neglected Art*, 2nd ed. (New York: W. W. Norton, 1992), 129; and Hickman, 8–12.

52. Rózsa, "Music in QUO VADIS," 6.

53. Whether Rózsa's arrangement of the hymns constituted a radical or minor alteration depends on the description one reads. See both Rózsa, "Music in QUO VADIS" and *Story Behind Quo Vadis*, MGM.

54. See, e.g., Mathiesen, 160.

55. David Schulenberg comments that "some of the most illuminating performances of early music have tried to replicate particular parameters, especially the performing forces, of specific performances or venues: Handel's 1754 *Messiah* . . . Bach's 1727 *St. Matthew Passion*. . . . Of course these were no more or less authentic than those reenactments of Civil War battles that so engage military-history buffs; some things doubtless accorded with what actually happened, others not." It is easy to think of a historical film such as *Quo Vadis* as another such reenactment. See David Schulenberg, review of *The End of Early Music: A Period Performer's History of Music for the Twenty-First Century* by Bruce Haynes, in *The Journal of the American Musicological Society* 63, no. 1 (Spring 2010): 176.

5 "Whatever Will Be, Will Be"

Gender Equality and the Music of Alfred Hitchcock's The Man Who Knew Too Much *(1956)*

JOSHUA NEUMANN

ALFRED HITCHCOCK, THE undisputed master of suspense, frequently examined individual psychologies and social structures in his iconic films of the mid-twentieth century.[1] In addition to *Psycho* (1960), films such as *Shadow of a Doubt* (1943), *Rope* (1948), and *Dial M for Murder* (1954) explore the individual psyche, each in relationship to crime. Alternatively, films such as *Saboteur* (1942), *Rear Window* (1954), and *North by Northwest* (1959) provide insight into the collective, social psyche of midcentury America, and these mostly in relationship to political interests. *Vertigo* (1958) and *Marnie* (1964) examine troubled relationships between couples in which at least one domestic partner battles personal demons.

In Hitchcock's oeuvre, one film stands as a testament to the growing empowerment of women, particularly as wives and mothers: the 1956 remake of *The Man Who Knew Too Much*. This film is part of a trilogy—preceded by *Rear Window* and followed by *Vertigo*—that encompasses Hitchcock's commentary on the victimization of women in marriage.[2] It critiques a male-centered society and stereotypical gender roles in 1950s America by considering the ways in which society benefits when women pursue both career and family. As such, it reveals both the positive and negative consequences for proponents and opponents, respectively, of its subject.

Hitchcock's controversial reputation provides insight into the significance of the use of music in this film. Many critics argue that Hitchcock projected his personal feelings and ambitions onto his male leads. Others, by contrast, refuse to acknowledge any ambiguity and see his works as completely negative portrayals of society. Still others believe that he offers no comment on society at all. In any case, ambiguity surrounds his worldview—particularly his sexual politics—and leads to ambiguous treatment of his subjects.[3] The general scholarly view concedes that "the charge of misogyny constantly recurs, and at all levels of critical writing," and that "the films dramatize and foreground not merely tensions personal to Hitchcock, but tensions central to our culture and to its construction and organization of sexual difference."[4] The popular view tends to range from wholly negative—"Hitchcock derived a great deal of pleasure through humiliating his heroines,"[5]—to more moderate, if sarcastic—"Of course Alfred Hitchcock was a misogynist, or at least had a neurotic compulsion to mistreat women in his films: everyone knows that."[6]

Conversely, few scholars have attempted to consider Hitchcock's films as feminist texts. A notable exception is Thomas Hemmeter, who reads *Shadow of a Doubt* "as a critique of the patriarchal ideology it represents, as a text that shows the cracks and fissures in the sexual roles born and existing in the institution of the family. From this perspective the film becomes a feminist text."[7] I read the remake of *The Man Who Knew Too Much* with the same "cracks and fissures" in mind. The film critiques the stereotypical attitude toward women (housewives and mothers, and nothing else) of the 1950s, suggesting Hitchcock actually supported female empowerment. While Hitchcock's employment of music in the film might indicate either a general recognition of social change, on the one hand, or his specific, personal feelings about women in the mid-1950s on the other, the truth probably lies somewhere in the middle: Hitchcock likely meant to serve as commentator rather than polemicist. In this chapter I explore some of the ways in which Hitchcock's use of music in this influential film may offer a "critique of gender roles."[8]

Representation

The Man Who Knew Too Much comes closer than many of Alfred Hitchcock's films of the 1950s to standing as a feminist critique of American society. Robin Wood asserts that it examines sexual identity and ideology.[9] Like *Rear Window*, this film "is crucially about marriage."[10] It also carries considerable intertextual qualities with several other collaborations between Alfred Hitchcock and James Stewart. At the heart of this film lies "the impossibility of successful human relations within an ideological system that constructs men and women in hopelessly incompatible roles," where one role is privileged over the other.[11]

Singer Doris Day was an appropriate choice to portray Jo McKenna, who gave up an international singing career as Josephine Conway to become a wife and mother.

While it is obvious that "Hitchcock had used her . . . in a very purposeful manner, matching [her] against Jimmy Stewart's Midwestern charm," he nevertheless
managed "to produce a frightening portrait of the 1950s American family."[12] The
differences between the maternal characters of this version and the 1934 original
highlight the stereotype of oppressive culture in Fifties American families. Wood
believes, "We can see that the structure of the patriarchal nuclear family, and the
supposedly monogamous marriage that guarantees it, has always been an institution for the subordination of women."[13] This sentiment leads to similar claims about
Alfred Hitchcock's view of gender roles: "Hitchcock's movies suggest that the submission of personality required of a film actress is akin to the submission required of
a 'good' wife or mistress."[14] Wendy Lesser then modifies this assertion: Hitchcock
may have reluctantly accepted that women were unable to be remade or formed into
whatever image their husbands might desire.[15] Even so, she falls short of considering that Hitchcock may have embraced the supposed intuition and emotional
attachment of femininity as different from the supposed objectivity and emotional
detachment of masculinity yet one as equally valuable to society.

In many analyses of music and gender, two points relevant to Hitchcock's
examination of gender roles in 1950s America emerge. First, Lacanian psychoanalysis establishes the link between subjectivity and the voice.[16] Second, philosopher and cultural critic Slavoj Žižek posits that a "song's power is in its
resonance with the maternal voice."[17] Therefore, the mother's voice both incorporates and heightens musical elements.[18] By virtue of her musicianship and
motherhood, Jo McKenna is, according to widespread attitudes in the 1950s
regarding gender roles, entirely feminine and incapable of functioning outside
her home because she is "defined according to (her) emotions and the effect of
those emotions."[19] In this light, Hitchcock's alteration of the female protagonist
from a hobbyist target shooter (played by actress Edna Best in the film's original
version) to a semi-retired singer, played by a real-life singer, provides reason to
believe that Hitchcock embraced the empowered femininity of Jo McKenna/
Doris Day. Also, the ending suggests that the film demonstrates a new possible
reality for American families in which professional pursuits are balanced with
shared domestic responsibility.

Dr. McKenna's Growing Pains

While the first portion of *The Man Who Knew Too Much* focuses primarily on Ben
McKenna (James Stewart), it does so to display the inherent limitations of a society
in which men have absolute social power, including the right to restrict their wives'
activities. From the outset of the film, the revised script wastes little time in pitting

the conservative Dr. McKenna against the progressive Jo Conway. Despite her identity as an independent, internationally renowned musician, Jo Conway occupied an enigmatic existence, one needing refurbishment according to stereotypical social archetypes in which the virtuous woman exhibited emotional and sexual self-control.[20] When a husband introduced a woman to others, nothing was unique about her appearance to the outside world other than the specificity of a particular man who had claimed her. Ben erroneously asserts on the bus that he has called Jo by her abbreviated first name for so long that no one calls her anything else.[21] This is pure fabrication: the Draytons, who had never previously met the McKennas, later address her as Jo Conway, as do her friends as they enter the McKennas' hotel room in London. Ben's insistence on prolonging this misrepresentation likely reflects his own beliefs and, by extension, those of the society in which he operates. For example, upon exiting the bus, Louis Bernard (Daniel Gélin) ignores Jo's question and instead addresses her husband; this elicits no redress from Ben on behalf of his obviously affronted wife. These aspects of the film reinforce the male domination of familial relations in 1950s America. Their son Hank's contradiction about addressing Jo as "Mommy" further delineates the perceived place of wives: each subsumed her identity into that of her husband's to everyone except her own children.[22] Thus, we see the clear boundaries that are drawn between men and women, with men being superior and immune from feminine displeasure with their actions.

The portrayal of typical Fifties attitudes toward women continues when, en route to the hotel, Jo voices her concern at Ben's forthrightness in response to Louis Bernard's questions. Her uneasiness here is not the result of an intuitive sensation or an emotional inclination (supposed feminine traits). Rather, Jo raises valid questions and makes an astute and accurate assessment of Ben's relative ignorance of Bernard's odd behavior and his unnerving knowledge of the McKenna family. She arrives at her conclusions by logical and relatively objective observation, which is ordinarily considered a masculine characteristic.[23] Ben dismisses Jo's aptitude for observation, patronizingly chiding, "Even though this is mysterious Morocco, let's not lose our heads." Upon arriving at the hotel and later at dinner, it is again Jo who notices the Draytons' voyeurism. Ben dismisses her concerns, this time more brusquely, as he exclaims with frustration, "Would you please stop imagining things!"[24]

Hitchcock privileges the viewer to what modern audiences might consider a stark dichotomy as the McKennas prepare to attend dinner with Louis Bernard. After Jo sings with Hank and puts him to bed, she joins Monsieur Bernard on the balcony of the suite and asks him questions in the same manner he used when he spoke to the McKennas on the bus. Rather than answering forthrightly, Bernard offers evasive, obfuscating answers to "Mrs. McKenna" (not "Jo"). Addressing her by her married name might serve as a subtle reminder that she is subservient to her husband, and that her proper place and interest should be on domestic, femininely appropriate matters, not on the activities of any man.[25]

The scene in the restaurant offers the first critique of male dominance. Bernard Herrmann, the film's composer, elucidates this point through the scene's (implicitly) diegetic music. Reminiscent of Hollywood's musical treatment of the exotic Middle East, the violin's and clarinet's solo lines nevertheless have a subtly comical character, as if mocking Ben's bumbling attempts to sit at the table. By extension, one might conclude that Hitchcock's use of this particular music here mocks Dr. McKenna's conservative gender role. Ben's discomfort is evident in his facial expressions, which make obvious his growing frustration with his inability to exert any control over a situation that has reduced him "to humiliating buffoonery" for the first time in the film, as Figures 5.1a–b illustrate.[26] Recalling that the McKennas are representatives of perceived 1950s American gender roles, this scene insinuates that culturally appropriate behavior can cause discomfort or humiliation. As Mr. Drayton (Bernard Miles) and the assassin eventually discover, bodily harm can come to those refusing to accept it.

The ensuing dialogue between Jo and Lucy (Brenda de Banzie) and Edward Drayton further alludes to the issues of gender equality:

LUCY: Good evening. You must think me awfully rude, I've been staring at you
    ever since I saw you at the Hotel. You are Jo Conway, *the* Jo Conway?
JO: Yes, I am.
LUCY: Didn't I tell you, I knew I was right. I'm Lucy Drayton and this is my
    husband.
ALL: How do you do?
BEN: We're Dr. and Mrs. *McKenna.*
EDWARD: My wife tells me Mrs. McKenna appeared at the London
    Palladium a few years ago.
LUCY: Of course we hardly ever see a show now, Edward is such an old stick in
    the mud. I have to console myself with your records.
EDWARD: I must admit I love them. I'm not one for this terrible Bebop.
JO: Thank you.
LUCY: When are you coming back to London?
JO: Possibly never again, professionally.
LUCY: Don't tell me you're giving up the stage.
JO: Temporarily.
BEN: Well it's just that I'm a doctor, and a doctor's wife never has much time.

JO: What my husband's trying to say is that Broadway musical shows are not produced in Indianapolis, Indiana. Of course we could live in New York. I hear the doctors aren't starving there either.

BEN: Well it's not that I have any objection to working in New York. It's just that it would be kind of hard for *my* patients to come all the way from Indianapolis for treatment.[27]

FIGURES 5.1A–B Ben McKenna (James Stewart) demonstrates the inherent foolishness of a gender-centric society first by his bumbling attempt to situate himself at the table, then by sulking. Jo's (Doris Day) knowing glance in the second frame fails to veil her frustration with Ben and the social conventions he embodies.

By asking if Mrs. McKenna is "Jo Conway, *the* Jo Conway," Mrs. Drayton raises the main point of contention in the McKennas' marriage and, by extension, American society: career versus family. Sensing Jo's frustration with her present position in life, Mr. Drayton confesses, "I'm not one for this terrible Bebop"; in so doing, he recognizes Jo's professional expertise and attempts to converse with her on recent developments in music. It is evident by these conversations that Jo is "poignantly aware she would still be a star were it not for the sexist culture she represents."[28] Jo's terse reply indicates she views herself as an equal and expects that Ben does too. Ben's comment about a doctor's wife having little time reiterates the seeming imbalance of marriages in 1950s society. Jo's response indicates she has either tried to forsake her own identity and has found it untenable, or she has married Ben despite this glaring character flaw, but with an eye toward his future awakening to the equality of the sexes. Furthermore, Ben's tantrums at dinner regarding correction in his attitude and behavior by both Jo and the waiter are, in the filmic sense, natural results of a man who is clearly out of his comfort zone. On one level, Ben's discomfort could easily result from his refusal to accept the viability of the existence of something outside himself and his control. This scene implies that such thought and action are immature. As Ben discovers later, it is only by working with Jo that he will reclaim any control over family life. Jo's professional life—improper though it is because she is not subservient to a man within it—is no accident in this version of the film.

By the end of the next day in the film, Hitchcock invites the viewer to consider the more nefarious aspects of the male-dominated society of the 1950s as Louis Bernard is murdered and Ben admits that he has lost control of the situation. Because losing his power is an affront to his conservative views, he "imposes control on his wife in compensation."[29] Upon returning to the hotel from the police station, Ben insists Jo take a prescription sedative in exchange for learning the truth about Hank, demonstrating a ruthlessly self-serving attitude and implicating him as desperate to maintain control at any cost. Through both chemical and physical restraint of his wife, Ben McKenna embodies an exaggeration of the conservative world of 1950s America at this juncture of the film. However, the film does not conclude with a final image of James Stewart restraining Doris Day. More importantly, it does not conclude with Ben attaining his desires regardless of the consequences to, or the involvement of, his wife. Instead, the film's ending does the opposite.

Even as the story shifts to London, Ben continues to display the belief that women are inept at sleuthing and all other nondomestic activities. He insists Jo should only mind the home, even if "home" is a hotel room, and minding it means entertaining friends instead of seeking to reunite her family. What is both revealing and troubling about Ben's actions here is that although he knows London is like Jo's second home, he takes noticeable offense to the affection showered on Jo rather than on him. This becomes particularly apparent when the press asks him to stand aside so that the photographer can capture an image of Jo. In this exchange it is clear that, to the assembled fan club, Jo is the more important figure in the couple. This is untenable for Dr. McKenna, who suddenly finds himself in the role of the (feminized) tagalong.

At Scotland Yard, Ben again tries vehemently to reassert his centrality and authority in both his marriage and society by retorting to Inspector Buchanan (Ralph Truman), "You worked on the wrong McKenna, Mr. Buchanan. Louis Bernard talked to me, not my wife."[30] His emphasis on the word "me" is distinct. Because the McKennas represent the idealized family unit, this seems to convey a negative view of couples' roles in 1950s marriages: self-centeredness by the man and self-deprecation by the woman to the point of worthlessness apart from the man. More conservative men in 1950s America would be understandably apprehensive about critiques that might diminish their power. It is entirely due to "Stewart's brilliantly awkward performance" that Hitchcock "illustrates the extent to which [Ben] is a fish out of water, ill-attuned to his environment and unable to see, to anticipate what is about to happen."[31] Even so, Ben continues his futile attempts at sleuthing around London, including the fruitless and wryly humorous endeavor at the business of taxidermist Ambrose Chappell. This scene reiterates the resulting reduction to "humiliating buffoonery" for those who would cling to the tenets of a society based upon control of others (Figure 5.2).[32]

FIGURE 5.2 The innocuous result of the "humiliating buffoonery" of trying to cling to a male-centric society: men bumbling about in a struggle for power.

Steady Insistence

The subsequent sequence at Ambrose Chapel is critical and may point to Hitchcock's advocacy for neither strictly feminine nor masculine dominance, but of greater gender equality and cooperation. This scene is the first in which Ben does not demonstrate evidence of antipathy for Jo having disobeyed his orders. Once inside the chapel, however, Ben reverts and irascibly shushes Jo as she attempts to get his attention. Furthermore, Ben's first direct interaction with diegetic music is to completely dismiss his wife's intuition (Figure 5.3), this time by using music, Jo's professional craft, to rashly inform her that her leading them to the chapel is nothing more than "just another wild goose chase."[33] Jo's response, "Let's wa-it . . . and look around," given in the robust and accurately tuned manner of a trained singer and on notes of the harmony easily drowns out the uniformly subdued and discordant congregational singing.[34] Her response draws both a dour expression from Ben and reproachful glares from two older women in front of her (Figure 5.4). Ben's subsequent, similarly intoned instruction to "Look who's coming down the aisle" carries with it a subtext of concession (Figure 5.5).[35] By admitting that Jo's hunch was correct, Ben shows for the first time that he is starting to believe in Jo's equal partnership in sleuthing. It is appropriate to understand this exchange as Ben's concession of control in their relationship for restoring their family. While at first a temporary compromise, Ben eventually realizes he is more effective working beside Jo, rather than in control of her.

FIGURE 5.3 Ben first uses music to mock the most important woman in his life.

FIGURE 5.4 The trained voice of a "progressive" woman draws consternation from her conservative husband and other "proper" women.

FIGURE 5.5 Ben is "feminine" in how he admits that his wife was successful in her foray into the "masculine" activity of sleuthing.

By the same reasoning, the sermon offered by Mr. Drayton seems to serve as a repudiation of Ben's defection from the status quo of sexist culture. This parallels the growing dichotomy between opponents and proponents of gender equality. His assertion that "strangely enough, it is often the things beyond our control which help to make us better beings" extols the virtues of a good wife in an effort to overwhelm the relative and perceived radicalism of women's rights.[36] Drayton's dramatic, effective change in tone and the termination of his address upon seeing Jo further emphasize the conflicting ideologies Hitchcock explores in this film. Drayton is a staunch proponent of women's subjugation to domesticity and masculine discernment. His words, while superficially addressed to his largely mid-dle-aged (perhaps "good") female congregation, are directed at Jo: they are a chastising insistence that she mind her place in the home and gratefully accept the offer to have her son safely returned if she only stays out of the affairs of men:

> Few of us pause to think how life's adversities work in our behalf, to make better men and women of us. But I believe we should pause now to do a little stock-taking—to look into our own hearts and see what we find there. Therefore instead of continuing the service, I think we should all return to our homes for private meditation, remembering how little we have to complain of and how much to be grateful for.[37]

This scene represents the confrontation of ideologies regarding gender roles, played out on the intimate level of a wife and husband. Jo is the American symbol of gender equality; the British congregation is the conservative establishment whose members view Jo as a radical. The vacillation in Ben's demeanor and in his responses to Jo represent his shift from a staunch supporter of the conservative order to a sympathizer for interdependence and cooperation between the genders. Ben's growth from a domineering husband in Morocco to an equal partner with his wife in Ambrose Chapel resolves the familial issues and so offered a model of gender equality to 1950s audiences.

The McKennas Get Their Act Together

A familiar story about the making of this film is that Hitchcock complained that he could not hear the music of the London Symphony Orchestra because of the dialogue between Stewart and Day. He chided the actors for "talking far too much" and subsequently instructed the screenwriter to "cut the talking so we can hear the music." These comments propose an exquisite allegory for the film's social tensions.[38] Facing the prospect of allowing an assassination in exchange for the assurance of the safety of her son, Jo follows both the trail of objective evidence and an intuitive hunch to a performance of Arthur Benjamin's *Storm Clouds* Cantata at Royal Albert Hall.[39] This musical performance shares the stage, as the background, with Jo's inaugural social performance as a married woman taking a prominent role outside of the home. Despite the last-minute admonition that she has a "very nice little boy . . . [whose] safety will depend on [her]," Jo goes into the auditorium and searches for the ambassador and assassin (Figure 5.6).[40] While she anxiously waits for what she does not entirely know, the viewer witnesses her immense personal turmoil regarding saving the prime minister or Hank, as Robin Wood, Murray Pomerance,

FIGURE 5.6   Jo's two worlds collide and she, entirely alone, must breach one aspect of her "femininity" to save the life of another, despite assurances that such a desecration will violate the other.

and Jack Sullivan have noted. The view held by Fereydoun Hoveyda is that this sequence shows Jo's struggle to overcome her "devotion to her own family in order to take a socially responsible action that protects the life of a stranger." Pomerance's dismissal of this view is on target, though it merits further consideration.[41]

Pomerance refutes Hoveyda's assertion that there is an apparent lack of social conscience preceding Jo's scream at Albert Hall. Hoveyda's greater offense is that he characterizes the location of the McKennas' rediscovery of a social conscience as coincidence.[42] The simple fact is that without Jo's engagement in her professional activities—first by anticipating the climactic cymbal crash, and later by singing—Hank McKenna would not have been reunited with his parents. Indeed, the McKennas' pursuit of their son does lead them to the verge of forsaking their entire world for Hank's safety, but it is not because either has lost a sense of social responsibility. If Jo had remained silent and acted according to social conventions, she would have violated her "maternal" responsibility to protect the life of another. But she asserts her role of strength, acting profoundly by screaming aloud in Royal Albert Hall. Hitchcock's intricate camera work builds the suspense by requiring audiences to focus on Jo, the assassin, his target, and the music that will mask the gunshot. Despite the overwhelming number of variables demanding Jo's focus, she does not falter in the task before her. Nor does she scream by chance or because of irrepressible anxiety or emotionality. As she later informs the police, she realized the assassin was "pointing at the Prime Minister, and I, and he was going to kill him and I realized that I had to scream."[43] This line does not appear in the final draft of the script, which suggests it might have been an on-set direction from Hitchcock or improvisation by Doris Day.[44] Either way, its presence in the final version of the film reveals Hitchcock's approval and strengthens the argument that Jo had full control of herself and made a decision that proved beneficial to a comparatively benevolent member of society.[45] Together with Ben, Jo is a detective and the protagonist who makes the most appropriate decision in the midst of both social and private moral chaos.[46]

Even after escaping from the imprisonment in one bastion of conservative society, Ambrose Chapel, Ben makes futile attempts to reason with the masculine instruments that enforce the existing social order: the police officers assigned to patrol Albert Hall.[47] At this point, Benjamin's *Storm Clouds* Cantata shifts from the lyrical, yet foreboding, A section to the turbulent bravado fanfares of the B section. While the musical agitation closely mimics the McKennas' apprehensive knowledge of an impending assassination attempt, the police officers' willful idleness reinforces their oblivion to the threat against the prime minister. In contrast, Ben assists Jo by running from box to box searching for the assassin. Ben's actions here, while generating only mild disruptions to a relative few concertgoers, perhaps mirror the equally minor disruption that he is willing to cause, whether or not he fully understands the magnitude of disruption necessary to achieve all of his desired results.

Finally, after viewers experience what may be Hitchcock's most dramatic and effective editing and directing work, in which he married sight and non-verbal sound, Jo McKenna lets loose the scream of her release. Her scream is alarming to those around her, but it is also a significant violation: it upsets the concert experience for many concertgoers, but considering again film's representational nature, it is also a multifaceted and heavily loaded element of Hitchcock's narrative.

The events at Ambrose Chapel and those at the taxidermist demonstrate the disruption of the social order within the McKenna marriage. In the same way, Jo's scream represents the intrusion upon the upper class society that likely supported her international singing career before she was married. Everything surrounding Jo at this juncture exists in support of societal conservatism: (1) formal dress and decorum befitting (2) an evening of comparatively conservative music, (3) led, of course, by a man (Bernard Herrmann), (4) and attended by a dignitary receiving special attention, (5) as well as the apparent presence of more men than women. Nonetheless, Jo's violation of the performers' collective right to be heard bears considerable weight because she, too, is a musician and would also, under normal circumstances, expect the same professional courtesies she violates. Alternatively, the accepted social practices for audience members are very similar in both the highbrow classical concert and the middlebrow Broadway musicals in which Jo starred and by which she accrued international acclaim. By directing such a violation to both screenwriter and actress, Hitchcock eliminates any plausibility that this is merely an exploration of one of his favorite social tensions: classism.[48]

Jo also contravenes her secondary social identifier: motherhood. This is noteworthy because Jo demonstrates a willingness to sacrifice her family for the good of others. Thus, she is also willing to abandon her closest emotional and physical relationships for the benefit of a complete stranger's life. Yet, given her femininity and expected sentimentality, her action represents instead a testament to the enormity of her decision to act on behalf of a person outside of her family, as well as to the immense value of equal partnering. Such relationships require compromise and unity of emotional and rational reasoning, which the McKennas have begun to embody.

Contrary to the generalized Fifties notion that women are overly emotional and therefore incapable of social strength and identity, Jo has used her well-trained voice in a manner that others do not immediately appreciate: the resounding scream to save a life. In doing so, she demonstrates that she is bound neither by her conventional gender role nor by the emotionalism associated with it. Likewise, Ben has disregarded social conventions by allowing his wife to join him in sleuthing, accepting her as his equal outside the home. Through her interaction with music, Jo plays one crucial role in assuring the safety of the ambassador; Ben plays the other by confronting the would-be assassin. The other primary person interacting with music in this sequence is Bernard Herrmann, who, appearing as himself, conducts the London Symphony Orchestra. This is significant because Herrmann serves as Hitchcock's on-screen alter-ego.[49] Together with the emphasis in the Albert Hall sequence on the feminine act of music making, Hitchcock's symbolic presence on-screen seems to represent Hitchcock leading gender equality forward in American society.

The Tranquil Coda

Understandably, such basic changes to society do not occur without pain, as the flesh wound to the prime minister might suggest. The assassin and Mr. Drayton discover the consequences of resisting such changes by dying violently in Albert Hall and in the embassy, respectively.

With the crisis averted, but the expected repose and closure supplanted by disturbance, Hitchcock places the task of reuniting the McKenna family in Ben and Jo's newfound joint and capable authority. Here "the order of music finally displaces the uncertainty of life."[50] Upon discovering that the Draytons are hiding at the embassy, Ben and Jo embark on their second true collaborative quest. Each has a task: Jo's is to "hold their attention," while Ben goes to search the embassy for the

Draytons and Hank.[51] As Jo sings the Jay Livingston song, "Whatever Will Be, Will Be," which she sang earlier as Hank's lullaby, the camera follows the sound of her voice up the stairs and around corners until her voice, very faintly, reaches Hank and Mrs. Drayton, who is attending him at this moment (Figure 5.7). In addition to "the shots of Doris Day's voice travelling up the stairs (so to speak)," which "are among the most moving in the whole of Hitchcock,"[52] the camera work shows the distance that Jo's voice carries and the lengths to which it has impact outside of her immediate surroundings. A mother is capable of representing home to her child, reaching out to him even when he is out of her view and, more importantly, while she is engaged in professional activities.

Jo and Ben have assumed this protective responsibility together, and through their joint activity, they subvert Mr. Drayton's malice. This unique juxtaposition of male and female characters and characteristics, especially their musical treatments by Hitchcock, provides a uniquely incisive commentary on gendered social anxiet-ies. Jo, the musician, wife, and mother, is an invaluable member of the duo who saves first the foreign dignitary and later her son. The ambassador, entirely passive at the time of Jo's intervention and again during her performance, is part of the ironically jostled status quo. Conversely, Hank mostly does what he is told, like a well-behaved child, until he hears his mother singing. Then, he tries to open the door holding him and Mrs. Drayton captive and zealously exclaims, "That's my mother's voice!"[53] Hank's sudden change reflects the unsuppressed individualism of an excited child,

FIGURE 5.7 Jo, having proven she is capable of social responsibility, now uses her premarital professional craft to save her son and reunite her family.

and here, one desperate to be rescued. He represents the second life that is saved by his mother, a figure of strength. By inverting the accepted societal functions assigned to the different genders, Hitchcock's only film remake demonstrates the advantages of both public and domestic gender equality.

Jo's first song of the evening, "Whatever Will Be, Will Be," famously loathed by Doris Day as "silly and embarrassing,"[54] carries with it a lesson directed at anyone who would seek to maintain authoritarian control or perpetuate the gender inequality of 1950s America. The song's narrator-as-singer asks different people with whom she is in different relationships (as mother, teacher, sweetheart) about the future, before finally becoming the questioned mother in the cyclic text. Each time, the reply of the familiar chorus is the same, cautioning against the ultimately futile quest for control over one's destiny:

> Que sera, sera;
> Whatever will be, will be:
> The future's not ours to see.
> Que sera, sera,
> What will be, will be.[55]

Further advancing the notion of feminine achievement outside the home, Jo's singing reawakens Lucy Drayton's maternal emotions and instincts, which here are also beneficial to the life of another, the child of a stranger. By telling Hank to "whistle it as loud as you can," fully realizing what likely awaits her, she provides him a way to safety.[56] Lucy thereby partially restores her culturally constructed and approved femininity, but, perhaps more importantly, her true humanity. Full restoration comes moments later with Lucy's "redemptive scream" as Ben bursts through the door to the room (which perhaps represents her personal prison of repression).[57] Here Lucy has dreaded the impending murder of a child to whom she has become a surrogate mother; her scream, which does not guarantee safety for Hank, but rather alerts others to her presence, mirrors Jo's lifesaving scream at Albert Hall. Lucy decides she must also scream to save the life of another woman's child, regardless of the cost to her; her action perhaps symbolizes her response to an unjust society that has damaged her own convictions and surrogate femininity.

Jo's concluding song, "We'll Love Again," while not confirming a pleasant resolution to the strife in the McKennas' marriage, leads viewers to expect that such a conclusion is in store.[58] Given the centrality of diegetic music to this film, Hitchcock's use of it throughout, the symbolism of the film's characters (and Herrmann being an alter-ego of Hitchcock), there seems to be no stronger possibility for the McKennas' life after their eventful vacation than Jo reviving her career and Ben becoming more equitable in his view of their respective roles. If any doubt remains, Hitchcock dismisses it at the close of the film through his musical alter ego: "'After Jimmy Stewart's line about going to pick up Hank, Mr. Herrmann will take over.' This he does, booming away with brass-timpani flourishes reprising the main title, but now in a happy major key."[59] Sullivan's characterization of the key as "happy" is indeed on target, and it leaves little room for alternatives to post-movie life for the McKennas.

Together with Ben following the sound of Hank's whistling, Jo's impromptu recital does more than merely enable the reunion of her family; it offers redemption to another human being (Lucy). In accomplishing both, Jo offers the answers to any questions that her actions throughout the film might have raised: she proves that she, as a woman, is fully capable of maintaining a career and/or raising her family. This encouraging affirmation to women is not, however, the only moral to glean from this film. Perhaps a more pertinent lesson for 1950s viewers was that a person's intrinsic value is not determined by gender and, as such, gender is not a legitimate basis for determining individual potential. By extension then, this film advocates the belief that the most good for society comes from the unity of (familial) cooperation, not (spousal) subjugation.[60] In short, this version of *The Man Who Knew Too Much* highlights the benefits of gender equality, in rights *and* responsibilities, as the basis for a more diverse, enriched, and enriching society.

Some maintain that Hitchcock is guilty of opulence and decadence in this film. If so, that is because he used everything at his directorial disposal to demonstrate the richness possible in an equal-gendered society, the requirements to form and support it, and the danger to those who would seek to prevent it. Perhaps Hitchcock did know too much. While he sumptuously depicts 1950s American society, its personal relationships, and the quest for authoritarian control, having two major personae for his hero and heroine help make *The Man Who Knew Too Much* an iconic reflection of the world Hitchcock saw. While it seems unlikely that the whole truth about Hitchcock's notoriously ambiguous views on gender roles will ever become clear, his only film remake postulated a unique justification for the empowerment of women.

NOTES

1. For helpful comments and suggestions, I wish to thank Stanley Pelkey, Anthony Bushard, Margaret Butler, and the anonymous readers of this essay.

2. Elise B. Michie, "Unveiling Maternal Desires: Hitchcock and American Domesticity," in *Hitchcock's America*, ed. Jonathan Freedman and Richard Millington (New York: Oxford University Press, 1999), 52.

3. Robin Wood, *Hitchcock's Films Revisited* (New York: Columbia University Press, 1989), 376.

4. Robin Wood, "Male Desire, Male Anxiety," in *A Hitchcock Reader*, ed. Marshall Deutelbaum and Leland Poague (Ames: Iowa Sate University Press, 1986), 221.

5. Jessica Coen, "Alfred Hitchcock: Genius? Misogynist?" accessed March 29, 2010, http://jezebel.com/5078382/alfred-hitchcock-genius-misogynist. According to Google, this is one of among approximately 124,000 hits that appear with the search terms "Hitchcock and misogyny." The majority of these are in editorials, blogs, and other personal websites, suggesting that an interest in or concern with Alfred Hitchcock's sexual politics permeates both scholarly and popular reception of his films.

6. John Russell Taylor, "Was Alfred Hitchcock a Misogynist? He Was Adored by Actresses," accessed March 29, 2010, http://entertainment.timesonline.co.uk/tol/arts_and_entertainment/film/article4666530.ece.

7. Thomas Hemmeter, "Hitchcock the Feminist: Rereading *Shadow of a Doubt*," in *Framing Hitchcock*, ed. Sidney Gottlieb and Christopher Brookhouse (Detroit, MI: Wayne State University Press, 2002), 221–233.

8. Paula Marantz Cohen, *Alfred Hitchcock: The Legacy of Victorianism* (Lexington: The University Press of Kentucky, 1995), 116.

9. Wood's chapter, while insightful and revelatory, stops short of acknowledging elements of autobiographical insight offered by Hitchcock through the ulterior messages, subliminal or not, in this film.

10. Wood, "Male Desire," 223.

11. Ibid.

12. Wendy Lesser, "Second Thoughts," *The Threepenny Review* 24 (1986): 17.

13. Wood, *Hitchcock's Films Revisited*, 366.

14. Lesser, 16.

15. Ibid. This remaking of a woman by a man is a central exploration *Vertigo*.

16. Ibid., 22–23. See also Julia Kristeva, *Powers of Horror: An Essay on Abjection*, trans. Leon Roudiez (New York: Columbia University Press, 1982).

17. Michal Grover-Friedlander, *Vocal Apparitions: The Attraction of Cinema to Opera* (Princeton, NJ: Princeton University Press, 2005), 156. See also Slavoj Žižek, *Enjoy Your Symptom: Jacques Lacan in Hollywood and Out* (New York: Routledge, 1992).

18. Kathryn Kalinak, *Settling the Score* (Madison: The University of Wisconsin Press, 1992), 36–37.

19. Heather Laing, *The Gendered Score: Music in 1940s Melodrama and the Woman's Film* (Burlington, VT: Ashgate Publishing Company, 2007), 23.

20. Laing, 23.

21. *The Man Who Knew Too Much*, DVD, directed by Alfred Hitchcock (1956; Universal City, CA: Universal Studios Home Entertainment, 2006), 5:55–6:01.

22. *The Man Who Knew Too Much*, 6:02–6:05.

23. Richard Allen, *Hitchcock's Romantic Irony* (New York: Columbia University Press, 2007), 82.

24. *The Man Who Knew Too Much*, 19:30–19:35.

25. Using her married name is a reminder of her subservience: the title of "Mrs." can only come as the result of a woman giving up her unique identity (Jo's was "Ms. Conway") for the sake of being subsumed into the man's (here it is "Dr. and Mrs. McKenna," or "Mrs. Benjamin McKenna").

26. Wood, *Hitchcock's Films Revisited*, 369.

27. *The Man Who Knew Too Much*, 19:36–20:36. Italics added by the author for emphasis.

28. Jack Sullivan, *Hitchcock's Music* (New Haven, CT: Yale University Press, 2006), 204.

29. Allen, 91.

30. *The Man Who Knew Too Much*, 52:58–53:04.

31. Allen, 90–91.

32. Wood, *Hitchcock's Films Revisited*, 369.

33. John Michael Hayes, Angus MacPhail, and Alfred Hitchcock, *The Man Who Knew Too Much* (Hollywood, CA: RC Entertainment, 1955), 106.

34. *The Man Who Knew Too Much*, 1:17:22–1:17:30.

35. Ibid., 1:17:36–1:17:42; and Hayes, 106.

36. *The Man Who Knew Too Much*, 1:19:39–1:19:44; and Hayes, 107.

37. Hayes, 108–109.

38. Sullivan, 199.

39. Benjamin originally composed *Storm Clouds* for the 1934 version of *The Man Who Knew Too Much*. Herrmann made some changes to Benjamin's orchestrations for the later version. Ibid., 32, 192–195.

40. *The Man Who Knew Too Much*, 1:30:41–1:30:49.

41. Murray Pomerance, *"Finding Release*: "Storm Clouds" and *The Man Who Knew Too Much*, in *Music and Cinema*, ed. James Buhler, Caryl Flinn, and David Neumeyer (Hanover, NH: Wesleyan University Press, 2000), 208. Pomerance refers to Hoveyda's review of the film in *Cahiers du Cinéma* 60 (1956) and notes that the idea of rediscovered or newly generated social conscience has received attention in Elisabeth Weis's *The Silent Scream* (Rutherford, NJ: Farleigh Dickinson University Press, 1985).

42. Ibid., 209.

43. *The Man Who Knew Too Much*, 1:41:35–1:41:39.

44. Hayes, 133–134. This is the portion of the script where these events occur, and there is no mention of Jo having her explanatory line to the police, or even about the camera angle capturing this moment.

45. While the prime minister's qualities are not assessed, it is reasonable to presume his benevolence based on his interactions with Jo, especially when compared to his country's duplicitous ambassador.

46. Sullivan, 197.

47. Ibid., 198.

48. Sullivan, 193.

49. Ibid., 204.

50. Ibid., 201.

51. *The Man Who Knew Too Much*, 1:49:43–1:49:45.

52. Wood, *Hitchcock's Films Revisited*, 370.

53. *The Man Who Knew Too Much*, 1:53:17–1:53:19.

54. Sullivan, 206.

55. *The Man Who Knew Too Much*, 1:51:46–1:52:06.

56. Ibid., 1:53:49–1:54:02.

57. Pomerance, 242.

58. Sullivan, 204.

59. Ibid.

60. This demonstration of the need for unity over isolation can also be projected onto the sociopolitical climate of the United States in the late 1950s, particularly with respect to McCarthyism and the Cold War.

6 Music, Maturity, and the Moral Geography in *Leave It to Beaver* (1957–1963)

STANLEY C. PELKEY II

LEAVE IT TO BEAVER (1957–1963) can be described as an overly idealized and sentimental portrayal of family life that masked the actual diversity of American families in the 1950s and early 1960s.[1] Books on child psychology, parenting, and the American family published in the 1940s and 1950s address a more diverse range of family configurations and experiences than depicted in *Leave It to Beaver*; nevertheless, plots and themes in the series echo those publications.[2] Furthermore, thorough investigation of all episodes uncovers reasonably nuanced depictions of moral maturation in the Cleaver household. These depictions and their musical accompaniment may provide new insights about the program and the history of representations of the Fifties suburban family.[3]

Leave It to Beaver did not escape the biases of its era: it presented conservative gender roles, although the relationship between Ward (Hugh Beaumont) and June (Barbara Billingsley) Cleaver is more complex than people may remember.[4] But *Leave It to Beaver* is not as regressive as later decades' (mis)representations of the series would suggest.[5] The moral dilemmas in some episodes involve more than simplistic notions of compliance; some require characters (even Ward and June) to balance competing social and moral demands to achieve deepening perspective and virtue. Most significantly, Wally (Tony Dow) and Beaver (Jerry Mathers) repeatedly observe that Ward is not like other fathers, which Larry Mondello (Rusty Stevens), Eddie Haskill (Ken Osmond), and Gilbert Bates (Stephen Talbot) reinforce with negative comments about their fathers. Considered against the backdrop of 1950s publications about the American family, the series can be read as a prescription for moral maturity and modern parenting during its time, rather than as an idealized fantasy of the American suburban family at a particular point in time. It may even suggest a more nuanced understanding of suburbia, community, and conformity in 1950s television culture is needed.[6]

In this chapter, I discuss how recurring musical materials punctuate the "moral geography" of *Leave It to Beaver*, mapping key moments as characters move through it. I then use these findings while exploring the extent to which the program exemplified moral maturation in the 1950s. Among the most important of the recurring musical materials are two variations on the main theme of the series. As aural indices, they point to affection and resolution of conflict between Beaver and Ward and the deepening of their personal perspectives. The manner in which music supervisors employed them suggests that while affection and sentimentality are essential components of the corporate lives of the Cleavers and their moral universe, an underlying tension exists between sentiment and (masculine) moral maturity. Because Ward functions as the most potent cipher of the program's prescriptive vision, he will occupy a central place in my discussion.

Leave It to Beaver's Moral Geography

> WALLY: Now, isn't that easy?
>
> BEAVER: Yeah, but there are a lot of things that sound easy in the kitchen that you can't say in the living room.
>
> From "The Younger Brother"[7]

Episodes across all six seasons of *Leave It to Beaver* turn on a moment when a character has to decide whether or not to take a particular action. Others must then react or make decisions, and conflict ensues as competing moralities collide. During the second half of episodes, consequences of decisions are explored and resolution occurs. The program's moral geography takes shape as this pattern of decisions, conflicts, consequences, and resolution unfolds across a predictable cycle of private and public spaces that usually concludes in the Cleaver home.[8]

Bad decisions and conflicts do occur in the Cleaver home, but as the principal site of resolution, it is the center of the moral geography and reinforces a significant theme: the formation of moral character within the family. As members of the Cleaver family move through the moral geography, they are changed and their personal moral perspectives mature. The benefits flow outward into the community, as is seen in later seasons during which Wally increasingly acts on behalf of his friends.[9]

Specific narrative functions tend to occur in particular places both inside and outside the home. While we may learn of poor decisions in the boys' bedroom, it is also the focal point for their development and the location where they process their feelings, conceive of (often flawed) problem-solving strategies, and share most openly. Conflicts regularly become apparent in the dining room as family members voice their frustrations, the boys obfuscate issues and evade questions, or Ward and June thwart such behavior. The framing of several resolution/growth scenes by the living room fireplace, as in "The Bank Account" (1.19) and "Beaver's Graduation" (6.34), is reminiscent of the (democratic) "family councils" described in the 1950s.[10] Furthermore, Ward and June process their feelings or discuss parenting insights in the living room, frequently toward the end of episodes, such as "Music Lesson" (1.30), "Beaver's House Guest" (4.2), and "Beaver's Doll Buggy" (4.38). These moments, when Ward almost addresses the camera, and his introductory voice-overs in early episodes of season 1 suggest this was not simply a children's program. (Lighter closing scenes between the boys in their bedroom are common, even after living room family councils or debriefs.)

While moral and social tensions exist in the Cleaver home and may lead to poor decision making there, they frequently originate outside the nuclear family. Aunt Martha (Madge Kennedy) and Uncle Billy (Edgar Buchanan), on-screen characters closest to grandparents, disrupt the Cleavers' negotiations of space, values, expectations, and gender roles when they visit. The boys' friends generate even greater conflict in the Cleaver home.[11] Other problems occur in the garage, at school, in the neighborhood; many arise because of conflicting behavioral codes expected at home versus by "the gang." Those who view *Leave It to Beaver* as an uncomplicated representation of suburbia's emphasis on the centrality of the nuclear family are justified in their conclusions, given these narrative tropes, yet 1950s parenting books did address the potentially disruptive influence of grandparents and conformity among school-aged friends.[12]

The series' vision of the family and the importance of home has flaws. Although mothers are reported to have worked before marriage and June reminds Beaver that girls can also become doctors and lawyers, gender and moral geography are strongly linked.[13] June holds her own against Ward, even putting him in his place at times, yet she is more constricted in her movement through narrative space than is Ward.

Scenes from "Wally Stays at Lumpy's" (5.24) highlight the most significant consequence of the gendering of the moral geography. Beaver and Gilbert enter the kitchen, where June is making yet another cake, to ask if Gilbert can spend the night. At the same time, Wally approaches Ward, who is balancing bank statements in his den, to ask if he can spend the night at Lumpy's (Figures 6.1a–b). The pattern throughout the series, reflected here, is that Ward's den is a male place

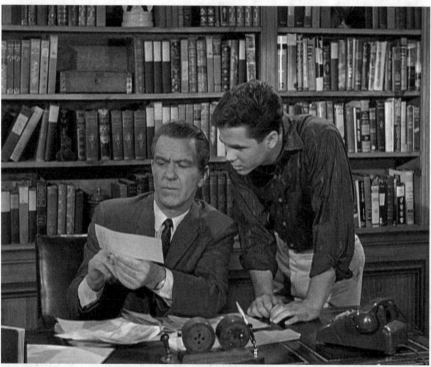

FIGURES 6.1A–B Gender and the "moral geography": June (Barbara Billingsley) is in the kitchen with the boys, while the men are in the den.

where important conversations about morality and character occur. The kitchen, contrarily, is the site for less substantive conversations between June and the boys. Furthermore, Ward is just as apt to convey his wisdom in the boys' room, where he appears more often than does June. While his purpose is almost always to "pass judgment" or discuss choices and consequences, June usually enters the boys' room to kiss them good night or check on them when they are sick. June functions as the linchpin in the family's network of sentimental relationships; Ward nurtures the boys' minds and characters. Beaver recognizes this: in "Beaver's First Date" (5.13), he asserts that "Moms are better for mushy stuff" while helping June with the dishes. The series thus construes thoughtful conversation about character and moral maturity as masculine, while it portrays sentiment (and banter) as feminine, and these constructions are reinforced musically.

Music and the Moral Geography

In *Leave It to Beaver*, music establishes time, place, situation, and mood while punctuating the characters' journeys through the moral geography. Several music supervisors worked on the series, including Stanley Wilson (the pilot; seasons 1 and 6), Frederick Herbert (most of season 2), Joseph Romero (season 2, two episodes), Michael F. Johnson (seasons 3 and 4 through 4.11), Frank Morriss (season 4, two episodes), and Jack B. Wadsworth (the second half of season 4, season 5, and season 6, one episode). Each maintained the same general narrative functions and middlebrow quality, but other aspects differed. Johnson, for example, utilized recurring musical materials introduced in season 1 (see below), but his later underscores feature several new cues. Wadsworth did not retain Johnson's new material, and his early episodes often include older recurring cues oddly spliced together. A jazzed-up version of the opening theme and new cues composed by Paul Smith and Pete Rugolo are featured in season 6. Thus some differences in the soundscape were due to the work of individual musical supervisors, but others may reflect the Cleaver boys' increasing maturity and alterations to the program's tone and types of stories.

Diegetic music that establishes time, place, situation, or mood is usually straightforward. In "Wally Stays at Lumpy's," Beaver and Gilbert watch a movie with music that sounds like that of 1950s science fiction films. When June calls home from a cocktail party, we hear piano music in the background. In "Beaver's Fear" (5.21), amusement park music, including an arrangement of Walzer II from *The Blue Danube Waltz* by Johann Strauss Jr., is heard at the Bellport Amusement Park. And in "Box Office Attraction" (6.23), twist music accompanies dancing and drinking at Hank's Place, where Wally and an older girl have gone for a date (Figure 6.2).

FIGURE 6.2 A more mature Wally (Tony Dow) has not touched his beer while on a date at Hank's Place.

Nondiegetic cues that reinforce situations are tied to specific visual material. In "Beaver's Laundry" (5.25), chase music accompanies Beaver and Richard (Rich Correll), who pursue a dog that nabbed some shorts, while in "Wally's Play" (3.37), Western-like saloon music plays as Beaver and Gilbert find Wally's costume—a dancehall girl's dress—for an upcoming school show. Hollywood musical *topoi* that evoke the "exotic" are also common: tribal drumming occurs in "Voodoo Magic" (1.13), "Next Door Indians" (1.28), and "Beaver's Sweater" (2.31), with its numerous references to "Eskimos," while in "Kite Day" (4.37), "Indianist" music rumbles as Beaver mentions rain dances. Spanish-style guitar music is heard in "Beaver and Poncho" (1.23) and "Three Boys and a Burro" (5.22), while Herbert quotes "Cielito Lindo" in "Beaver and Chuey."

Like "Cielito Lindo," many recurring nondiegetic cues that reflect the mood or punctuate movement through the moral geography are quotations of familiar music from outside the *Beaverse*. Musical quotations compel attention by directing us back from the cultural artifact in which they occur to the musical source material, and, once recognized, by highlighting us as listening subjects in the act of hearing. Quotations may also cause layers of personal associations to accumulate onto quoting artifacts. Among the most common in *Leave It to Beaver* are "Westminster Chimes," which occurs seven times, usually at night and midway through episodes (including "Beaver's Guest" 1.38, "Price of Fame" 2.26, and "Beaver, the Magician" 3.12), and a humorous version of the funeral march from Chopin's Piano Sonata in B-flat Minor, Op. 35. An index of both Beaver's emotional state and the point in the plot when he has been "caught" and conflict is about to ensue, the "funeral march" was first introduced in the pilot, returned in "Beaver and Poncho," and then recurred nine times before disappearing after "Beaver's Dance" (3.21). Thus three music supervisors used it. Nevertheless, these and other light-hearted quotations were gradually muted, as was a recurring, humorous variation of the theme song that accompanied montages featuring Beaver "on the move" during the first three years of the program (e.g., in "Beaver Gets 'Spelled'" 1.1 and "Beaver the Athlete" 2.37).[14]

The most important recurring musical material in *Leave It to Beaver* are phrases from what I refer to as the "Primary Sentimental Theme" (PST; Example 6.1), a contemplative variation of "The Toy Parade," the title theme of the series. While "The Toy Parade" is boisterous and in a faster compound meter, the PST is set in a slower triple meter.[15] Its phrases regularly accompany scenes of resolution and reaffirmation of family affection, the vast majority of which involve Ward and Beaver. Portions of the PST appeared as cues as early as "Beaver Gets 'Spelled.'" Until "Beaver's Short Pants" (1.11), their use was somewhat flexible; even after that, they occasionally denoted Beaver's sadness, including in episodes with PST-accompanied resolution scenes.

The full PST consists of 8 phrases, each 8 measures long and differentiated by melodic and harmonic content, cadences, and instrumentation (e.g., strings or solo oboe on the melody). Music supervisors used the PST's phrases modularly, employing only as many as were dramatically required for a particular scene or its most affectionate moment.[16]

The entire PST never occurs as a cue in the program, although Johnson employed all of phrases 2–8, about two minutes of music, for the resolution scene in "June's Birthday" (3.13), and Herbert began at the sixth bar of phrase 2, then continued through to the conclusion of the PST, in "Beaver's Hero" (2.28). These are the two longest occurrences in the series. Romero, Herbert, and Johnson used phrases 4–8 in "The Visiting Aunts" (2.12), "The Cookie Fund" (2.35), and "Beaver Takes a Bath" (3.2) respectively, while Wilson included slightly shorter cues that started in the middle of phrase 5 and went to the end of phrase 8 three times in season 1. Phrase 1 occurs only seven times and typically in cues that demonstrate that music supervisors cut the PST to the scene at hand, sometimes with peculiar musical results. In "Beaver Says Good-bye" (2.29), Herbert incorporated phrases 1–3 but stopped with phrase 3's half cadence before shifting into a humorous "bumper" for the fade to the final commercial break. Likewise, in "Beaver's Sweater," he began with

EXAMPLE 6.1 *Leave It to Beaver*, Primary Sentimental Theme. (Transcribed by S. Pelkey.)

phrases 3–4, and then he created an awkward harmonic shift by jumping to phrases 6–8. Johnson's editing was more successful in "Beaver's Fortune" (3.10): phrase 8 follows directly after phrases 1–3, which works because phrases 3 and 7 share the same melodic material and half cadence that propels the music into phrases 4 or 8. Nevertheless, the difference in volume between phrases 3 and 8 in this cue reveals the editing process.

Portions of the PST appear in 35 episodes during seasons 1 and 2. Johnson included the PST in eight episodes during seasons 3 and 4, but he also expanded the scoring of resolution and affection, most significantly by introducing a "Secondary Sentimental Theme" (SST) in "Last Day of School" (3.38), which he then recycled four times in season 4 (Example 6.2). The SST is also modular, with five 8-measure phrases, and it incorporates an alternative reworking of the middle portion of the main theme (comparable to phrases 5 and 6 from the PST). Unlike the PST, the SST does not include a variation of the opening phrase of "The Toy Parade."

EXAMPLE 6.2 *Leave It to Beaver,* Secondary Sentimental Theme, second and fifth phrase. (Transcribed by S. Pelkey.)

In all, 48 episodes from season 1 through the beginning of season 4 contain portions of the PST or SST to reinforce scenes of resolution and/or family affection. Two occurrences (one simple, one more developed) demonstrate how different music supervisors exploited the sentimental themes and their modular characteristics; how music, sentiment, maturity/morality, and gender are coordinated across the series; and how Ward's unique character shapes the program.

"Beaver's Short Pants" introduces Aunt Martha, a maternal figure to June. It follows the general narrative trajectory through the moral geography: when the proper, elderly woman arrives, she decides to gentrify Beaver's clothes, though they conform to those worn by his peers. Before long, she has dressed Beaver in an old-fashioned short pants suit.[17] Neither Ward nor Beaver can openly challenge Martha over the suit, even though it leads to teasing and a fight at school, because June (away visiting her sister) expects Ward and the boys to do what Aunt Martha asks. Ward saves the day: pretending to leave early for work, he hides in the garage and then calls Beaver in with him after Martha has seen her grandnephew out the door. Father and son slip normal clothing over Martha's beloved suit before sharing a moment of mutual affection, including a kiss (Figure 6.3), accompanied by only phrase 4 of the PST (23:52–24:10).

Ward could have sacrificed Beaver's feelings for Martha's (and June's), demanding obedience while giving a fatherly lecture on how goodness is its own reward and children must learn to ignore classmates' comments. Instead, Ward creates a new moral-social equilibrium in the home that protects Beaver's feelings and dignity without offending Martha or June, who have their own perspectives shaped by forces he cannot now change.

"Beaver's House Guest" is unique because Johnson incorporated portions of both the PST and the SST into an unusually rich underscore. The episode features Chopper (Barry Gordon), Beaver's weekend houseguest. Chopper's parents are divorced, and Beaver spends much of the episode thinking it would be wonderful to get all the gifts Chopper receives from his various (step) families. Unexpectedly, Chopper's mother phones: she has the "weepies" and wants him to come home. Beaver asks his parents for an explanation, and Ward admits that even men get the "weepies" sometimes. In the boys' room, Chopper interrupts his packing to assure Beaver that he has the better domestic arrangement, especially because Beaver has

FIGURE 6.3 Ward (Hugh Beaumont) has saved the day for Beaver (Jerry Mathers).

two parents who love each other. He tells Beaver he saw Ward and June "standing close like you see in the movies" (20:58). Johnson brings in the closing phrase of the SST as Chopper explains things to Wally and gives him the extra baseball mitt he had brought with him before heading downstairs (21:44). Wally then puts his arm around his distraught brother.

After a break, we see Ward and June, arm-in-arm, as Chopper had observed (off screen) earlier, before they enter the boys' room. June tells Beaver she is sorry Chopper had to leave early, then kisses both boys. Beaver reaches for Ward, kisses him, then says, "I'm really too big for that, Dad, but I did it because I don't want you to ever get the weepies." Ward now speechless, June wishes them a final good night. Johnson scored the scene from June's words about Chopper to her final good night with phrases 3–4 of the PST (23:29).

In this episode, recurring musical materials (PST and SST) punctuate characters' journeys through the moral geography and reflect their emotional states. But Beaver's reference to "being too big" for demonstrations of affection toward Ward is critical for teasing out the gendered relationships among music, sentiment, and maturity. In earlier episodes such as "Beaver's Short Pants," "Music Lesson," "Beaver Runs Away" (1.37), and "Beaver's Ring" (2.7), when Beaver remains young and small, the appropriateness of expressions of affection, including kissing, between Ward and Beaver is never questioned.[18] As late as "The Silent Treatment" (6.25), displays of affection toward June remain routine, yet by "The Cookie Fund," Beaver kisses June instead of Ward during a resolution/affection scene; Ward speculates that Beaver "had to hug someone, and I guess he feels he's getting a little too big to hug his father" (23:20). Being too old for affection is picked up again in "Kite Day": Ward, surprised by another kiss, indicates he thought Beaver was "getting too big to kiss your father." The fundamental difference between these two episodes is that by season 4's "Kite Day," all sentimental music, including the PST and SST, has been muted.

After Wadsworth became music supervisor in "Beaver's Accordion" (4.13), sentimental music was phased out of the series. Even in episodes with profoundly important resolutions involving Ward and Beaver, such as "Uncle Billy" (4.14) and "Ward's Millions" (4.16), not to mention the significant episode, "Nobody Loves Me" (5.20), music does not participate in dramatic presentations of resolution and familial affection. The change in supervisors probably played a part, but so did the aging Cleaver sons. Beaver's age in relation to displays of affection for his father had already been foregrounded; by "Beaver's Electric Trains" (5.17), Beaver realizes he's in a confusing place between being a child and being responsible (22:07). In "Beaver, the Sheepdog" (6.11), Ward tells June that Beaver is "growing up. . . . We can't hold his hand and baby him all through life" (10:10). Wally had matured even more. In "Wally's Big Date" (5.8), Ward tells him he has become too old to be told what to do; as an adult, he needs to use his "own good judgment" (16:34).[19] The series finale, "The Scrapbook" (6.39), emphasizes this maturity. Ward says Wally and Beaver are "responsible individuals now," "practically grown men," not "little boys anymore," which is visually reinforced as the young men are juxtaposed with younger selves in ten retrospective scenes from seasons 1–3. For these scenes, original soundtracks are removed or replaced; most significantly, in the last flashback, the resolution/affection scene from "Wally's Election" (3.19), phrases 1–4 of the PST from the scene's original soundtrack are completely excised (new music is not added). (See Figure 6.4.)

Sentimentality and overt displays of affection are thus marked as youthful and non-masculine; the absence of music in resolution scenes in the later seasons implies that music is too. Indeed, on-screen singing further infantilizes and feminizes musical utterance. School children sing "Hark, the Herald Angels Sing" ("The Haircut," 1.4), and "Row, Row, Row Your Boat" ("Teacher Comes to Dinner," 3.9), among other songs. Larry sings "You Always Hurt the One You Love" ("Beaver Makes a Loan," 3.11), while Beaver, the most regular vocalist, performs songs such as "Oh the Monkeys Have No Tails in Zamboanga" ("Lonesome Beaver," 1.20) and "Oh My Darling, Clementine" ("Beaver and Andy," 3.20). His renditions of "Alouette" (with mispronunciations) and "Jeanie With the Light Brown Hair" in "Teacher's Daughter" (4.15) and "Mother's Helper" (4.23), respectively, create a strong contrast

FIGURE 6.4 Ward admits he was wrong during "Wally's Election."

between the still youthful Beaver and the rapidly maturing Wally (with his intensifying romantic relationships). Women (for example, June in "Pet Fair," 3.16) or economically and socially vulnerable men, such as the alcoholic Andy, who also sings "Oh My Darling, Clementine," and the tramp in "Beaver's Good Deed" (6.19), sing all other diegetic songs.[20]

Because moral maturity is construed as masculine, while sentiment and music are infantilized and feminized, masculine anxiety requires that both be put away as a boy becomes a man. Youthful self-expression (e.g., Beaver singing) and musically rich depictions of sentimentality (e.g., the PST and SST) are muted after season 4, while season 6 offers increasingly common representations of consumer consumption among teens (e.g., twist and bossa nova recordings).

Not Like Other Dads: Ward, Moral Maturity, and Another Fifties

To make the development of one's highest powers the end of living, and to make learning from free choice and consequences the chief means of that development, is a doctrine of individualism. Great virtue is a product of conventional deviation, not of conventional conformity.

Lyman Bryson (1952)[21]

Throughout *Leave It to Beaver*, differences over hygiene, grooming, and clothing among the Cleavers lead to conflicts, as in "Wally's Haircomb" (2.34), "Sweatshirt Monsters" (5.35), and "Beaver's Football Award" (6.2). In earlier seasons, Wally is as likely as Beaver to be negligent about hygiene and appearance, though in later seasons, he becomes fastidious about his looks. These episodes and others, such as "Borrowed Boat" (3.7), "Wally's Track Meet" (4.18), and "Beaver Takes a Drive" (5.7), in which even getting into trouble when innocent or for relatively trivial reasons are causes for family embarrassment, open Wally up to the charge of finally embracing bland conformity, and Ward and June to confusing social shame with right and wrong. Thus "Substitute Father" (4.39), which shows the more positive development of Wally taking appropriate responsibility for others, is marred because Miss Landers (Sue Randall) is more concerned that Beaver swore than that he was bullied. Such episodes undermine those moments when Ward and June do take a stand against social embarrassment, as in "Wally and Dudley" (4.25), or openly oppose the thirst for popularity, as in "Beaver and Kenneth" (4.12), and they speak to the worst accusations concerning Fifties suburban conformity.[22]

The series places the viewer in a world in which conservative gender expectations shape peer group formation, behavior, and sexuality. Given the era, the role of advertising in early television production, and the target audience,[23] heterosexuality is assumed to be the norm for romantic and sexual relationships and is the only type depicted. June often frets about how involved Wally might become with young women, yet both girls and parents regard Wally as "safe."[24] "Wally Goes Steady" (5.1), "Tennis, Anyone?" and "Box Office Attraction" are among the few episodes that hint at an emerging Sixties sexual revolution.

These expectations and limitations, though consistent with the broader Cold War masculinity addressed in chapter 1, are cause for complaint about suburbia, and in *Leave It to Beaver*, deviation causes anxiety and even violence. In "Beaver's Doll Buggy," Wally and June acknowledge that children who are different are picked on, while Ward admits that he would have "clobbered" a boy pushing a buggy when he was a little fella. Meanwhile, as Beaver pushes a buggy home, one man says to another, "I can remember when boys played with coasters and bikes. Ed, we're really in trouble with this younger generation. They've gone sissy on us" (15:49).

Despite these shortcomings, *Leave It to Beaver* demonstrates prescriptive qualities and provides a basis for a more nuanced reading of 1950s television culture through Ward. He is on a journey of moral self-discovery and is the father who best models a more progressive vision of parent–child relationships. Whether intentionally or not, writers created a figure consistent with Lyman Bryson's ideal democratic citizen who offered his sons a vision of better possibilities while embodying "great virtue" in his own life.

Many episodes suggest violence lurks among Mayfield's families; this negative and forgotten subtext highlights a network of related characteristics that make Ward unusual. During a conversation about responsibility and parenting in "Larry Hides Out" (3.15), Wally tells Ward, "There's a lot of worse fathers around than you." Wally's awkwardly phrased compliment is an understatement: youth regularly confess that their fathers "clobber" them. In "Borrowed Boat," Larry and Beaver, mistakenly accused of stealing a boat, end up at a police station. Larry later reports his father "hit me, the minute he got home" (24:27), despite their innocence. Likewise, Eddie tells Wally and Beaver, "You'd think differently [about how fathers behave] if you'd been pushed around as much as I have."[25] Some adults admit they strike their children. Fred Rutherford (Richard Deacon) informs Ward that after his son Lumpy (Frank Bank) spoke back to him, Fred "smacked him right in the mouth."[26] Two seasons later, Wally tells his father, "Lumpy isn't as lucky as I am. . . . He's kinda got a feeling that his father's against him."[27]

In contrast, Ward models progressive parenting, particularly in terms of punishment, which was under scrutiny in the 1950s and was believed to foster conformist behavior in later life.[28] Beaver repeatedly tells Wally he's happy their father does not strike them,[29] which Ward confirms in "Tire Trouble" when he reminds Beaver, "You know I'd never hit you." Yet other children in Mayfield assume that Ward spanks his sons. Gilbert asks Beaver, "How hard [did] he [Ward] whack you?" in "Beaver's English Test" (5.11) after Beaver admitted to their English teacher that they had innocently studied one of Wally's old tests before it was given to them. Gilbert is not only incapable of imagining that a parent might respond to this incident without hitting, his moral perception is too simplistic: he views what they did as "cheating"; Ward identifies it as "misrepresentation."

Ward marshals memories of his childhood to better understand his sons and his role as their father. This is the foundation of his character.[30] Remembering his own fear and pain, Ward commits himself to avoiding the mistakes his father made.[31] One morning over breakfast, Ward reminisces that as a boy he had to wake up early to milk the cows on his family's dairy farm. Beaver pipes up, "You had a hittin' father, didn't you?"[32] After Beaver leaves, June corrects Ward, reminding him that his father had electric milking machines, but she does not question that his father was overly stern. June and Ward consider generational differences in parenting styles again during "Ward's Golf Clubs" (5.14). Treated with the humor typical of their end-of-episode exchanges, the dialogue is nonetheless poignant:

JUNE: Ward, when you were Beaver's age, if you'd broken something of your
   father's would you have tried to hide it from him?

WARD: Yeah, I think like Beaver, I'd have gone to most any lengths to avoid a fuss.

JUNE: Well when he found out about it, would he have sat down and let you explain it to him?

WARD: Well, no, my father had a very practical shortcut to child psychology: a razor strap. Sure cut down on the conversation around our house.[33]

Ward is unique among Mayfield's citizens: deeply self-aware, his memories and experiences shape his character, insights about others, and parenting.[34] So does his love of reading. June refers to him as a "kitchen philosopher,"[35] and the walls of Ward's den (seasons 3–6) and the living room near the side card table are filled with novels, collected volumes of "the classics," and books on history, sociology, and anthropology, such as *Male and Female*.[36] He purchases new books to "improve his mind,"[37] and we often see Ward and June reading.

They have clearly been exposed to modern psychology;[38] their comments suggest its insights have seeped into the general marketplace of ideas, probably through parenting books, magazine articles, and radio programs.[39] Just as Ward is the most self-reflective character and most progressive father in *Leave It to Beaver*, he also possesses the most robust understanding of psychology, which provides additional insights into contemporary childhood. In an age fascinated with psychoanalysis, Ward tells Beaver to analyze his feelings.[40] Ward does not fight with June in front of the boys because of things he has read,[41] and this is probably another cause of his aversion to spanking.

Ward's reception of modern psychology is not uncritical, and he admits that the moral lessons he conveys to his sons—and their source in his beloved books—have their limits.[42] Nevertheless, Ward takes the insights of modern child psychology seriously, unlike Fred Rutherford, who adamantly assures Ward that he'll have "none of that psychology" in the same scene in which he admits to hitting Lumpy.[43] This plus Ward's self-awareness, reflections on his present feelings, and memories of his childhood enable him to empathize with his sons and act with nurturing warmth and affection.

The many references to child psychology suggest a purposeful, reflexive link between text and context. This is strengthened when characters refer to "togetherness," "like you read about in the magazines," a beloved idea in the 1950s,[44] in "Three Boys and a Burro" (7:11), "Wally's Dream Girl" (4.29), and even "Un-togetherness" (5.39). Through its plot and visual surfaces, "Nobody Loves Me" points forcefully toward this reflexive link and the series' prescriptive quality. Beaver and Richard view parenting books on display in a bookstore as the episode begins. Visible titles include *You and Your Child*, *Understanding Your Teenager*, *The Problem Child*, and

The Awkward Age. Richard tellingly says these books exist to explain "what's wrong with kids" (0:35), and throughout the episode, Beaver feels unloved and unwanted by Wally, his parents, and even the fireman Gus (Burt Mustin). Eventually, Ward, June, and Wally realize that Beaver's hurting because they have picked on him (though unintentionally and without malice). As Ward and June go upstairs to comfort Beaver, Ward asserts they'll know exactly what to say, "if we just remember a boy Beaver's age needs more assurance of love and understanding than he ever has before" (20:25). The episode concludes with significant symmetry: Beaver and Richard are back at the bookstore, which has a new window display. As the camera pans across the window, *Parents: Do You Know Yourself?*, *Parenting: The Ultimate Insecurity*, *The Road to Maturity*, and *Facing Forty Without Fear* are revealed.

Ward knows himself, and he is doing all he can to help his sons come to know themselves too. He embodies Bryson's ideals, teaching his sons about choices and consequences, but also living out a life of Brysonian individualism, one marked by "conventional deviation," that is choice in the service of an ideal personality and real commitment to personal excellence and virtue, in contrast to "conventional conformity" and its obsession with materialism and "gross pleasures."[45] More engaged in nurturing his sons than his own father was or other Mayfield fathers are, Ward wants his sons' experiences to be better than his were and for them to become better than he was.[46] That shapes his parenting decisions and ultimately seems to have succeeded. Most of his, Beaver's, and Wally's friends never change or improve.[47] Contrarily, by Season 5, Wally is a morally serious, mature adult who begins to care for Lumpy and Eddie in ways Ward (whom he calls one of his "best friends") has done for him.[48] Wally is becoming Ward's son in the deepest sense. "A Night in the Woods" (5.36) demonstrates the fundamental difference in character formation and maturation between Wally and his "gang": Wally is prepared to defend Beaver and his friends from a wolf if need be; however, Eddie, who had been using a recorded wolf call to try to scare Wally and the younger guys, is spooked by a real one (Figures 6.5a–b).

Ward's tutelage also gradually transforms Beaver. During the closing scene of "Beaver's Sweater," which follows the resolution scene at home, Beaver refrains from taunting Judy (Jeri Weil), who is wearing a hideous sweater with totem poles and war shields, because Beaver considers how he would have felt if schoolmates had done that to him when he was wearing the same sweater. Likewise, in "Beaver's Ring," he reaches a new level of empathy as he realizes how Aunt Martha would feel if she knew he had broken the ring she sent him. Most importantly, in "Beaver, the Caddy" (6.21), Beaver stands up to Mr. Langley, who cheated another golfer out of $500, while in "Uncle Billy," Beaver realizes why his granduncle brags so much. Sharing his insight with his father helps Ward to feel sympathy rather than anger

FIGURES 6.5A–B Responsible Wally Cleaver is prepared to defend the boys from threats, real or imagined.

at his uncle, who failed to keep his promises to Ward when he was a boy and is now doing the same to Beaver.

This is not the only time that Ward's perspective changes after talking to Wally and Beaver; sometimes he even acknowledges his fallibility. During "Wally's Election," Ward encourages Wally to more aggressively campaign for class president, but Wally's awkward attempts alienate his classmates and cost him the election. Ward apologizes (accompanied by the PST, as noted earlier),[49] but when Wally reports to Lumpy and Eddie that his father "even said it was kind of his own fault," Lumpy reacts incredulously: "No Dad would ever say that in a million years."

Conclusion

Leave It to Beaver can be read as a naive, sanitized, and idealized reflection of the American suburban family of the late 1950s and early 1960s, one that functions merely as a "celebration of suburban life" in which "dads dispense sage advice to compliant wives and children."[50] But this fails to capture much of its detail, musical profile, and overall trajectory.

The full diversity of the 1950s American family is not evident in this iconic Fifties sitcom, yet there is trouble in paradise. Some fathers are absent or barely engaged, as Principal Rayburn (Doris Packer) confesses to Ward.[51] Parents such as Mr. Rutherford and Mrs. Mondello (Madge Blake) are Ward's antitheses: they strike their children and have generally poor relations with them.

The recurring references to modern child psychology, Ward's introductory voiceovers in episodes 1–16 of season 1 (which are directed at adult viewers), the many times he and June share their insights about parenting in debriefing scenes, and, most importantly, the construction of Ward himself as an ideal, progressive father (well-read, nonviolent, affectionate), and of Wally as a newly mature and moral man, suggest *Leave It to Beaver* offered a prescriptive vision of what the American family (and the individuals therein) could be if the insights of modern psychology and parenting were embraced.[52] Given the representation of Ward's many books and the importance attached by the series to the family and home as sites of moral development, it is not too far fetched to imagine the writings of Lyman Bryson on family, morality, and democracy gracing Ward's den and shaping his perspectives, and through him, those of the viewer.

Nevertheless, this prescriptive vision had its shortcomings. The series projected moral maturity as masculine and construed sentiment and, by extension, the music that had accompanied affection and resolution during earlier seasons as feminine. The muting of affection and musicality was the price of moral maturity.

NOTES

1. See chapter 1 (and sources listed in chapter 1, note 24) for additional discussion.

2. See, for example, Gertrude E. Chittenden, *Living With Children* (New York: MacMillan, 1944); James H. S. Bossard and Eleanor S. Boll, *Ritual in Family Living: A Contemporary Study* (Philadelphia: University of Pennsylvania Press, 1950); Robert Geib Foster, *Marriage and Family Relationships* (New York: MacMillan, 1950); Sidonie Matsner Gruenberg, ed., *Our Children Today: A Guide to Their Needs From Infancy Through Adolescence* (New York: Viking Press, 1952); and Barney Katz, *How to Be a Better Parent: Understanding Yourself and Your Child* (New York: Ronald Press, 1953).

3. The history of the representation of the American family is not merely a historical curiosity. For a survey of the academic study of suburbia, as well as a compelling argument that "representations that reinforce suburban ideals" (e.g., "female subordination, class stratification, and racial segregation") "abound both on television and in the movies," have done so since the 1950s, and remain "a significant force shaping ideas about suburbia today," see William Sharpe and Leonard Wallock, "Bold New City or Built-Up 'Burb? Redefining Suburbia," *American Quarterly* 46, no. 1 (1994): 1–30, 17; and Sharpe and Wallock, "Contextualizing Suburbia," *American Quarterly* 46, no. 1 (1994): 55–61; 57. Stuart C. Aitken has also found that "nostalgia for the nuclear family and the small town" and "family and community relations that probably never existed" influence attitudes about child rearing (11); parents he interviewed indicated that television families, including the Cleavers, had shaped their perspectives on what family life should be like. Aitken, *Family Fantasies and Community Space* (New Brunswick, NJ: Rutgers University Press, 1998), 21, 35.

4. My phrase "conservative gender roles" is intentionally vague. Although the gender roles in *Leave It to Beaver* are clearly conservative by today's standards, they were also becoming conservative for an increasing number of women in the late 1950s and early 1960s, even if they remained typical for many of the program's viewers when it was first broadcast. Nevertheless, I want to avoid the easy assumption that our popular understanding—as evident in many retrospective films and television programs—of women's lives and their social, cultural, and economic roles in the 1950s are completely accurate. Joanne Meyerowitz summarizes the "well-entrenched stereotype of American women in the post-Word War II years"—which is often tied to cultural icons such as June Cleaver—as "domestic and quiescent," forging "family togetherness." Joanne Meyerowitz, ed., *Not June Cleaver: Women and Gender in Postwar America, 1945–1960* (Philadelphia: Temple University Press, 1994), 1. Yet Meyerowitz also argues that accepting this stereotype as universally applicable for the 1950s "flattens the history of women" (2), while focusing solely on "women's subordination erases much of the history of the postwar years." (4) In short, not all women in the 1950s fit this stereotype. (2) See, for example, statistics regarding working women in the 1950s in Susan M. Hartmann, "Women's Employment and the Domestic Ideal in the Early Cold War Years," in *Not June Cleaver*, ed. Meyerowitz, 84–87. At the same time, it would also be inaccurate to assume that nothing has changed for the majority of American women since the 1950s and 1960s. For an excellent summary, see Bruce J. Schulman, "Battles of the Sexes: Women, Men, and the Family," in *The Seventies: The Great Shift in American Culture, Society, and Politics* (Cambridge, MA: Da Capo Press, 2002), 159–176.

5. Verbal or visual references to Beaver and June often shift the Cleavers from representatives of an age of innocence to signifiers of an age of ignorance. See "Shake The Dust" by Anis

Mojgani, accessed April 28, 2013, http://www.youtube.com/watch?v=1PWrlOgrzHQ; *Mars Attacks!* (1996); *8 Mile* (2002); "Arrow" (2006) from *Smallville*; "Slacker Mom" (2007) from *Life with Derek*; and the "Meet the Buttertons" commercial for "I Can't Believe It's Not Butter" (2008).

6. Margaret Marsh asserts that Sharpe and Wallock overemphasize suburbia's cultural stagnation at the expense of its functional transformations (40) and argues that the "suburban domestic ideal" (42) was widespread in the United States before World War II and was never limited to the suburbs. See Marsh, "(Ms)Reading the Suburbs," *American Quarterly* 46, no. 1 (1994): 40–48. (The similar domestic roles of Lucy Ricardo and June Cleaver may support Marsh's point.) Likewise, Robert Bruegmann, "The Twenty-Three Percent Solution," *American Quarterly* 46, no. 1 (1994): 31–34, argues that the conception of a "privatized, restrictive, consumption-minded, culturally impoverished" suburbia ignores the complexity and diversity of suburban communities since World War II (31).

7. "The Younger Brother" (season 5, episode 28), 20:30ff. Time indices in this chapter are from *Leave It to Beaver*, DVD (seasons 1–2, Universal City, CA: Universal Studios Home Entertainment, 2005–2006; seasons 3–6, Los Angeles: NBC Universal, 2010).

8. My thinking about the "moral geography" has been shaped in part by Paul C. Adams, "Television as Gathering Place," *Annals of the Association of American Geographers* 82, no. 1 (1992): 117–135; Aitken (see especially pages 18–23, 107–108); Stephen C. Levinson, "Language and Space," *Annual Review of Anthropology* 25 (1996): 352–382; Andrew Leyshon, David Matless, and George Revill, "The Place of Music: [Introduction]," *Transactions of the Institute of British Geographers* 20, no. 4 (1995): 423–433; and Sara Cohen, "Sounding the City: Music and the Sensuous Production of Place," *Transactions of the Institute of British Geographers* 20, no. 4 (1995): 434–446.

9. Gruenberg argued that maturity is not conformity (or "adjustment") to adult expectations but rather acceptance of others and a willingness to work with and for them. (208)

10. Chittenden, 78–82; Foster, 158.

11. Eddie, for example, causes a falling out between Beaver and a new friend who only speaks Spanish in "Beaver and Chuey" (2.4).

12. For discussion of the gang's competing values and childhood peer pressure, see Chittenden, 1–2, 43; Katz, 56, 59; and Gruenberg, 184; see Katz, 221, regarding disruptive grandparents.

13. See "Mother's Day Composition" (3.31) and "Beaver's I.Q." (4.9).

14. It reappears, uncharacteristically, in "Tennis, Anyone?" (5.33).

15. For a partial transcription of "The Toy Parade," as well as a differently focused discussion of the music and its role in *Leave It to Beaver*, see Ron Rodman, *Tuning In: American Narrative Television Music* (New York: Oxford University Press, 2010), 114–116.

16. The relationship between strings and the sentimental was well established before *Leave It to Beaver*; the oboe may suggest suburbia's (presumed) idyllic, quasi-rural, pastoral character. See Rodman, 120.

17. See Chittenden, 43–44, regarding inappropriate clothing.

18. Chittenden notes many American parents are "reluctant to show their love for their children. . . . There are some fathers who would have hesitated to bestow the second kiss; and there are many who would have failed to bestow the first." (82) Yet in "Music Lesson," Ward and Beaver even share that second kiss. For more on 1950s fathers and displays of affection, see Katz, 23–28.

19. See Foster, 63.

20. Ward sings "Juanita!" (1855), but does so while reminiscing about childhood; the boys are stunned by this unusual behavior. See "Happy Weekend" (2.13).

21. Lyman Bryson, *The New America: Prophecy and Faith* (New York: Harper and Brothers, 1952), 144, 202.

22. See Foster, 263.

23. Regarding television sponsorship and purposeful orientation of programming toward the (suburban) family, see William Boddy, *Fifties Television: The Industry and Its Critics* (Urbana: University of Illinois Press, 1990), 155.

24. See "Wally's Chauffer" (5.12) and "The All-Night Party" (6.36).

25. "Beaver's Big Contest" (4.6), 9:55.

26. "Tire Trouble" (3.14), 8:51.

27. "The Merchant Marine" (5.30), 15:37.

28. Paul Henry Mussen and Jerome Kagan, "Group Conformity and Perceptions of Parents," *Child Development* 29, no. 1 (March 1958): 57–60.

29. See "School Bus" (3.3), "The School Picture" (4.30), and "Beaver's Jacket" (5.19).

30. Parenting and family books from the 1950s noted childhood experiences shape adult behavior and urged parents to recognize how their childhood influenced their interaction with their children. See Chittenden, 1; Katz, 118; and Gruenberg, 20.

31. See also "The Haircut" (1.4), "Wally's Pug Nose" (2.19), "Beaver's I.Q.", and "Beaver's Football Award."

32. "Beaver's Freckles" (4.5), 2:12.

33. "Ward's Golf Clubs" (5.14), 23:09.

34. Nostalgia can momentarily warp Ward's perspective: in "Happy Weekend," he attempts to reshape his sons' lives in the image of his own, supposedly better childhood. Ward's nostalgic turns sometimes cause the boys trouble. At such times, June calls Ward out with humor, telling him not to "glamorize" his "Romantic past" in "Beaver Takes a Walk" (3.6), and gently mocking Ward's claim that he read three or four books a week when he was Beaver's age in "Beaver's Library Book" (3.18). In "Wally's Election," June chides Ward for his concern regarding Wally's lack of "gumption," responding, "Gumption? Well, for land's sake, Grannie." (12:05)

35. "Beaver and Violet" (3.32) and "Eddie's Double-Cross" (4.8).

36. For titles, see "Wally's New Suit" (2.10) and "One of the Boys" (5.34). During the former, we see the book *Male and Female*, perhaps intended to represent Margaret Mead's *Male and Female: A Study of Sexes in a Changing World* (1949), while Ward and June dance. For an exploration of "the classics," mass media, and juvenile delinquency, see Jed Rasula, "Nietzsche in the Nursery: Naive Classics and Surrogate Parents in Postwar American Cultural Debates," *Representations* 29 (1990): 50–77.

37. "Beaver's Library Book." In "Ward's Millions" (4.16), Beaver, assuming his father can do anything once he's read a book about it, buys *How I Became a Millionaire in 12 Months* for Ward.

38. See Eli Zaretsky, "Charisma or Rationalization? Domesticity and Psychoanalysis in the United States in the 1950s," *Critical Inquiry* 26, no. 2 (Winter 2000): 328–354, for an exploration of psychoanalysis and how it supported both the "cold war project of normalization" and the counter tendency to "criticize social control and conformity."

39. Foster, 186.

40. "Wally, the Lifeguard" (4.4) and "Community Chest" (4.33).

41. "Beaver's Laundry," 15:11.

42. See "Beaver's Library Book," "Community Chest," "Weekend Invitation" (5.10), and "Beaver's Electric Trains" for negative comments; and "Eddie's Double-Cross," 17:15, and "Ward's Millions," 22:05, for these limitations.

43. "Tire Trouble."

44. Lynn Spigel, *Make Room for TV: Television and the Family Ideal in Postwar America* (Chicago: University of Chicago Press, 1992), 37.

45. Bryson, 1, 202–203.

46. See Ward's actions in "Beaver Becomes a Hero" (4.3) and the conclusion of "Wally's Track Meet" (4.18).

47. Eddie does try in "Eddie Spends the Night" (4.26) and "The Spot Removers" (3.33).

48. See "Eddie's Double-Cross," "The Merchant Marine," "Eddie Quits School" (5.23), "Bachelor at Large" (6.8), and "Summer in Alaska" (6.33); for Wally's friendship with Ward, see "Wally's Glamour Girl" (4.10) and "Stocks and Bonds" (5.38). Katz told 1950s parents that "you will enjoy your child more if you can be a real friend to him." (241)

49. Ward admits that parents should not try to live through their children; see also Katz, 3; Foster, 149.

50. Sharpe and Wallock, "Bold New City," 17.

51. See "Ward's Problem" (2.3) and "Beaver's Poem" (2.1), respectively.

52. A sea change in parenting was occurring at the time; see Katz, 49, 61, 102, 118; and Gruenberg, 246. *Leave It to Beaver* may have been suggesting it needed to be hastened. For a pessimistic retrospective history of these changes and their broad impact on American society, see Christopher Lasch, "The Socialization of Reproduction and the Collapse of Authority," in *The Culture of Narcissism: American Life in An Age of Diminishing Expectations* (New York: W. W. Norton, 1979), 154–186.

7 The Whole Truth

Music as Truth in The Twilight Zone *(1959–1964)*

REBA WISSNER

FROM 1959 TO 1964, the CBS Television Network ran *The Twilight Zone*, one of the most iconic television series of the twentieth century. Much has been written about the series, and scholars have offered numerous interpretations of the show, often highlighting the ways the program explored issues of concern in postwar society. For example, Peter Wolfe asserts, "By testing our imagination, *The Twilight Zone* heightens our apprehension of reality."[1] The music composed for the *Twilight Zone* served to enhance the anxieties that episodes invoked, often conveyed insight into an episode's subtext, and even contradicted the visuals, thereby preparing the viewer for the series' trademark "twist ending." Nevertheless, the vital relationship between the music and the moving images in many episodes of *The Twilight Zone* has often been overlooked. In this chapter I examine several soundtracks for *The Twilight* Zone and investigate how the music functions as a narrative tool. The music of these episodes fulfills suspenseful and atmospheric roles, but careful examination reveals that the soundtracks also contribute to the series' sense that things are not always what they seem.

The Twilight Zone was not simply a fantasy or science fiction program meant solely to entertain; it was also intended to be thought provoking and to argue philosophical issues, such as "skepticism in its various forms, the ethics of war and peace, the nature and value of knowledge (and of ignorance), the nature of love, the objectivity of judgments of value, [and] the nature of happiness, of freedom, and of justice."[2] The show was famous for treating these topics within the context of impossible events set in everyday places, thus subverting the audience's expectations. It did so effectively, since audience members willingly suspended their disbelief regarding the archetypes that were more freely treated on-screen.[3] Additionally, the series provided cautionary tales, warning viewers of what might happen if they routinely accepted everything they saw and heard; after all, the majority is not always right.[4]

The series is akin to absurdist drama in that both require the suspension of natural law in order to examine reality differently.[5] Many episodes offered a twist ending in the manner of O. Henry that was intended as social commentary to inspire self-reflection. This "twist ending" turned viewer expectation on its head; it also affirmed that one's actions can affect the overall outcome of a situation.

A number of scholars have addressed relationships between the series and Cold War politics and have noted how series writers presented various social anxieties allegorically rather than explicitly. Rod Serling himself readily admitted this. He "understood that because [science fiction] is taken seriously by so few people, it's an ideal vehicle for social comment that, in other contexts, might be unacceptable to audiences."[6] As he recounted in his 1959 interview with Mike Wallace, "network censors would not allow two senators to engage in current political debate, but they could not stand in the way of two Martians saying the same things in allegorical terms."[7] After the pilot, Serling began "inflecting the series with social, economic, and political commentary that reflected issues plaguing late 1950s and early 1960s."[8] In this way, Serling could express the anxieties of current events in a muted manner.

The series mirrored the five main sources of stress that the American people felt during this tumultuous time in history: alienation, fear of "The Other," fear of war and mass destruction, fear of the erosion of traditional values, and fear of totalitarian regimes.[9] Like other anthology shows of the time, it mirrored these sources of stress by addressing issues such as civil rights, McCarthyism, Communism, racial prejudice, corporate culture, and fame.[10] Serling substituted parable for realism in terms of confrontational subjects.[11] For example, scholars often interpret certain episodes as expressions of fear of "The Other," with the aliens representing Communists, the most feared Other at the time.[12]

Like much television of the era, *The Twilight Zone* became an agent of contemporary myth.[13] In essence, the series, in all of its components, played on the reversal of the normal and the abnormal.[14] As a result, in most episodes, it becomes increasingly difficult to ascertain what is real and what is fiction.[15] Don Presnell and Marty McGee have succinctly summed up this point in their study of the series, noting, "At the most basic aesthetic level, *The Twilight Zone* can best be described as the ultimate Rorschach: no matter how many people have seen the series, they all see something different."[16] Furthermore, one of the key themes that *The Twilight Zone* exploits is that reality often conflicts with the images that pervade everyday television programs.[17] As Steven Stark points out, "*The Twilight Zone* implicitly dealt with our newfound national inability to trust anyone or anything—even reality itself."[18]

Thomas E. Wartenberg elaborates on this idea: each episode "plays with the fact that television is both an audio and a visual medium, so that it is possible to record a sound- and an image-track that require different and contradictory assumptions about [how] its content should be interpreted."[19] Like other science fiction television series from the 1960s, such as *The Outer Limits* (1963–1965) and *Lost in Space* (1965–1968), *The Twilight Zone* "had signature tunes and incidental music that were strongly evocative of their genre."[20]

Visual, musical, and dialogic elements each contain varying layers of meaning within a moving image, with the visual as a reproduction of what is absent and the aural as what is present.[21] As Janet Halfyard intimates:

> In theory, any piece of music and any visual image or sequence has a set of potential meanings: but put a specific piece of music with a specific image and they will tend to imply mutually a particular meaning, one that they both have in common: any music will do (something), but the temporal coincidence of music and scene creates different effects according to the dynamics and structure of the music.[22]

In the case of *The Twilight Zone*, therefore, seeing should not be the only prerequisite to believing; hearing should be taken into account as well. It is important to pay as much attention to the nonverbal elements, especially music, as to the visual elements.[23]

The episodes that I examine in this chapter fall into four subcategories: those that use pre-existing music to help demonstrate truth; those that employ music as an indicator of hallucination; those with music that suggests illusion at work; and those in which music indicates that individuals are being controlled by powerful forces outside of themselves. Within the first subcategory, some episodes, like the first that I will examine, use several pieces of music to demonstrate the truth, while others, such as the second episode to be considered, use a single pre-existing classical, popular, folk, or jazz piece throughout.

Pre-existing Music as Truth

The most overt example of music as truth in *The Twilight Zone* occurs in "A Piano in the House" (season 3, episode by Earl Hamner Jr., stock music).[24] This episode, which features stock music consisting of famous songs, is an unusual music-themed special that provides a model for the series' overall musical approaches. As it opens, misanthropic theater critic Fitzgerald Fortune (Barry Morse) enters an antique shop in search of a birthday present for his wife, Esther (Joan Hackett), who is roughly fifteen years his junior. Because Esther wants to learn to play the piano, Fortune buys her a player piano so that she will not have to bother practicing only to realize she has no talent; instead, all she will have to do is replace a roll. Neither he nor others recognize that the piano has a special quality: each roll has the power to affect someone as it plays, thus revealing the person's true self. The piano's ability to strip away masks is visually prefigured by the appearance of the masks in the antique shop (Figure 7.1).[25]

The first victim of the piano's power is the shop owner (Phil Coolidge), who goes from curtness to kindness when the piano begins to play Jimmy McHugh's "I'm in the Mood for Love" (3:15). Fortune asks the shop owner, "Are you aware that you are extraordinarily susceptible to the power of music?" to which he replies, "Isn't everybody?" (4:27). As soon as the roll runs out and the music stops, the shop owner reverts to his earlier stuffy, belligerent demeanor (4:40).

The piano is delivered in time for Esther's birthday party that evening. The butler, Marvin (Cyril Delevanti), is its second victim; when Fortune inserts the roll for Charlie Chaplin's "Smiles," the dour Marvin, who never smiles, becomes jubilant. While laughing and dancing around, he makes fun of the abysmal way that Fortune treats him (7:53). After the music stops, he returns to his normal demeanor, apologizing to Fortune for speaking out of place. Though aware of what just happened,

FIGURE 7.1 The masks in the antique shop.

he was unable to control himself (9:00). A telling remark by Fortune regarding Martin's reaction to the music demonstrates that the piano brings the truth out of people (9:30):

> Who would have known that beyond that gloomy exterior, the man exudes a sunny nature? Of course I've always believed that we have two faces: one that we wear, and the other that we keep hidden. The problem has always been to find some method to make people reveal their hidden faces. It also helps if you know what particular hidden face you're looking for.

At this point, Fortune inserts the roll that plays Aram Khachaturian's "The Sabre Dance," and Esther's true feelings for her husband emerge (10:03). She reveals the pent-up anger that she has felt for the six years she has been married to a man she calls a "beast" and a "sadistic fiend." Like Marvin, she returns to her previous demeanor after it stops playing and she realizes that it had just taken complete control over her (11:14).

During the birthday party, the piano claims more victims. The first guest, Greg (Don Durant), expresses his love for Esther upon the insertion of a roll that plays Jack Strachey's "Those Foolish Things (Remind Me of You)"; she apparently loves him too (13:11). Before the next guest arrives, Esther implores Fortune not to use the piano that evening because it is "not something you fool with." His reply is frank: "I'm not fooling with it dear; I'm using it with deadly accuracy" (15:15). As the party gets underway, Fortune turns to the piano again, referring to it as a party game. Upon hearing Claude Debussy's "Claire de Lune," Marge (Muriel Landers) transforms into her inner child, Tina, who loves to dance. As she twirls around the room, inciting the guests' laughter (17:44), she reveals that she is not always Tina: sometimes she pretends she is a floating snowflake and she is not lonely, but loved (18:07).

After exploiting Marge, Fortune asks Esther to put in a specific roll to find "the devil among them," but she switches it, instead inserting Johannes Brahms's "Lullaby," which turns Fortune into "a poor, frightened kid" (21:10). Greg implores Fortune to tell them his secret, and he reveals his fear of everyone. Inside he is nothing but a small, frightened boy whom he has kept hidden—a boy who only likes to hurt people. He explains that he cannot stop himself, thus enlightening everyone as to the reasons for his behavior. Before everyone, including Esther, walks out on him, he admits that jealousy drove him to hurt Marge, Greg, and Esther. Rod Serling's closing monologue encapsulates the entire episode: "Mr. Fitzgerald Fortune: a man who went looking for concealed persons. And found himself . . ."

While "A Piano in the House" uses a number of pre-existing pieces of music as it explores the truth behind people's masks, the underscore of "Miniature" (season 4, episode by Charles Beaumont, music by Fred Steiner) repeatedly employs the first movement of Mozart's Piano Sonata No. 11 in A Major, K. 331, to reveal the reality of the emotional life of Charley Parks (Robert Duvall), a middle-aged bachelor. Likewise, a newly composed cue and a recurring folk tune help to elucidate the actual condition of characters in "The Passersby" (season 3, episode by Rod Serling, music by Fred Steiner).[26] "The Passersby" takes place in the American south immediately after the Civil War and features characters who do not know until the end of the episode that they are casualties of the war.

As the episode begins, Lavinia (Joanne Linville) sits on her porch watching soldiers walk past her house. An injured confederate sergeant (James Gregory) stops to ask if he can drink from her well, and she gives him permission to do so. The opening cue, "Passing By," accompanies the soldiers who walk by; it is based on an ostinato, juxtaposed with somber music (0:40). Fred Steiner noted that this cue was inspired by Sergei Rachmaninoff's tone poem "Island of the Dead," and that "a tune detective" would be able to notice this quotation here.[27] The quotation is one way the truth about the soldiers who are passing by is implicitly revealed. This music appears several times throughout the episode and conveys both sadness because these men were fatally injured in battle and a revelation that they will not return home. There is an eerie quality to the chromatic motion of the violin when they discuss how beautiful their town once was (1:55). The music gets increasingly unsettling and dissonant as Lavinia talks to the sergeant about the passersby and remarks, "Wouldn't you think with all those men, my Jud would be among them?" (5:09). Unfortunately, her husband Jud (Warren Kemmerling) is dead. The sergeant sings and plays on his guitar "Black Is the Color of My True Love's Hair," which also pervades the episode (5:41).[28]

A sudden, jolting chord sounds when Lavinia sees her neighbor Charlie Constable (Rex Holman), whom everyone thought had been killed during the war. Dissonant guitar chords accompany her attempts to greet him. When he finally responds to her, he tells her that he does not need all the weight that he carries and that he has to keep moving because he is almost "there." Here the violin leaps between registers, accompanied by the harp, which once again presents the disarming music (7:14). Lavinia remarks that she is glad that they were mistaken that Charlie was shot in the head at Gettysburg, but once she discovers blood on Charlie's cap, the violins in their upper register play a minor second accompanied by violin tremolos, a motive commonly used in horror films (7:57).

As Lavinia tells the sergeant about her husband, he continues to play "Black Is the Color of My True Love's Hair." Often, he hums between what should be two adjacent lines. The moments when he sings text rather than hums as he strums are lines directly related to Lavinia's story. For example, when he sings, "I love my love and well she knows," Lavinia says of her husband, "He was a gentle man" (10:28). When he sings, "I love the ground whereon she goes," she says, "Well I remember nights, why he would sit here on this very porch. Play. And sing" (10:42). When he sings, "My life would quickly fade away," she says at the same time, "And then the Yankees came. And the blue locusts had to eat away the trees, the land, and everything on it" (11:05). At this point the music completely stops.

The unsettling music returns as a dark stranger on horseback (David Garcia), who turns out to be a Yankee lieutenant, stops and asks for water. The string tremolos return when Lavinia shoots the Yankee, but he does not react (13:54). The tension of the music increases as the sergeant remembers that the lieutenant, who attempted to help him, was actually killed. As the lieutenant drinks water from the well, the ascending intervals played by the violins become wider and more dissonant (16:45). Finally the violins begin to repeatedly play a dissonant interval, which grows louder until the sergeant shines the light onto the lieutenant's face and we can see that his eye is maimed (17:13). After the sergeant tells Lavinia that he needs to keep going down the road to wherever it leads, Jud emerges from the distance singing "Black Is the Color of My True Love's Hair" (20:05). When Jud asks the sergeant if "he knows," there is a lilting, longing violin solo, which is the point of revelation for him that they are all dead (21:05). This music continues as the last casualty of the Civil War, Abraham Lincoln (Austin Green), tries to persuade Lavinia to walk down the road with him and not remain alone. This finally convinces her that she, too, is dead (22:33).

Music as Dreams and Hallucination

Peter Wolfe reminds us, "Truth in *The Twilight Zone* comes more often in delirium, hallucination, or nightmares than in fact."[29] The second subcategory of episodes features music as an indicator of hallucination. Here, the music foreshadows the revelation that the character is dreaming or hallucinating.

Like many episodes in the series that feature space travel, "Where is Everybody?" (season 1, episode by Rod Serling, music by Bernard Herrmann)[30] is an allegory for alienation, a widespread feeling among Americans during the late 1950s and early 1960s.[31] Here, appropriately unstable harmonies accompany the increasing mental instability of the main character, Mike Ferris (Earl Holliman), a lone Air Force pilot who spends the episode wandering around an empty town trying to rediscover who he is and seeking answers to such questions as "Is anybody here?" after he discovers a mannequin in a car (6:32), or "Who's watching any of the stores?" (9:08), "Who's the wise guy who locked the doors?" (9:37), and "How about a hand, somebody; a little assistance?" (9:46).

The music, which becomes increasingly frantic as Ferris fails to find someone in the town to tell him where he is, reaches its most tense near the end of the episode as Ferris begins to incessantly press the crosswalk button and shout repeatedly, "Help me, please, somebody help me!" When the camera finally turns to those who are, in fact, watching him, the music ceases, grounding the viewer in reality (19:23). In actuality, Mike Ferris has been confined in a tiny isolation box for 484 hours and 36 minutes to simulate a lunar orbit in preparation for his solo trip to the moon. In his loneliness, his mind has created a place for him, but it lacks inhabitants.

Although there is no score for this work among Herrmann's papers at the University of California, Los Angeles, where the CBS scores reside, or at the University of California, Santa Barbara, where the composer's papers are stored, a handwritten piano reduction by someone other than Herrmann exists, and each cue includes a description.[32] For example, cue no. 1563 is labeled "soft, static suspense, sense of loneliness"; cue no. 1564 is described as "dark, lonely, static; elements of suspense and fantasy." All of the cues give the viewer an insight into Ferris's situation of being stuck in an endless cycle with no way out, and each highlights one of the abandoned places—a diner, an alleyway, a phone booth, a police station—where Ferris finds himself.

"The Midnight Sun" (season 3, episode by Rod Serling, music by Nathan Van Cleave) features two neighbors, Norma (Lois Nettleton) and Mrs. Bronson (Betty Garde), struggling through a major heat wave as the Earth moves closer to the sun.[33] At several points, such as in the opening scene, a descending whole-tone scale, which often accompanies dreams, is played on the piano while a flute melody is juxtaposed over it. The music suggests that all is not right, even though the viewer sees Norma calmly painting at the opening of the episode (0:40).

The opening music, which recurs throughout the episode, stops as the last family evacuates Norma's building, but it returns as she says that she is not going to leave. She then says that she has a feeling that she will "wake up in a cool bed. It will be night outside. And there'll be a wind—branches rustling" (3:53). Nevertheless, the heat soon becomes so strong that both Norma and Mrs. Bronson begin to hallucinate. The descending music resumes when Mrs. Bronson sees Norma's painting of the waterfall (18:00).

At the end of the episode, there is a very dramatic moment: simultaneously, Norma's paintings begin to melt, she sweats profusely, and the mercury rises in the thermometer so high the glass shatters. While all of this occurs, the music gets louder, ascends by half steps (while the piano line continues to reiterate its descending motive), and increases in tempo with each iteration. Ironically, what the viewer sees directly conflicts with what is actually happening. Humanity is not doomed to burn because the Earth is not actually moving closer to the sun; rather, it is moving farther from the sun, and everyone will soon freeze to death. Norma is actually ill and has been dreaming (20:00), as the dreamlike music suggested all along, and the rising music that accompanied the rising temperature can, in retrospect, be heard to mirror her state of delirium.

Music as Illusion

One of Serling's favorite motifs in the series is the confusion of the animate and the inanimate. He not only makes inanimate objects come alive, he also treats them anthropomorphically.[34] Several episodes thus deal with illusion, specifically the false impression that inanimate objects or machines are human. In such episodes, the music either reminds us or tells us that the human-looking figure on screen merely appears to be alive, despite the human qualities that this object or machine exudes. Thus in "Five Characters in Search of an Exit" (season 3, episode by Rod Serling, stock music), music evokes the feeling that the eponymous characters are in a strange, unexpected place. But the dreamlike music also informs the viewer that the characters or situations are somehow not real. In fact, in the end, we discover that they are nothing more than dolls in a charity bin for Christmas donations.

In "The Lonely" (season 1, episode by Rod Serling, music by Bernard Herrmann), James A. Corry (Jack Warden) serves a sentence of solitary confinement on an asteroid for murder in self-defense.[35] Four times a year, a supply-ship captain named Allenby (John Dehner) arrives to deliver supplies. The visit that the viewer witnesses is different, however, because Allenby brings Corry something that could simultaneously quell Corry's loneliness but also cause Allenby to lose his job: a robot named Alicia (Jean Marsh) that looks, acts, and feels like a woman. At first, Corry dismisses her as nothing but a machine, but when she begins to cry, he not only accepts her as a woman, he also falls in love with her (Figure 7.2).

While the episode has some music taken from the CBS stock music shelves, it also features an original score composed by Herrmann. Like the majority of Herrmann's film and television scores, the episode exploits the characteristics of several small motivic cells that develop constantly throughout the episode, simultaneously expressing the strangeness and eeriness of the story as well as its romantic elements.[36] Herrmann accompanies the beginning of the episode—a panning image of the asteroid and its desert-like emptiness—with muted horns and strings, both consisting of descending half-steps and accompanied by a whole-tone scale played by the vibraphone (1:40). This music returns with the very same panning images at the end, with one addition: Alicia's legs sprawled out on the sandy ground (23:37).

FIGURE 7.2 Corry (Jack Warden) and Alicia (Jean Marsh).

Herrmann's trademark half-diminished seventh chords also pervade this episode. The muted brass plays the first in their low register at the point when Allenby's spaceship lands on the asteroid (3:10). When Alicia's crate is opened, the two-note semitone motive in the brass is expanded into half-diminished seventh chords moving in the same way with the vibraphone playing whole-tone glissandos underneath. When the chords stop, the vibraphone continues playing, soon suspended over the Hammond organ (10:26). When the vibraphone stops, the organ continues alone and the crate is completely opened, but its contents are not yet revealed. Further development of the music continues as Alicia is exposed and Corry reads aloud the information about her. The camera cuts to Allenby and his crew boarding the ship, and the descending minor second motive is played by the trombones, but alternates with the same motive—this time ascending—in the trumpets. These two motives are developed into hazy music as Allenby's crewmate asks what the crate contains. Allenby replies, "I don't know. Maybe it's an illusion," thus mirroring the accompanying music (10:46).

After cohabitating with Alicia for eleven months, Corry writes in his journal, "It's difficult to write down what has been the sum total of this very strange and bizarre relationship. Is it man and woman? Or man and machine? I don't really know myself." At this point, for the first time, the music—the "Eleven Months" cue (Example 7.1)—is quasi-tonal, suggesting Corry's acceptance of Alicia and her adaptation to Corry's likes and dislikes as she becomes an extension of Corry (16:15).[37]

EXAMPLE 7.1   Bernard Herrmann, *The Twilight Zone*, "Eleven Months" cue, VII no. 2065, mm. 1–11.

Corry thus faces a difficult decision several months later. Allenby returns ahead of schedule, but not with supplies. Instead, he bears the news that Corry has been pardoned and can return to Earth. There is one stipulation, however: he can only bring fifteen pounds of belongings with him, which precludes Alicia. Forgetting that she is only a robot, Corry protests and says that they cannot desert her, but Allenby stops Corry in his tracks when he takes out a gun and shoots Alicia in the face, which reveals nothing but wires and circuits. Corry remembers her true identity, boards the ship bound for Earth, and leaves only his loneliness behind.

Music and Control

The final subcategory concerns episodes in which the main character is controlled by something. Music indicates the source of that control, which is often at odds with what the viewer expects based upon the on-screen action or visuals. In the two episodes discussed here, the main characters are controlled by powerful social forces in one and inanimate objects in the other.

The series as a whole requires the viewer to reevaluate the laws of reality, and no episode demonstrates this more clearly than "The Eye of the Beholder" (season 2, episode by Rod Serling, music by Bernard Herrmann).[38] Remarkably, this reality is veiled not only for the viewer, who cannot see any of the characters' faces until near the episode's end, but it is also the only episode of the series in which the protagonist also is unable to see until the end.[39] Douglas Heyes has likened the episode to a radio show, in that the sound, rather than the image, is most important,[40] while Tony Albarella notes, "sparse and methodical to build tension early on, the score becomes a resonant force at the point of Janet Tyler's unmasking and accentuates her nightmarish run through the hospital."[41]

The episode opens with Tyler (masked: Maxine Stuart; unmasked: Donna Douglas) in a hospital bed: her face is wrapped in bandages and a nurse (Jennifer Howard) is taking her pulse and temperature. Throughout the episode, everyone's faces are hidden by shadows. When Janet convinces her doctor (William D. Gordon) to remove the bandages, a vibraphone plays a whole-tone melody (11:20). This dreamlike music continues through the episode until the end, at which point Janet's "ugly" face is revealed to the accompaniment of a dissonant chord played by low brass (19:20).[42] As it turns out, from our perspective Janet is actually quite beautiful, but all of the doctors and nurses that surround her have pig-like faces (Figure 7.3). What seems ugly by our standards is the norm for that society. According to them, Janet is not simply ugly: she is hideously deformed. Because she has undergone eleven unsuccessful state-sponsored treatments for her "disfigurement," she will now be segregated into a ghetto for similar people who, we can assume, are all beautiful, given the appearance of Walter Smith (Edson Stroll), the representative of the group.

FIGURE 7.3 The "ugly" Janet Tyler (Donna Douglas) and the "normal" Doctor and Nurse.

Realizing her fate is sealed, Janet runs frantically down the hall to try to escape what awaits her. As she runs, she repeatedly encounters television screens featuring a leader preaching "glorious conformity" (19:47). As his speech progresses, the music gets louder, and it becomes increasingly difficult to understand him. Just before Janet runs unexpectedly into Mr. Smith's arms, the background music drowns out all but the important phrases (20:54).

Throughout the episode, Herrmann milks the theme of anti-conformity by composing a sparse score based on a relentless ostinato, using the harp and vibraphone to intone repeated chromatic fragments with distant muted brass to create rising and falling gestures that are first buried in the texture, and then appear more prominently on the surface.[43] Like the diminished seventh chord, the ostinato resists resolution and creates tension because of its ability to combine with disparate harmonies. Herrmann often employs an ostinato in episodes such as this one that require a build-up of tension but lack dialogue.[44]

The second episode, "The Whole Truth" (season 2, episode by Rod Serling, stock music), opens with music representing a rush of people.[45] Harvey Hunnicut (Jack Carson), a shady car salesman notorious for lying, approaches a couple (Jack Ging and Nan Peterson) looking to buy a vehicle. His accompanying music seems to indicate that although Hunnicut feigns kindness and truth, he is as devious as his music (0:46). After a soliloquy about how commerce has gone wrong and that the older models that he sells are better than the new ones, he kicks the fender of one of the cars; it promptly falls off, and circus-like music, indicating that Hunnicut has just made a fool of himself (3:33), begins to play.

Soon after, an old man (George Chandler) sells Hunnicut a Model A; the old man warns him that the car has a unique quality: anyone who possesses it becomes incapable of lying. Hunnicut is doubtful at first, until his next attempt to lie fails. During each subsequent attempt, the music shifts to a haunted-like quality (Example 7.2), as if he is possessed (9:40).[46]

Remembering what the old man said about the car, Hunnicut looks inside it. Accompanying music built on a whole-tone scale suggests that the car has a spell-like quality, though subsequent comical bassoon music shows that the joke is on Hunnicut (11:35). Later, while looking at the newspaper, a friend suggests to Hunnicut that it would be a great joke if he could get a certain person who appears in the paper—his name is never mentioned—to buy the car. Toward the end of the episode, a march theme plays while someone important enters (21:24); we soon see that it is Nikita Khrushchev (Lee Sabinson). The Soviet Premier and his aide purchase the car, then drive it off the lot. Serling's closing monologue is accompanied by the haunted theme, highlighting Serling's punch line: Khrushchev, the proud new owner of the car, will now no longer be able to lie until he sells the car (23:43). This places the political commentary into the episode in a very overt manner.

EXAMPLE 7.2 *The Twilight Zone*, "Brouillards" cue, mm. 1–5, flutes only. (Transcribed by R. Wissner.)

Conclusion

Douglas Brode reminds us that "at its best, *The Twilight Zone* did not tell us what to think. Instead, Serling's series forced us to think for ourselves."[47] No element of these episodes—and the above episode inventory is far from exhaustive—exemplifies this more than the relationship between the music and the visuals. As we have seen, examining the dialogue and images on screen can elucidate an episode's specific meaning. But paying close attention to the music, its placement, and its characteristics adds another level to the episode and helps us to understand things that seem to be beyond understanding. For example, several episodes considered in this chapter use the whole-tone scale to reveal the reality of the situation. Music was also used to suggest dream states and illusions, to control characters, or to highlight how they were being controlled by elements in their environment. Other features not discussed, such as the use of anachronistic music, which often provides insight into a character's innermost thoughts and depicts a reversal in time that is not obviously apparent, will have to await further consideration.[48] Nevertheless, the episodes addressed in this chapter suggest that Serling succeeded in his mission to make television that could be simultaneously entertaining and intellectually worthwhile.

NOTES

1. Pete Wolfe, *In The Zone: The Twilight World of Rod Serling* (Bowling Green, OH: Bowling Green State University Press, 1997), 202.

2. Lester Hunt, "Introduction," in *Philosophy in The Twilight Zone*, ed. Noel Carrol and Lester H. Hunt (Chichester, UK: Wiley-Blackwell, 2009), 1.

3. Joel Engel, *Rod Serling: The Dreams and Nightmares of Life in The Twilight Zone* (Chicago and New York: Contemporary Books, 1989), 186–187.

4. Carl Plantinga, "Frame Shifters: Surprise Endings and Spectator Imagination in *The Twilight Zone*," in Carrol and Hunt, *Philosophy in The Twilight Zone*, 39.

5. Wolfe, 97.

6. Jon Kraszewski, "Television Anthology Writers and Authorship: The Work and Identity of Rod Serling, Reginald Rose, and Paddy Chayefsky in 1950s and 1960s Media Industries" (PhD diss., Indiana University, 2004), 151.

7. Mike Wallace Interview, 1959, quoted in Novotny Lawrence, "Reflections of a Nation's Angst; or How I Learned to Stop Worrying and Love *The Twilight Zone*," in *Space and Time: Essays on Visions of History in Science Fiction and Fantasy Television*, ed. David C. Wright and Allan W. Austin (Jefferson, NC: McFarland, 2010), 11.

8. Ibid., 12–13.

9. Crista D. Scaturro, " 'Between the Pit of Man's Fears and the Summit of His Knowledge:' Cold War America and the *Twilight Zone*" (master's thesis, The George Washington University, 2009), 46. David Hogan notes, "explorations of gender issues, war, xenophobia, and other

difficult topics are more easily accepted by viewers if the tale's protagonists exist in future times in alien places with discernible, but not too literal, links to our own world. If the protagonists are only vaguely human, a writer can achieve especially pointed comment because audiences will nod and absorb the lesson without having been made to feel morally deficient or unfairly put upon." See "Introduction: Science Fiction and the Actual," in *Science Fiction America: Essays on SF Cinema*, ed. David J. Hogan (Jefferson, NC: McFarland, 2006), 3–4.

10. Jon Kraszewski, "Do Not Go Gentle Into That Twilight: Rod Serling's Challenge to 1960s Television Production," *The Review of Film and Television Studies* 6 (2008): 343. Examples of these anthologies include *Kraft Television Theater* (ABC, 1953–1955), *Kraft Suspense Theater* (NBC, 1963–1965), *Lux Video Theater* (NBC, 1954–1957), *Ford Theater* (NBC, 1952–1956), *Four Star Playhouse* (CBS, 1952–1956), and *Alfred Hitchcock Presents* (CBS/NBC, 1955–1965).

11. Douglas Brode and Carol Serling, *Rod Serling and The Twilight Zone: The 50th Anniversary Tribute* (Fort Lee, NJ: Barricade Books, 2009), xvi.

12. Lincoln Geraghty, "Painted Men and Salt Monsters: The Alien Body in 50s and 60s American Television," *Intensities* 4 (2007): 6.

13. Rodney Hill, "Anthology Drama: Mapping the *Twilight Zone*'s Cultural and Mythological Terrain," in *The Essential Science Fiction Television Reader*, ed. J. P. Telotte (Lexington: University of Kentucky Press, 2008), 111.

14. M. Keith Booker, *Strange TV: Innovative Television Series from The Twilight Zone to the X-Files* (Westport, CT: Greenwood Press, 2002), 61.

15. Steward Stanyard, *Dimensions Behind The Twilight Zone: A Backstage Tribute to Television's Groundbreaking Series* (Toronto: ECW Press, 2007), 42.

16. Don Presnell and Marty McGee, *A Critical History of Television's The Twilight Zone, 1959–1964* (Jefferson, NC: McFarland, 1998), 6.

17. Brode and Serling, 165.

18. Steven D. Stark, *Glued to the Set: The 60 Television Shows and Events that Made Us Who We Are Today* (New York: The Free Press, 1998), 89.

19. Thomas E. Wartenberg, "Blending Fiction and Reality: The Odyssey of Flight 33," in Carrol and Hunt, *Philosophy in The Twilight Zone*, 134.

20. Philip Hayward, *Off The Planet: Music, Sound, and Science Fiction Cinema* (Bloomington: Indiana University Press, 2004), 12–13.

21. William A. Gamson, et al., "Media Images and the Social Construction of Reality," *Annual Review of Sociology* 18 (1992): 374.

22. Janet K. Halfyard, "Mischief Afoot: Supernatural Horror-Comedies and the Diabolus in Musica," in *Music in the Horror Film: Listening to Fear*, ed. Neil Lerner (New York: Routledge, 2010), 25.

23. Scatturo, 50.

24. *The Twilight Zone: The Complete Definitive Collection*, DVD, Disc 14, produced by Rod Serling (Chatsworth, CA: Image Entertainment, 2006).

25. Wolfe, 166.

26. *The Twilight Zone*, Disc 12.

27. Fred Steiner, "Interview, Archive of American Television," http://www.emmytvlegends.org/interviews/people/fred-steiner.

28. The song's use in the episode is likely an anachronism. See Martin Grams, *The Twilight Zone: Unlocking the Door to a Television Classic* (Churchville, MD: OTR Publishing, 2008), 427.

29. Wolfe, 14.

30. *The Twilight Zone*, Disc 6.

31. M. Keith Booker, *Science Fiction Television* (Westport, CT: Praeger, 2004), 13.

32. William Wrobel, "Television Works of Bernard Herrmann," Unpublished paper, 21.

33. *The Twilight Zone*, Disc 13.

34. Booker, 63.

35. *The Twilight Zone*, Disc 1.

36. Steven C. Smith, *A Heart at Fire's Center: The Life and Music of Bernard Herrmann* (Berkeley: University of California Press, 1991), 231.

37. In the manuscript score, it is spelled, "Elven Months." See the manuscript score in the Bernard Herrmann Papers, 1927–1977, Department of Special Collections, University of California, Santa Barbara.

38. Geraghty, 6; *The Twilight Zone*, Disc 7.

39. Brode and Serling, 204.

40. Tony Albarella, "Truth in Beauty," in *As Timeless As Infinity: The Complete Twilight Zone Scripts of Rod Serling*, Vol. 1, ed. Tony Albarella (Colorado Springs, CO: Gauntlet Press, 2004), 331.

41. Ibid., 330.

42. In science fiction and horror, those who conform to society are often accompanied by tonal music, while outsiders (and in the case of horror films, aliens or monsters) by atonal music. See Halfyard, 22; and chapter 9 in this collection.

43. Smith, 234.

44. Graham Donald Bruce, "Bernard Herrmann: Film Music and Narrative" (PhD diss., New York University, 1982), 256.

45. *The Twilight Zone*, Disc 9.

46. CBS Collection, UCLA.

47. Brode and Serling, 163.

48. David Butler, "The Days that Do Not End: Film Music, Time, and Bernard Herrmann," *Film Studies* 9 (2001): 55.

8   "Living in Harmony"?

American Music and Individualism in The Prisoner *(1967–1968)*

JOANNA SMOLKO AND TIM SMOLKO

THOUGH A BRITISH production, the 17-episode television series *The Prisoner* (1967–1968) uses specifically American music and themes in two of its most controversial episodes, "Living in Harmony" and "Fall Out." The series features a recently resigned British Intelligence Agent (Patrick McGoohan) who is abducted and sent to a prison disguised as a pleasant seaside village. There, individual identities are suppressed by replacing people's names with numbers. McGoohan—unnamed throughout the series—is labeled Number Six. He learns that a succession of Number Twos rules the Village, and each reports to the mysterious and unseen Number One. In every episode, Number Six seeks to retain his identity and escape the unbarred prison. He pits himself against those in control who want to dissolve him into the collective and extract information about his intelligence career. Music is used both to reflect the village community in lockstep and to emphasize Number Six's quest to preserve his personhood.

"Living in Harmony" characterizes Number Six as a lone sheriff who initially refuses to carry a gun but then arms himself against a threatening populace. His quest for individuality is exemplified aurally by Phrygian-laced, solo acoustic guitar passages, which reinforce a cinematic trope often employed in Westerns to portray an outsider. In the final episode, "Fall Out," the series reaches a climax when Prisoner Number Forty-Eight bursts into the African-American spiritual "Dem

Bones" to defy a Ku Klux Klan-like hooded jury. The raucous song, with its biblical allusion to the body's resurrection, accrues apocalyptic significance as it initiates the prison's surreal dissolution.

An overview of the cross-pollination between British and American television, film, and music in the 1960s will provide context for understanding the use of American music and themes in "Living in Harmony" and "Fall Out." In particular, this chapter will explore the ways in which American music is used to evoke concerns held by both American and British audience members about the preservation of freedom and individuality in the midst of the Cold War, the Vietnam War, and the civil rights movement.

Cross-Pollination Between British and American Popular Culture

The shared language and mutual experience of fighting World War II facilitated a commonality between American and British culture that can readily be seen in film, television, and music. The presence of thousands of American GIs in England during and after World War II resulted in an increasing American influence on the British.[1] American television and radio were influential, but American film had the greatest impact on British culture through musicals, gangster films, and especially Westerns.[2] Generations of Britons recount in their memoirs that as schoolchildren in the 1910s–1950s they flocked to Saturday morning matinees to watch cowboy movies.[3] Yet despite the popularity of American Westerns in England, "Living in Harmony" was among the first Western-themed television episodes or films produced within the UK.

Likewise, the British public became entranced by American popular music. In the late 1950s, young Britons shaped their identities by imitating singers and musicians of American popular, country, and R&B music. Though the BBC remained aloof to American artists such as Little Richard, Chuck Berry, and Elvis Presley, their new sounds were disseminated by Radio Luxembourg, the Armed Forces Network, and the pirate station Radio Caroline.

British culture had its own allure for post–World War II Americans. One of the major television events of 1953 in America was the coronation of Queen Elizabeth II. Throughout the 1950s, a steady stream of British films and television programs were shown on American television. Many were highbrow dramas and Sherlock Holmes-type mysteries, giving British film an air of sophistication, and even superiority. In the 1960s, Beatlemania, the British Invasion, and James Bond films were the major catalysts in exporting British popular culture into the ears and eyes of practically every American.

The Cold War and Spy Dramas

Among the most popular television genres in the 1960s on both sides of the Atlantic was the spy drama. Americans produced *The Man from U.N.C.L.E.* (1964–1968), *I Spy* (1965–1968), and *Mission: Impossible* (1966–1973), while the British produced *The Avengers* (1961–1969), *Espionage* (1963–1964), *The Saint* (1962–1969), and two series starring Patrick McGoohan, *Danger Man/Secret Agent* (1960–1966) and *The Prisoner* (1967–1968). The ascendancy of this genre is hardly surprising given the events of the previous two decades: increased state-sponsored espionage, onset of the Cold War, anti-Communism, inception of NATO, nuclear proliferation, construction of the Berlin Wall, and the Cuban Missile Crisis.

Wesley Britton links the Cold War and spy dramas succinctly: "As the rise of television began almost precisely with the growth of Cold War thinking, the two new developments in American culture were quickly joined at the hip."[4] Cold War espionage was also a frequent subject in novels and films, as the iconic James Bond demonstrates. In 1953, Ian Fleming published his first Bond novel, *Casino Royale*, and the first Bond movie (*Dr. No*) was released in 1962. The continuing James Bond film series has become one of the highest-grossing film franchises in history and has only recently been challenged by the Harry Potter films. Bond spawned an entire industry of movies and television shows with Cold War espionage as its theme. Jeffrey S. Miller writes, "The post-Kennedy popularity of James Bond in the United States acted as a major vector in introducing the spy series to American television, and it was a significant part of the entrée given John Drake and *Secret Agent* to American audiences."[5]

Danger Man/Secret Agent[6] starred Patrick McGoohan first as a Washington, DC-based NATO investigator, then as a British Secret Service agent, and was broadcast in America intermittently from 1961 to 1967. Like Bond, McGoohan's character was a spy, yet Drake never killed, rarely carried a gun, and had a strict code of morals. He was more interested in Cold War politics and less in stylish clothes, women, and martinis. The first *Danger Man* was broadcast in America in April 1961, two years before the American premiere of *Dr. No*. Yet the success of the subsequent Bond movies in America in the 1960s bolstered the popularity of *Danger Man/Secret Agent* and, ultimately, *The Prisoner*.

For Your Ears Only: Music for Spies

The Prisoner's music fits neatly within the music used in 1960s spy films and television shows. Bebop jazz, lounge music, brassy fanfares, sensuous string melodies, and instrumental rock featuring electric guitar appear most often in main themes and incidental music to portray intrigue, suspense, and danger. Opening themes frequently feature highly syncopated rhythms played on bongos (*Mission: Impossible*), bold melodies with wide intervallic leaps (*The Avengers*), and jazzy chromaticism (*Secret Agent*). These spy music tropes were crystallized by John Barry, who composed the soundtracks for eleven James Bond films. *The Prisoner*'s music borrows much from the Bond formula, except for the seductive, female-sung torch-songs like Shirley Bassey's rendition of "Goldfinger." This musical absence reinforces Number Six's sharp contrast with 007's playboy lifestyle: McGoohan's character never consummates a romantic relationship with any woman in the Village.

The electric guitar is prominent in this genre, evoking the danger and "electricity" of the spy lifestyle, as in the "Peter Gunn Theme" and especially the "James Bond Theme." Composed by Monty Norman and arranged by Barry, the Bond theme features reverb and staccato picking by Vic Flick, whose riff appears in every Bond film and came to define the lifestyle ethos of the spy.[7] The riff most likely had an influence on the one played by Chuck Day in Johnny Rivers's "Secret Agent Man," the theme for *Secret Agent*'s broadcast in the mid-1960s. The song was a hit on the U.S. *Billboard* chart in 1966 and is widely regarded as the quintessential opening theme of the spy television genre. Flick also played the electric guitar on Ron Grainer's *The Prisoner* theme, employing reverb and staccato passages similar to those heard in the Bond theme.

Overview of the Music in *The Prisoner*

In his book on *The Prisoner*, Robert Fairclough aptly names one of the chapters "Cinema for the Small Screen"[8] because the scope and style of the show broadened television's dimensions in the 1960s and approached the proportions of cinema. The same can be said for its music, which is deliberately used as a signifier and subtext, and in some instances approaches film score proportions. In a scene from the episode "Anvil into Hammer," Number Six sees two signs in the window of the Village shop: "Music says all" and "Music begins where words leave off." Here, even within the fictional world of the Village, the series acknowledges music's importance as an interpreter of the narrative, and even as an *actor* within the drama. In this episode, after a fellow prisoner is killed, Number Six uses music to chip away at the totalitarian control of the Village: he deceives Number Two into believing that a recording of George Bizet's *Suite L'Arlésienne* (1872) contains a hidden code. Driven to the brink of insanity by his inability to decode it, Number Two turns himself in to Number One for his "breakdown in control."

Repeatedly, crucial dramatic moments in the series are structured around musical devices. For example, in the penultimate episode "Once Upon a Time," Number Two sings nursery rhymes to lull Number Six into a childlike state for interrogation purposes. Music thus becomes a psychological weapon. Yet, at the same time, the nursery rhymes depict Number Two's own downward spiral into madness, which eventually leads to the Village's destruction.

Roger Langley, author of the definitive biography on McGoohan, writes, "The series star and mentor McGoohan was closely involved with all aspects of production, not the least of all the music."[9] Ron Grainer, Albert Elms, Robert Farnon, and Wilfred Josephs composed the music for the show, and editors Robert Dearberg and Eric Mival selected incidental music from the Chappell Music Library[10] to fit the mood of various scenes.[11] For example, fight scenes contain brisk, jazz-inflected "action music," romantic scenes feature soft, alluring music, and suspense-filled scenes include dissonant, fragmented music. According to Joseph Lanza, libraries such as Chappell provided music that was "not easily recognizable but that, after frequent exposure, came to have a hypnotic and subliminal impact."[12] As discussed below, the incidental music for the series was chosen carefully to subtly reinforce the themes and action, and the compilers deliberately avoided music that would hit the listener "like a ton of bricks." Instead, they used "subtle" music that subconsciously shapes viewers' interpretations of the scene.[13]

When diegetic music appears in the series, it is sometimes employed (as in "Hammer into Anvil") as a subversive force, demonstrating prisoners' attempts to escape or overthrow the system. However, those in control use source music more frequently to lull their subjects into blissful submission. For example, in the first *Prisoner* episode "Arrival," Number Six hears a brass band—which reappears in many episodes—playing the bright and bouncy "Radetzky March" by Johann Strauss Sr. (17:00).[14] The music portrays the carnivalesque atmosphere of the Village, reinforcing in the prisoners a sense of peace and well-being. Later (22:00), Number Six realizes that the soporific lullaby[15] piped into his apartment is impossible to turn off, even after he crushes the speaker to bits with his feet. This demonstrates McGoohan's intention, even from the first episode, to show how music can manipulate characters on screen.

Kristopher Spencer effectively sums up the soundscape of the series: "Much of this music captures the whimsical character of the Village itself—particularly the marching band numbers—but a few tracks venture into territory as disparate as exotica, Moog electronica, sitar psychedelia, funky soul and groovy pop."[16] In the remainder of this chapter we will explore more closely the ways in which specifically American music is used to symbolize resistance in the episodes "Living in Harmony" and "Fall Out." In the larger cultural view, it appears that within this

British drama, America itself—as represented through music—is a potent symbol of rebellion, anarchy, and hope.

"Living in Harmony"

After the first thirteen episodes of the series had been conceived, McGoohan searched for innovative directions to bring the series to its grand finale. Ian Rakoff presented McGoohan with his conception of a Western-themed episode, and McGoohan gave him permission to develop the idea. The episode, co-written and directed by David Tomblin, employs many of the easily identifiable tropes found in cinematic portrayals of the Old West. Number Six is depicted as a sheriff who relinquishes his badge and gun and tries to leave a rural town called Harmony, which parallels the opening sequences of Number Six resigning his Secret Service position in the other episodes. He is captured, taken back to the town, and thrown into prison by an evil Judge and his men. For the first time in the series we see the Prisoner in an actual prison. He is conned into being the town's sheriff again and drawn into a duel to save the life of a woman who befriends him. He eventually lays down his sheriff's badge, picks up his gun, and kills the Judge's hit man, The Kid. Number Six is apparently killed by the Judge but awakens to find himself within the confines of the Village. It is revealed that the entire Western scenario has been an elaborate hallucination induced so the keepers of the Village can probe his reactions.

Rakoff's working episode title was "Do Not Forsake Me Oh My Darling," in reference to the theme song of the classic Western *High Noon* (1952), composed by Dmitri Tiomkin and sung by Tex Ritter.[17] Rakoff states, "There were, in fact, aspects of *High Noon* which I had born [*sic*] in mind when writing the script."[18] Fragments of "Do Not Forsake Me" are woven throughout the film, even representing different characters in turn, as Anthony Bushard discusses.[19] The reference to the song in the working title highlights the image of McGoohan's Number Six as a solitary lawman who follows his own conscience, even when forsaken by all others.

High Noon appears to be the central source of inspiration for the episode, but Rakoff discusses three additional influences. First, the name of the town "Harmony" was taken from a Gene Autry comic, entitled "Guns of Chance," which evokes the pacifist theme present in both "Living in Harmony" and *High Noon* (at least in their beginnings).[20] The alliteration between the town's name "Harmony" and *High Noon*'s Hadleyville suggests a reference between them. Second, Rakoff had worked in 1960 as assistant director for the Western-themed movie *The Hellions* (1961). Set in South Africa and similar to *High Noon*, "one brave man" inspires townsfolk to drive out a family of outlaws who "live by the gun." Rakoff's experience working on the movie, and witnessing apartheid firsthand, had chilling resonances with the themes of control and manipulation in *The Prisoner* and fueled his conception of "Living in Harmony." He recounts, "Under the draconian laws of apartheid, the entire population was rigidly controlled. The religiously white government claimed biblical motivation as its excuse for their own experiment in social engineering."[21] A final source for the episode was Rakoff's musings on the parallels between the violence inherent in the Western film genre and America's involvement in the Vietnam War:

> Well, it's America, it's the West. There's shooting and killing. You can't have a western without action or one that's only psychological. Right now they're going crazy in Vietnam, in the war that everybody says they won't win. But the stranger [McGoohan's character] is not a pacifist or a conscientious objector. His position comes from strength, not weakness.[22] Vietnam and the burning of draft cards were big in the news. The call to arms was being resisted across America. I deliberately did not try to separate my ideas from these events.[23]

Rakoff envisioned this episode realistically and felt there was no room for parody or caricature. The gritty realism of "Living in Harmony" contrasts with the surreal and fanciful world of The Village featured in most episodes. Although the setting for "Living in Harmony" isn't real either, as it is the product of a drug-induced hallucination, the Prisoner and viewer do not discover this until the end. "My West was no jokey affair. It was a serious place," Rakoff writes.[24] The music is vital in projecting this realism.

The Music in "Living in Harmony"

Just as the plot of "Living in Harmony" models common elements of cinematic Westerns, so its music, composed entirely by Albert Elms, is comparable to a Western film score. Elms eschewed the Eurocentric music of the Chappell Library and employed musical devices that evoke the American Southwest. The music of the episode borrows not only from tropes heard in *High Noon* (solo guitar, Phrygian melodies, a central recurring melody), but also from the scores of Ennio Morricone, especially *The Good, the Bad and the Ugly* (1966). All three scores are characterized by variations on a single melody. *High Noon* is dominated by the melody of "Do Not Forsake Me." *The Good, the Bad and the Ugly* is infused with its unforgettable main theme, variations on which serve to represent the three main characters: soprano recorder for Blondie ("Good"), bass ocarina for Angel Eyes ("Bad"), and two male voices imitating a coyote call for Tuco ("Ugly").[25] One hears the main theme of "Living in Harmony" on acoustic guitar over 20 times in the episode, and it symbolizes the struggle of the solitary stranger against the town of Harmony. As the narratives of *High Noon, The Good, The Bad and the Ugly*, and "Living in Harmony" unfold, the motives accumulate meanings and help to build tension for the climaxes of each.

The opening sequence and music of "Living in Harmony" is a striking departure from the show's usual opening. Instead of the bird's-eye view of a London cityscape, we see from ground view a broad expanse of land with a solitary rider on a galloping steed approaching the camera. This dichotomy between the open landscape and the solitary figure was made famous by John Ford in his Westerns from the 1940s and 1950s and became a cinematic trope for individualism. As the opening scene unfolds, the broad land is depicted aurally by an organ or harmonium that lays down a hollow-sounding pedal point. Elms depicts the rider with an acoustic guitar and oboe playing mournful, Phrygian-laced melodic fragments, while a timpani riff foreshadows an impending confrontation. The solitary rider is Number Six, who has come to surrender his badge and gun to the Judge. The music and images have thrust the viewer and the Prisoner into a new paradigm, yet the connection with the plot and mood of the series is still quite clear.

As noted above, the music that Elms composed for this episode has striking similarities to the scores of Morricone, especially three "Spaghetti Westerns" directed by Sergio Leone: *A Fistful of Dollars* (1964), *For a Few Dollars More* (1965), and *The Good, the Bad and the Ugly* (1966).[26] Morricone represented a generation of film composers who were moving beyond singing cowboys, such as Gene Autry and Roy Rogers, the use of folk and popular songs (as found in *Stagecoach* [1939]), and the employment of large orchestras, which were prominent in the Westerns of John Ford and others from the 1930s to the 1950s. One of Morricone's innovations was his augmentation of orchestral arrangements with instruments such as organ, acoustic and electric guitars, and electronically treated sounds. These elements are heard in "Living in Harmony." Early in *The Good, the Bad and the Ugly* Lee Van Cleef's character Angel Eyes ("The Bad") approaches the camera on horseback to the accompaniment of strings, organ, and acoustic guitar. This cue, titled "The Sundown," is similar to the opening music of "Living in Harmony." They both feature an acoustic guitar playing stepwise ascending and descending lines over a hollow-sounding pedal point. The solo guitar is a Western trope frequently used to pit the one against the many (often represented through a full orchestral score). Here, it represents the Prisoner's isolation from the town of Harmony. This is extremely effective, and distinctive, when compared to the musical landscape of the other episodes that take place in the Village. The diegetic music of the Village most frequently represents a collective identity: the lockstep music of the marching band, the cheery trumpet fanfare that precedes announcements on the loudspeakers, and the carnival music in episodes such as "Dance of the Dead." Throughout the series, Number Six's individualism is portrayed musically in the Village with a distorted electric guitar playing minor seconds, but this motif is also used broadly to represent tension or suspense. Only in the solo acoustic guitar of "Living in Harmony" is the individuality of Number Six portrayed with precision. Because the musical tropes portraying the outsider in Westerns were established in film and television by 1967, it only takes a few seconds of watching the opening of "Living in Harmony" for viewers to identify Number Six as an outsider.[27]

Like the Leone films and other Westerns, "Living in Harmony" features a strategic use of silence and natural diegetic sounds unencumbered by music to build tension when a confrontation is about to take place. While this is a common technique in Westerns, Leone and McGoohan give it an added emphasis by highlighting the ominous footfalls on saloon floorboards, the striking of a match, and the cocking of a revolver's hammer to create the soundtrack by themselves.

While an affinity exists between the style, music, and violence of the Leone films and "Living in Harmony," one way they differ is in their tone. "Living in Harmony" lacks the comic elements of the Leone films, which, as Robert J. Landry notes, are "one mouthful of blood short of parody."[28] Similarly, many of Morricone's musical themes instantly strike the listener as cowboy camp, such as the mouth harp, Indian drumbeats, and chanting in *For a Few Dollars More*, and the squawk box, coyote imitations, and banshee yodel in *The Good, the Bad and the Ugly*. Conversely, Elms's incidental music for "Living in Harmony" is as serious throughout as the dialogue, acting, and plot.

To the British television audience, "Living in Harmony" was a dramatic foray into the romance of the American Old West. The music augmented this sense of escapism and fantasy. But to the American television censors at CBS in 1968, its gritty realism and vivid portrayal of a sheriff who tries to clean up a corrupt town—without a gun—hit too close to home, and they chose not to show this episode in the series' first American run. At first they claimed that the use of hallucinatory drugs was objectionable, even though many of the other *Prisoner* episodes include drug-induced hallucinations as a major plot device. But as Matthew White and Jaffer Ali write, "Official spokesmen for both CBS and ITC are on the record as saying that the Vietnam issue killed the episode."[29] Similarly, Eric v. d. Luft shares the fan's perspective: "As soon as we at last saw it, we recognized its pacifist political allegory, just the kind of thing that pro-Vietnam War hawks would hate."[30] Thus, music in "Living in Harmony" plays a vital role in situating *The Prisoner* in the Old West, portraying Number Six as an outsider against the establishment, creating resonances with the film scores of 1960s Westerns, and giving the episode a gritty realism that contributed to its initial censorship in America.

"Fall Out"

Written and directed by Patrick McGoohan, "Fall Out" was first broadcast in the UK on February 4, 1968, and in America on September 21, 1968. It is a continuation of the penultimate episode of the series "Once Upon a Time," in which Number Six and Number Two (Leo McKern) face off in a psychological battle to the death. In a series full of enigmatic episodes, "Fall Out" is the most perplexing and controversial. Its ambiguous and surreal ending outraged fans after its premiere and caused McGoohan to flee England and live in Switzerland for a time until the uproar died down.

The most significant musical element in this episode is the use of well-known popular music, which enters the diegetic soundscape for the first time in the series. The Beatles' "All You Need Is Love" and an upbeat rendition of James Weldon Johnson's spiritual, "Dem Bones,"[31] are used in complex ways to provide frameworks through which to view the episode's events. Explicit musical references in the other episodes typically draw from music of the past (classical music or children's songs) and tend to generalize or mythologize the setting. Here, the music contemporizes and personalizes the prison's setting, drawing the viewer into a visceral confrontation with critical issues of the 1960s.

All You Need Is Love?

After Number Six "wins" his psychological battle with Number Two, he is escorted into the Village's inner sanctum. The Beatles' "All You Need Is Love" plays while Number Six is led through a jukebox-lined corridor.[32] Despite the song's accessibility, its presence within the context of the Village is surprising. First heard by 400 million people via live television broadcast on June 25, 1967, on the UK television show *Our World*, the song hit No. 1 on the charts in both Britain and America shortly after its release and became emblematic of the "Summer of Love" in both countries. George Harrison summed up the song's cultural importance by saying, "It was a perfect song because it was so simple. It was a great excuse to go right in the middle of that whole culture that was happening and give them a theme tune."[33]

The original script for Number Six's walk through the corridor called for a pastiche of several popular songs blasting from the jukeboxes. Fairclough writes, "There would have been the Beatles songs 'All You Need Is Love' and 'Yellow Submarine,'

Sandie Shaw's 'Puppet on a String' [and] 'Little Boxes,' Al Jolson's 'Toot-Toot-Tootsie Goodbye' and 'Hello, Dolly.'"[34] Record sleeves for some of these are seen briefly in the scene within the jukeboxes. Though the songs were not retained in the soundtrack, it is useful to examine what they suggest about McGoohan's intentions. Including these songs demonstrates that McGoohan and his collaborators chose popular music deliberately, not because the individual songs created meaning, but because popular music itself acted as a symbolic force. Popular music of the period represents both individual freedom and youth culture, particularly in its revolt against the mores of the previous generation. While songs such as "Yellow Submarine" provide a humorous counterpoint to the surreality of life in the Village, others directly critique "group-think" within contemporary culture. Specifically, Shaw's songs tackle this issue: the title of "Puppet on a String" evokes the manipulation of ordinary people by nameless cultural authorities, while the cultural conformity depicted in "Little Boxes" ensures that "ticky tacky houses"—and the people inside them—all look the same. Finally, the inclusion of both British and American songs highlights the international language of popular music that was developing through cross-cultural influences. Whatever McGoohan's reason for narrowing the choices down to a single song, "All You Need Is Love" provides a narrative framework for the episode, from its first appearance leading Number Six (and the viewer) into the underbelly of the Village to its return after the courtroom scenario of the episode.

A Klandestine Jury

Number Six emerges from the tunnel into a large cavern, where a judge and jury are seated for the trials of prisoners charged with crimes against the Village. The jury is dressed in white robes and triangular hoods, their faces cloaked behind bilateral masks: one side is a frowning white tragedy mask, the other a grinning black comedy mask. They appear to have no individual wills or consciences and assent and dissent as a unit. The white robes and hoods instantly recall the Ku Klux Klan. Though the Klan was not a dominant cultural influence in Britain, American Klansmen lectured there from the turn of the twentieth century, and media depictions of the Klan in Britain date back at least to showings of *The Birth of a Nation* in British theaters (1915–1916). By the 1960s, the Klan was viewed by most as an anonymous and menacing mob, an appropriate symbol of the despotic keepers of the Village.

Throughout the 1960s, the American civil rights movement and Dr. Martin Luther King Jr.'s speeches were applauded in Britain. Some of Britain's own civil rights legislation was modeled on similar American laws.[35] The year 1968 was tumultuous for race relations on both sides of the Atlantic, as can be seen in three major events that occurred between the British and American premieres of "Fall Out" (February 4 and September 21, 1968 respectively). Dr. Martin Luther King Jr. was assassinated on April 4, British MP Enoch Powell gave his "Rivers of Blood" speech denouncing immigration and racial integration on April 20, and Robert Kennedy was assassinated on June 6.

Bells of Freedom

The first trial is that of Number Forty-Eight (Alexis Kanner). Though white, he deliberately invokes stereotyped black mannerisms, dialect, and street slang. He insolently calls the judge "Dad," simultaneously invoking the image of a child speaking to a parent, while undermining the relationship through his rudeness.

Four times during his trial, Number Forty-Eight rings a small bell around his neck while sporting a wry look on his face. When considered along with his invocation of black dialect and the white-hooded jury, as well as the significance of bells within the civil rights movement, this bell can be read as a visual and aural symbol of freedom. The popular civil rights anthem "If I Had a Hammer" (1949), penned by Lee Hayes and Pete Seeger, refers to "the bell of freedom," evoking the image of the Liberty Bell. Dr. Martin Luther King Jr.'s 1963 "I Have a Dream" speech climaxes on the repeated refrain of "Let freedom ring"; not only had this speech been eagerly received in England, Dr. King met several times in the late 1950s and early 1960s with British activists who were seeking solutions to their own nation's racial tensions.[36]

The bell's association with freedom had previously appeared in the episode "The Chimes of Big Ben." Here, Number Six is duped into thinking he has escaped from the Village. In what he believes to be his office in Westminster, he hears Big Ben's chimes from the window, a poignant sonic symbol of his newfound freedom. Yet it is simply a recording; as he leaves the office, the Village marching band confirms his imprisonment.

"Dem Bones Gonna Walk Around"

Number Forty-Eight's trial evokes nineteenth- and early twentieth-century blackface minstrelsy, especially through its use of exaggerated Southern black dialect spoken by a white man. However, this moment inverts the racial mockery present in much blackface minstrelsy, and, instead, frames a sincere plea for freedom and defiance of oppressive forces, here represented by the jury in Klan garb. Forty-Eight continues, "The bones is yours, Dad. They came from you my Daddy." The judge commands Number Forty-Eight to confess and, imitating Forty-Eight's dialect, he offers to "hep" him. Number Forty-Eight takes "hep" not as "help" but as "hip," as in hip bone. He starts to recite, and then sings, "Dem Bones."

"Dem Bones"—set by brothers James Weldon Johnson and J. Rosamund Johnson—is based on the biblical story of a valley filled with dry bones (Ezekiel 37:1–14). The lyrics may have been traditional or may have been derived from sermons on the topic.[37] In Ezekiel's story, the bones join together, are covered in flesh, stand upright, and come to life. While many commentators on *The Prisoner* have noted that "Dem Bones" is significant to the episode, few have speculated on its meaning. Chris Gregory writes that the song depicts the Village as "a whole nation of skeletons . . . with its forced gaiety, its brainwashed population, its isolation and destruction of a real humanity."[38] To Eric v. d. Luft, the song connotes resurrection, causing the jury to dance and "apparently identify with the dead, dry bones that were given new life."[39] Dennis Redmond, emphasizing the psychedelic milieu of the late 1960s, sees the song as just another surreal element in an episode full of surreal elements.[40] Tony Williams interprets the song as encapsulating one of the central themes of the series: the illusion of and false quest for individuality. The union of the bones becomes a "motif of the interconnectedness of all elements within society."[41]

One viewpoint has not been sufficiently addressed: the song's invocation of the civil rights movement. While McGoohan made it clear that *The Prisoner* was an allegory[42] and discouraged any singular interpretation, the Klannish jury, the freedom bell, the black mannerisms of Number Forty-Eight, and Johnson's "Dem Bones" evoke the racial struggles of the 1960s. When Number Forty-Eight first sings, the jury members stand up and express their outrage by waving their fists. Yet the second time he sings (lip-synching to the recording by The Four Lads), the jury begins a convulsive and involuntary dance along with the music. They appear to be the bones that are brought to life by another's will. In the context of contemporary civil rights battles, it could imply that the power structures of those in authority will be changed with or without their assent. The scene dissolves into chaos, with Number Forty-Eight shouting, singing, and running around the room. Angered, the judge condemns him and the hippie culture he represents as "uncoordinated youth, rebelling against nothing it can define." Number Forty-Eight rings his bell one last time and sings a few more lines of "Dem Bones" before two soldiers physically remove him from the courtroom. As he is carried away, his posture and locked legs evoke the passive resistance of American civil rights sit-ins.

Number Two is then brought before the jury. We become aware that he, like Number Six, was also abducted. He is not subjected to questioning, but instead gives a speech condemning himself for capitulating to the Village authorities: "What is deplorable is that I resisted for so short a time—a fine tribute to your methods." He seems to represent those who give up the battle for personal freedom before they achieve it. Lastly, Number Six is brought before the jury and is praised for his actions as an individual. Several times he tries to begin a speech—beginning with "I..."—but each time he is drowned out by the jury who shout "I" repeatedly. Piling irony upon irony, Number Six is simultaneously praised and mocked by the judge and jury.

All You Need Is Anarchy

The episode concludes with a dark journey that questions individual autonomy. At the end of the courtroom scene, Number Six is "set free" to go wherever he pleases, or to rule the Village if that is his choice. He chooses to meet Number One, the Village's ruler, who seemingly resides within a giant rocket with a single ominous, blinking eye. Entering the rocket, Number Six walks past the re-imprisoned Number Two, laughing maniacally, and Number Forty-Eight, who continues to sing and scat "Dem Bones." Number Six enters an inner chamber, climbs up a spiral staircase, and confronts Number One, also hidden behind a white hood and comedy–tragedy mask. Number Six tears at the mask, only to be confronted by a gorilla mask, perhaps the face of animal instinct. He rips at the gorilla mask, only to see himself cackling back at him. Number One is Number Six. The last enemy to be conquered is himself. In the end, the individual, as well as any collective, has the potential for ultimate corruption. Horrified and dazed, he chases after his alter ego but cannot catch him.

Number Six returns to the courtroom after arming himself, Number Two, Number Forty-Eight, and the Butler with machine guns. Ironically, the four are dressed in white robes they have stolen from the jury. Here we are challenged to question the show's central premise from its opening episode: the prioritization of the individual against the many. At times it is not enough for the individual conscience to rebel; it becomes necessary for the many to come together against oppression. It was not when Rosa Parks sat in the front of the bus that discriminatory laws changed, but rather when the entire African American community of Birmingham joined together in a boycott. The individual must be involved, and many times he or she instigates the fight, but results require everyone.

The Village's soldiers and jurors battle the rebels, accompanied nondiegetically by "All You Need Is Love." The incongruity between the song's bright mood and uplifting lyrics and the violent machine-gun barrage creates a jarring audiovisual dissonance for the viewer. Sue Short suggests the scene "question[s] the very tenets of 1960s' pacifism, not to mention the pacifism that McGoohan had equally striven to uphold in the series."[43] Number Six confronts evil throughout the series without employing deadly force, relying instead on his wits. There are only two times when he takes up arms. The first is his hallucinatory shooting of The Kid in "Living in Harmony"; the second occurs in this Village shoot-out. What remains unclear is whether this rebellion against "the machine" is allegoric (whether it be subduing the self or standing up against injustice), or whether there is actual violence and anarchy advocated within the scene.

Ironically, the four rebels use a prison cell on wheels to break out of the Village. Their journey is accompanied by "Dem Bones," which emanates from a passing car; to this, they perform a jubilant dance.[44] The song has become an apocalyptic force: the resurrected prisoners are returning to a new life. Number Forty-Eight jumps out of the cell to hitch a ride from passing cars (an iconic gesture associated both with beatniks and hippies); Number Two returns to the Houses of Parliament; and Number Six to his apartment with the Butler. But is it a happy ending? The last thing that is shown is Number Six driving his Lotus Seven, the scene that opens almost every episode and spirals him back into the Village. The end becomes the beginning.

"Fall Out" invites introspective examination for the potential of good and evil present not only within cultural groups, but within every individual. The conflict is no longer merely the one (Number Six) against the many (the Village), but it is located within every soul, even Number Six. In television and in war, protagonists frequently are read as morally upright because they are on "our side." "Fall Out" subverts that assumption, and viewers were scandalized not only by the episode's violence, but also by the inversion of Number Six's role as hero. He—and we—are not only Number Six, but also Number One. McGoohan elaborates: "The greatest evil that one has to fight constantly every minute of the day until one dies is the worser part of oneself."[45]

Conclusion

The Prisoner incorporates American music as a symbol of freedom and individuality, and it summons up resonances with the Cold War, the Vietnam War, and the civil rights movement. Yet the music in *The Prisoner* is just as ambiguous, inversive, and challenging as the series itself and intentionally defies any simple explanation or interpretation. In "Living in Harmony," American music augments the episode's Old West setting and gritty realism. Yet ironically, the Old West setting is not real; it is fabricated, a drug-induced hallucination. "Fall Out" employs "Dem Bones" to depict Number Forty-Eight's pursuit of freedom. Yet the episode's denouement, which suggests that Number One resides within us, questions the privileging of individual freedom. "All You Need Is Love" represents a sincere anthem of the peace-loving counterculture yet it is rendered sardonically as the soundtrack of a machine-gun battle. Ultimately, the music reinforces *The Prisoner*'s multivalent nature and helps establish its reception as one of the most culturally insightful series of the 1960s.

NOTES

1. In tracing this influence, some have used such strong terms as "saturated" and "flooded." See Howard L. Malchow, *Special Relations: The Americanization of Britain?* (Stanford, CA: Stanford University Press, 2011), 17; and Alexander Stephen, ed., *The Americanization of Europe: Culture, Diplomacy, and Anti-Americanism after 1945* (New York: Berghahn Books, 2006), 3.

2. Richard Abel, *Americanizing the Movies and "Movie-Mad" Audiences, 1910–1914* (Berkeley: University of California Press, 2006), 106.

3. Holly George-Warren, *Public Cowboy No. 1: The Life and Times of Gene Autry* (New York: Oxford University Press, 2007), 180–181.

4. Wesley Britton, *Spy Television* (Westport, CT: Praeger, 2004), 13.

5. Jeffrey S. Miller, *Something Completely Different: British Television and American Culture* (Minneapolis: University of Minnesota Press, 2000), 39.

6. The show was called *Danger Man* in England and America from 1961–1962. Helped in part by Johnny Rivers's "Secret Agent Man," the program was renamed *Secret Agent* in America from 1964–1967.

7. Ironically, Flick played the "electric" Bond theme on an acoustic guitar with a pickup, rather than on an electric guitar. See Jon Burlingame, *The Music of James Bond* (New York: Oxford University Press, 2012), 15.

8. Robert Fairclough, *The Prisoner: The Official Companion to the Classic TV Series* (London: Carlton Books, 2002), 21.

9. Roger Langley, liner notes, *Original Music from The Prisoner Volume Two*, CD, FILMCD 084. Silva Screen, 1991; accessed August 19, 2011, http://www.the-prisoner-6.freeserve.co.uk/arch_2_cd2.htm.

10. The Chappell Music Library was one of several repositories of inexpensive and copyright-free "mood music" used by television directors for background music.

11. Dearberg edited "Arrival," "The Chimes of Big Ben," and "Checkmate"; Eric Mival edited the remaining fourteen episodes.

12. Joseph Lanza, *Elevator Music: A Surreal History of Muzak, Easy-Listening, and Other Moodsong*, rev. and expanded ed. (Ann Arbor: University of Michigan Press, 2004), 63.

13. Derek Lawton interview on *KQEK* website, "Derek Lawton/The Prisoner-Chappell Music Library," accessed August 1, 2011, http://www.kqek.com/exclusives/Exclusives_Lawton_2.htm.

14. *The Prisoner: The Complete Series*, DVD, produced by Patrick McGoohan (New York: A&E Home Video, 2009).

15. The music is Mark Lubbock's "Moon Lullaby" from the Chappell Music Library.

16. Kristopher Spencer, *Film and Television Scores, 1950-1979: A Critical Survey by Genre* (Jefferson, NC: McFarland, 2008), 60.

17. Ian Rakoff, *Inside the Prisoner: Radical Television and Film in the 1960s* (London: Batsford, 1998), 40, 59, 80.

18. Ibid., 59.

19. See chapter 3 in this collection.

20. In *High Noon*, Amy Kane forgoes her pacifist principles at the film's conclusion in order to save her husband's life; her difficult internal battle is a major theme in the film.

21. Rakoff, 41–42.

22. Ibid., 58.

23. Ibid., 42.

24. Ibid., 59.

25. Charles Leinberger, *Ennio Morricone's The Good, the Bad and the Ugly: A Film Score Guide* (Lanham, MD: Scarecrow Press, 2004), 71.

26. Paralleling McGoohan's nameless "Number Six," these movies are commonly referred to as "The Man with No Name Trilogy," since Clint Eastwood portrays outsiders with no name. Moreover, the lyrics from "Secret Agent Man" remind us, "They've given you a number and taken away your name."

27. Cinematic Westerns frequently center on the cowboy as a lone outsider, a rugged individual who may be a hero or antihero. The repertoire drew from cowboy songs presented in publications such as John A. Lomax's *Cowboy Songs and Other Frontier Ballads* (1910), as well as newly composed songs. By the early 1930s, a solitary cowboy singing on his horse was a frequent trope in these pictures. Even in films that lack a singing cowboy, the use of the solo guitar within the nondiegetic score evokes this established sonic representation of a solitary figure. See Peter Stanfield, *Hollywood, Westerns and the 1930s: The Lost Trail* (Exeter, UK: University of Exeter Press, 2001), 70.

28. Robert J. Landry, "It's Murder, Italian Style," *Variety*, February 8, 1967, 30.

29. Matthew White and Jaffer Ali, *The Official Prisoner Companion* (New York: Warner Books, 1988), 148.

30. Eric v. d. Luft, *Die at the Right Time!: A Subjective Cultural History of the American Sixties* (North Syracuse, NY: Gegensatz Press, 2009), 312.

31. This version of "Dem Bones" is a recording by The Four Lads from their album *Dixieland Doin's* (1962).

32. Interestingly, "All You Need Is Love" begins with a quotation of "La Marseillaise," an iconic symbol of resistance and revolt.

33. Gorge Harrison, "The Beatles: The Mini-documentaries, Yellow Submarine," *The Beatles Stereo Box Set*, DVD 5099969944994 (EMI Records, 2009), 38:46–38:57.

34. Fairclough, 106.

35. Malchow, 170.

36. Ibid., 171.

37. In his autobiography, Johnson specifically references the Ezekiel passage, writing, "I remember . . . sermons that passed with only slight modifications from preacher to preacher, [including] 'The Valley of the Dry Bones.'" James Weldon Johnson, *Complete Poems*, ed. Sondra Kathryn Wilson (New York: Penguin Books, 2000), 5.

38. Chris Gregory, *Be Seeing You . . . . : Decoding the Prisoner* (Luton, Bedfordshire, UK:University of Luton Press, 1997), 167.

39. Luft, 314.

40. Dennis Redmond, *The World is Watching: Video as Multinational Aesthetics, 1968–1995* (Carbondale: Southern Illinois University Press, 2004), 53.

41. Tony Williams, "Authorship Conflict in *The Prisoner*," in *Making Television: Authorship and the Production Process*, ed. Robert J. Thompson and Gary Burns (New York: Praeger, 1990), 75.

42. From Patrick McGoohan interview "The L.A. Tape, 1983" quoted in Roger Langley, *Patrick McGoohan: Danger Man or Prisoner?* (London: Tomahawk Press, 2007), 232.

43. Sue Short, "Countering the Counterculture: The Prisoner and the 1960s," in *British Science Fiction Television: A Hitchhiker's Guide*, ed. John R. Cook and Peter Wright (London: I.B. Tauris, 2006), 83.

44. Interestingly, the black car looks suspiciously like the black hearse that pulls up to Number Six's apartment in the series' opening sequence.

45. McGoohan interview, as quoted in Langley, 232.

9   The Sound of Disability

Music, the Obsessive Avenger, and Eugenics in America

MEGHAN SCHRADER

> One might say that the true subject of the horror genre is all that our civilization represses
> or oppresses.
>
> —Robin Wood[1]

THERE ARE SEVERAL historical connections between what Tobin Siebers calls "disability aesthetics," the horror film, and the ongoing influence of eugenic thought in American society. Eugenics began in the nineteenth century and reached its zenith during the 1930s; its reputation was then sullied by the Nuremberg trials.[2] Yet the science of eugenics continued to influence postwar conceptions of family, gender, and cultural homogeneity, which were strongly connected to particular notions of physical beauty and health prevalent in Western society. A cultural emphasis on *physical* homogeneity thus evolved to embody these values, as can be seen in the cinematic portrayal of disability.

In this chapter, I will argue that some postwar horror films are rooted, at least in part, in widespread perceptions of, reactions to, and anxieties concerning disability in America in the 1950s. These perceptions and reactions were influenced by prewar eugenic theories and reflect what Siebers calls "the aesthetics of human disqualification."[3] Furthermore, musical representations of disability in horror films can also be heard to reinforce this system of disability anxiety, its underlying source in eugenics, and ultimately ableism within society.[4] Musical cues frequently augment the visual and narrative portrayals of the many disabled characters encountered in this genre.

Film music itself is not responsible for perpetuating eugenic ideas and ableism, but the emotional response it tends to elicit can make related behaviors seem more palpable to filmgoers. Analysis of music in this way also reflects what disability studies scholars might call a "cultural logic of euthanasia,"[5] in which disability is viewed as a fate worse than death. Such logic is related to the ableist association between disability and suffering, and many horror films reflect the influence of this trend.

My analysis will focus on the use of the "Monster Theme," which alienates viewers from disabled characters or elicits feelings of revulsion toward them, and the "Love Theme," which sanctions the demise of those characters. These terms are my own and are intended to reflect the respective narrative role of each theme type. Examples will be drawn from *The Spiral Staircase* (1946), *The Bad Seed* (1956), *The Fly* (1958), and *The Fly* (1986). Throughout the chapter, I will consider social conventions related to gender, emasculation, xenophobia, euthanasia, and selective procreation as these illuminate representations of disability. Finally, I will conclude by discussing how film music helps reinforce cultural stereotypes of the disabled and ableist cinematic tropes more broadly.

Historical Background

The ableist conceptions of disability reflected in 1950s horror films and their music are related to eugenic tropes. Horror film's on-screen relationship with anti-disability stereotypes began with *The Cabinet of Dr. Caligari* (1920), which concluded with the revelation that the narrative takes place in the mind of a mental patient. This ending established a lasting connection between horror and disability in Western audiovisual culture. During the early twentieth century, eugenics became more prominent in the United States with the passage of the country's first compulsory sterilization law in 1907[6] and the publicity surrounding physician Harry Haiselden's 1916 crusade to withhold treatment from disabled infants, which he hoped would lead to active euthanasia.[7] The silent film *The Black Stork* (1916), rereleased as *Are You Fit to Marry?* (1927), dramatized these decisions, featured Haiselden in one of the primary roles, and used inter-titles that he wrote.[8] Manipulative cinematography and dialogue that portrayed disabled people as otherworldly and threatening promoted his crusade. In the film, a woman named Anne (Elsie Esmond) gives birth to a disabled infant and then has a vision from God in which her child grows up and shoots the doctor whose ministrations "condemned me to this life of torture and shame" (1:11:04). Anne therefore decides to forgo life-saving surgery, and Jesus welcomes the baby's soul as he dies. This decision precludes the infant from growing up to become what Norden calls "the Obsessive Avenger," a disabled person whose desire for vengeance makes him dangerous to others.[9]

Although the film's soundtrack appears to be lost, music did play a role in emphasizing the film's theme of reproductive morality and foreshadowing the disabled baby's birth. While the child's father, Claude (Hamilton Revelle), is aware that he carries "defective" genes, he does not tell Anne and follows through on his plan to marry her. Meanwhile, Anne sings and plays the piano, and the instrument's association with domesticity contrasts with Claude's unsuitability for marriage and the felicity enjoyed in unions between nondisabled individuals (26:46–29:03). Comparing this film to an instructional movie that promoted eugenics, *The Science of Life* (1922), Martin Pernick writes, "Both films selectively highlighted the repulsive ugliness of defectives, in dimly lit shots of dingy beggars, stark clinical scenes of retarded and physically disabled patients, and close-ups of babies severely disfigured by congenital syphilis."[10]

This "repulsive ugliness" is repeatedly found among horror film monsters whose features are indicative of disability. For example, the monster that appears in James Whales's *Frankenstein* (1931) has a lumbering gait, is unable to speak, and seems unaware of his physical strength. Furthermore, because those who become monsters frequently exhibit characteristics associated with various disabilities, the transformation from "normal" to "monster" may reflect the fear of becoming disabled or carrying some aspect of disability within oneself. All this suggests a longstanding association between horror film and eugenics through their mutually degrading portrayals of the disabled. Indeed, Angela Marie Smith has argued that early horror films adapted Gothic conventions to eugenic ideas that were popular in the early 1930s.[11] Thus in the case of Dr. Frankenstein's experiment, the monster's murderous tendencies are attributed to the use of a "criminal brain," which was acquired by Fritz, the doctor's disabled assistant.

The continuing influence of and critical respect for 1930s cinema in the 1950s helped preserve the eugenic presumptions expressed in later horror films.[12] Moreover, the support for eugenics expressed in *The Black Stork* was not unique to the early twentieth century, nor did it end with the 1930s or 1940s. With the exception of Nazi crimes against the disabled, euthanasia was covered favorably in the press. Examples include coverage in the *New York Times* of Bishop E. W. Barnes's 1950 address to the British Association for the Advancement of Science in which he defended euthanasia on the premise that disabled people were not made in the image of God.[13] Haiselden's crusade remained in the public consciousness, as it was mentioned in a 1950s article that cited "hopeless mental retardation" in the case of one euthanasia victim.[14]

Moreover, eugenicists continued to work in the fields of family counseling, reproductive health, and biology.[15] In a study on the procreative habits of mentally disabled people published in the *Eugenics Quarterly* in 1954, researchers found that patients who were committed after puberty had produced more children than those who had been committed beforehand, and they encouraged institutionalization as a means of reproductive control and ultimately as a way to avoid "considerable misery and expense."[16]

Eugenics and ableism remained a significant force in discussions of health, marriage, and gender during the 1950s. Disabled people who did not meet their assigned gender or social roles stood on the edge of a society that sought physical and cultural homogeneity. This desire had a significant impact on the nascent disability advocacy of the 1950s. The first parents' groups for children with developmental disabilities focused on proving that affected families were "nice, normal Americans." Other groups, such as the American League Against Epilepsy, used recent scientific evidence to argue that those with epilepsy should not be sterilized and sought to reform antiquated terminology.[17] Despite this increasing awareness, such advocacy actually demonstrated the continuing prevalence of eugenic ideology. The desire to exempt those with epilepsy from existing sterilization laws rested on the knowledge that epilepsy was not hereditary. However, those with congenital disabilities were not included in this advocacy. Such inconsistencies were partially responsible for the increased institutionalization of disabled children during the 1950s, a phenomenon caused by growing concern that such children threatened wholesome family life.[18]

Those with disabilities thus shared the plight of poor, foreign, gay, or nonwhite individuals who were often ostracized in 1950s society. This connection becomes more significant when one considers that such differences were often regarded as forms of biological inferiority. Hence, eugenic presumptions about disabled individuals remained prominent and were incorporated into films, and those films often included music that helped to reinforce the portrayal of societal attitudes toward disability.

Musical and Aesthetic Links between Horror and Disability

Musical moments associated with the Monster Theme reflect the horror genre's preoccupation with disability through auditory elements that represent deformity. Unresolved dissonance is paramount in evoking a sense of auditory monstrosity that corresponds to imagery on-screen. There are usually significant melodic and harmonic clashes within the musical texture, and distorted timbres are common. Moreover, rapid changes of pitch and extremely fast or slow tempos communicate a sense of unease. Descending motifs are prevalent and suggest a personal de-evolution of disabled characters. Such works may also incorporate atonality. Many of these musical traits are derived from modernist and expressionist musical experimentation of the early twentieth century.

The Love Theme, contrarily, more closely evokes the musical characteristics of the Common Practice Period. Harmonic experimentation is less prevalent and atonality is rare; consonance is more common, and when dissonance occurs, it eventually resolves. Ascending motifs are also significant in enhancing depictions of well-being that precede the onset of disability. This theme can thus be heard as an auditory representation of able-bodiedness.

Of course, these musical tropes are not static. For example, a Monster Theme may possess rapid intervallic changes, descending motifs, atonality, low pedal tones, rapidly shifting tempo, and hairpin dynamics. But if rapid leaps appear in conjunction with an ascending motif, a strong tonal center, *rubato*, ornamental triplets, and a rich, smooth timbre, they are likely part of a Love Theme. Moreover, cinematography and setting significantly influence each theme's narrative impact. Either theme may soften, intensify, and change to connote character development (such as the changes that occur in Kong's Monster Theme throughout *King Kong*, [1933]), but they tend to retain a set of intersecting (and distinguishing) musical characteristics.

Monster Themes are also present in horror films that do not explicitly feature disabled characters. This reflects the significant role of disability in horror film aesthetics. Sickness, decay, injury, and mental instability are frequently encountered in the horror genre. The fact that Monster Themes can be associated with ostensibly nondisabled characters suggests that often music must be "deformed" in order to evoke horror. When Monster Themes are combined with visual and narrative representations of disability, the resulting effect draws on ableist stereotypes that are present in audiovisual culture.[19] Furthermore, films such as *The Spiral Staircase* (1946), *The Bad Seed* (1956), and *The Fly* (1958) that incorporate a character who transforms into a monster may reveal an even stronger connection between audiovisual tropes and anti-disability anxiety.

The Spiral Staircase is significant for its unique meditation on the involuntary euthanasia of disabled individuals and for its feminization of disability.[20] It tells the story of Helen (Dorothy McGuire), a young woman who works as a nurse for the elderly matriarch, Mrs. Warren (Ethel Barrymore). Helen, mute as a result of trauma, becomes the target of a serial killer obsessed with murdering disabled women, whose presence is suggested by the Monster Theme (12:45–13:03). She is also in love with the town physician, Dr. Parry (Kent Smith), whose interactions with Helen are distinguished by the Love Theme (8:07–8:19; Example 9.1).

Melodic strings are accompanied by woodwinds, while the harp accentuates the theme. The music's intervallic structure is particularly significant, as is the melodic vacillation

EXAMPLE 9.1 Roy Webb, *The Spiral Staircase*, Love Theme, mm. 1–5. (Transcribed by M. Wirt and T. Wilfong.)

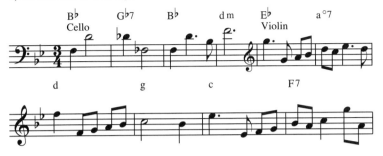

between an ascending major and descending minor sixth. This common diatonic interval appears as the harmony shifts from the tonic (B-flat major) to an essentially unrelated dominant-seventh chord built on the flat-6 scale degree (G flat) before returning to B-flat major. Perhaps the shifting manifestation of this common or "normal" interval suggests tension between Helen's identity as a woman with romantic interests in Dr. Parry and her identity as a disabled person whom he wants to cure. Ultimately, the harmonic suggestion of struggle seems to be resolved when the cue moves to the dominant. The upward leaps in the melody also imply a sense of freedom (such as that evoked by the ascending sixths in Tamino's aria "Dies Bildnis ist bezaubernd schön" [This Image is Enchantingly Lovely] from Act I of Mozart's *Die Zäuberflöte*). The first time we hear the theme, Helen is outside with Dr. Parry; this setting conflicts with the notion that romantic relationships are not part of disabled people's lives and suggests that through her relationship with Dr. Parry, Helen is freed from the constraints of her disability.

Helen's interactions reveal the influence of eugenics and disability stereotypes on gender norms. Disabled men, such as Claude in *The Black Stork*, are usually portrayed as impotent or dangerous to female partners, but females are likely to be cast in the role of "Sweet Innocent," a passive victim easily dominated by a male caretaker.[21] Helen's appeal depends on her status as a submissive "innocent" and our expectation that she will be cured. Moreover, her inability to speak mimics the powerlessness traditionally ascribed to her gender. The Love Theme underlines all of this as it characterizes Helen as sympathetic.[22] Helen's disability is less conspicuous than is that of the disabled male protagonists considered in this chapter because hers is in accordance with perceptions of her gender as a disability in itself.

In contrast to Helen's desirability, the film's antagonist is the widely respected Professor Albert Warren (George Brent), whose presence on-screen is emphasized by a close-up of his eye and a dissonant, haunting motif—the Monster Theme—performed by *pizzicato* strings and a reverberating theremin with an eerie, wide vibrato (Example 9.2). The harmony moves from a fifth to a tritone, generating an extremely dissonant and unstable phrase that suggests insanity (17:43–18:01).

EXAMPLE 9.2 Roy Webb, *The Spiral Staircase*, Monster Theme, mm. 1–7. (Transcribed by M. Wirt and T. Wilfong.)

This implication is strengthened by the theremin's association with monsters in other 1950s horror films, such as *The Day the Earth Stood Still* (1951) and *The Thing From Another World* (1951). Although Professor Warren does not look disabled, the theremin and the extreme close-ups of his eye suggest that he may be; furthermore, he identifies his own failings in the disabilities of others. Discussions about his father reveal that Professor Warren views his own weaknesses as a form of disability, which he attempts to purge by murdering disabled people. During one discussion, his brother Steven (Gordon Oliver) says:

You know, I'm inclined to think that Father was disappointed in both of us. Neither of us fitted his concept of what a real man should be: a gun-toting, hard-drinking, God-fearing citizen. He used to say: "The strong survive, the weak die." How wrong he was, Albert, because you and I, the meek, have inherited the earth.[23]

This film's emphasis on the professor's alleged lack of masculinity is central to the connection between the professor and his victims. The film's climax highlights Helen's vulnerability as the professor reveals himself (Figure 9.1) and says, "You tried the telephone, didn't you? I'm glad you couldn't." As he says this, the same unstable motif plays that accompanied him as he watched from the shadows, suggesting that his hidden deformities are about to manifest themselves (1:11:45–1:12:16). Warren continues:

The only person who could have prevented you from achieving the quiet that I can give you is Steven, and you locked him up. What a pity my father didn't live to see me become strong, to see me dispose of the weak and imperfects of the world whom he detested.[24]

FIGURE 9.1 Professor Warren (George Brent) threatens Helen (Dorothy McGuire).

In his perverted logic, the professor sees death as providing deliverance (e.g., "the quiet") to his victims.

Because Professor Warren's serial killing is eventually stopped, we might conclude that the film offers a narrative disapproval of mercy killing and a relatively positive view of disability. The latter is undermined, however, by the movie's conclusion. Helen is saved from the professor as Mrs. Warren miraculously regains the ability to walk and shoots him. The shock causes Helen's voice to return, and as she calls Dr. Parry for help (the first time she has actually spoken to him), the Love Theme begins to play (1:21:59–1:23:18). As it passes from single violin to *tutti* strings and then triumphant brass, the Love Theme signifies Helen's triumph over infirmity and implies that survival and happiness depend on curing or otherwise "overcoming" disability (Example 9.3). Perhaps this attitude accounts for the fact that, of the four protagonists discussed in this essay, Helen is the only one who does not die. In contrast to the professor's murderous obsessions, Helen represents society's ideal disabled person: an innocent who can be cured and rejoin "normal" society.

Of the films considered in this chapter, *The Bad Seed* has the strongest connections to eugenics. It tells the story of Christine (Nancy Kelly), a mother who discovers that her child, Rhoda (Patty McCormack), is a serial killer. Rhoda's actions are relevant to cinematic portrayals of disability because the eugenics movement viewed criminality as an inherited mental disorder. The movie was based on the popular 1954 novel by William March; his biographer, Roy S. Simmonds, suggests that March personally embraced these theories.[25] Moreover, March had lived during the

EXAMPLE 9.3 Roy Webb, *The Spiral Staircase*, Triumph/Love Theme, mm. 1–17. (Transcribed by M. Wirt.)

eugenic movement's heyday and would likely have seen much of the propaganda that was distributed through fairs, movie theaters, and other venues. Whatever the sources of his influences, eugenic theories regarding heredity, criminality, and mental disorder are prominent in his novel.

In the film, the Love Theme accompanies scenes of affection between Rhoda and her mother, while the Monster Theme suggests Rhoda's wicked nature.[26] "Au Claire de la Lune" is periodically superimposed over the Monster Theme, which enhances the contrast between Rhoda's cruel behavior and her youth. The piece also suggests the congenital nature of Rhoda's drive to kill, as its connotation of innocence implies that this behavior lies beyond her control. It is particularly prominent in the opening title sequence during which it is heard in counterpoint with the erratic pitches of the orchestral Monster Theme (0:17–0:26).

The cue begins with rolling thunder and snare drum, accompanied by pizzicato strings (0:08–1:11). During mm. 1–4, blaring horns and strings play the first section of the movie's primary Monster Theme, while "Au Claire de la Lune" joins in underneath the cacophony in mm. 6–11. (See the alto register in Example 9.4.) Discordant strings rise and fall at a rapid tempo, accompanying the *agitato* piano piece. As the strings play underneath the piano melody, the clash between the two instrumental timbres creates an element of distortion and friction, a musical emblem of Rhoda's "deformed" conscience.

As the camera moves from the frightening outdoor scene to one of Rhoda playing the piano, the piece connotes an air of wholesome normalcy (1:34–2:24), which contrasts greatly with the threatening music that preceded it. Blond-haired Rhoda is wearing a frilly dress and new shoes as she plays on the piano, an instrument that has long been associated with female domesticity. Like Helen, Rhoda appears to embody mid-century idealization of the feminine, but she is an inversion of the Sweet Innocent stereotype. In contrast to Helen's demure behavior, Rhoda is driven to kill in order to obtain trinkets and other things she desires. This is a significant violation of Rhoda's expected role as a female, but it also reflects the belief common to eugenics theory that to transgress gender roles indicated psychological infirmity. The periodic superimposition of the piano tune in the opening Monster Theme enhances the narrative's suggestion that Rhoda's ostensibly "healthy" appearance hides a "sick" nature, which will later be attributed to a psychological illness.

The Love Theme helps establish the relationship between mother and daughter and drives the film's pro-euthanasia message. It is notable that the Love Theme does not play during interactions between Rhoda and her father, suggesting that Christine bears the mantel of responsibility for Rhoda's birth, upbringing, and criminal nature. During a discussion between Christine and her neighbors about inherited criminality, the Love Theme enters for the first time (19:22–20:19).

The Love Theme plays a significant role during scenes of affection (Example 9.5). It is performed by an organ and strings as Rhoda asks her mother, "What will you give me for a basket of kisses?" and Christine answers, "I'll give you a basket of hugs!"[27] The wistful theme also plays during scenes of Christine reading to Rhoda

EXAMPLE 9.4 Alex North, *The Bad Seed*, Monster Theme, mm. 1–13. (Transcribed by M. Wirt.) © 1956 (Renewed) WB Music Corp. (ASCAP). All Rights Reserved.

EXAMPLE 9.5 Alex North, *The Bad Seed*, Love Theme, mm. 6–23. (Transcribed by
T. Wilfong.) © 1956 (Renewed) WB Music Corp. (ASCAP). All Rights Reserved.

and tucking her into bed (29:11–29:32). These occurrences are indicative of their
close, loving relationship.

The theme's earlier appearance during Christine's conversation with the neighbors points to the connection between Rhoda and the criminality being discussed.
During the course of the film, Christine learns that she is the child of an infamous
murderess and comes to believe that Rhoda has inherited criminal tendencies from
her grandmother. The film's narrative connection between criminality and disability is reinforced when a psychiatrist friend says:

> Fellow criminologists and behavioral scientists have been saying that we've all
> been putting too much emphasis on environment, and too little on hereditary.

They cite a type of criminal born with no capacity for remorse or guilt, with a kind of brain that might have been normal fifty thousand years ago. It's as if these children were born blind, permanently. It's just that they are bad seeds.[28]

Having learned that Rhoda is a murderer, Christine decides to kill her with a lethal dose of sedatives. Christine's actions reflect notions of female responsibility for reproduction and children common in the 1950s, as well as eugenic protestations of responsibility for ensuring that one did not procreate if one had an undesirable family history.[29] Because Christine is responsible for transmitting defective genes to her daughter and bringing her into the world, she is responsible for eliminating her bad genes by removing Rhoda from society. Rhoda's father, in contrast, bears no responsibility and is therefore not involved in the decision.

Christine gives Rhoda a handful of pills as she carries on with their normal routine of reading aloud before bed, and she later tells her sleeping daughter, "Rhoda, Rhoda, you're mine. And I carried you. And I can't let them hurt you. They'd shut you up and make a show of you. And no one can save you from that unless I save you. So sleep well, and dream well my only child and the one that I love. I shall sleep, too." Thus the overdose becomes associated with Christine's other motherly actions (Figure 9.2). Alex North's music helps to reinforce the characterization of Christine's

FIGURE 9.2 Christine (Nancy Kelly) speaks to an unconscious Rhoda (Patty McCormack) after poisoning her.

attempt to euthanize Rhoda as a loving and holy act, one which may even enjoy heavenly approval, as an unseen choir reprises the Love Theme (1:54:40–1:56:04).

This scenario resonates with *The Black Stork* in which a mother, faced with a disabled child whose future is a life of crime, chooses to end the child's life with divine approval. However, the Motion Picture Production Code precluded the use of the novel's original ending. In that version, Christine commits suicide and Rhoda survives the poisoning attempt.[30] In the film, both survive, but Rhoda is later killed in an accident. The opening sequence is reprised as Rhoda walks outside during a storm. Once again, "Au Clair de la Lune" highlights the disparity between Rhoda's innate depravity and her innocent appearance (2:04:30–2:04:59). She is then struck by lightning, at which point the Monster Theme re-enters and ends the film (2:06:29–2:07:25).

Disability takes on a more metaphorical dimension in Kurt Neumann's *The Fly*, in which the head and hand of Andre Delambre (David Hedison) switch with those of a fly during a teleportation experiment.[31] Although Andre's disability is caused by misadventure rather than genetics, his subsequent degradation suggests that cultural associations between disability and emasculation were not unique to the eugenics era and continued to intersect with ableist conceptions of suffering in the 1950s.

Of the soundtracks considered in this chapter, this one has the strongest relationship to both emasculation and xenophobia, as Andre's disability turns him into an alien being. Prior to Andre's injury, his American nuclear family's idyllic existence is represented musically by a bright, carefree Love Theme (28:21). Played with *rubato* and in an expressive tempo in the harps, woodwinds, and strings, it includes an ascending motif in a moderate registral range, replete with joyful-sounding triplets that recall Siegmund's and Sieglinde's love duet in Act I of Richard Wagner's *Die Walküre* (Example 9.6). This theme most often underscores Andre's loving relationship with his wife, Helene Delambre (Patricia Owen). As he explains his experiments to her, their theme enters, signifying the strength of their mutual affection and commitment (34:26).

EXAMPLE 9.6 Paul Sawtell and Bert Shefter, *The Fly*, Love Theme, mm. 1–5. (Transcribed by M. Wirt and T. Wilfong.)

After his accident, however, Andre is represented musically by the Monster Theme, which indicates his transformation into an alien "Other" (1:13:25). As in *The Bad Seed*, the movie's score reinforces anti-disability attitudes. The tagline for the film reads, "Once it was human, even as you and I!" This points toward society-wide fear of becoming disabled or otherwise "monstrous." Such attitudes are not difficult to find in other media. In 1966, Erving Goffman documented the impact of this fear of disability on suicide in a letter from a sixteen-year-old girl to an advice columnist, in which she writes: "My mother loves me, but she cries terrible [*sic*] when she looks at me. Ought I commit suicide?"[32] This quote, which introduces Goffman's theories on stigma in human society, shows how associations between disability and transformation into a foreign and frightening being have been made.

The use of the Love and Monster Themes also traces the protagonist's emasculation. The family musical motif mentioned above celebrates each member's ability to fulfill his or her expected familial role, which Andre loses through his metamorphosis. After his transformation, Andre adopts different eating habits and becomes mute, which compromises his ability to fulfill his socially ordained function of husband and provider. Thus, Andre's transformation is another representation of the postwar "crisis of masculinity" discussed by Mike Chopra-Gant.[33] Because he is disabled, Andre's wife must take the dominant role in their relationship; she is unable to do so alone, so Andre's brother, François (Vincent Price), becomes involved. The tendency to substitute non-disabled men for disabled men in interpersonal relationships was common in films of the original eugenics era (e.g., *Freaks* [1932] and *The Phantom of the Opera* [1943]) and is a significant step along the narrative's path of legitimizing Andre's death. After Helene kills Andre, François supplants him as husband and father by helping Helene talk to the police and shielding their son, Philippe (Charles Herbert), from the ensuing chaos.

As in *The Bad Seed*, the contrasting Monster and Love Themes help bring the topic of mercy killing into full relief. One of the music's most significant roles is enhancing the visual shock of Andre's transformation. After the accident Andre is suicidal, but Helene vows that she will never help him kill himself. Her resolve crumbles, however, when she sees that her husband's head has been switched with a fly's. At the climactic scene in which Andre reveals his condition, horns and percussion crash in a violent, threatening motif that signifies the ominous nature of Andre's disability (1:13:42).

Accentuating her shock, a *tremolando* in the strings precedes diminished chords ascending chromatically, accompanied by strident brass, jarring percussion, and a descending motif. Helene faints, and Andre tenderly carries her to bed. He then kneels over her, caressing her with his uninjured hand while the Love Theme plays (1:14:15). A sense of trepidation is preserved, however, by a low pedal tone held by cello and bassoon, which lends a sense of foreboding as Andre's fly hand reaches menacingly toward Helene. He yanks it away, at which point the Monster Theme re-enters (1:14:38), and his hand moves independently to strangle her. Thus, the Obsessive Avenger stereotype becomes integral to Andre's transformation, for his disabled part is independently imbued with the instinct to kill.

Having been confronted with Andre's disability, Helene loses touch with her earlier affirmation of his humanity and becomes willing to facilitate his suicide. Her change of attitude is indicated when the Love Theme plays over Andre's plaintive message, "No use now. Help me . . . Kill fly, please. Love you."[34] Because the Love Theme is associated with the couple's happiness together, it construes assisting suicide as a natural outgrowth of their marital relationship. Moreover, the Love Theme in this sequence enhances narrative approval of Andre's death, while the Monster motif suggests disapproval of Andre himself.

Helene's dialogue with the police reinforces the idea that Andre was less than human:

HELENE: Inspector, it wasn't wrong to destroy the thing?

INSPECTOR: A fly-headed human? No.

HELENE: It wasn't Andre. I couldn't have hurt Andre, but I'm glad, I'm glad the thing's dead.[35]

Characterizing Andre as a "thing" implies his disability changed him into a subhuman entity. During this discussion, the violin subtly suggests the Love Theme against the predominantly low, foreboding tones of an oboe. Because of the violin's strong association with the Love Theme, it can be heard to enhance the film's narrative suggestion that killing Andre was the right decision. Ultimately the inspector comes to support Helene's actions, and she is free to begin a new life with François.

The continuing influence of this constellation of ideas concerning disability, the monstrous, and mercy killing is demonstrated by David Cronenberg's 1986 remake of *The Fly*, in which the Love and Monster Themes are also used to vilify the disabled protagonist and seemingly endorse neo-eugenic practices.[36] Unlike the 1958 film, Cronenberg's *The Fly* addresses the theme of selective procreation in addition to euthanasia. While there is a significant progression in how Cronenberg portrays women, there is no change in the way he depicts disabled people. In Cronenberg's film, the traditional family structure is absent, and inventor Seth Brundle (Jeff Goldblum) develops a romantic relationship with Veronica (Geena Davis), the reporter covering his work. Unlike Helene's passive persona, Veronica is confident and independent. Brookover and Silver note, "As a professional woman of the '80s paired with a social throwback, Veronica is definitely in charge."[37] In contrast, Seth becomes a dangerous antagonist as his transformation into a fly slowly emasculates and kills him. The film's depiction of this process is enhanced by two Love Themes that differentiate Seth's relationship with Veronica before and after he becomes disabled. The movie also employs several different Monster Themes, which are distinguished by atonality, profound dissonance, large registral spans, and jarring instrumentation that collectively contribute to representations of Seth's mangled body.

As the couple makes love for the first time, saxophone, piano, and strings join to create a gentle, ascending Love Theme that connotes sexual awakening (22:23–22:47). In contrast to the Doomed Love Theme, this motif's ascending arpeggios, tonal stability, and upward scalar motion complement the couple's physical closeness in this scene (Example 9.7). Visual and auditory elements seem to connote an

EXAMPLE 9.7 Love Theme, mm. 1–10. (Transcribed by M. Wirt.) *The Fly*. Words and Music by Howard Shore. Copyright © 1986 Brooksfilms Music. All Rights Reserved. Used by Permission. Reprinted with Permission of Hal Leonard Corporation.

association between being able-bodied and having healthy relationships. The theme plays again when the couple first acknowledges that their feelings have developed into passionate love (30:02–30:33).

This relationship is gradually spoiled, however, as Seth changes into a fly and Veronica's former boyfriend, Stathis (John Getz), continues to have a significant role in her life. The impact of these elements on their relationship is represented by the Doomed Love Theme played by timpani, brass, and strings (Example 9.8). The texture that supports the theme includes low brass pedal tones and a constant timpani roll underneath the melody. This theme accompanies scenes of Veronica and Seth after his accident to highlight the transformation of their relationship into one doomed by circumstance. For example, this theme is used during Seth's "Insect Politics" speech (Figure 9.3). When Veronica attempts to tell Seth that she is pregnant, he says:

> Have you ever heard of insect politics? Neither have I. Insects don't have politics. They're very brutal. No compassion, no compromise. I'm an insect who dreamt he was a man, and loved it. But now the dream is over, and the insect is awake. I'm saying I'll hurt you if you stay.[38]

The Doomed Love Theme plays as Seth utters this last sentence, indicating that his disability has endangered him and their child (18:20–18:59).

EXAMPLE 9.8 Doomed Love Theme, mm. 1–8. (Transcribed by M. Wirt and T. Wilfong.) *The Fly*. Words and Music by Howard Shore. Copyright © 1986 Brooksfilms Music. All Rights Reserved. Used by Permission. Reprinted with Permission of Hal Leonard Corporation.

FIGURE 9.3 An increasingly deteriorating Seth (Jeff Goldblum) tells a distraught Veronica (Geena Davis) about "Insect Politics."

In contrast to the Love Theme's moderate registral span, the pitches are widely spread in an uneven pattern of dramatic leaps and descents. When heard in combination with the low drone of the timpani and brass, this cue enhances the hopelessness evoked by the scene's predominantly gray palette. Veronica's pregnancy becomes integral to the theme's significance when she chooses to have an abortion, because she has "reason to believe that this child will be deformed."[39]

Hence, eugenics ideas and ableist attitudes manifest themselves in a contemporary situation. In the 1950s, women did not have the option of abortion; forced sterilization was the primary bone of contention. Today, many disability rights activists are concerned that prenatal screenings to identify congenital disabilities encourage abortion, which some view as a form of *voluntary* eugenics. In a culture of saccharine pleas for the "right of [disabled] fetuses not to be born,"[40] 90 percent of women who learn they are carrying a fetus with Down Syndrome have an abortion.[41] This is concurrent with the rise of Wrongful Birth lawsuits, in which parents sue obstetricians for the birth of a disabled child.[42] Writing in "Disability Rights and Selective Abortion," Marsha Saxton asserts: "The medical system, unable to cure or fix us, exaggerates the suffering and burden of disability. The media, especially the movies, distort our lives by using disability as a metaphor for evil, impotence, eternal dependence, or tragedy."[43] In an example of how music can underscore a scene that reflects this phenomenon, the Doomed Love Theme accompanies Seth's speech, further suggesting that Veronica's fetus might be an "insect without compassion," suffer due to its disability, and share Seth's fate.

Ultimately, both Love Themes are pivotal at the conclusion of the story as Seth kidnaps Veronica and attempts to force her into an experiment that would fuse her body with his and create a human–fly hybrid. As he kidnaps her, the Doomed Love motif becomes a representation of monstrosity as it is played piercingly and quickly in strings that rise into a series of dissonant pitches with disjointed rhythm (Example 9.9). His actions and the music demonstrate that Seth has been transformed into a dangerous, morally deformed menace (1:21:34–1:21:56).

With this version of the Monster Theme, the soundtrack moves away from the tonality that previously characterized Seth and his experiences. The score's massive registral span and lack of a tonal center aid aurally in projecting deformity. The subsequent contrast between Stathis and Seth reflects the influence of cultural associations between disability and impotence. After Seth kidnaps Veronica, a rifle-carrying Stathis follows them to his lab and rescues her. As he enters Seth's lab, the Monster Theme contributes to the visual impression of a monster's lair (1:22:53–1:24:18). The musical texture moves from a unison statement of the dissonant,

EXAMPLE 9.9 Monster Theme, mm. 1–10. (Transcribed by M. Wirt.) *The Fly.* Words and Music by Howard Shore. Copyright © 1986 Brooksfilms Music. All Rights Reserved. Used by Permission. Reprinted with Permission of Hal Leonard Corporation.

suspenseful theme to more contrapuntal treatment, creating a progressively discon-certing texture indicative of deformity. The music reaches its highest intensity as Seth attacks him. The dense, bombastic texture of brass, percussion, strings, and increasingly disjunct rhythms help to represent Seth's deformed body. The music rakes back and forth over falling and ascending dissonances, while woodwind trills, string tremolos, shrieking violin *glissandi*, blaring brass, and percussive cymbal swells emit intermittent "screams" to suggest Seth's horrific condition and Stathis's revulsion (1:25:06–1:26:21).

The rising and falling dissonances also imitate Seth's stifled gait as he drags his mutated body across the floor to inflict further harm. Ultimately, the Doomed Love Theme's relationship to the film's visual and narrative elements helps to characterize Seth's suicide as the final act of his humanity. When Stathis destroys the wires con-necting the two telepods during the experiment and saves Veronica, Seth's body is fused with portions of the telepod. As he emerges with chunks of metal in his back, the soundtrack veers into atonality for the final time before using a massive registral span, though tonally conceived, to represent Seth's final transformation. Repulsed, Veronica picks up the rifle as he crawls toward her. Seth silently begs Veronica to end his life, and the Doomed Love Theme crescendos, ending the film as Veronica hysterically pulls the trigger (1:31:21).

Like Andre, Seth loses his humanity. Director David Cronenberg notes, "If you tried to sell a story about two attractive, eccentric people who fall in love, and then one of them contracts a hideous, wasting disease, and the other one watches as he deteriorates and then helps him commit suicide at the end, this is a tough sell for a movie. But that is what the plot of this movie is, and yet it doesn't feel quite like that."[44] Cronenberg's comment again points to a connection between horror cin-ema and eugenic ideas: the intentionally hyperbolic depictions of suffering expected by consumers of the genre allowed him to create an uncensored portrayal of Seth's degradation and destruction. The Doomed Love Theme also helps to facilitate acceptance of Seth's fate, as its connotation of love suggests deliverance from the gruesome scenario portrayed on-screen. As their transformations into flies progress and their respective Monster Themes present Andre and Seth as shadows of their former selves, they are dehumanized, and their Love Themes make their facilitated suicides more easily acceptable, narratively and emotionally.[45]

Conclusion

People of the 1950s lived in the aftermath of the eugenics era; hence, 1950s horror films partly reflected its influence. Society has changed significantly since then, but cultural associations between disability and suffering influence current narrative tropes related to perceptions of what constitutes a valuable life. This one chapter does not permit discussion of other recent horror films, such as *It's Alive* (1974), *Audition* (1999), *Session 9* (2001), and *May* (2002), in which music enhances the Obsessive Avenger stereotype or helps sanction the demise of disabled characters. Knowingly or not, the role of disability in such films suggests that ableist and eugenic criteria continue to define the perceived value of disabled people's lives.

In *Privilege, Power, and Difference*, Allan G. Johnson argues that "isms" are systemic *phenomena* that individuals participate in regardless of their personal beliefs.[46] Contemporary individuals are usually quick to decry the eugenics movement, yet ableism persists and makes eugenic ideas seem humane. Film music and other art forms are subject to these trends, because the musical characteristics composers choose to represent disability are conditioned by their immersion in an ableist society.

Music employed in cinematic representations of disability remains consistent in *The Fly* and other contemporary horror films, and so ableist ideas that were fundamental to the eugenics movement, including aversion to disability, the desire for physical homogeneity, and the belief that related choices will impact social welfare, would seem to remain present in our social consciousness, despite changes in how such values are applied. Because the basic narrative surrounding disability since the 1950s remains unchanged, these stereotypes will continue to be echoed in films and film music until our society's understanding of disability evolves into a more positive one.

NOTES

1. Robin Wood, "An Introduction to the American Horror Film," in *Planks of Reason: Essays on the Horror Film*, rev. ed., ed. Barry Keith Grant and Christopher Sharrett (Lanham, MD: Scarecrow Press, 2004), 113.

2. Joseph P. Shapiro, *No Pity: People with Disabilities Forging a New Civil Rights Movement* (New York: Three Rivers Press, 1994), 159.

3. Tobin Siebers, *Disability Aesthetics* (Ann Arbor: University of Michigan Press, 2010), 23.

4. Ableism is a social system in which able-bodied people are privileged over those with a disability.

5. Rosemarie Garland Thompson, "The Cultural Logic of Euthanasia: 'Sad Fancyings' in Herman Melvilles's "Bartleby," *American Literature* 76, no. 4 (2004): 777–806.

6. Ruth Cliffoer Engs, *The Eugenics Movement: An Encyclopedia* (Westport, CT: Greenwood Press, 2005), 237.

7. Martin Pernick, *The Black Stork: Eugenics and the Death of "Defective" Babies in American Medicine and Motion Pictures Since 1915* (New York: Oxford University Press, 1996), 87.

8. *Are You Fit to Marry?*, DVD, directed by Leopold Wharton (1927; Newfoundland, PA: John E. Allen Inc., 1996).

9. Martin F. Norden, *The Cinema of Isolation: A History of Physical Disability in the Movies* (New Brunswick, NJ: Rutgers University Press, 1994), 18.

10. Pernick, 64.

11. Angela Marie Smith, "Monsters in the Bed: The Horror Film Eugenics of *Dracula* and *Frankenstein*," in *Popular Eugenics: National Efficiency and American Mass Culture in the 1930s*, ed. Christina Cogdell (Athens: Ohio University Press, 2006), 333.

12. William K. Everson, "The Horror Film," in *The Horror Film Reader*, ed. Alain Silver and James Ursini (New York: Limelight Editions, 2000), 21–38.

13. "Bishop Questions Life's Sacredness: Mercy Killings Defended by British Prelate, Who Cites Danger of Overpopulation," *New York Times*, September 4, 1950.

14. "Mercy or Murder?" *New York Times*, January 8, 1950.

15. Rebecca M. Kluchin, *Fit to be Tied: Sterilization and Reproductive Rights in America, 1950–1980* (New Brunswick, NJ: Rutgers University Press, 2009), 28.

16. S. C. Reed, Elizabeth Reed, and J. D. Palm, "Fertility and Intelligence among Families of the Mentally Deficient," *Eugenics Quarterly* 1 (1954): 49.

17. "Epilepsy Law Reform: Conference Urges Changes in Outmoded Statutes," *New York Times*, December 12, 1954; "Study Lists Needs of Retarded Child: Parents Ask Doctors to be Honest, Schools and Public Helpful and Kind," *New York Times*, June 8, 1953.

18. Katherine Castles, "Nice Average Americans," in *Mental Retardation in America: A Historical Reader*, ed. Steven Noll and James W. Trent (New York: New York University Press, 2004), 352–353.

19. See *Rear Window* (1954), *Vertigo* (1958), *The Tingler* (1959), *Peeping Tom* (1960), *Psycho* (1960), *Whatever Happened to Baby Jane?* (1962), and *Wait until Dark* (1967).

20. *The Spiral Staircase*, DVD, directed by Robert Siodmak (1942: Los Angeles: MGM Home Video, 2005).

21. Norden, 18.

22. The Love Theme sometimes plays when Helen is alone, indicating the narrative's sympathetic stance toward her.

23. *The Spiral Staircase*, 35:19–35:46.

24. Ibid., 1:12:23–1:13:33.

25. Roy S. Simmonds, *The Two Worlds of William March* (Tuscaloosa: University of Alabama Press, 1984), 270.

26. *The Bad Seed*, DVD, directed by Mervyn LeRoy (1942; Burbank, CA: Warner Home Videos, 2004).

27. *The Bad Seed*, 25:38–26:25. The organ has often been used in horror films. Moreover, its religious connotations may anticipate the plot's forthcoming inversion of maternal love.

28. *The Bad Seed*, 1:06:57–1:07:57.

29. Kluchin, 18–19.

30. Thomas M. Pryor, "Hollywood Secret: Outline for 'Bad Seed' Mystery—Other Items," *New York Times*, October 23, 1955.

31. *The Fly*, DVD, directed by Kurt Neumann (1958; Los Angeles: Twentieth Century Fox Home Video, 2007).

32. Erving Goffman, *Stigma: Notes on the Management of Spoiled Identity* (Englewood Cliffs, NJ: Prentice-Hall, 1963), i.

33. Mike Chopra-Gant, *Cinema and History: The Telling of Stories* (London: Wallflower, 2008), 34–35.

34. *The Fly* (1958), 1:17:55.

35. Ibid., 1:21:46–1:22:03.

36. *The Fly*, DVD, directed by David Cronenberg (1986; Los Angeles: Twentieth Century Fox Home Video, 2005).

37. Linda Brookover and Alain Silver, "What Rough Beast? Insect Politics and *The Fly*," in Silver and Ursini, *The Horror Film Reader*, 238.

38. *The Fly* (1986), 1:16:59–1:18:20.

39. Ibid., 1:20:15.

40. Mary Steichen Calderone, "Fetuses' Right Not to be Born," *New York Times*, September 21, 1989.

41. Amy Harmon, "Prenatal Test Puts Down Syndrome in Hard Focus," *New York Times*, May 7, 2007, accessed May 1, 2010, http://www.nytimes.com/2007/05/09/us/09down.html.

42. Meena Hart Duerson, "Parents Awarded 2.9M in 'Wrongful Birth,'" *New York Daily News*, March 11, 2012, http://articles.nydailynews.com/2012-03-11/news/31146217_1_doctors-baby-syndrome.

43. Marsha Saxton, "Disability Rights and Selective Abortion," in *The Disability Studies Reader*, ed. Leonard J. Davis (New York: Routledge, 2006), 109.

44. *The Fly* (1986), audio commentary, 1:01:25–1:01:49.

45. In *Disability Aesthetics*, Siebers discusses the disability community's concern about the use of art to portray disabled people as "Others" in respect to euthanasia. See in particular Peter Singer's contention that some disabled individuals are not "persons" and can thus be killed without their consent (Siebers, 23). "Futile Care" laws and offers of assisted suicide in lieu of chemotherapy lend credence to these kinds of community concerns. See Mary Ann Rosner, "Senators Hear Passionate Arguments on 'Medical Futility' Proposal," *Austin Statesman*, April 13, 2007, accessed May 2, 2010, https://groups.yahoo.com/neo/groups/Bioethics/conversations/topics/10731]; and Wesley J. Smith, "Covering the Cost of Assisted Suicide but Not Chemotherapy in Oregon," *First Things* June 3, 2008, accessed May 17, 2010, http://www.firstthings.com/blogs/secondhandsmoke/2008/06/03/covering-the-cost-of-assisted-suicide-but-not-chemotherapy-in-oregon.

46. Allan G. Johnson, *Privilege, Power, and Difference*, 2nd ed. (New York: McGraw Hill, 2006), 10–11.

10 Masculinity, Race, and the Blues in the Bizpic *Cadillac Records* (2008)

JESSE SCHLOTTERBECK

ONE OF THE most distinctive aspects of *Cadillac Records* (2008), a portrayal of the blues record label Chess Records, is its emphasis on the manufacturing of popular music. As Joshua Clover points out, this film represents a different kind of biopic: "The film is more the biography of a business than a person. (Don't we need a subgenre for this—the *bizpic*, maybe?)."[1] By foregrounding the history of the record label, the production of songs, and the management of black talent—it would seem that the bizpic must, effectively, be a more truthful mode of biography than the individualistic, star-celebrating form that biopics more commonly assume. True to this description, *Cadillac Records* makes the exploitation of Chess Records recording artists—Chuck Berry, Muddy Waters, Etta James, and Little Walter—a central part of its narrative. For example, Len Chess (Adrien Brody) bribes radio stations to play the music of his black talent, then compensates himself at a far higher rate than his artists, all of whom openly discuss this subject.

According to John C. Tibbetts, the musical biopic has commonly been identified as a "producer's genre."[2] George Custen writes that the classical Hollywood biopic tends to "cultivate the interests of their producers, presenting a worldview that naturalizes certain lives and specific values over alternative ones."[3] The ambivalent depiction of Len Chess in *Cadillac Records* is atypical for this genre in which producers and the entertainment industry are too often uncritically glamorized. Chess, by contrast, is portrayed here as a deeply conflicted and contradictory producer-character.

This, of course, is only half the story; for *Cadillac Records* to attract a mass audience the film must offer at least as many guilt-free spectacles as sobering revelations. Thus, emphasis on injustice is counterbalanced by exuberant passages in which artistry, commercialism, and social progress are celebrated. *Cadillac Records*, incongruously, acknowledges the exploitation of these artists and is also a nostalgic film, which results in startlingly divergent scenes. In my analysis, I explicate the film's contradictory tendencies, attending to critical literature on the blues, the musical biopic genre, and representations of race and masculinity on screen. The title of this anthology prompts us to think about the anxiety that attends our engagement with Fifties culture. *Cadillac Records* appeals to a mass audience by both provoking and allaying such anxiety.

Robert Ray's work on Hollywood cinema provides us with a theoretical framework that can account for the incongruity of *Cadillac Records*, which appears, alternately, to be a liberal social-problem film and a celebration of American entertainment and consumerism. Ray argues that the most successful Hollywood films are not those that are the most conservative or liberal, but those that are maximally ambivalent or ambiguous. While Ray retains ideological criticism's reading of movies as "massively overdetermined"—that is, their content should not be regarded as arbitrary, but as the compacted expression of many dominant economic and social forces—he also distinguishes his approach from the tendency of other ideological critics to "simply ignore American Cinema with its 'realist,' 'transparent' style whose political effect can be read in advance."[4] He asserts that we must regard the film text as "decentered," as so overdetermined in multiple ways that it eludes any one-sided analysis: "The film historian, in other words, has an array of factors to consider, each of them 'right' as an object of study, each becoming 'wrong' only if the historian's attention fixes on one as the sole explanation of cinema."[5]

Ray's attentive criticism explains the popularity of *The Godfather* (1972) by way of its appeal to diverse, seemingly oppositional segments, of the audience.[6] For Ray, it is little coincidence that *The Godfather* was both extraordinarily profitable—setting a new box office record of $86 million in 1972—and successfully combined "right" and "left" qualities of early 1970s film cycles—defined on the right by Steve McQueen (*Bullitt*, 1968), Clint Eastwood (*Dirty Harry*, 1971), and Charles Bronson (*Death Wish*, 1974), and on the left by films like *Bonnie and Clyde* (1967), *The Graduate* (1967), and *Easy Rider* (1969). Late 1960s and early 1970s production was split between left and right films whose potential for success was limited by appeal to certain audience segments. In right action films, often called "street Westerns," protagonists use vigilante violence to restore social order. In left films like *Bonnie and Clyde*, outlaw heroes attempt to escape the dominant social order. *The Godfather's* Italian-American mob family unites this split audience by portraying the systemic corruption in America for those on the left, as well as an organized, hierarchical patriarchal culture for those on the right. Further oppositions are held in balance: the left fantasy of rebellion and freedom is balanced by the right fantasy of authority and control. *The Godfather* features outlaw heroes, yet is offset by their placement in a family with tradition.

Close analysis of the musical biopic—a popular genre which has consistently drawn greater interest from the audience and the industry than from critics or academics—reveals similarly ambivalent texts. Just as Ray explains *The Godfather*'s efficacy by way of its management of contradictory ideologies, we can read *Cadillac Records* as a contradictory, equally left and right text. *Cadillac Records*, like *The Godfather*, works by weighting its oppositions against one another. The pathos of the minority musicians who suffer in racist social and economic contexts is measured against the more transcendent achievements of their cultural production. In an account of the biopic's increasingly frequent depiction of minorities in films, such as *Malcolm X* (1992) and *Ali* (2001), Carolyn Anderson and Jon Lupo note the reasons for the mass appeal of this subject:

> Placing individual and institutional racism in the past, which must be the setting for at least part of every biopic, appeals to Hollywood. A narrative can easily be constructed that denounces (past) racism while celebrating the protagonist's personal triumph over such racism and entry into what is presented as a contemporary American meritocracy.[7]

While the biopic must, by definition, situate racism historically, this does not negate the significance of this representational shift. Anderson and Lupo also credit the minority-centered biopic for adding a "rich social context" to a genre that "has traditionally taken a psychological approach to explain its protagonist's life."[8]

I will now survey how the film exposes past injustices before considering the film's more nostalgic investment in race, music, and the Fifties. Such an analytical approach, which emphasizes tension in lieu of a more unified reading, accurately attends to the contradictory textuality of *Cadillac Records*. Portrayals of racial discrimination figure prominently in numerous scenes: Etta James (Beyoncé Knowles), the child of a brief biracial affair, is unable to get her white father to take an interest in her, and Little Walter (Columbus Short) is roughed up by the police for doing little else but driving an expensive car. I begin my analysis of *Cadillac Records* with a scene depicting the appropriation of black musical styles by white artists.

Cadillac Records positions Chuck Berry (Mos Def) as the first practitioner of rock 'n' roll, hybridizing two racially divided popular music styles, blues and country. In the scene that introduces Berry, he is blocked from performing at a club because he

FIGURE 10.1 Fans briefly climb on stage and dance with Chuck Berry (Mos Def) before the police shut down the performance.

does not fit the racial profile the staff expected. When Berry and his band arrive to play a contracted gig, the club management, having assumed that the booked "country singer" was white, is incredulous. Though Berry is turned away, his records continue to receive more radio play and the popularity of rock 'n' roll grows. His concerts begin to draw increasingly large audiences. At a particularly raucous, large concert, barriers separating the young white and black crowds from one another are perfunctorily pushed aside, and both audiences happily dance together to Berry's music. The police at the function allow this, but draw the line when white teenage girls climb onstage and dance along with Berry (Figure 10.1).

Racial tensions continue to plague Berry as his fame increases. The singer exploits the enthusiasm of his young fans, relishing his ability to attract the same sort of young white girls who danced on stage with him for sexual liaisons. We, of course, expect Berry to receive his comeuppance for pursuing these women, and he does. Yet, rather than depicting his dispute with the police in an isolated scene, *Cadillac Records* dynamically pairs Berry's arrest with his discovery that white pop artists are imitating and profiting from the very style of rock 'n' roll that he devised. This sequence begins with Berry in a carload of nearly naked girls. Their encounter is interrupted when the singer suddenly hears a pop song whose instrumental track duplicates his "Maybelline" on the car stereo. To this point—token resistance from two-dimensional promoters or policemen aside—Berry's music and ascendant stardom had enabled him considerable freedom in transcending racial boundaries. The singer's escapades with young women, which the narrator playfully refers to as his "recruitment of new talent," had been portrayed more with bemusement (at Fifties backwardness) than seriousness (regarding its potential consequences). Yet, it is the moment at which Berry, in the car full of white girls, hears The Beach Boys' "Surfin'

USA" that marks a shift in the film. Berry's music, once his source of freedom, will from this point forward be managed and performed by white entertainers. After the elliptical edit that follows this scene, Berry is arrested for taking these juveniles across state lines.

For their part, Berry's companions are baffled by his response when he hears the instrumental tracks of "Maybelline" on the car stereo. When Berry angrily says, "That's my song!" one of the girls, at once naive and knowing, replies, "No darlin', that's The Beach Boys."[9] These straw girls do not recognize the significance of Berry's decision to take them out of state or of the Beach Boys' unauthorized appropriation. Berry, by contrast, is immediately incensed by the musical thievery, but he is seemingly unaware of any problems his sexual forays may cause him.

The film forces viewers to compare the severity of these crimes by depicting his arrest in the following scene: Berry barges into the recording studio filled with righteous indignation. In this relatively safe space he delivers an angry monologue: "That is 'Sweet Sixteen,' note for note ... not one change. Aside, apart from the lyrics, about the new lyrics about ... surfing. I've provided them the soundtrack unbeknownst to myself." The engineer asks him if he's ready to lay down some new tracks, to which he sarcastically responds, "I'm ready. I'm very ready to make more songs for the Beach Boys and all other manner of white folks to steal. Yes, I'm quite ready. [Len walks in.] You say the devil's name, he appears. You heard this? You know what's going on? I'm not laying down for this. First, Freed gets a third for 'Maybelline,' for what? ... Did he write one part of the song?" But Chess has come with more pressing news. After curtly responding to Berry's agitation with the Beach Boys—"Freed put us on the map"—Chess warns Berry that the police are about to arrest him for transporting a (white) minor across state lines. If the pairing of the car and the studio scenes has not already made these points of contrast explicit enough, Berry argues with the police as they cuff him and escort him from the room: "Jerry Lee Lewis has a thirteen-year-old wife; are we stopping by his house on the way? Emmit Till gets murdered for whistling at a white woman. I know you're pleased to get Chuck Berry."[10] A montage sequence, featuring songs by the Beach Boys and clips from "beach movies" follows Berry's arrest.[11] In a particularly deliberate juxtaposition of images, Berry's arrest photos are paired with footage of elated, white beach-goers from these films (Figure 10.2). Note how the following frame clearly suggests that Berry, who has been effectively removed from the public eye and the realm of performance, has been relegated to the secret (or suppressed) center of the surfin' safari.

By aligning the spectator with Berry—who links one scene to the next and speaks most eloquently on the subject—and closing with this three-part image, the following reading is made clear: in the Fifties, mixed race affairs were regarded as criminal,

FIGURE 10.2   Chuck Berry and the beach movie collage.

but now we can see that the Beach Boys' unauthorized use of Berry's music is the far greater crime.

Cadillac Records clearly and obviously draws attention to the phenomena of musical appropriation and inadequate compensation, yet it is hard to know what to make of this contradictory film: at the same time as it condemns the exploitation of black artists, it is also deeply nostalgic. While the sequence on the appropriation of Chuck Berry's music works in exposé-mode, the opening credit sequence illustrates the tendency of the film to treat its historical period in a more romantic, nostalgic manner. Here, a sleek montage introduces the key semantic elements of the movie. Film stock flickers, analogue records hiss and pop, and a series of shots show vintage promotional material, photographs, concert tickets, gold records, guitars, record players, and, of course, Cadillacs. These items are lovingly introduced in a syrupy voice-over by Willie Dixon (Cedric the Entertainer): "I'm making this here recording so when you visit Chess Records studio you know the history. Now, the first time a gal took off her underwear and threw them on stage it was on account of the blues. Now when the white girls started doing it, they called that rock 'n' roll. Took a whole lot of people to make the music that changed the world."[12] By coincidence, the nostalgic bent of the film—in particular, its portrayal of extravagant and guilt-less enjoyment of luxury American cars—was enhanced by its uncanny timing with the economic crisis of 2008.

The effect of this curious combination is difficult to judge or situate with finality. How can we make sense of the film's double-sided quality—its equal presentation of alternately dystopic and utopic moments of the Fifties? In Joshua Clover's less-than-charitable summation of the film, he writes that the label's talent "make more hits than money under the shrewd patronage of Leonard Chess, though he seems to love them one and all; it's a family, albeit one where the black children get screwed. Surely this is meant to fire our liberal hearts with outrage."[13] While Clover misstates many specific points about *Cadillac Records* in his short column, he is right to point to the curiously ritualistic function of the film: why do we need to see this story again?[14] What is the social or political function of *Cadillac Records*' moral story when everybody already knows?

The fact that African American recording artists were compensated at vastly unfair sums has been widely reported in scholarly sources, in pop culture, and in the autobiographies of many popular performers. As Brian Ward writes:

> Many black artists were locked into extraordinarily exploitative contracts which substantially reduced their capacity to profit from even the records they did sell. When lawyer Howell Begle investigated claims by a number of R&B veterans that they have routinely been deprived of proper payments by their record companies, he discovered that in the 1940s and 1950s most had contracts which paid royalties at a meager rate of between 1 and 4 percent of the retail price of recordings sold, or else provided one-off payments of around $200 in return for performances which sometimes made millions.[15]

Glenn Altschuler, who also draws on Begle's investigation, cites a portion of Chuck Berry's autobiography that would later be dramatized in *Cadillac Records*:

> What Berry was told was a "standard contract," in fact, shorted him on royalties to a much greater extent than standard contracts for white artists: "Berry noticed that Alan Freed and a disc jockey named Russ Fratto were listed as co-composers of the song. Chess told him that the song would get more attention if big names in the industry had an interest in it. 'With me being unknown,' Berry recalled, 'this made sense to me, especially since he failed to mention that there would be a split in the royalties as well.'"[16]

The exploitation of black artists became such common knowledge that it could be knowingly cited in pop culture. For example, a 1978 *Saturday Night Live* sketch parodies the appropriation of blues music. In "Beach Blanket Bimbo from Outer Space," Carrie Fisher and other white friends dance to rock music on the beach, in a clear parody of "beach movies." Where the adaptation of blues to lighter rock is an invisible part of the original films, *SNL*'s writers make this painfully, and comically, obvious in what follows:

> VINCENT PRICE: Hi, kids. Remember that recording artist friend I was telling you about? Well, here he is.
> ANNETTE [excited]: Hey look, everybody! It's Chubby Checker!

EVERYONE: CHUBBY CHECKER?!! WOWWW!!!

CHUBBY CHECKER: Hi, gang! Do you kids like to have fun?!

EVERYONE: YEAHHHH!!!

CHUBBY CHECKER: Great! 'Cause there's nothing I like better than entertaining white, middle-class kids on the beach! So come on, everybody! Let's Twist![17]

Here, *SNL* confidently parodies the typical social cast of popular music consumption: black musician (Chubby Checker), white manager (Vincent Price), and white audience (Carrie Fisher and others). The sketch implies that the style of music Checker plays is designed to maximize profit, which will then be split heavily with his white manager. Yet, there is also a key distinction between exploitation and appropriation. Where the exploitative nature of the economic relationships is acknowledged by nearly all popular music scholars and critics, there is less agreement as to the legacy of appropriation, to what extent the aesthetic and artistic legacies of these musicians have been overshadowed and copied by others. Even Steve Perry, who has written one of the strongest arguments for a history of popular music which emphasizes black and white partnerships in predominantly positive tones, also qualifies that he is speaking in terms of formal collaboration, not payment of royalties: "I don't mean to imply that black and white musicians have received anything approaching equal rewards—either in money or acclaim—for their talents. They have not. But to jump from that fact to the conclusion that the story of American music is the story of 'original' black music and 'derivative' white imitations is too far a leap."[18] Perry cites Greil Marcus's account of the writing and performance of "Hound Dog" as an example of the racially entangled history of musical production in the twentieth century: "Whites wrote it; a white made it a hit. And yet there is no denying that 'Hound Dog' is a 'black' song, unthinkable outside the impulses of black music, and probably a rewrite of an old piece of juke joint fury that dated back far beyond the birth of any of these people. Can you pull justice out of *that* maze?"[19]

Cadillac Records illustrates how a contemporary, retrospective account of these practices can present an equally difficult "maze" to sort through. In some scenes, the film unambiguously portrays these popular musicians as unfairly exploited and angry about it. In addition to his frustration with the appropriation of "Sweet Sixteen," Chuck Berry challenges Len for dividing royalties unfairly. On both accounts, the grounds for his objection are rational and clear.[20] Other scenes represent this history in a more problematic way. For example, Willie Dixon's voice-over makes light of rock's co-optation of the blues. In the diegesis, Dixon's jocular narrative is an audio recording to guide tourists through Chess Records as a historical site. It both illustrates and participates with the compromises necessary to make such shameful or threatening aspects of history palatable to contemporary consumption.

Further summary of *Cadillac Records* does more to illustrate the ambivalent and contradictory aspects of the film than to firmly situate any political tendency or argument. In many cases, *Cadillac*'s portrayal of race and music is remarkably resonant with historically dominant modes of representing these subjects. Krin Gabbard notes, for example, how jazz films in the post-blackface era routinely continued to narrativize blackness in a similar manner to *The Jazz Singer*. In the 1927 Jolson film, the lead applies blackface at a pivotal moment in the film, which marks the beginning of his successful management and eventual mastery of multiple threats to his masculine identity. Unable to resolve disputes about his career path with his family, or work up the confidence to fully pursue his love interest, blackface performance provides him with the courage to resolve these problems: "At a crucial moment in the story the son masquerades as an African American male just as he must simultaneously confront both his romantic ties to the Gentile woman and the Oedipal crises in his own family."[21] The efficacy of this narrative marker would seem to expire at the same time that blackface performances fell out of favor. Arthur Knight reports that Hollywood made its last blackface films in 1953.[22] The most comprehensive study of *The Jolson Story* (1946) quotes a review from its re-release in the late 1960s, which describes how blackface had fallen out of favor by this time:

> *The Al Jolson Story* [sic] today is an anachronism, a rather mediocre film biography of one who was a great entertainer in an era now irrevocably past. We cannot unwrite history, so there is no point in pretending it didn't happen: not so many decades ago singers and actors did blacken their faces and audiences were amused by it. But the reaction to the re-run of *The Al Jolson Story* is proof enough that it can't happen in America any more. The owners of the film may as well put it back in the vault to stay.[23]

Yet, as Gabbard argues, while blackface performance had fallen out of fashion, the narrative template that *The Jazz Singer* defined could be retained in films from the 1950s on. In *The Benny Goodman Story* (1956), "The hero never puts on blackface, but he does have critical encounters with black musicians who seem to affect his sexuality and emotional expressivity. The mythological characteristics of African Americans that Jack Robin puts on along with burnt cork are acquired by Goodman when blacks are simply nearby."[24] Here, Goodman's mastery of black musical forms, particularly his performance alongside black musicians, provides him a similar form of surrogate masculinity.

This characterization also fits Adrien Brody's performance as Chess Records producer Leonard Chess in *Cadillac Records*. In the scenes that introduce Brody's character, we see an overhead shot of him vigorously making love to a young woman. This shot, along with Brody's star persona as one of the more handsome actors to debut in the late 2000s,[25] would seem, rather obviously, to establish him as a virile and desirable man. This brief introduction to Brody as Len Chess is shortly followed by a scene in which he is emasculated by his fiancée's father. Dubious of Chess's plans to start a recording studio, he threatens Chess to make good on his promise to take care of his daughter. From the start, then, Chess's masculine identity is equated with his relative success or failure as a businessman and producer. As viewers of the film, both specifically (Chess Records is well known) and generically (musical biopics tend toward hagiography), we know that Chess will do well. He will provide for his wife and become a successful businessman, thereby proving his manhood.

Obviously, Chess's record label provides an income that allows him to succeed and prove his masculine worth, but, as a Jewish American managing a roster of African American talent, the racial dynamic of his ownership fits a tendency of filmic representation established with *The Jazz Singer*. Much like the positive correlation of blacks and masculinity in films removed from explicit blackface performances, such as *The Benny Goodman Story*, Chess's interaction with his bluesmen solidifies his status as a *man*.

Two blues classics featured in both the film and on the soundtrack—"I'm A Man" and "(I'm Your) Hoochie Coochie Man"—portray a typically exaggerated masculine persona: a man of great sexual prowess and unlimited access to sexual gratification. Consider the following lyrics:

"(I'm Your) Hoochie Coochie Man" (Muddy Waters)
Gypsy woman told my momma, before I was born
You got a boy-child comin', gonna be a son-of-a-gun
Gonna make these pretty women, jump and shout
And the world will know, what it's all about
Y'know I'm here
Everybody knows I'm here
And I'm the hoochie-coochie man
Everybody knows I'm here.

"I'm A Man" (Bo Diddley)
I'm a man,
I spell *M-A-N*.
Man.
All you pretty women,
Stand in line,

I can make love to you baby,
In an hour's time.
The line I shoot,
Will never miss,
The way I make love to 'em,
They can't resist.

Ove Sernhede notes two exaggerated personas—absolutely powerful or abso-lutely powerless—that characterize most blues songs: "Blues thematizes adolescent vacillation between 'progressive,' self-reinforcing and 'regressive,' ego-dissolving processes."[26] "I'm a Man" and "Hoochie Coochie Man" feature "self-reinforcing" identifications addressed to a broad audience. These singer-characters are less invested in persuading a potential lover than in the self-assurance that "the world will know, what it's all about." This "self-reinforcing" blues song, as defined by Sernhede, is characterized by "the offensive macho-text's grandiose representations and by the music's declamatory aggression and sexual actions."[27] That Chess is intro-duced with his masculinity under threat by his fiancée's father helps to explain his attraction to the exaggerated macho figures at the center of these songs. While he does not have access to these personas through his own musical expression, Chess performs a "macho-text" via deportment, language, and interpersonal interactions.

As Chess becomes more comfortable with the musicians on his label, he walks with more of a macho swagger and talks with slangy bravado, dropping an ever-increasing number of "motherfuckers" as his status as both a producer and a man grows.[28] The masculine effect of blackness is traceable to the performances of white Americans in the blackface tradition in the nineteenth century. In his study of this theatrical tradition, which had too often been easily written off as simply a crude, two-dimensional stereo-type, Eric Lott explores the macho affect that blackface provided for white performers:

What appears in fact to have been appropriated were certain kinds of mas-culinity. To put on the cultural forms of "blackness" was to engage in a com-plex affair of manly mimicry. Examples of this dynamic since the heyday of minstrelsy are ready enough at hand—Elvis, Mailer . . . To wear or even enjoy blackface was literally, for a time, to become black to inherit the cool, virility, humiliation, abandon, or *gaité de coeur* that were the prime components of white ideologies of black manhood.[29]

This description aptly accounts for Chess's increasing bravado and his appropria-tion of increasingly "black" characteristics. Like his contracted musicians, he has a large sexual appetite, which he feeds with affairs on the road. Where Etta James's white father will have little to do with her, Chess lavishes attention on the singer and nearly has an affair with her as well. Beyond these descriptions of Chess's sexuality and his increasing command of a "black" vernacular, the scene—which motivates the hiring of volatile harmonica player Little Walter—most revealingly intersects with discourses of white fascination with black masculinity.

Len approaches Muddy Waters (Jeffrey Wright) after his bandmate, harpist Little Walter, had, just the night before, nearly gotten in a duel with other club patrons and caused significant damage to the club. Waters is bashful, half-expecting some request of restitution from Chess, who approaches the guitarist as he is working as a truck-loader:

> WATERS: We're just here working sir. I thought we was alright boss?
> CHESS: C'mon, stop talking to me like I'm a damn plantation owner, huh? . . .
>   I wanna put you on a record.
> WATERS: A record, you're kidding?[30]

Waters is baffled by both the timing and enthusiasm of Chess's request. The condensed narration of the film nearly begs the viewer to conclude that—far from dissuading Chess from associating with him and Walter—the violent spectacle of the nightclub incident actually arouses the interest of the club owner who had to foot the bill for Little Walter's outburst just the night before.

Here, too, we can situate Chess's seemingly incongruous decision within the history of racial representations. Lott also describes the historical foundation behind the double-sided attraction of blackness—as a mix of a pleasure and fear—to the white audience:

> Ideologies of working-class manhood . . . shaped white men's contradictory feelings about black men. Because of the power of the black penis in white American psychic life, the pleasure of minstrelsy's largely white and male audiences derived from their investment in "blackness" always carried a threat of castration—a threat obsessively reversed in white lynching rituals.[31]

In this case, Len's ownership and management of Chess Records grants him both proximity to violence and danger—which he courts by mimicking the macho exploits of his roster of talent, imitating black vernacular, pursuing affairs, and seeking to dominate his professional field—yet, as the producer, he retains the ability to master and control the same cast of characters that threaten to destroy him.

It may come as some surprise that Leonard Chess is so ambiguously portrayed. While this draws out some subtleties in his characterization, it is by no means an against-the-grain reading. Although, as Clover also notes, the record label is often referred to as a family, this metaphor—really a power-play by Chess that his recording artists resist, with varying degrees of subtlety—is presented unevenly throughout the film. Consider the following scenes: When Muddy Waters gives a radio interview in the South, he effusively praises his white producer, introducing him as the man who gave a poor field hand a shot. He says, "When I was out there I used to sing, 'Time don't get no better up the road I'm going,' so I want to thank old Len Chess here for giving Muddy Waters a chance to shine."[32] Yet, as they leave the station, Chess thanks him in return, but Waters is less inclined to repeat his praise, reflecting the fact that such comments, perhaps, were intended to appease a Southern audience more than convey his true feelings. Chess, ignoring the fact that Waters has just declined to repeat his deferential compliment, then presses on about his idea of the label as family. In a gesture meant to signify how much he intends to "take care" of this family, Chess offers Waters an extravagant gift, his own Cadillac. Little Walter's response to the same gift draws even more attention to its manipulative function. The more explosive of the two musicians hugs Chess and, while holding him aloft, exclaims, "You my white daddy!"[33] Later in the film, the label is no longer so flush with cash, and when Waters asks his boss for payment, Chess reveals that he routed much of their royalties to the purchase of these cars (even though they had previously been presented as gifts or bonuses).[34] The extravagant cars figure as promises of fatherly care and omnipotence, which eventually fall short.

There is an additional portrayal of production-within-the-production in *Cadillac Records*, which emphasizes the centrality of Alan Lomax in the rise of blues. As in Gordon Park Sr.'s biopic *Leadbelly* (1976), the work of Lomax provides a convenient framing story for the rise-to-fame of these African American musicians. Yet, where the Parks film portrays Lomax with a degree of ambivalence, in *Cadillac Records* Lomax (Tony Bentley), in contrast to Chess, selflessly launches Waters's career. Their original meeting is portrayed with a sense of predetermination, with Lomax clearly positioned as the primary reason that Waters would become a musical star. The soundtrack conveys a sense of Waters's destiny, now that Lomax has chosen him: an electric guitar riff, at a time when Waters only played acoustic, accompanies the Lomax car as it speeds to Muddy's modest, rural home.

McKinley Morganfield, as Lomax will address him shortly, is portrayed as unrefined and ignorant. He is startled by Lomax's approaching vehicle, and, with a tremor in his voice, tells his wife to get inside. He sidles away from the front of the house and, as if the passengers would not see him, retreats to the water well to get a drink, averting eye-contact. Lomax exits the car and addresses him confidently: "I'm Alan Lomax . . . I'm recording folk music for the Library of Congress." Waters is initially nonplussed. "Folk music?" he asks. Morganfield, though, is a quick study, and soon accepts the value of committing his music to record. For Chess, closeness to and management of black talent confers his masculinity. The film suggests that Waters receives a similar effect from electrification. When Lomax, visibly pleased with the results, plays back the record for Waters, he says, "That's what I sound like, huh?" Lomax replies, "Yes, sir, that's what you sound like," to which Waters says, "Feels like I'm meeting myself for the first time." Thus, the future Muddy Waters's reluctance is overcome in a matter of seconds.[35] The voice-over affirms and extends the transformation that Lomax's recording effected: "And he was [meeting himself for the first time], and he knew it was a man he was meeting, too big for that slave shack he was born in, and too big for that plantation."[36] Lomax, it seems, has not only conferred musical stardom or a new musical style on Waters, but also masculinity and independence. Now that he has been recorded and electrified, Waters walks confidently down the train tracks, fated to succeed.

Thus *Cadillac Records* invokes a befuddling range of references and exemplifies a no less vexing range of readings and portrayals of race relations, musical production, and economic exploitation. On the one hand, Len Chess receives the ambivalent characterization that he deserves, as he is perpetually challenged by his exploited roster of talent; for Chess, as the voice-over informs us, "It was the color of them bills that mattered."[37] On the other hand, numerous aspects of Chess's characterization point to a more regressive project: the casting of Adrien Brody shapes the reception of this character, and his ability to access a surrogate masculinity through his work with expressive black musicians places the film more in concert with (than opposition to) the history of black/white relations in numerous Hollywood films. Likewise, the portrayal of the manufacture of commercial music stands out as a progressive development. Yet the commercial industry, here, is not just a mere launch pad for great talents, but is lingered upon at numerous crucial plot points: radio play is enabled with bribery; Muddy Waters's career is launched when the Lomax brothers decide he ought to be recorded and electrified; Waters resists recording the Willie Dixon tune "Hoochie Coochie Man," which would become his most popular song, because he believes it is too simple.

Cadillac Records effectively illustrates that popular music is the collaborative effort of many to manufacture a commercial product. Yet, at what cost do these numerous qualifications come? In a style that has more frequently aggrandized the lead's foresight in predicting popular taste, Waters is so often wrong, and in an era that has just recently allowed the extensive portrayal of African American musicians, must they be denied the fluid and immediate access to spontaneous expression that has historically been granted to those who sing in Hollywood musicals? How can we reconcile the musical's characteristic investment in feeling and emotional intensity with the presence of such persistently pessimistic contextualization and qualifications? Bruce Babington and Peter Williams Evans offer us a way out of this dilemma:

> What we see [in musicals since the 1970s] is the encounter between a utopian urge (without which the musical, as we know it, would be unrecognizable) and a dystopian reality given prominence, even predominance, in a way that it never was done before. It is the dynamic of the encounter that is essential, the tension between two conflicting impulses as the utopian drive makes of a more pressing reality what it can. If the bias towards affirmation has to respect the difficulties of less malleable interpretations of reality, the impulse to de-idealization in turn respects the power and nostalgia . . . of the old mythologies.[38]

The film's double-sided treatment of race, music, and the Fifties ought to be read not as incoherent or contradictory in a pejorative sense, but as channeling the kind of productive ambivalence, however purposefully, that explains the popularity of so many Hollywood films. *Cadillac Records*, as such an open text, could conceivably lead to a wide variety of audience responses.

This film is able to both function as a social-problem film and a celebration of popular music's artistry. Here, the vexed history of the appropriation of the blues is treated fairly and openly in a film that is also entertaining. Whether this allays, indulges, or strikes an appropriate balance in negotiating the anxieties that attend this subject is ultimately as dependent on the viewer as any specifics of the film-text. Returning to Ray's insight about Hollywood films combining left and right ideologies, left viewers of *Cadillac Records* are more likely to applaud (or find fault in) its treatment of racism, while right viewers are more likely to attend to its entertaining qualities and celebrating of American enterprise. It is the task of the critic to see how it makes both readings possible. Ray reminds us to regard the "decentered" popular film as so multiply overdetermined that it eludes any one-sided analysis.[39] Whether *Cadillac Records* is right, left, both, or neither rests ultimately with individual viewers and interpretive communities. As a popular film, its purpose is to make each response possible.

NOTES

1. Joshua Clover, "Based on Actual Events," *Film Quarterly* 62, no. 3 (March 2009): 8.

2. Tibbetts draws this conclusion from study of the production memos behind numerous musical biopics. See John C. Tibbetts, *Composers in the Movies: Studies in Musical Biography* (New Haven, CT: Yale University Press, 2005), 110.

3. George F. Custen, *Bio/Pics: How Hollywood Constructed Public History* (New Brunswick, NJ: Rutgers University Press, 1992), 4.

4. Robert B. Ray, *A Certain Tendency of the Hollywood Cinema, 1930–1980* (Princeton, NJ: Princeton University Press, 1985), 8.

5. Ibid., 7.

6. See "Chapter 10: *The Godfather* and *Taxi Driver*," in Ray, 326–360.

7. Carolyn Anderson and Jon Lupo, "Hollywood Lives: The State of the Bio-Pic at the Turn of the Century," in *Genre and Contemporary Hollywood*, ed. Steve Neale (London: British Film Institute, 2002): 93.

8. Ibid.

9. *Cadillac Records*, DVD, directed by Darnell Martin (2008; Culver City, CA: Sony Pictures Home Entertainment, 2009), 1:11:30–1:11:50.

10. Ibid., 1:12:45–1:13:10.

11. For a discussion of the use of rock music in so-called "beach movies" of the early 1960s, see Michael Dunne, *American Film Musical Themes and Forms* (London: McFarland, 2004), 58–63.

12. *Cadillac Records*, 2:00–2:40.

13. Clover, 8–9.

14. Clover mischaracterizes the supposed absence of Elvis in the film; he appears twice, not once, and is explicitly discussed by characters in *Cadillac Records*. Clover also inaccurately describes the film's African American performers as being more sexual than white figures, even though Chess's sexuality is a central focus of the film.

15. Brian Ward, *Just My Soul Responding: Rhythm and Blues, Black Consciousness, and Race Relations* (Berkeley: University of California Press, 1998), 48.

16. Glenn Altschuler, *All Shook Up: How Rock 'n' Roll Changed America* (New York: Oxford University Press, 2003), 55. Altschuler cites Berry's autobiography in this quote: Chuck Berry, *The Autobiography* (New York: Harmony, 1987), 104, 110.

17. Dunne cites "Beach Blanket Bimbo from Outer Space" in his study of "beach movies" of the early 1960s. Dunne, 58–63. See also the full transcript of the *SNL* sketch, accessed May 21, 2014, http://snltranscripts.jt.org/78/78fbeach.phtml.

18. Steve Perry, "Ain't No Mountain High Enough: The Politics of Crossover" in *Facing the Music*, ed. Simon Frith (New York: Pantheon, 1988), 66.

19. Greil Marcus, *Mystery Train: Images of America in Rock & Roll Music* (New York: Penguin, 1990), 155, as quoted by Perry, 65. (Emphasis in the original.)

20. Altschuler's description of Berry's frustration with his contract confirms the historical basis for the scene in which Berry confronts Len for giving DJs and promoters a large percentage of their profits; see Altschuler, 55.

21. Krin Gabbard, *Jammin' at the Margins: Jazz and the American Cinema* (Chicago: University of Chicago Press, 1996), 38.

22. Arthur Knight, *Disintegrating the Musical: Black Performance and the American Musical Film* (Durham, NC: Duke University Press, 2002), 91.

23. Review from *Portland Oregonian*, 1968, as quoted in Doug McClelland, *Blackface to Blacklist: Al Jolson, Larry Parks, and "The Jolson Story"* (Lanham, MD: Scarecrow Press, 1998), 257.

24. Gabbard, 54–55.

25. Profiles in popular magazines included *People*, "Adrien Brody," June 30, 2003, 71; and *Rolling Stone*, "Adrien Brody: An Oscar Star Is Born," May 1, 2003, 63.

26. Ove Sernhede, "Black Music and White Adolescence," in *Negotiating Identities: Essays on Immigration and Culture in Present-Day Europe*, ed. Aleksandra Alund and Raoul Granqvist (Atlanta, GA: Rodopoi, 1995), 190.

27. Ibid.

28. *Screen It!*, which tracks instances of sex, violence, and illegal behavior in popular films, reports that the script for *Cadillac Records* includes "at least 78 'f' words (38 used with 'mother,')"; Len drops many of these after he successfully recruits and establishes friendly relationships with his roster of black talent. *"Cadillac Records" Screen It! Parental Review*, accessed April 24, 2009, http://www.screenit.com/movies/2008/cadillac_records.html. According to Palmer's account of Chess's studio manner, the late 2000s film use of colorful language is verified by the oral history. An engineer who worked at the studio told Palmer, "With some of the blues players, the whole session would be Leonard and whoever it was calling each other stacks of mother-fuckers." Robert Palmer, *Deep Blues: A Musical and Cultural History of the Mississippi Delta* (New York: Penguin, 1982), 162.

29. Eric Lott, *Love and Theft: Blackface Minstrelsy and the American Working Class* (New York: Oxford University Press, 1993), 52.

30. *Cadillac Records*, 16:10–16:30.

31. Lott, 9.

32. *Cadillac Records*, 22:00–22:45.

33. Ibid., 28:25–28:45.

34. Chess's use of these extravagant gifts as a way of conferring value on their relationship recalls the exchange of cigars in *Young Man With a Horn* (1950). See Gabbard, 71. Dixon's voice-over makes the function of the lavish gift quite explicit: "Now, Leonard Chess didn't worry none about skin color. It was the color of them bills that mattered. Just get you enough green to cover yourself and then you ain't no Jew-boy no more, and you ain't no colored boy either. You're just a man, with a Cadillac."

35. *Leadbelly* (1976) presents a significantly different reading of Lomax's work. Here, the lead is deeply skeptical of the Library of Congress project, and these recording scenes are portrayed with a greater sense of tension than discovery or triumph.

36. *Cadillac Records*, 5:45–7:15.

37. Ibid., 17:10–17:30.

38. Bruce Babington and Peter Williams Evans, *Blue Skies and Silver Linings: Aspects of the Hollywood Musical* (Dover, NH: Manchester University Press, 1985), 226.

39. Ray, 6–7.

11 Comin' Back to the Sixties

Mobilizing Music and Performing Politics, 1988–1990

CHRISTOPHER D. STONE

Beyond *The Big Chill*

IN *THE BIG CHILL* (1983), seven friends reunite to bury Alex Marshall, the idealist who brought them together as college students at the University of Michigan during the 1960s. During a dinner on the second night of their reunion, aside from Nick Carlton (William Hurt) and Harold Cooper (Kevin Kline), they talk of ideals betrayed, promises broken, and identities lost. Anxiety and self-recrimination abound. With the meal complete and the mood heavy, Harold cues up the Temptations' "Ain't Too Proud to Beg" (1966). Suddenly David Ruffin's gritty tenor issues forth a passionate call to arms: "I know you want to leave me/But I refuse to let you go." On cue, the mood lifts and anxieties temporarily abate as the gang begins dancing to one of the Funk Brothers' most infectious grooves.[1]

That scene likely sold a lot of tickets and moved scores of soundtrack albums.[2] Certainly, it remains closely associated with *The Big Chill*—as evinced by the American Film Institute (AFI) ranking the scene as the 94th most iconic musical moment in American cinema.[3] Yet, despite such acclaim, for those interested in the Sixties as a site of memory, for those deeply invested in that era's vision of a more democratic and authentic America, that scene, the character of Harold, and *The Big Chill*'s overall trajectory carries a host of troubling implications.

On one level, Harold seems stuck in the Sixties. Accompanied by Procol Harum's elegiac "A Whiter Shade of Pale" (1967), Michael Gold (Jeff Goldblum) critiques his host's all-Sixties, all-the-time playlist. He urges Harold to invest in some music from "this century." Unmoved, Harold reaffirms his fidelity to the music of youth, proclaiming: "There is no other music, not in my house."[4]

Yet aside from the era's music, the Sixties exhibit little meaning to Harold. He has adapted to the more conservative, materialistic ethos of post-Sixties America. In fact, most of his friends have prospered as well, usually in ways they would have deemed repellent in 1968. What distinguishes Harold is not the course he has charted, but his feelings about it. He does not flagellate himself or talk of ideals abandoned. Nor does he discuss the Sixties as something still living, as a set of values and goals that remain applicable to the present. For Harold, the Sixties belong to the past and cannot be revived. In contrast, before his suicide, Alex clung to his ideals, choosing death over living in a world opposed to his values. Or as director and co-writer Kasdan bluntly notes: "Alex fell by the wayside because he could not adjust."[5]

Such messages have not endeared *The Big Chill* to many academics. Tony Williams accused the film of trying to discredit Sixties activism by furnishing it with "a comfortable 'yuppie' conclusion."[6] James Miller believes the film illustrates "the neoconservative scorn and facile nostalgia" that has infused remembrances of the Sixties in mass media.[7] Rebecca Klatch and Ted Morgan have cited *The Big Chill* as an example of the media's penchant for promoting the myth that former activists withdrew from politics, abandoned their ideals, and "sold out."[8] Other scholars, while not explicitly singling out *The Big Chill*, have echoed Klatch's broader point about dismissive representations of Sixties activism in the media.[9]

These indictments ring true; indeed, *The Big Chill*'s message is even more pernicious. The film suggests that Sixties activism was merely fashion. As fashions changed, boomers became their parents, forsaking activism, striving for economic success, and reveling in consumerism. In short, the film takes a sad song (boomers betray their ideals) and makes it even sadder (boomers had no ideals to forsake).

In this chapter, I seek not to re-evaluate *The Big Chill*. Rather, I seek to reframe the discussion by examining similar titles that belong to a cluster of films I term "Sixties Postscripts." Emerging in the 1970s, this cluster reached its peak in the late 1980s and early 1990s, as Reaganism ebbed cinematically and politically and as interest in the Sixties and its music grew.[10] This chapter focuses on four films released during these years: *Running on Empty* (1988), *Rude Awakening* (1989), *Flashback* (1990), and *Pump Up the Volume* (1990). It examines how these texts imagined and mobilized the Sixties. In so doing, it highlights the ways filmmakers embedded their political and cultural interventions through songs and performers associated with the Sixties. It argues that these films rejected the message of *The Big Chill* as they consciously worked to configure the Sixties not as a spent force, not as a relic every bit as obsolete as Harold's vinyl records, but as an endlessly renewable source of inspiration.

To analyze these films, I have divided the chapter into two sections. "(What's So Funny 'Bout) Peace, Love, and Understanding" introduces readers to the Sixties Postscript. It defines the cluster, surveys its development, examines its political implications, and identifies its principal narrative trajectories. "Stealing It Back" considers a series of texts from the cluster's peak. It mixes synopses with extended discussions of the films' principal themes, with special attention given to music's role in establishing context, driving narratives, and defining characters.

"(What's So Funny 'Bout) Peace, Love, and Understanding": The Sixties Postscript in American Cinema

To begin, it might be useful to proffer some definitions, starting with the distinction between the "1960s" and "the Sixties." The 1960s is a decade; the Sixties is an era. As employed by pundits, academics, and filmmakers alike, the Sixties generally excludes the early 1960s (defined as part of the "Long Fifties") and stretches into the 1970s (with 1973, 1974, or 1975 the most common endpoints). The Sixties is a construction; it is a complex mixture of fact, myth, and simplification. In terms of historical analysis, the Sixties can obscure or distort the 1960s. However, in terms of memory, the Sixties—the way it has been articulated, contested, and deployed—has a history, which I engage.

Sixties Postscripts are films set in the present that examine the era's meaning and legacy. More than any other subset of films, this cluster speaks to the unique position of the Sixties in American cinema. This position may seem obvious, considering the legions of films that engage the Sixties, but numbers alone do not fully tell the tale. After all, if filmmakers have screened the Sixties with great frequency, the same holds true, albeit to varying degrees, for the 1940s, 1950s, and 1970s. What these other eras lack, however, is the equivalent of the Sixties Postscript.

Certainly, other eras have inspired "reunion" films such as *That Championship Season* (1982), *The Best of Times* (1986), or *Grown Ups* (2010). These films, however, make little use of the past/present binary; indeed, the past and present do not appear that dissimilar. These films have little to say about the 1950s or 1970s. Characters do not assign any overriding political meaning to their youth, reference political movements, figures, causes, or issues, or speak of idealism or ideology. Herein is where Sixties Postscripts differ: they foreground politics, idealism, and activism, while reinforcing the notion of the Sixties as a singularly activist era.

The Big Chill, the most famous of the Sixties Postscripts, certainly associated the Sixties with activism, but it also embraced a stereotype beloved by mass media in the late 1970s and early 1980s: the "Yippie Gone Yuppie." Other Sixties Postscripts would tread down different paths. Indeed, of the dozens of cinematic commentaries on the fate of Sixties activism, only *The Big Fix* (1978) features another unreconstructed Yippie Gone Yuppie, and even in that film, he is an oddity. The film's other activists, including protagonist Moses Wine (Richard Dreyfuss), chart different trajectories, functioning as either "Enduring Idealists" or "Revived/Redeemed Reformers." These trajectories, not the Yippie Gone Yuppie, dominate Sixties Postscripts.

Enduring Idealists continue to adhere to their youthful beliefs, albeit with caveats. Some have dialed back the intensity of their political involvement. Others have sacrificed ideological purity for political pragmatism or have dropped out of a society they see as beyond redemption. Whatever their path, these characters end the movie where they began, on the margins of American society. As such, films that employ this template carry either a pessimistic or tempered appraisal of the contemporary relevance of the Sixties and the future of progressive politics.

In contrast, films that contain Revived/Redeemed Reformers speak of renewal and recommitment. These reclamation projects proceed along one of two paths. In the first, exiled or chastened activists return to the public sphere. Having kept their faith even while hiding out on the margins of American life, Revived Reformers reenter public spaces and reassert their voices. In the second, Redeemed Reformers, having strayed from the politics of their youth, regain their moral footing and reconnect with their social conscience. Films with Revived/Redeemed Reformers tend to conclude on a hopeful note, although some, most notably *Bulworth* (1998), amend or even undercut this optimism.

All of these archetypes figured into the first Sixties Postscript to achieve wide release, the moderately successful *The Big Fix*. Over the next nine years, there was a smattering of similarly themed films. Enduring Idealists appeared in *Return of the Secaucus 7* (1980) and *River's Edge* (1986).[11] Revived Reformers headlined *Second Thoughts* (1983), *Teachers* (1984), and *Power* (1986), although only *Teachers* met with any degree of commercial success.

Taken as a whole, Sixties Postscripts released before 1988 interpreted the years since the Sixties as a time of progressive retreat; only *The Big Chill* defined acquiescence to Reaganism as a virtue. The other films cast former activists as sympathetic figures. *The Big Fix*, *Return of the Secaucus 7*, *Second Thoughts*, *Teachers*, and *River's Edge* all suggest that activists acted out of deep conviction rather than radical chic, nihilism, oedipal complexes, or white guilt, as did Sixties Postscripts from after 1987.

Like their predecessors, the Sixties Postscripts released between 1988 and 1990 defended, performed, and mobilized the Sixties. They departed from these earlier films on several key points. They exhibited greater confidence and optimism—a difference expressed most clearly in the ways these films dealt with younger Americans.

Here the first decade of Sixties Postscripts alternated between disdain and disinterest. *The Big Fix* ignores post-Sixties youth. *Teachers* fails to explore the relationship of American youth to the Sixties. *Return of the Secaucus 7* laments their disinterest in politics. *River's Edge* levels the same charge, but ups the ante, portraying American youth as bored, nihilistic, and possibly sociopathic. That said, for our purposes, the most critical difference between the Sixties Postscripts of 1988–1990 and the films that preceded them is this: the earlier films, *The Big Chill* aside, made little use of Sixties music. Such will not be the case for the films of 1988–1990, starting with *Running on Empty*, a film named after one of Jackson Browne's meditations on the place of the Sixties in a post-Sixties world.

"Stealing It Back": Sixties Postscripts, 1988–1990

Running on Empty was Sidney Lumet's second Sixties Postscript. If more successful than the ill-fated *Power*, *Running on Empty*, despite solid reviews and Academy Award and Golden Globe nominations, failed to achieve wide release.[12] The film's most honored participant was Naomi Foner (née Achs), who won a Golden Globe for Best Screenplay. Unlike Lumet, who remained partial to the Old Left, Foner strongly identified with the movement.[13] She joined the SDS chapter at Columbia (where she met and married historian Eric Foner), registered voters in South Carolina, taught in Harlem through Head Start, and campaigned for Eugene McCarthy.[14]

These commitments informed a script that revolves around a pair of interpersonal conflicts. The first pits Arthur Pope (Judd Hirsch) against his wife, Annie Pope (Christine Lahti). The couple bombed the Military Research Lab at the University of Massachusetts in 1971, blinding a custodian in the process.[15] Since then, they and their sons Danny (River Phoenix) and Harry (Jonas Abry) have been on the run. While Arthur has no interest in turning himself in, Annie's resolve is crumbling. She is tired of the constant relocations and weary of Arthur's sometimes overbearing, dictatorial ways. Guilt also gnaws at her. She thinks of the janitor she maimed, the anguish she caused her parents, and the burdens her choices have imposed upon her children. The second conflict pits Arthur against Danny. Having spent virtually his entire life on the lam, constantly changing names, schools, and identities, Danny longs to stop running and begin his own life.

Music underscores these fault lines. As a young woman, Annie, a gifted pianist, studied at Juilliard. Her involvement in the movement led her to turn her back on school and her father, a wealthy industrialist. Yet she never abandoned her love of classical music, nor her practice board, which she gave to Danny, who inherited her passion and talent for music. None of this pleases Arthur, a red diaper baby from a working-class background. Preferring rock 'n' roll, he dismisses classical music as "decadent, white-skinned, privileged crap" and forbids Danny from attending a recital. His words elicit scorn from spouse and son alike. Annie mocks his hubris ("When did you become the minister of culture?"), while Danny underscores the scene's implicit irony: Arthur expects his sons to obey him without question even as he continually urges them to question authority.[16]

These musical cues might unwittingly emit a conservative riposte to the progressive leanings of Foner and Lumet. After all, by film's end, Danny will choose to travel the very path his mother rejected, leaving his parents to attend Julliard and live with his maternal grandparents (Figure 11.1). Such a trajectory might suggest that the Sixties were an unwelcome rupture, a retreat from a better past (embodied by the Fifties), a mistake that must be remedied posthaste—which is exactly the narrative conservative figures such as Newt Gingrich and Dick Armey have aggressively advanced.[17]

Such a reading does not jibe with the rest of the film. Neither Annie nor Arthur renounces the Sixties. Arthur may be standoffish, but he is also a nurturing father and principled man. He remains socially engaged, organizing a food co-op, canvassing for environmental issues, attempting to unionize the restaurant at which

FIGURE 11.1 As three members of the Pope family dance to James Taylor's "Fire and Rain" (1970), the clan's eldest son, Danny (River Phoenix), dances with Lorna (Martha Plimpton), his girlfriend. The widely spaced blocking of this scene foreshadows the film's conclusion. Indeed, at film's end, after the Popes bid farewell to Danny, the soundtrack harkens back to this sequence by replaying "Fire and Rain."

he works. Annie, meanwhile, despite being contrite about the suffering she caused and skeptical of the efficacy of revolutionary violence, stands firm when her father scorns the movement as a whole. To him, she replies, "If you do not believe [the bombing] was an act of conscience to stop the war, there is nothing more I can say."[18] The importance of her words becomes more apparent when placed alongside an earlier exchange prompted by a newspaper article about the manhunt for the Popes, which is the moment when the audience learns why the Popes are fugitives. Confused, Harry, no doubt speaking for many filmgoers, asks Danny why their parents bombed a lab. Without hesitation, Danny informs his brother that the U.S. government was dropping tons of napalm on civilians.[19] Taken together, these scenes enable the filmmakers to foreground the principles that guided Annie (and the antiwar movement) while subtly hinting that the real purveyors of violence were not those who protested the war but those who conducted it.

Even more critically, if Danny breaks rank to lead the life his mom rejected, he does so with the blessing and the values of his parents. Indeed, as he departs, his father offers a final benediction for not only Danny, but also for the young viewers for whom Danny functions as a surrogate. He urges them to "go out there and make a difference. Your mother and I tried. And don't let anyone tell you any different."[20] In other words, future generations should ignore the libels leveled against the movement and recognize that it fought the good fight and remains a relevant model of social responsibility and political engagement.

Similar messages inform *Rude Awakening*, a painfully earnest attempt to reignite Sixties-style activism.[21] Harassed by the federal government, Fred Wook (Eric Roberts) and Jesus Monteya (Cheech Marin), draft evaders, antiwar activists, and members of the underground press, bid farewell to Sammy Margolin (Robert Carradine), a writer, and Petra Black (Julie Hagerty), an artist. From 1969 the film then jumps to 1989. Fred and Jesus live on a small commune in the fictional Central American country of Managuador. After learning of an American plan to invade Managuador, they return to New York and seek the aid of Petra and Sammy, both of whom have "sold out." With time, Fred and Jesus bring Petra and Sammy back into the activist fold. However, when their efforts seem to yield little success, a dispirited Fred considers returning to exile only to be stopped by a group of students who assure him: "Some of us did hear you."[22] Fred, Sammy, and Petra agree to assist the students, who have already begun organizing. The film concludes with a dedication to "all people who care about the planet."

The film underscores or, perhaps undercuts, that dedication with a cover of the Beatles' "Revolution."[23] It is unclear whether the filmmakers grasp the irony in ending a film that champions activism with a song fairly dismissive of efforts to transform existing social and political arrangements: "You say you'll change the constitution/Well, you know/We all want to change your head/You tell me it's the institution/Well, you know/You better free your mind instead."[24] Like Bob Dylan's "It's Alright, Ma (I'm Only Bleeding)," "Revolution" seems to suggest that organized politics, whatever its ideological orientation, deadens the spirit and constrains the individual.

Rude Awakening makes better use of music in furthering another one of its chief preoccupations: lampooning the conservative "Other." Here the filmmakers tip their hand almost immediately. In a sequence bearing the imprints of *A Clockwork Orange* (1971) and *The Parallax View* (1974), a team of federally funded researchers, intending to transform antiwar activists into compliant soldiers, feed Jesus massive doses of LSD while subjecting him to a series of images. While exaggerated for comic effect, this sequence does hint at the government's very real efforts to disrupt the antiwar movement (a point frequently made in films set in the Sixties). The sequence also lays out a key cultural project of the Right: the desire to preserve the Fifties from the onslaught of the Sixties. The film's brainwashing montage differentiates the Fifties and Sixties in large part through competing renditions of "The Star Spangled Banner."[25] One is by Pat Boone, the other by Jimi Hendrix. By drawing on Boone's public persona, the film defines the Fifties as bland, pious, prudish, and conservative.[26] In contrast, Hendrix's image casts the Sixties as Boone's inverse, while allowing the filmmakers to pledge allegiance to an America open to creativity, individuality, and dissent. In so doing, the film employs "rock" not just as a signifier for the Sixties, but as a spark for that era's politics.[27]

Rude Awakening's most original use of music occurs as a wounded CIA agent dashes through the dense foliage of Managuador. The soundtrack scores his flight to a cover of Creedence Clearwater Revival's "Run Through the Jungle" by the Georgia Satellites.[28] Like many of the film's soundtrack choices, the song exhibits a literal connection. Yet here the film operates more subtly by forging a sonic link between the Vietnam War and American adventurism in Central America during the 1980s—a connection rendered explicit by subsequent dialogue. Ironically, while the filmmakers draw on that song's association with Vietnam, songwriter John Fogerty intended no such connection. For him, despite being "adopted by the guys in country," "Run Through the Jungle" served as a metaphor for domestic politics.[29]

Flashback shares certain similarities with *Rude Awakening*. Both revolve around activists who emerge from exile to fight for a vision of America now deemed unfashionable. Both sought to address and inspire Reagan/Bush-era youth.[30] *Flashback* opens with upright, conservative agent John Buckner (Kiefer Sutherland) receiving his next assignment: to escort Huey Walker (Dennis Hopper), an activist once heralded as the "Court Jester of the Radical Left." Walker's greatest notoriety came at the expense of Spiro Agnew. Legend credited Walker with disconnecting the vice president's railroad car, thereby stranding Agnew when the train embarked. Since escaping from FBI custody in 1969, Walker has remained underground. Twenty years later, having turned himself in, Walker has a plan. If he can escape from FBI custody a second time, he believes the resulting headlines will enable him to publish the manifesto he has been writing for two decades. The wily Walker manages to give Buckner the slip, but Buckner tracks him down in the wilderness. Searching for a phone, Buckner stumbles upon a commune whose sole inhabitant is Maggie (Carol Kane). There Buckner reconnects with the past and helps Walker. The resulting publicity propels Walker's book, *Flashback*, into a bestseller.

In telling this story, the film employs Sixties music in multiple ways. It introduces and contextualizes Huey Walker during a briefing by Buckner's superior, Stark (John Dooley). Since Buckner claims to know nothing of Walker, Stark brings him up to speed. Upon the younger agent's departure, Dooley studies a picture of Walker, his musing offset by the extended introduction of Jimi Hendrix's "All Along the Watchtower" (1968). The introduction continues as the film shifts—over a superimposed image of Walker's face—to its next scene: Buckner's arrival at Walker's prison. When the agent reaches Walker's cell, Hendrix declaims the song's famous opening lines: " 'There must be some kind of way out of here,' said the joker to the thief/'There's too much confusion, I can't get no relief.' "[31]

This sequence enjoins Walker to the Sixties and permits the filmmakers to cast the Sixties as a time of nearly apocalyptic urgency—an interpretation of the era that feels entirely plausible when one weds Dylan's biblical imagery to Hendrix's forceful playing. Moreover, in using the song's opening lyrics to frame the initial meeting between Buckner and Walker, the film hints that a desire to transcend constraints will be central to its narrative. At this early juncture in the film, such sentiments would seem to apply to the incarcerated Walker, but as the movie progresses, they better illuminate Buckner's predicament.

The film continues to link Walker to Sixties music as he and Buckner travel to "On the Road Again" (1968) by Canned Heat, "All Down the Line" (1971) by the Rolling Stones, and "Last of the Steam-Powered Trains" (1968) by the Kinks. Here, however, the soundtrack takes a backseat to the script as the film contrasts its two leads and the eras they personify. An Enduring Idealist, Walker is quick to defend the movement and its accomplishments, while lambasting Reagan's America as a land awash in greed, inequality, empty consumerism, and sexual repression. On the other hand, Buckner defends Reagan, while mocking Walker as a dimly remembered relic. Buckner also assails the memory of the Sixties, which he characterizes as an irresponsible era when activists dishonored the flag and assisted America's enemies abroad while true patriots, including Buckner's father, fought and died in Vietnam.

Soon after these exchanges, Walker convinces Buckner that he spiked his mineral water with LSD. To counteract the nonexistent acid, Buckner imbibes copious amounts of alcohol. Once plastered, Buckner unleashes a spirited, albeit off-key and garbled, version of "White Rabbit" (1967), Jefferson Airplane's ode to acid and Lewis Carroll.[32] While functioning as comic commentary on Buckner's situation, the FBI agent's drunken rendition of "White Rabbit" also foreshadows his trajectory. It speaks to the resurfacing of repressed memories and identities.

The tension between Buckner's constructed self and his actual background grows more pronounced when Buckner brings Walker to "Rainbow Zen," an all-but abandoned commune. The ensuing sequence forces both characters to examine their relationship to the Sixties: Buckner will have to confront his inheritance, while Walker rethinks his legacy.

Maggie, the commune's last denizen, helps initiate these reflections. She upbraids Walker for referring to his "creative railroading" as his defining moment. His pride wounded, Walker laments: "That's the one thing I'm remembered for." Maggie scolds him for trivializing his legacy. His words mattered, not an "immature stunt." "You set our minds on fire," Maggie reassures him. "You made us understand that if we really cared individually each of us could make a difference, but collectively we could change the world."[33] Maggie's speech defends the legacy of the Sixties in general and the memory of Abbie Hoffman, a clear inspiration for Huey Walker, in particular. Maggie argues that Sixties activism should not be remembered for its sometimes juvenile excesses, but rather for its willingness to speak truth to power, quest for personal authenticity, and fight against social injustice.

If Maggie tries to set the historical record straight, she also tries to reach the wayward Buckner. The filmmakers use "Comin' Back to Me," a song cut from *Surrealistic Pillow* (1967), Jefferson Airplane's breakthrough album, to comment on this process. The song first plays as Buckner and Walker enter the commune, gently accompanying Buckner as he unveils his true backstory: he grew up on this commune. As he matured, he became increasingly embarrassed by his parents and their lifestyle. He rebelled, ran away, changed his name, and forged a new identity replete with the middle-class upbringing he coveted.[34]

At this point, Maggie enters the conversation, outing Buckner as "Free," in yet another of the script's allusions to Hoffman (he used this pseudonym for his 1968 manifesto *Revolution for the Hell of It*). With her appearance, Marty Balin's wistful ballad recedes. Agitated and defensive, Buckner bitterly recalls the taunting he endured as a hippie kid in a straight world.

Maggie responds to Buckner's intransigence by striking a bargain: she will reveal the whereabouts of the commune's only phone if he watches footage of the commune in 1967. Once Buckner agrees, the audience glimpses Free's childhood. Against an understated, meditative instrumental, we see him playing with his mother and Maggie; we see the commune celebrating his fourth birthday; we see him strumming a guitar with his dad; we see them imitating Chuck Berry's iconic "duck walk." At this point, the filmmakers underscore the sequence's meaning by shifting back into "Comin' Back to Me." As the home movies continue, Balin sings: "I saw you; I saw you, comin' back to me."[35]

The filmmakers use "Comin' Back to Me" to speak of returns, reckonings, and reawakenings. Its haunting melody adds emotional heft to the entire sequence. Its lyrics reference Free's past and Buckner's present. The line "I realize I've been here before" alludes to Buckner's homecoming, while "Whatever happened to wishes, wished on a star" comments on the birthday party (Maggie and Huey alike talk of "wishes" as they watch the footage). Moreover, the song's very title highlights the film's reclamation project. It asks contemporary youth, the children of the children of the Sixties, for whom Buckner is a surrogate, to reexamine their inheritance. In so doing, it offered a counterpoint to another, more popular cultural text from Reagan's America, *Family Ties* (1982–1989), which, like *Flashback*, centered on a young man who rebelled against his countercultural parents by embracing conservatism.[36] Unlike Alex P. Keaton, Buckner re-evaluates his beliefs: "comin' back" to his parents and their values.

Unlike *Flashback* or *Rude Awakening*, *Pump Up the Volume* does not revolve largely or almost entirely around former Sixties activists.[37] Instead, it focuses on an important topic addressed in the other two films: the relationship of the Sixties to contemporary youth. A pirate radio show hosted by "Hard Harry," the alias of Mark Hunter (Christian Slater), lies at the center of *Pump Up the Volume*. As Mark's popularity grows among teens disenchanted with school, suburbia, and American life, parents become increasingly alarmed. Fear also grips the tyrannical administration of Mark's school. Even the FCC gets involved after tapes of Harry's show begin circulating in other states (Figure 11.2). In his final broadcast, Harry abandons the harmonizer that disguises his voice and challenges his audience: "It's not over. It's just beginning. The rest is up to you. Speak up. Steal air. It belongs to you. Take charge. Try anything. Say fuck and shit a million times. You decide. It's up to you." The film concludes on a hopeful note as pirate broadcasters sign on across the nation. The last line urges listeners to "turn on the truth."[38]

While *Pump Up the Volume* centers on the young, Mark's parents, both former activists, are also critical to the film's narrative. Mark terms Brian (Scott Paulin) and Marla (Mimi Kennedy) "sell-outs." Marla fears he's right. Projecting her anxiety upon Brian, she scolds him: "When you were a young radical, you did not care about power and money. You opposed the system and now you're part of it."[39] The film buttresses her words by lingering upon a Grateful Dead poster in his office, a

FIGURE 11.2 During a pivotal juncture of *Pump Up the Volume*, with the press, local police, and feds turning up the heat, Mark Hunter (Christian Slater) ruminates on what course he should chart. As he begins walking through the construction of another cookie-cutter suburb—the very embodiment of the bland, conformist, security-obsessed, spiritually impoverished culture against which he rails—the soundtrack plays "Wave of Mutilation" by the Pixies. In the song's opening line, which coincides with the image above, Black Francis sings "cease to resist." If Hunter contemplates that injunction, he and his listeners ultimately choose to "Stand!"

shot that echoes Don Henley's "The Boys of Summer" (1984) and its famous lament about "a Dead Head sticker on a Cadillac."[40]

Once a free spirit, now older and with a touch of grey, Brian works as a school superintendent for a system obsessed with standardized tests. However, as Mark and his classmates recognize, this qualitative approach dehumanizes and alienates learners, while giving administrators an incentive to expel underperforming students. Brian's redemption comes when he taps into the spirit of resistance infusing his son's school and starts questioning the administration. Eventually, after a teacher—also emboldened by Harry—filches incriminating documents, Brian dismisses the school's domineering principal.

The trajectory charted by *Pump Up the Volume*—insurgent youth redeem fallen activist—echoes another Sixties Postscript, *True Believer* (1989). Compared to that film, however, *Pump Up the Volume* offers a far more nuanced portrait of the relationship between youth and the Sixties. As Mark's Hard Harry alter ego muses: "Parents always talk about the 1960s and how cool it was. Where did it get them?" After a sardonic chorus of the Youngbloods' "Get Together," Mark announces, "I hate the Sixties, schools, and principals," before unleashing "Weiner

Schnitzel" (1981), an eleven-second assault on fast-food culture by the Descendents, an American punk band.[41] Interestingly, Nirvana would echo Hard Harry on its landmark album *Nevermind* (1991). Urged to sing something as the band recorded "Territorial Pissings," Krist Novoselic opted to mock "corny hippie idealism" by snarling the chorus of "Get Together." Yet, as the bassist conceded, he actually liked the song; he even speculated that his ad lib might have been a half-conscious nod toward "lost ideals."[42]

Novoselic and the makers of *Pump Up the Volume* were not the only cultural producers from this time to exhibit a conflicted relationship to the Sixties. U2's Bono, although a little too mainstream for Hard Harry, lodged a similar complaint in "God Part II": "I don't believe in the '60s in the golden age of pop/You glorify the past when the future dries up."[43] Of course, Bono registers his complaint in a song dedicated to John Lennon that references "Instant Karma (We All Shine On)" (1970), denounces Albert Goldman, author of an unflattering biography of Lennon, and, as the song's title suggests, serves as a sequel to one of the most celebrated tracks from *John Lennon/Plastic Ono Band* (1970). And if these allusions are insufficient to document the band's fascination with the Sixties, "God Part II" appears on an album that features a splice of Jimi Hendrix's "The Star-Spangled Banner," a cover of Dylan's "All Along the Watchtower" (in the style of Hendrix's more famous cover version), and a remake of "Helter Skelter" replete with Bono boasting: "This is a song Charles Manson stole from The Beatles. We're stealing it back."[44]

In short, U2, like Mark, is both alienated from and attracted to the Sixties. Each is annoyed by the self-importance of boomers yet also drawn to the era's spirit, ideas, and energy. More so than Bono, however, Mark seems embittered by what he perceives as the failure of the Sixties. It is no accident that he opens his broadcasts with Leonard Cohen's mournful elegy "Everybody Knows" and its bleak inscription for the post-Sixties world: "Everybody knows the war is over/Everybody knows the good guys lost."

But what's to be done? After sending teen bodies into a frenzy with a blistering cover of "Kick Out the Jams," a listener confronts Hard Harry with that very question, challenging him to go beyond laments. Hard Harry has no answer. The question continues to vex him as he walks through a suburban development being erected to "Wave of Mutilation" by the Pixies.[45] (See Figure 11.2.) With the homogenized America that he detests sprawling forth unimpeded, Mark might surrender to despair and, in the words of Black Francis, "cease to resist."

Mark neither gives into despair nor the mounting attacks on his show. The film seems to attribute Mark's resolve to his knowledge of Sixties-era icons and rhetoric. In one scene he borrows a Lenny Bruce book from the school library. Nora Diniro (Samantha Mathis) works the circulation desk. Although she is Hard Harry's most avid listener, she has never heard of the groundbreaking comedian.[46] This short sequence suggests two things. First, the traces of Bruce, Hoffman, Mario Savio, and Tom Hayden evident in Hard Harry's broadcasts were products of emulation, not happenstance. Second, Mark's knowledge of past cultural insurgencies enables him to express his generation's alienation. Another, perhaps even more revealing illustration of this theme occurs when Mark announces: "Society is mutating so rapidly that anyone over the age of twenty really has no idea."[47] Here he references an iconic quotation from the Sixties but updates it, giving it an angrier, more desperate tone than the original, which was playful and ironic.

This particular move—revisiting while revising the Sixties—challenges the young to become more creative, more spontaneous, more politically engaged, and more critical of the status quo. Mark endorses these goals in his final broadcast. He beseeches the "'Why bother?' generation" to awaken from their apathy: "It's time. It begins with us. Not with the politicians, or the experts, or the teachers, but with us." Soon after, the credits roll as the Liquid Jesus cover of Sly and the Family Stone's "Stand!" plays—a move that allows writer, director, and boomer Allan Moyle one last chance to implore young people not to look back longingly or dismissively on the Sixties but to instead create a new cultural insurgency that might improve upon and even eclipse its earlier model.[48]

Conclusion

With Reaganism seemingly on the ropes in the late 1980s, films such as *Running on Empty*, *Rude Awakening*, *Flashback*, and *Pump Up the Volume* sought to mobilize an imagined past to promote political action and social change. They not only critiqued the Reagan-Bush era, they communicated the need for such a critique. They not only forged spaces for imagining alternatives, they insisted that alternatives existed. In so doing, they asserted that the status quo was indeterminate, not immutable—a conceptual shift that creates opportunities to model practices that break from prevailing norms.

In advancing these various cultural projects, these films frequently tapped into the immense cultural capital vested in the music of the Sixties. Sometimes filmmakers employed music to amplify divergences between characters, as in *Running on Empty* and *Rude Awakening*. Other times filmmakers used music to underscore a character's reconnection with the spirit of the Sixties. Such a move informed one of the most critical scenes in *True Believer*. In it, Eddie Dodd (James Woods)—once a crusading leftist, now a jaded burnout—spends an evening ruminating how he might yet reconnect with his better, truer self. To ensure that audiences linked

Dodd's brooding with the Sixties, the filmmakers scored the sequence to Hendrix's "All Along the Watchtower."[49] *Rude Awakening* went a step further. In it, the image of John Lennon inspired Fred to speak truth to power in a kind of boomer variation on the iconography of earlier films, such as *Gabriel Over the White House* (1933), *Mr. Smith Goes to Washington* (1939), or *Wilson* (1944), which used Abraham Lincoln, another martyred icon, to prod the protagonists into action.

Of course, such moves can be problematic. They assume rather than demonstrate a relationship between the social movements of the Sixties and that era's music. A relationship between the two exists, but it is more subtle than the films often allow. Moreover, at their worst, these films can reduce the Sixties, culturally and politically, into kitsch, with *Flashback*'s "hippie shrine" perhaps the most egregious offender.[50] They can also lapse into uncritical celebrity worship, as does *Rude Awakening* when it deifies Lennon despite the fact that the iconoclastic singer mocked such benedictions in one of his finest songs, "God."[51]

The Sixties Postscripts of the late 1980s and early 1990s both exhibit these flaws and transcend them. Perhaps no film better illustrates this paradox than *Married to It* (1991). One of its protagonists, John Morden (Beau Bridges), an Enduring Idealist, speaks to his son's class about the 1960s in an important scene. He grows agitated, however, when the teacher insists that he should limit his remarks to music and clothes. Channeling Abbie Hoffman, who once asserted that if music alone became the message, the message was lost, John announces that he wants to provide the class with the truth, "not a watered-down version of revisionist history."[52] He foregrounds the importance of politics, noting that his generation rose up in opposition to an immoral war being waged by a psychopath who killed and maimed hundreds of thousands of people to affirm his masculinity. Ironically, the film does not heed John's advice; instead, it ends with kids costumed as hippies singing Joni Mitchell's "The Circle Game" (1970) in a school pageant—a conclusion even more cloying than it sounds.[53]

If *Married to It* concludes on a poor note, John's pointed rejoinder insists that very real ideas, grievances, and commitments propelled the social movements of the Sixties. It also posits a critique of mass media (which makes the film's conclusion even more baffling). Hard Harry issued his own critique by eviscerating "Get Together." His caustic rebuke targets not just the song and the hubris of boomers, but also the media's tendency to equate the Sixties with the "Summer of Love," which, even in benign accounts, gets encoded as fun and colorful but ultimately silly and inconsequential. *Flashback*, meanwhile, mocks two boomers for reducing the Sixties to commodity as they rock out to Steppenwolf's "Born to Be Wild" (1968) and brag about owning *Easy Rider* (1969).[54] In a bit of intertextual commentary, the mockery comes from Huey Walker, a character played by Dennis Hopper, famous for his role in *Easy Rider*.

At the same time, *Flashback* uses Walker to caution against reducing the social movements of the Sixties to the sometimes clever, sometimes goofy media stunts of the Yippies, which brings us to the real significance of the Sixties Postscripts. Realizing how contested the legacy of the Sixties is, realizing that the issue at stake is not just what happened then, but what should happen now, these films enjoined the very public, pitched battle over the meaning of the Sixties. In so doing, they sought to preserve a certain vision of what the Sixties represented. Over and over, these films cast activists in a sympathetic light, touting their commitment, idealism, and principles, while dramatizing the harassment they faced and the costs they often bore. Just as critically, they interpreted the Sixties not as a bygone historical era, but as something living, a spirit, a dream, a metaphor, a vision, that can continue to inspire.

NOTES

1. *The Big Chill*, DVD, directed by Lawrence Kasdan (1983; Culver City, CA: Sony Pictures Home Entertainment, 1999), 55:06–56:31.

2. The film was 1983's thirteenth highest grosser. "*The Big Chill*," Box Office Mojo, accessed April 12, 2009, http://www.boxofficemojo.com/movies/?id=bigchill.htm.

3. "America's Greatest Music in the Movies," American Film Institute, accessed May 17, 2014, http://afi.com/100years/songs.asp.

4. *The Big Chill*, 29:01–29:11.

5. *The Big Chill: A Reunion*, directed by Laurent Bouzereau (Columbia/TriStar Home Video, 1998).

6. Tony Williams, "Narrative Patterns and Mythic Trajectories in Mid-1980s Vietnam Movies," in *From Hanoi to Hollywood: The Vietnam War in American Film*, ed. Linda Dittmar and Gene Michaud (New Brunswick, NJ: Rutgers University Press, 1990), 115.

7. James Miller, *Democracy in the Streets: From Port Huron to the Siege of Chicago* (New York: Simon and Schuster, 1987), 17.

8. Rebecca E. Klatch, *A Generation Divided: The New Left, the New Right* (Berkeley: University of California Press, 1999), 328; Edward P. Morgan, "Who Controls the Past?: Propaganda and the Demonised Sixties," *Irish Association for American Studies* 5 (December 1996): 48.

9. Wini Breines, *Community and Organization in the New Left, 1962–1966* (Brunswick, NJ: Rutgers University Press, 1989), xii, 151; Lauren Kessler, *After All These Years: Sixties Ideals in a Different World* (New York: Thunder Mouth's Press, 1990), xi–xii; Jack Whalen and Richard Flacks, *Beyond the Barricades: The Sixties Generation Grows Up* (Philadelphia: Temple University Press, 1990), 273.

10. For the political decline of Reaganism, see Philip Jenkins, *Decade of Nightmares: The End of the Sixties and the Making of Eighties America* (New York: Oxford University Press, 2006), 273; Gil Troy, *Morning in America: How Ronald Reagan Invented the 1980s* (Princeton: Princeton University Press, 2005), 233–264; Robert M. Collins, *Transforming America: Politics and Culture in the Reagan Years* (New York: Columbia University Press, 2007), 82–87, 93–100, 227–234; John Ehrman, *The Eighties: America in the Age of Reagan*

(New Haven, CT: Yale University Press, 2005), 128–149. For growing interest in the Sixties, see Daniel Marcus, *Happy Days and Wonder Years: The Fifties and the Sixties in Contemporary Cultural Politics* (New Brunswick, NJ: Rutgers University Press, 2004), 128–135.

11. *Rolling Stone* named *Return of the Secaucus 7* one of the ten best movies of the 1980s; the film was also enshrined by the National Film Registry in 1997. Peter Travers, "Movies of the Eighties," *Rolling Stone*, December 14 and 28, 1989, 23. In 1996, Entertainment Weekly ranked *River's Edge* among the 100 greatest dramas ever. *The Entertainment Weekly Guide to the Greatest Movies Ever Made* (New York: Warner Books, 1996), 36.

12. *Running on Empty* made a little over 2.8 million dollars in limited release, ranking 147 for 1988. "*Running on Empty*," Box Office Mojo, accessed March 25, 2009, http://www.box-officemojo.com/movies/?id=runningonempty.htm. Roger Ebert named it one of the year's ten best movies. "*Siskel and Ebert* Top Ten Lists (1968–1998)," *The Inner Mind*, accessed March 26, 2009, http://www.innermind.com/misc/s_e_top.htm#SE1998. Pans came from Hal Hinson, "*Running*: Out of Gas," *Washington Post*, September 30, 1988, B7; and Desson Howe, "*Running on Empty*: Too Much Gas," *Washington Post*, September 30, 1988, WE37.

13. Terry H. Anderson, *The Movement and the Sixties: Protest in America from Greensboro to Wounded Knee* (New York: Oxford University Press, 1995), xvi; Van Gosse, *Rethinking The New Left: An Interpretative History* (New York: Palgrave: 2005), 2.

14. Anne Thompson, "Naomi Foner: Radical on the Write," *Film Comment* 24 (July/August 1988): 33, 39, 42–43.

15. Here the film alludes to the 1970 killing of Robert Fassnacht, a University of Wisconsin-Madison postdoctorate researcher, but Foner altered the victim's socioeconomic status and lessened the crime by maiming rather than killing the bombing's unintended victim. Tom Bates, *Rads: The 1970 Bombing of the Army Math Research Center at the University of Wisconsin and Its Aftermath* (New York: HarperCollins, 1992); *The War at Home*, directed by Glenn Sibler, New Front Films, 1979.

16. *Running on Empty*, DVD, directed by Sidney Lumet (1988; Burbank, CA: Warner Brothers Home Video, 1999), 37:11–38:20.

17. Newt Gingrich, *To Renew America* (New York: HarperCollins, 1995), 3, 7, 78, 113; Fred Barnes, "Revenge of the Squares," *New Republic*, March 13, 1995, 29.

18. *Running on Empty*, 1:34:13–1:41:11.

19. Ibid., 8:50–10:54.

20. Ibid., 1:52:36–1:53:21.

21. With no box office draws, poor reviews, and a modest advertising campaign, it is not surprising that the film opened poorly and disappeared quickly, netting only 3.1 million dollars during its theatrical run. "*Rude Awakening*," Box Office Mojo, accessed March 26, 2009, http://www.boxofficemojo.com/movies/?id=rudeawakening.htm. Reviewers savaged the film. See, for example, Jay Carr, "*Awakening*: Go Back to Sleep," *Boston Globe*, August 16, 1989, 79.

22. *Rude Awakening*, VHS, directed by David Greenwalt and Aaron Russo (1989; Santa Monica, CA: HBO Home Video, 1995), 1:34:16–1:35:43.

23. *Rude Awakening*, 1:36:54–1:39:34.

24. The Beatles, "Revolution," *Past Masters, Vol. 2*, Capitol Records CDP 7 90044 2, 1988.

25. *Rude Awakening*, 2:28–3:51.

26. Glenn C. Altschuler, *All Shook Up: How Rock 'n' Roll Changed America* (New York: Oxford University Press, 2003), 78–81, 113–116.

27. I am using music critic Robert Christgau's definition of "rock" as "all music derived from the energy and influence of the Beatles—and maybe Bob Dylan, and maybe you should stick pretensions in there someplace." Quoted in Theodore Gracyk, *Rhythm and Noise: An Aesthetics of Rock* (Durham, NC: Duke University Press, 1996), 9.

28. *Rude Awakening*, 21:13–23:02.

29. Hank Bordowitz, *Bad Moon Rising: The Unofficial History of Creedence Clearwater Revival* (New York: Schirmer Books, 1998), 87–88.

30. At its widest release, *Flashback* played in 875 theatres, earning 6.4 million, making it the 113th highest grossing film of 1990. "*Flashback*," Box Office Mojo, accessed March 27, 2009, http://www.boxofficemojo.com/movies/?id=flashback.htm. *The New York Times* recommended the film, albeit with reservations. Vincent Canby, "Liberal Old vs. Conservative Young in *Flashback*," *New York Times*, February 2, 1990, 13C. Other critics panned it. See, for example, Peter Goddard, "*Flashback*'s Faulty Recall of '60s Shows Hopper in Revisionist Light," *Toronto Star*, February 2, 1990, E6.

31. *Flashback*, DVD, directed by Franco Amurri (1990; Hollywood, CA: Paramount Pictures, 2002), 4:19–4:55.

32. Ibid., 24:12–24:25.

33. Ibid., 1:05:11–1:06:25.

34. Ibid., 1:01:04–1:02:51.

35. Ibid., 1:14:01–1:15:14.

36. One of the most popular programs of the 1980s, *Family Ties* made Michael J. Fox a star. The show's popularity peaked between 1985 and 1987, after which its ratings fell in half, indicating, as elsewhere, that the icons of Reaganism, such as Alex P. Keaton, lost traction as the decade neared its end. Tim Brooks and Earle Marsh, *The Complete Directory to Prime Time Network and Cable TV Shows, 1946–Present*, 7th ed. (New York: Ballantine Books, 1999), 332, 1229–1231, 1254–1255.

37. *Pump Up the Volume* earned 11.5 million dollars or 92nd place for 1990. "*Pump Up the Volume*," Box Office Mojo, accessed May 2, 2009, http://www.boxofficemojo.com/movies/?id=pumpupthevolume.htm. Critics praised the film, and its reputation grew in the next few years. In 1991, Gene Siskel designated the film a "buried treasure" on a *Siskel and Ebert* tribute to "sleepers." *Entertainment Weekly* later ranked it as the 100th greatest drama ever. *Greatest Movies*, 39.

38. *Pump Up the Volume*, DVD, directed by Allan Moyle (1990; Los Angeles: New Line Home Videos, 1999), 1:32:52–1:37:11.

39. Ibid., 11:20.

40. Ibid., 12:36. See Don Henley, "The Boys of Summer," *Building the Perfect Beast*, Geffen 24026, 1984.

41. *Pump Up the Volume*, 17:28–18:22.

42. Michael Azerrad, *Come As You Are: The Story of Nirvana* (New York: Doubleday, 1993), 175.

43. U2, "God Part II," *Rattle and Hum*, Island 91003–2, 1988.

44. U2, "Helter Skelter," *Rattle and Hum*, Island 91003–2, 1988.

45. *Pump Up the Volume*, 51:58–52:51.

46. Ibid., 16:31.

47. Ibid., 21:04.

48. Ibid., 1:32:52–1:37:11.

49. *True Believer*, DVD, directed by Joseph Ruben (1989; Culver City, CA: Sony Pictures Home Entertainment, 2001), 19:17–20:16.

50. *Flashback*, 1:07:18–1:08:25.

51. John Lennon, "God," *John Lennon/Plastic Ono Band*, Apple 3372, 1970.

52. *Married to It*, DVD, directed by Arthur Hiller (1991; Beverly Hills, CA: MGM, 2003), 58:30–1:01:07; Jack Hoffman and Daniel Simon, *Run Run Run: The Lives of Abbie Hoffman* (New York: Jeremy P. Tarcher, 1994), 123.

53. *Married to It*, 1:43:43–1:47:51.

54. *Flashback*, 34:47–36:40.

12 Late-Adolescence in the American Sixties

"The Twist" and the Twentysomethings in AMC's
Mad Men *(2007–)*

SAMANTHA LONDON

Mad Men as Cultural Microscope

WHEN THE AMC series *Mad Men* debuted in 2007, it was lavished with praise for its authenticity—daring, shocking, and to many of its critics and viewers, exquisitely accurate. This period piece, created by Matthew Weiner, is set in New York City and portrays upper-middle class American life at the start of the 1960s. At its core the series is an anthropological study. Weiner excavates the most trying social issues from this tumultuous time—civil rights, gender roles, and sexual liberation—and renders them as real issues in the lives of his complex, conflicted characters.

The show's protagonist, Don Draper (Jon Hamm), best embodies the difficulties born of this revolutionary time. Don is the hinge joining the two worlds of *Mad Men*: suburban home life and cosmopolitan office life. In the show's first two seasons, the domestic environment represents the "old" Fifties, while the corporate setting depicts the "new" Sixties. The viewer learns a great deal about Don's private life, seeing him regularly at home in Ossining, New York. Here in suburbia, Don is, apparently, surrounded by perfection: his lawn is manicured, his children are charming, and his wife, Betty (January Jones), is beautiful and staunchly proper. This life on the home front paints the American Fifties, in all its surface-level perfection, with broad strokes.

The viewer has also seen Don outside of the home, and his activities in the murkier world of Manhattan shatter the façade of his suburban oasis. Don, a self-made ad man, works at Sterling Cooper, a fictitious Madison Avenue advertising agency. Due to his prodigious creative talent he is among the firm's highest-ranking employees; he reports only to the agency's partners and their ever-evolving roster of clients. Don's gift for advertising is rivaled only by his penchant for philandering. His eyes wander far and often, and his affairs flow with little moral reckoning. Though brooding and still unfulfilled, the "Sterling Cooper" Don is free, relishing the liberations sweeping through the Sixties. He is, however, still tied to Fifties rigidity through his life in Ossining. He is stuck straddling these two eras, conflicted and anxiety-ridden.

Matthew Weiner has dedicated much of *Mad Men*'s seven seasons to the changing tides between the Fifties and Sixties. He has paid special attention to that era's emerging block of twentysomethings, the generation that helmed these social and cultural shifts. Sterling Cooper overflows with these young adults who enjoy an extended adolescent period in Manhattan, where they have affairs, try out new ideologies and principles, and resist adulthood. What Don does under shrouded secrecy at dark-lit restaurants and in remote apartments, this younger generation often does in broad daylight.

These characters do not forge new paths easily, however, a dynamic Weiner especially captures in the show's first two seasons. In this chapter, I will examine two early scenes from *Mad Men* to untangle the complexities of this generation and their revolutions. These moments, one from "The Hobo Code" (season 1, episode 8),[1] the other from "For Those Who Think Young" (season 2, episode 1),[2] use versions of "The Twist" underneath activities of *Mad Men*'s twentysomethings. Through devices both explicit and implicit, these scenes distill the *Zeitgeist* of this generation and encapsulate the enormity of the adolescent wave sweeping through the 1960s that helped shape our understanding of the Sixties.

The Milieu of the Sixties and Its Pivotal Adolescents

The Sixties in America have come to epitomize social liberation. History often recalls the freedoms that ruled the cultural pulse of the 1960s, a pulse that beats even more loudly when compared to the preceding decade. Though radical, this shift, in hindsight, seems inevitable: one extreme was balanced by its antithesis. In 1977 Morris Dickstein reflected on this change from the vantage of his recent memory. He observed, "The tremors of the [S]ixties . . . were generated from society's own deep core, from all the problems neglected in the [F]ifties that could no longer be wished away."[3] The "moralism"[4] ruling the Fifties, he asserted, failed to create a healthy culture, so it was only natural that society would try a new direction.

From the Fifties to the Sixties, many social conventions were inverted. While the Fifties prized domesticity, the Sixties brought about "the death of the family," initiating such lifestyles as open marriage and communes.[5] Outside of the home, hallucinogens, "urban restlessness, and street violence" were ubiquitous. In further contrast to Fifties pragmatism, the Sixties promoted a democracy so idealized that it approached utopianism.[6]

Of all the manners in which the Sixties sought to correct the Fifties, perhaps the most reverberant was its attitude toward sexuality. Succeeding the deep sexual repression that came before, the emancipation of sex in the 1960s changed the cultural landscape immediately and indelibly. Dickstein reflected on the breadth of this shift: "Nowhere have our public values—and perhaps even our private conduct—changed more noticeably than here."[7] In both thought and practice, sexual emancipation generated wide-reaching effects.

Looking at the shift from an earlier vantage point, the theologian Harvey Cox wrote in 1965 that the traditional notions of "Girl" and "Boy" as basic gender models had been supplanted by sexualized "Miss America" and "Playboy" figures.[8] He deemed the newfound American sexuality incongruous with traditional Christian values[9] and ultimately posited that this attitude was a façade and that real sexual liberation had not truly arrived. Nevertheless, the very act of a theologian undertaking such a study demonstrates the breadth of this movement: it stretched to the most remote corners of American moralism.

The dominant force behind this sexual liberation movement—and the myriad others that blew through the 1960s—was the rise of adolescents. In this decade, adolescents not only gained a louder collective voice, but they began to dwell in this phase for a longer period, navigating the chasm between childhood and adulthood with unprecedented leisure. John Goodwin and Henrietta O'Connor understand adolescence as the time of "three interrelated transitions[:] from school to work, from family of origin to family of destination[,] and from childhood home to independent living."[10] As many of *Mad Men*'s younger characters illustrate, members of this burgeoning generation continued to sift through the ramifications of these transitions well into their twenties, distracted as they celebrated newfound liberties.

These particular twentysomethings also had time to develop a collective voice as they extended the period of their adolescence. As I will discuss, they embraced rock 'n' roll as one of their dominant voices. Rock 'n' roll not only told the world what and how this generation felt; as they consumed it, adolescents demonstrated their newfound fiscal power. Unlike members of preceding generations, the adolescents of the 1960s had stored a disposable income. Roy Shuker says this change resulted from the improved economy of the 1960s and, more significantly, from the rising average age of an adolescent.[11] Consequently, these late-adolescents could make a real impact when banding together, using their pooled resources to advance their liberalized agendas. Kennedy's 1960 presidential race is considered an early example of this burgeoning power,[12] as is the much broader "juvenocratization" of America's college campuses.[13] With more money and time spent in adolescence, this young generation of Americans wielded unprecedented power to affect change.

These twentysomethings are especially compelling because they married adolescence—a period of universal discomfort and transition—with the new forces taking shape in 1960s America. *Mad Men*, understandably drawn to this complex shift, generates a (retrospective) case study of its late-adolescents. The earlier of the two scenes that I will discuss, the one from "The Hobo Code," uses Chubby Checker's 1960 hit, "The Twist," as a diegetic background to these twentysomethings' interactions at an after-work bar.[14] In this scene, the soundtrack and the story unpeel layers of this generation's *Zeitgeist.* Weiner echoes this commentary later in the opening sequence of season 2, where he uses Chubby Checker's "Let's Twist Again" (1961) as the soundtrack to his characters' morning routines. He aurally grounds the new season in a specific time while also coloring the freshness of the characters' new days.[15]

"The Twist" and Early Rock 'n' Roll

Born in the late 1950s, "The Twist" was first a song (performed in its initial genesis by its composer Hank Ballard), then a chart-topping hit (popularized by Chubby Checker's 1960 cover), and finally a dance style that thrilled adolescents and spawned dozens of imitations.[16] The craze that Checker's version sparked became one of the first youth-defining sensations of rock 'n' roll's young life. So successful was "The Twist" that Checker recorded the commercially successful companion in 1961, aptly titled "Let's Twist Again." Another famous cousin of the original was "Twist and Shout," best remembered in renditions by both the Beatles and the Isley Brothers in 1962.

Rock 'n' roll, bold and youthful, was born in the 1950s. It foreshadowed many characteristics that would define the rebellion of many late-adolescents in the 1960s. In particular, it showed an early manifestation of the country's forthcoming fight for racial equality. The musical style was an outgrowth of the African American rhythm and blues tradition. In its infancy, however, the genre was also influenced by the white musical traditions of rockabilly and such 1930s balladeers as Cole Porter and George Gershwin.[17] It integrated America's variegated musical fibers before America was ready to come together socially.

Reflecting the colorblindness of its music, the fans of rock 'n' roll demonstrated strikingly progressive attitudes toward race relations. The earliest rock 'n' roll songs are remembered for "[capturing] the imagination of a whole generation of young teenagers, both black and white."[18] Rock 'n' roll did not confine itself to one color of audience, and through this music, the races began to co-mingle.

Women's liberation, another imminent social change, began to make its mark on the rock 'n' roll industry. As Arnold Shaw notes, this music's primary record buyers were young women. Therefore, from an economic perspective, women's roles were growing: as consumers, they were determining the majority of the record-buying demand, hence dictating the shape of the genre.[19]

The bond between rock 'n' roll and its liberal-leaning audience again emerges in the music's approach to teenagers. Whether using "teen" as a war cry or simply to tell its audience's story in hits such as Johnny Cash's "Ballad of a Teenage Queen," rock 'n' roll was unmistakably catering to the concerns of its adolescent consumers.[20] Bonded under this music, the teenagers of the 1950s found a collective voice that they would capitalize upon as they grew into the twentysomethings of the 1960s.

Whether as teens or twentysomethings, social awareness dominated members of this generation, and rock 'n' roll captured their passion. Arnold Shaw, writing of early rock 'n' roll lyrics, remarks, "Humorous songs were rare. The teenage song cosmos seemed weighted down with problems."[21] In hindsight, it is logical that this weighted-down, oppressed generation was poised to erupt in the 1960s. That early rock 'n' roll songs capture this boiling sentiment demonstrates the music's fascinating interplay with its consumers.

David R. Shumway explores this art–society relationship, proposing that, in rock 'n' roll, this bond is uniquely inseparable. Unlike other musical styles, this form has no widely accepted definition.[22] It does not have a true text:[23] there is no score; songs change identity in different artists' hands; and even recordings do not suffice, because the music is so heavily informed by the live-concert experience. Rock 'n' roll is as much affected by its audience as it is by its performers, resulting in a frustratingly elusive subject.[24] Shumway asserts, "Rock & roll is an impure musical form; it is not even mainly a musical form,"[25] which leads him to re-conceptualize this style as something else entirely, a "historically specific cultural practice."[26] This entanglement between music and culture enables one to use rock 'n' roll as a text when examining the Fifties and Sixties. Because it was so informed by its audience, it is an artifact of this particular demographic from this unique time.

The Convergence of Rock 'n' Roll, Late-Adolescence, and the Spirit of the Sixties in *Mad Men's* Twist Scenes

Weiner elegantly weaves the complex themes of Sixties late-adolescents throughout *Mad Men*. He returns to them regularly (the emergence of rock 'n' roll, the extension of adolescence, and the shift of cultural tides), reminding his viewer that the angst and enthusiasm of these twentysomethings have been constantly simmering in the background. Sometimes, as in the Twist scene in "The Hobo Code," their emotions come to the foreground and dominate the drama. Other times, as in the Twist sequence that opens season 2, their generational identity lies implicitly in the background, as gesture and soundtrack paint Weiner's social landscape. However, in both cases the use of the twist gracefully points the viewer to the struggles of this generation, simultaneously enriching the characters' stories and Weiner's larger, sociocultural reflection.

Both versions of the "Twist" are able to ground their respective scenes in a specific time, but Weiner calls on different techniques in incorporating them: he uses music diegetically in the earlier scene ("The Hobo Code") and nondiegetically in the later ("For Those Who Think Young"). The earlier, diegetic treatment of "The Twist" bears a different set of implications than does the later, nondiegetic use of "Let's Twist Again." In the former, the song highlights the many cultural shifts at play for the viewers. They can see the song selected on a jukebox and thus can discern who chose the song. Because the song plays diegetically, they can observe characters' reactions to the song itself. In short, viewers can peek into the year 1960 and watch the twentysomethings respond to this music within a milieu of their own creation. In the latter scene, viewers can react to the twist reference with nostalgia, remembering both bygone years (1961) and seasons (*Mad Men*'s season 1). Through more subtle suggestion, the nondiegetic music fortifies these themes of Sixties adolescence within the series.

Inside the Drama

"The Twist" in "The Hobo Code"

While the Twist scene in "The Hobo Code" does not even last two minutes, it captures the generation's revolutionary currents. The scene is set at P. J. Harvey's, a Manhattan bar, and shows Sterling Cooper's younger employees socializing at the end of a workday. The scene's first visual is a close shot of a woman's hand dropping a coin into the jukebox (31:16). Upon hearing the hit single begin, the girls at the bar shriek, jump, and clap their hands (31:19). Pairs of men and women promptly begin to dance the twist. After depicting their unalloyed joy, the scene transitions into story development (31:38).[27] Two of its principal twentysomethings, Peggy (Elisabeth Moss) and Peter (Vincent Kartheiser), wordlessly debate whether or not they should twist together. This moment is laden with significance: their interaction comes at the end of a critical day for their relationship, and the use of

"The Twist" advances the audience's understanding of them as individuals and as a couple.

Throughout season 1, Peggy and Peter are attracted to each other and to their generation's freedom-loving agenda. Their similarities, however, are often eclipsed by their differences. Peggy grew up in Brooklyn and was raised in a conservative, working-class, Catholic family. As she now forges her independence in Manhattan, her relationship with her family has turned tense. She wants to escape the oppressive moralism of her upbringing and desires personal validation through success in the workplace. There, she is at a gender disadvantage as a female, a hardship compounded by her training at Miss Deaver's Secretarial School rather than at a university. Thus, at Sterling Cooper, she fits in neither with her fellow secretaries, who are using the agency as a matchmaking service, nor with her career-oriented male peers.

Nevertheless, Peggy fights through these barriers with the same spirit she channels when giving up her baby for adoption or asking her doctor for birth control pills.[28] Despite being an outsider at Sterling Cooper in many respects—working-class, Brooklynite, female—Peggy is not afraid to assert herself as a forward-thinking woman, exemplary of the Sixties' women's liberation movement. Over large story arcs, Weiner lets her embody this movement's upward trajectory, but he is careful never to romanticize the process. It is only with good fortune, great tenacity, and abundant missteps that Peggy moves in the general direction of a "modern" career woman.

Although disadvantaged in many regards, Peggy is lucky to enter the world of Sterling Cooper free from familial expectations. In contrast, Peter Campbell is rich and white, very much an "insider," perhaps, too much an insider; his family's hopes and pressures burden him heavily. He hails from well-established Manhattan Protestants, a group that expects its offspring to continue propagating its wealth and good name. Advertising, the viewer gleans, is not a suitable field for a young man of such breeding. Thus, while Peggy has nothing to lose as she forges her way on Madison Avenue, Pete struggles constantly to stay afloat of the expectations of his upbringing. Moreover, Pete's marriage compounds his pressures. While the single Peggy is free to pursue ambitions for her personal edification, to be a "late-adolescent," Pete must already be an "adult" and provide for his wife.[29]

Despite their biographical differences, Peggy and Pete both subscribe to the new freedoms embraced by their generation. Peggy refuses to let her gender relegate her to secretarial roles forever; Pete refuses to let his upper-crust family dictate his path. Fundamentally compatible, they have an instant attraction, which they consummate at the end of the pilot episode. An almost-married Pete goes from his bachelor party to Peggy's apartment, and that night, to neither party's knowledge, they conceive a child. Their relationship, however, turns platonic by the next episode. Pete respects his union to wife Trudy (Alison Brie)—that is, until he and Peggy have the tryst that opens "The Hobo Code."

The Twist scene from that episode shows this relationship reaching a fever as both characters appear poised to consummate their attraction. Peggy, increasingly confident, is ready to embrace her sexual emancipation. As she looks seductively at Pete, it is clear that she wants to further the affair. Pete, however, seems increasingly stuck. He remains dour and glued to the wall while his recent lover dances the twist and embraces the emerging *Zeitgeist*. Married and laden with expectation, he bitterly rejects Peggy and the twisting generation. Weiner's diegetic use of this song allows his characters to react to the auditory layer of the scene, thereby guiding the viewer to a deeper appreciation for Peggy and Pete's incompatibilities.

"Let's Twist Again" in "For Those Who Think Young"

Weiner introduces *Mad Men*'s second season with hope and optimism through Chubby Checker's lively "Let's Twist Again," which harkens back to the gleeful high of the scene at P. J. Harvey's. The song underpins Weiner's visual suggestions of vitality and potential: a sequence of mini-scenes showing his principals preparing for a new day. The first character on-screen is Joan (Christina Hendricks), the quintessence of Sixties sexual liberation. Although a very late late-adolescent—Joan is already in her thirties—she is a trailblazer for the generation of twentysomethings; she uses her sexuality as currency without shame. Yet because she has yet to reach her "family of destination,"[30] one should still consider her a member of this extended adolescence. In this opening scene, Joan dresses and primps, zipping up her red dress and confronting her figure in the mirror (0:37–0:41). We then transition to Peggy, who has grown increasingly confident in her womanhood: she looks at her reflection squarely in the eyes as she applies perfume (0:54–1:03). Next, Trudy adoringly helps Pete get ready. Unlike her contemporaries Joan and Peggy, Trudy looks not into a mirror but gazes at Pete. She is a relic of the Fifties and serves her husband's needs, not her own. Pete, an especially conflicted member of this generation, hardly acknowledges his wife as he slicks his own hair. It is only in the fading moment of this mini-scene that he gives her a smile, perhaps exhibiting some gratitude for his Fifties-style family life (1:04–1:14).[31]

The remaining thirty seconds of the scene anachronistically juxtapose this late-adolescent anthem with Don and Betty, characters too old to be twentysomethings. While playing behind their morning preparations, "Let's Twist Again" takes on a new function: it shows the audience how Don and Betty have responded to the previous season's cliffhanger. At the end of season 1, their status quo—Don's shrouded secrecy and Betty's forced bliss—collapsed when Betty discovered Don's deepest secret. The audience's questions are answered immediately in "For Those Who Think Young" as Weiner reintroduces them with mini-scenes depicting their repression and denial. Don has a new lock installed on his door (1:15–1:23), suggesting his return to guarded mystery. Betty is shown working on her equestrian form at a riding ring (1:24–1:42), devoting herself anew to a façade of rigid perfection. Accompanied by the lyrics, "Let's twist again, like we did *last year*," Weiner tells the viewer that, for Don and Betty, business in season 2 will proceed as usual.[32]

Beyond the Drama

Matthew Weiner's use of Chubby Checker's "The Twist" and "Let's Twist Again" in these two scenes exemplifies his effective storytelling by shedding light on the interior lives of *Mad Men*'s characters and by adding weighty, allegorical depth to the series. Divorced from *Mad Men*, these songs act as lightning rods for this tumultuous time. They epitomize early rock 'n' roll and sing like an anthem for this budding generation. In an instant, they summon the *Zeitgeist* of the late-adolescents of the 1960s. Weiner uses "The Twist" and "Let's Twist Again" to till the themes of his twentysomethings and their revolution.

Racial Equality

As discussed earlier, racial equality emerged as a new and defining concern for this generation. Racial integration also shone through the mechanisms of early rock 'n' roll. "The Twist" and its sequel songs were wildly popular in the early 1960s, beloved by black and white audiences alike. This common ground shows an initial step toward racial integration. Weiner uses the "Twist" songs as cultural artifacts; through the music, he conjures up this generation's racial tolerance and enlightenment.

Rock 'n' roll stemmed largely from the African American musical tradition of rhythm and blues (see preceding). "The Twist" propelled Chubby Checker into stardom. He was featured on the *Ed Sullivan Show* in 1961 and was among the first African Americans to become a household name recognized by both whites and blacks.[33] The mechanics of this song, in particular, are distinctly black. Its "fast, pounding, evenly stressed beat in 4/4 meter" mimics the rhythm of African dance, a divergence from the Latin style that drove 1950s rock.[34] Significantly, the song enjoyed mass popularity despite its origins. It unearthed a color-blind audience of twentysomethings, and it brought races together during the early stages of the civil rights movement. Weiner approaches this phenomenon boldly in the Twist scene of "The Hobo Code," and he alludes to it more obliquely during the "Let's Twist

Again" sequence of "For Those Who Think Young." In both instances, he recreates Sixties late-adolescents and their path toward racial equality.

In "The Hobo Code," "The Twist" finds an ecstatic audience at P. J. Harvey's, despite the apparent absence of black people in the bar. The roots of this "black" song do not even seem to register for these white, carefree late-adolescents as they fall easily into the dance inspired by the song (31:24).[35] Their lack of awareness shows a marked departure from their parents' polarized racial relations. With this diegetic treatment of "The Twist," Weiner catches white members of this generation in candid response to "black" material, and he shows racial barriers beginning to dissolve.

This sense of racial fluidity continues through the "Let's Twist Again" sequence that opens "For Those Who Think Young." Again, Weiner presents this "black" music as an accepted part of white life: here "Let's Twist Again" plays behind whites' private morning routines. Infused in the background of their quotidian preparations, the "blackness" of the song seems as innocuous as, for example, putting on cuff links. This racial intermingling peaks when Weiner uses the song to accompany a shot of Betty posting atop her trotting horse (1:26), a stereotypically Caucasian pastime.[36] With this musical-visual medley, Weiner captures the early blur of racial boundaries—and the early impact of progressive late-adolescents of the 1960s.[37]

Women's Liberation

Women were another group whose cause was championed by this generation. Throughout the series, *Mad Men*'s Peggy and Joan represent two archetypes of the era's trailblazing women. Unlike the women of preceding generations, they have ambitions that extend beyond domestic life. Peggy and Joan have very different goals—and even more different means of pursuing them—but nevertheless, they both embody the era's newfound female empowerment.

Gender relations are central to the world of Sterling Cooper, and, throughout the series, Weiner delves deeply into women's issues. The Twist scene in "The Hobo Code" adds a powerful layer to this exploration where Weiner takes great care to show that this selection was the work of a woman—a new woman, emblematic of the Sixties. The opening visuals—a woman's hand, her coin, the jukebox—convey growing economic independence and assertion of taste (31:16).[38] As discussed earlier, rock 'n' roll contained some seeds of the women's liberation movement; as enthusiastic and leading consumers of this musical style, they were determining its course by how they spent their money. The musical preference of this "everywoman" at P. J. Harvey's—captured diegetically—represents the growing voice of women, the merging of this generation's gender gap.

The nondiegetic nature of "Let's Twist Again" is less specific in its evocation of women's liberation. Nevertheless, the scene advances this theme through underlying implication. Combining images of Peggy and Joan dressing with the song (0:37–1:03), Weiner privileges these women's preparations: now they, like their male counterparts, are dressing up for a day at the workplace. Weiner furthers this parallel by letting an image of Peggy adjusting her bangs fade into the glimpse of Pete slicking his hair (1:03, 1:04–1:14).[39] Joan and Peggy, Weiner implies, have just as much need as Pete to ready themselves for a day at Sterling Cooper. The union of this popular song with images of female empowerment orients the viewer to this time, and it specifies to which generation these work-ready women belong.

Sexual Emancipation

A cousin of women's liberation, the need for sexual emancipation also drove this generation of twentysomethings. Against the backdrop of the Fifties, this rebellion was especially glaring. Perhaps because of its shock value, or because it excluded no minority, this plight became particularly emblematic of the generation. As discussed above, these late-adolescents found an ally in their quest for sexual emancipation in rock 'n' roll music. Thanks largely to Elvis Presley's bodily gyrations and graphic insinuations, rock 'n' roll was considered boldly sexual in the 1950s and 1960s.[40] "The Twist," a song contemporaneous with Presley's career, delivered the sexuality from singer to the audience; it launched a dance craze considered so lewd that it was initially banned from dance halls.[41]

Used diegetically in "The Hobo Code," "The Twist" allows Weiner to portray these late-adolescents embracing their new, lascivious dance style. Following a very polite cha-cha (29:55–31:09), Chubby Checker's "The Twist" jolts the crowd to life when its first chords incite hip swiveling across the dance floor. Mirroring the switch from the Fifties to the Sixties, the cha-cha was cautious and polite, while the twist is sensual and fluid.

Peggy embodies this liberated spirit as she transforms in this Twist scene into an utter seductress. Once the song begins, she sees Pete sitting gloomily against the wall. Bold, she locks eyes with him and twists ever so slowly to his side, wordlessly inviting him to dance (31:38–32:06; Figure 12.1) When she finally reaches him and says, "Dance with me," her words seem superfluous—and an understatement (32:06). This one sequence covers almost 30 seconds of narrative time during which everything other than Peggy's shocking transformation fades away. Although Pete rejects her seduction (31:12), Peggy's sexual liberation continues. Upon dismissal, she composes herself, hints at a smile (32:26), and finds another dance partner (32:33).

FIGURE 12.1   Peggy (Elizabeth Moss) dances the twist for Peter (Vincent Kartheiser).

Although she wipes tears away (32:40–32:54), she forges ahead, an emancipated woman free to seduce someone new.[42] This transformation is remarkable for a girl who grew up under the Catholic moral code. But Peggy, like her late-adolescent peers, has been sexually freed. Standing for her generation of women in this scene, Peggy capitalizes on the shifting cultural tide.

Conversely, Pete reacts differently to "The Twist." While the song plays, Pete refuses to take part in the suggestive dancing, glowering from his seat against the wall. Although he hardly eschews sexual immorality—despite being a newlywed, he had slept with Peggy that morning—he rejects Peggy in this scene: "I don't like you like this" (32:12).[43] Perhaps the character regrets his actions earlier that day, or perhaps he, unlike the presiding spirit of his generation, is still not comfortable with public displays of sexuality. Alternately, perhaps Pete, already a married "adult,"[44] must distance himself from the extended adolescence that Peggy is embracing. Or possibly this opposing attitude reflects their divergent backgrounds. Peggy can afford to embrace Sixties radicalism because she is moving upwards and away from her working-class, Brooklyn childhood. In contrast, the wealthy Pete has much to lose if he strays too far from the status quo of the Fifties. Weiner adds depth to this theme by depicting Pete's resistance. Although his attitude was eclipsed by the presiding spirit of his generation, it captures the complexities of the issue during its evolutionary stages.

The issue of sexual emancipation surges into season 2 where the opening sequence of "For Those Who Think Young" juxtaposes Chubby Checker's "Let's Twist Again" against suggestive images of Joan. The first shot of the episode zooms in on Joan's lower back, following her hand up as she zips the deep zipper of a very red, very fitted dress. She smoothes her neckline and adjusts her breasts (0:43–0:46).[45] Joan is the epitome of these late-adolescents' sexual emancipation; she has learned the weight of her sexual currency, and, evidently, she realizes the value of strengthening it before going into the workplace.

The scene's next shots are of Peggy applying perfume to her neck and wrists. While Joan's preparations seem routine, Peggy gives deliberate attention to hers. She is still a novice to open sexuality, and a meaningful moment of eye contact with herself in the mirror reveals the special care she continues to take (1:02–1:03).[46] With this fleeting glance, she acknowledges the significance of what she is doing: she is breaking from preceding generations' approach to sexuality. She does not apply perfume to find a husband; rather, like Joan, she is using her sexuality to advance herself in the workplace. As a liberated woman, Peggy has professional goals, and as a sexually emancipated twentysomething, she has a new tool to achieve them.

Sexuality is present only discreetly in this opening sequence, but Weiner amplifies its voice through his use of "Let's Twist Again." This song, with its many sexual implications, reminds the audience of strong currents that were sweeping through this generation and stretching beyond dance halls and bars; they had infiltrated the private lives and the subconscious of these late-adolescents. Joan and Peggy show this movement's deep roots as they proceed through their preparations in a manner that is mostly mundane. By 1961, it seems, sexual emancipation had made such great strides that it could already be ignored.

This loss of pomp is also reflected in Weiner's treatment of the musical material. In "The Hobo Code," the diegetic presentation of "The Twist" causes an enormous spectacle. It launches a scene that is brimming with fun and enthusiasm, and with tension and drama. In contrast, the nondiegetic use of "Let's Twist Again" in "For Those Who Think Young" allows the sexual energy of the music to live only in the background. The characters are now oblivious to the music that is humming along. This later treatment of the material does not lessen the significance of the music or sexual emancipation; rather, it captures how the movement had thoroughly and permanently changed the generation.

Mad Men's greatest asset is its artful approach to a fastidiously well-researched history. Matthew Weiner's Sixties tapestry is rich with realism, and he employs an array of devices to transport his audience into it. The diegetic-versus-nondiegetic treatment of "The Twist" is but one example of his clever portals to the past. Moment after moment, scene after scene, he carries the viewer into and beyond the world of *Mad Men*; he brings alive the real time in history when "The Twist" was, simply, the rage.

NOTES

1. Matthew Weiner, "The Hobo Code," *Mad Men* (season 1), DVD, directed by Phil Abraham (Santa Monica, CA: Lions Gate Television, 2007), 31:15–33:00.

2. Matthew Weiner, "For Those Who Think Young," *Mad Men* (season 2), DVD, directed by Tim Hunter (Santa Monica, CA: Lions Gate Television, 2007), 0:37–1:42.

3. Morris Dickstein, *Gates of Eden: American Culture in the Sixties* (New York: Basic Books, 1977), 69.

4. Ibid., 51.

5. Ibid., 82.

6. Ibid., 80, 82.

7. Ibid., 82.

8. Harvey Cox, "Sex and Secularization," *The Secular City* (New York: Macmillan, 1965), reprinted in *The Sense of the 60's*, ed. Edward Quinn and Paul J. Dolan (New York: The Free Press, 1968), 150.

9. Ibid., 154, 160.

10. John Goodwin and Henrietta O'Connor, "Exploring Complex Transitions: Looking Back at the 'Golden Age' from School to Work," *Sociology* 39 (2005): 214.

11. Roy Shuker, *Understanding Popular Music*, 2nd ed. (New York: Routledge, 2001), 195.

12. Quinn and Dolan, 1.

13. Lewis S. Feuer, "The Risk Is Juvenocracy," *The New York Times Magazine*, September 18, 1966, 56–64, reprinted in Quinn and Dolan, 33.

14. Weiner, "The Hobo Code."

15. Weiner, "For Those Who Think Young."

16. "The Twist," in Grove Music Online, *Oxford Music Online*, last modified June 2, 2011, http://www.oxfordmusiconline.com.

17. Terence J. O'Grady, "A Rock Retrospective," *Music Educators Journal* 66, no. 4 (December 1979): 35–36.

18. Ibid., 41.

19. Arnold Shaw, *The Rock Revolution* (New York: Crowell-Collier Press, 1969), 45.

20. Ibid., 36.

21. Ibid., 37.

22. David R. Shumway, "Rock & Roll as a Cultural Practice," in *Present Tense: Rock & Roll and Culture*, ed. Anthony DeCurtis (Durham, NC: Duke University Press, 1992), 117.

23. Ibid., 118.

24. Ibid., 120.

25. Ibid., 123.

26. Ibid., 119.

27. Weiner, "The Hobo Code."

28. J. M. Tyree, "No Fun: Debunking the 1960s in *Mad Men* and *A Serious Man*," *Film Quarterly* 63, no. 4 (Summer 2010): 35.

29. Goodwin and O'Connor, 214.

30. Ibid.

31. Weiner, "For Those Who Think Young." For an alternative assessment of period detail, gender, and sexuality in *Mad Men*, see Mabel Rosenheck, "Swing Skirts and Swinging

Singles: *Mad Men*, Fashion, and Cultural Memory," in *Mad Men, Mad World: Sex, Politics, Style & the 1960s*, ed. Lauren M. E. Goodlad, Lilya Kaganovsky, and Robert A. Rushing (Durham, NC: Duke University Press, 2013), 161–162, 171–179.

32. Weiner, "For Those Who Think Young." Italics added by the author for emphasis.

33. "The Twist," Grove Music Online.

34. Ibid.

35. Weiner, "The Hobo Code."

36. Weiner, "For Those Who Think Young."

37. For an alternative reading of *Mad Men*'s approach to race, see Kent Ono, "*Mad Men*'s Postracial Figuration of a Racial Past," in Goodlad, Kaganovsky, and Rushing, 300–301, 305, 315.

38. Weiner, "The Hobo Code."

39. Weiner, "For Those Who Think Young."

40. Shumway, 126.

41. "The Twist," Grove Music Online.

42. Weiner, "The Hobo Code."

43. Ibid.

44. Goodwin and O'Connor, 214.

45. Weiner, "For Those Who Think Young."

46. Ibid.

13 Musically Recreating the Fifties in *Far From Heaven* (2002)

MARIANA WHITMER

> But if you're going to have music in a film at all, you have to understand that it's going to change the film, by pointing things up, supporting things, toning things down. It's going to *do* something. And therefore, the director really has to be ready to make it part of the process.
>
> —Elmer Bernstein[1]

TODD HAYNES'S *Far From Heaven* (2002) is not simply a re-make of *All That Heaven Allows* (1955), one of several significant melodramas directed by Douglas Sirk, but the result of inspiration from other sources as well. As James Morrison notes, "The film draws on a large fund of references . . . for its evocation of the era, from the stories of John Cheever or books like *The Man in the Gray Flannel Suit* (1955) or *The Organization Man* (1956), to other movies of the time like Max Ophus's *The Reckless Moment* (1949) . . . and the film version of *Peyton Place* (1957)."[2] With *All That Heaven Allows* as his primary model, however, Haynes intensifies the social commentary of the original by expanding its take on issues of class to include race and sexuality. While the earlier film deals with the romance between a widow and her gardener—the social *faux pas* being that he is her employee and thus socially beneath her—Haynes's re-creation adds complexity to the problematic relationship between a married woman, Cathy Whitaker (Julianne Moore), and her gardener, Raymond Deagen (Dennis Haysbert), by making the latter a Negro (to use the

239

identifier from the film). Complicating this situation is the revelation that Cathy's husband Frank (Dennis Quaid) is a homosexual who unsuccessfully attempts to treat this perceived aberration as a mental illness.

More than the title's retention of the word "heaven" recalls Sirk's 1955 film. Haynes consciously mimics Sirk's original wardrobe and set design, dialogue, and cinematography. Even the acting, which is tighter and almost forced in a repressed manner, is shaped from the perspective of looking back at the Fifties. Moreover, as Sharon Willis describes, "This film's credits and opening sequence feel almost 'traced,' as if superimposing its frame onto that of *All That Heaven Allows*."[3] The visual similarities belie the distinctions that quickly become apparent, however, as Haynes continues with a more multifaceted and nuanced presentation. Sirk introduces us to the social conflict almost immediately, as Cary Scott (Jane Wyman) meets Ron Kirby (Rock Hudson) at the beginning of the film, and keeps the conflict out in the open. Haynes initially keeps the problems hidden behind a portrayal of the seemingly idyllic life led by the Whitakers and their friends and only gradually lets the viewer discover the underlying conflicts.

In creating the narrative realities that form his films, Haynes demonstrates a special sensitivity for the entire soundscape, including the musical score and other sounds extraneous to the dialogue. For example, the minimal musical score in *Safe* (1995) forces ambient sounds to the foreground, supplemented by occasional synthesized washes of sound lacking distinctive musical elements. The resulting soundscape is a tense and surrealistic backdrop that forces us to share in the growing anxiety of affluent homemaker/wife Carol White (Julianne Moore) as she faces her unknown chemical sensitivities.

Haynes recognizes that melodrama, such as *Far From Heaven*, requires music to be an important part of the film's sonic landscape. So to complete his evocation of the Fifties with an appropriate musical accompaniment, Haynes asked Elmer Bernstein to compose the score, noting, "His career reaches back to encompass Hollywood filmmaking at its best."[4] Bernstein, in turn, was thrilled to be able to compose what he described as "the kind of score you don't hear any more."[5] *Far From Heaven* was Bernstein's last film score, allowing him to contribute belatedly and obliquely to the melodramatic repertoire of the 1950s. A digression into Bernstein's background before an examination of the score will enhance our understanding of this important aspect of Haynes's film.

Bernstein as Fifties Composer

The 1950s began as a rewarding time for Bernstein, which he remembered fondly in later interviews. He arrived in Hollywood in the fall of 1951 when the major studios still dominated and a supportive, close-knit environment existed where composers were appreciated. "The way that studios were organized, they gave you tremendous support because everything was there. Your orchestrators, your copyists, and your orchestra—they were all there."[6] Things were changing, however, due to aging studio heads, the introduction of television, and the Red Scare, which threatened the status quo. Bernstein recalled that Hitler was still on everyone's mind, and it was easy to generate fear. "One of the things that happened to everybody, on every level, was fear. It was a fascinating phenomenon, looking back at it now." The studio heads were the most vulnerable, concerned as they were with public perception of their films, especially sensitive since the days of the 1920s Production Code. "They were afraid that these Un-American Activities people would convince them (the public) that Hollywood had a communist hue."[7]

Although Bernstein generally distanced himself from political activities, he found himself unknowingly caught up in them. "Just the idea that you might be somebody left of centre was enough to get you blacklisted,"[8] he recalled, and his sympathy for "left-wing causes"[9] made him somewhat of a target. Because it was unclear whether or not Bernstein was a card-carrying member of the Communist Party, he was "graylisted," a nuanced distinction from being "blacklisted."[10] As Bernstein noted, "I didn't realize I was being listed at all. But I suddenly realized that I wasn't working."[11] When the studios did hire him, he was assigned documentaries and marginal films, like *Cat-Women of the Moon* (1953), *Robot Monster* (1953), and *It's a Dog's Life* (1955), which afforded him the opportunity to develop his chameleon-like talent for composing music for all kinds of films.

Bernstein was working for Cecil B. DeMille on *The Ten Commandments* (1956) when it became known he was listed.[12] DeMille asked Bernstein directly if he was a Communist; Bernstein recalled that he could not stand "on his constitutional rights" and refuse to answer, so he replied "No." After DeMille lectured Bernstein, warning him to be careful, he made a phone call to someone in Washington. Bernstein later admitted that without DeMille's intervention things could have been much harder for him.[13]

During an interruption in the production of *The Ten Commandments*, Otto Preminger asked Bernstein to score *The Man with the Golden Arm* (1955). With these two major scores completed, Bernstein's career was back on track. However, the experience of scoring the non-mainstream films during this period had an impact: Bernstein never again allowed himself to be boxed into one specific style of film, moving easily from jazz scores to drama and from Westerns to comedy.

Bernstein was not familiar with the films of Sirk or Haynes, nor had he previously scored any melodramas or "weepies," as he referred to them. Instead, he identified his work from the 1950s as being "on the other cutting edge" working with jazz film scores, particularly *The Man with the Golden Arm* and *Sweet Smell of Success* (1957).[14] Thus, Bernstein came to Haynes's project without knowledge of its conception but easily settled in and composed music that was similarly a throwback.

Having experienced the 1950s and its political and social undercurrents, Bernstein's score for *Far From Heaven* re-channels his impressions of the decade, just as Haynes reworks aspects of Sirk's film. While a younger composer might not appreciate the repressed mood and hidden social ills, Bernstein could relate to the themes Haynes addresses in the film. Bernstein's music complements Haynes's adaptation of the melodrama in his composition and development of musical materials by drawing on his personal recollection of the period, as well as the mannerisms of his earlier scores.

Moreover, Haynes's cinematic techniques and his complex reconstruction of Sirk's film inspired Bernstein to enhance the traditional approach to melodramatic accompaniment, adding subtleties not considered in scores from the era. For example, Haynes created a deliberate and careful color palette for *Far From Heaven* that enhances the narrative through the use of contrasts, primarily between cool ("moonlight blues") and warm (autumnal) colors.[15] Markedly standing out against these color combinations are the red and green color schemes of the gay bar and Eagen's Restaurant. The green tint, which Haynes describes as conveying something "forbidden,"[16] is also discernible at the police station at the beginning of the film and at the movie theater, particularly as we look up the steps to the men's lounge where assignations take place. As Scott Higgins aptly points out, "the cool/warm and red/green pairings take on strongly expressive roles" and assist viewers in understanding the social code of each scene's location.[17]

Bernstein's score complements this color scheme: lush melodies accompany the warm tones, while ominous music, characterized by chromatic melodic lines and lower registrations, is heard in those scenes with cool (particularly blue) colors. Meanwhile, the red/green of the bars (and those locations connected with "forbidden" activity) suggest contemporaneous jazz idioms. Further, the gradual revelation of the film's social problems is echoed in the development of melodic material. Bernstein alters the themes as the drama unfolds, making them unsettling through the addition of dissonances or altered rhythms. The music thus parallels the narrative's growing tensions as the social conflicts are revealed.

While we hear musical echoes of *The Man with the Golden Arm* in *Far From Heaven*, it was Bernstein's favorite film score, *To Kill a Mockingbird* (1962), that guided his hand while collaborating with Haynes. Comparable to *Far From Heaven* in its consideration of issues of class and race, Bernstein's Oscar-nominated score for *Mockingbird* is sensitively crafted and orchestrated, primarily with the intention of maintaining the children's viewpoint.[18] Although *Far From Heaven* deals with adult themes, Bernstein calls upon similarly simplistic melodic construction, transparent orchestration, and generally consonant harmonies. In both films he fashions the musical cues to underscore the significant points in the films, enhancing the drama by expressing the emotional core of the scene, insinuating atmosphere, enhancing sub-textual connections, and developing tension, particularly during scenes with action.

The most obvious evocation of the Fifties is the orchestration of Bernstein's score, which recalls *Mockingbird* in several ways. In a departure from the (almost) exclusive string sound of the 1940s, the instruments are combined in small groups, most often arranged as a solo melodic line with accompaniment. The woodwinds most often express this transparent texture with little brass, and the strings are relegated to the background, lending an air of intimacy to the drama. When tutti strings do appear, it becomes a dramatic statement recalling the lush romanticism of classic Hollywood films. The best example of this is the party scene, which Haynes describes as "one of the beautiful girly and swirly moments of the film . . . [as] the music rises and we crane in."[19]

Tutti strings also reiterate the simplistic, naive melodic lines that comprise the instances of happy or perky music that accompany Cathy and Frank as they go about their routine lives, differentiated further by the upbeat tempo, major tonality, and regular phrasing. Cathy's cheery music is heard at the film's beginning as she pulls into the driveway, the following morning as she sees the children off to school, and again as she is seen entering the art exhibit. Frank's melody is heard each time we see him walking into his office, although the second time it is subdued, occurring after his meeting with the psychiatrist.

As in *Mockingbird*, Bernstein juxtaposes the high and low instrumental registers with stunning effects. For example, in an emotionally charged scene, Frank admits to Cathy that he has fallen in love (1:23:11).[20] As Frank begins to cry, the low strings play a halting and trembling accompaniment figure that contrasts with the solo oboe in a high register.[21] With this approach to orchestration, Bernstein recreates his scores from the post-classic period in Hollywood when smaller and distinctive sounding assortments of instruments, as well as jazz combinations, became prevalent.

Bernstein's use of piano also recalls his music for *Mockingbird*, especially as it infuses the drama with an atmosphere of intimacy and domesticity. The piano's popularity in the nineteenth century as a parlor instrument and its prominent role in home performances evokes the familial, a focal point of the narrative in *Far From Heaven*. In both films the main title theme begins with solo piano, a quiet, intimate presentation that subtly draws us into the drama. In *Mockingbird*, a child's humming interrupts the theme, though the piano is used throughout the film to recall the children's simplistic innocence. In *Far From Heaven*, however, the theme follows a more cohesive trajectory during the main title as it is repeated in the strings and grows in intensity, culminating in a stylized romantic statement that is more consistent with the film's adult nature.

Bernstein's Melodramatic Score

Bernstein's score features three significant musical ideas, each connected to an emotional situation, specifically those circumstances that triangulate throughout the film. The two main themes, notably associated with Cathy, represent the sexual and racial conflicts. The first, "Autumn in Connecticut,"[22] appears during the main title and symbolizes the ostensibly idyllic life led by the Whitakers. The second is a theme associated with the emerging relationship between Cathy and her gardener, Raymond. The third melody correlates with Frank's homosexuality. The lack of clear tonal center, dissonant intervals, and disjunct motion that characterize Frank's music underline the confusion he is experiencing, as well as the turmoil it creates in his family's life. The three melodies complement one another, yet they are different in ways that underscore the film's various emotional currents. By recalling these thematic elements in a subtle and sensitive fashion throughout the soundtrack, Bernstein links different scenes and the relationships that are presented therein while providing a cohesive feel to the film.

The main title theme, which I will refer to simply as "Autumn" (Example 13.1),[23] is reminiscent of the long, languid melodies of 1950s melodrama. While the initial statement is heard in the solo piano (with a chime), Bernstein develops the melodic material and expands the instrumentation with each repetition. The climactic statement is heard in the strings with a timpani roll and cymbal crash reminiscent of the melodramatic scores of the 1940s (such as *Rebecca*). Although tonally organized in C-sharp minor, the harmony is unsettled by the subdominant accompaniment and the emphasis on the dominant (G-sharp) in the first phrase of the melody. The absence of the leading tone (B-sharp) makes the harmonic motion even more uncertain, and it isn't until the end of the theme that the tonality is affirmed with a cadence on the tonic. The vague harmonic motion hints at the sadness that lies just below the surface in this perfect family we are about to meet.

"Autumn" is heard most often in scenes that depict the Whitakers' perfect life, primarily involving Cathy as the successful wife and mother. We hear this theme during the main title sequence, which accompanies Cathy bringing her daughter

EXAMPLE 13.1 Elmer Bernstein, *Far From Heaven*, "Autumn in Connecticut." (Transcribed by M. Whitmer.)

home from ballet class. One notices the theme again in its entirety as Cathy goes to Frank's office to take him his dinner and again at the important office party at the Whitakers' home. If Haynes's film had been titled "The Surface of Things" (one of several alternatives considered), this theme would represent the "surface," signifying heteronormativity, conformity, and a middle-class life.[24] However, by its recapitulation at the film's closing, the ugliness below the surface has been revealed, and the theme now epitomizes Cathy's loneliness.

In addition to these complete statements of the theme, Bernstein recalls this melody either as a fragment or in an altered form at dramatically important points in the narrative. For example, parts of "Autumn" bookend Cathy's ill-fated visit to Frank's office, and while the initial presentation is upbeat (23:32), the version that accompanies her return home is truncated and more subdued (25:27). It ends with a fragment of the contrasting phrase (Example 13.1, m. 12) played by a solo cello. The music stops at this point to allow the stammered conversation between Frank and Cathy to dominate the soundtrack (except for the crickets in the background). This melody in the solo cello continues briefly, however, after the argument outside the psychiatrist's office (32:30), and the theme is partially restated by a solo oboe. The melancholy tone of this particular instance reflects the futility of the visit to the psychiatrist and the inevitable disintegration of their perfect life. "Autumn" is heard again in the scene where Cathy tells Raymond she cannot be friends with him, this time in a fragmented, rhythmically altered version, insistently reminding us of her obligation to her marriage and her family (1:10:21; Example 13.2).

Their perfect world, and the melody, is disrupted again as Frank confesses to his new relationship (1:24:18). A fragment of "Autumn" is heard in yet a different version, this time with strikingly different accompaniment and a "wrong" note (the C-sharp), as Frank reveals how he has tried for the sake of the family to maintain appearances (Example 13.3). While the sour note underscores the flaws in their perfect world,[25] a descending arpeggio in the celli, heard just before Frank reiterates, "I can't, I can't," symbolizes the final disintegration of their perfect life.

A more contemplative version of the theme is heard as Cathy wanders around her darkened living room, gazing at the branch of witch hazel Raymond gave her (1:28:16; Example 13.4). Notably, the accompaniment in this statement is based on a motive from Frank's theme, an ascending fifth followed by a minor second (Example 13.8, m. 1; and Example 13.9, mm. 4–5). At this point her relationship

EXAMPLE 13.2 Elmer Bernstein, *Far From Heaven*, "Walk Away." (Transcribed by M. Whitmer.)

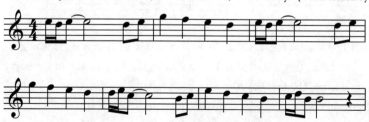

EXAMPLE 13.3 Elmer Bernstein, *Far From Heaven*, "Revelation." (Transcribed by M. Whitmer.)

EXAMPLE 13.4 Elmer Bernstein, *Far From Heaven*, "Remembrance." (Transcribed by M. Whitmer.)

with Frank is irreparable and the one with Raymond impossible, so the presence of Frank's motive underscores the sadness/loneliness she feels and hints at the impetus behind her altered life.

"Autumn" is heard twice more at the end of the film, effectively bringing the drama to a close in much the same way as it began, with Cathy driving around Hartford, although things have changed and it is now spring (note the blossoming tree branch) rather than autumn. The theme begins as Cathy, preparing to leave the house, pulls the lavender scarf out of her pocket (1:38:31). The scarf reminds us of her first lengthy conversation with Raymond, while the music transports us to an earlier time in her life before events irrevocably changed her world.

At the train station, the theme stops abruptly just after Cathy sees Raymond and approaches his train car (1:40:03). As Raymond and Cathy sadly gaze at one another, the emotional depth of their interaction is made even more intense by the complete lack of music. The whistle blows and as the train begins to move, low strings and winds enter with a pulsating motive (minor seconds) that seems to echo the train sounds. These are joined by a high solo trumpet, which projects the loneliness both have already begun to feel. The music then segues into "Autumn," and although it is the same as the main title, Bernstein titled the cue "Beginnings," alluding to the beginning of Cathy's new life. Unlike the main title, the last section of this cue is allowed to continue and conclude on a final cadence, but with another false note. In this instance Bernstein ends the ascending A-flat arpeggio on a held C/D and then resolves the D to E-flat.[26]

Bernstein contrasts the melancholy "Autumn" with the sensitive and sultry melody that accompanies the growing emotional intimacy of the relationship between Cathy and Raymond. This tune, in F major, is romantic and hopeful, not sad or foreboding like "Autumn." Their theme (Example 13.5), stated initially in the oboe and then strings, emerges for the first time as Cathy and Raymond spend an afternoon together in the country (53:43).

As Raymond and Cathy's friendship deepens and they share personal observations about life and race, their music changes slightly. When it turns to questions of race (Cathy says, "We all have our troubles . . . I kept wondering what it must be like to be the only [colored] one in the room"), we hear their theme in a transformed version, beginning in the low strings and continuing in the oboe. Once Raymond becomes less serious, we hear the original, optimistic version of the theme, but transposed down a minor third (56:39). It ends ominously, signaling trouble as the town gossip, Mona, sees Cathy and Raymond together. Bernstein emphasizes the cadential F-sharp in octaves and reiterates the last three notes of the theme (F-sharp–E–F-sharp) as a pivot to a rhythmically altered reference to "Autumn." While the emphasis on the descending/ascending major second alerts us to impending trouble for Cathy and Raymond, the fragmentary reference to "Autumn" suggests a collision of Cathy's two worlds.

We hear Cathy and Raymond's theme in its original form only once more, as Cathy drives past Raymond's store in a subsequent scene. Bernstein alters the subsequent presentations as it becomes evident that their relationship is impossible. For example, when Cathy tells Raymond they can no longer be friends, the theme plays twice, each time changing to reflect the scene's emotional content. As Raymond finishes the (poetic yet fake) quote, "Just beyond the fall from grace . . ." the theme begins in the flute and clarinet above strings (1:11:26). In this instance, the slower tempo deprives it of its positive hopefulness and it ends abruptly in mid-statement

EXAMPLE 13.5 Elmer Bernstein, *Far From Heaven*, Cathy and Raymond's Theme. (Transcribed by M. Whitmer.)

(Example 13.5, m.8). The cadence is slightly altered and comes to rest on G-sharp, anticipating a similar gesture in the theme's subsequent statement (Example 13.6), heard after the passersby have taken offense at Raymond holding Cathy's arm. This time we hear a melancholy, augmented variant of the theme, imbuing a sense of finality.

EXAMPLE 13.6 Elmer Bernstein, *Far From Heaven*, Variation of Cathy and Raymond's Theme. (Transcribed by M. Whitmer.)

Cathy and Raymond's theme is developed extensively in the cue that accompanies the emotional scene when Cathy goes to visit Raymond at his house. Due to an edit in the film, the audience does not hear the cue as Bernstein conceived it, starting at the point when Raymond discloses that he and his daughter are leaving town (1:31:10). Bernstein's original version, entitled "More Pain," begins with a strident statement of the theme's first five notes in the strings. The oboe plays the same melodic fragment twice, very slowly, and then just the first four notes are reiterated in the low strings.[27]

In the film the music begins as Cathy talks hopefully of visiting Raymond in Baltimore (1:31:53). At this point (42 seconds into the original cue) the flute plays the ascending A minor triad twice (Example 13.5, mm. 4–5) before the theme continues in a slightly varied form. After several measures of underscoring based on the original contrasting section (Example 13.5, m. 14), the theme is heard one more time (played by a solo oboe followed by strings and solo flute) as Raymond puts his hand on Cathy's shoulder (1:33:32). At the end of the theme, in lieu of a cadence, a transitional phrase (heard in the piano accompanied by a low cello) leads to the theme's final statement, which is altered melodically and rhythmically (Example 13.7) and heard as a transition to the scene where Cathy cries (1:34:19). The relationship is over and this is the last time we will hear this melodic material, as Bernstein implies with the vague and dwindling ending.

Bernstein sets "Autumn" and Cathy and Raymond's theme, both related to Cathy, diegetically as dance music, thereby enhancing his conception of the classic score in two ways—by making them jazzy and by keeping the themes within the diegesis. When Frank and Cathy are in Miami, a Latin dance band performs the main title theme, "Autumn in Connecticut." Bernstein recasts the melody with appropriate

EXAMPLE 13.7 Elmer Bernstein, *Far From Heaven*, Final variant of Cathy and Raymond's Theme. (Transcribed by M. Whitmer.)

rhythm and instrumentation, including Conga drums, guitar, and trumpet, reflecting the predominantly Cuban demographics of Miami in the late 1950s. In a much more romantic setting, a jazz band plays Cathy and Raymond's theme in Eagan's Bar as they dance. The cue begins with an introduction featuring brushed cymbal, guitar, and piano and continues with a seductive rendition of the theme on the saxophone. Referring to this diegetic presentation of this melody, Todd Haynes remarks, "All these wonderful old conventions . . . have been so completely disregarded over the years [but] we got to gleefully reappoint [them] for this movie."[28] These two cues remind us of Bernstein's talent for jazz composition (exemplified in his innovative score for *The Man With the Golden Arm*) and his appreciation for an idiom that flourished in the 1950s, thus strengthening his evocation of the era.

Haynes talks about the "hermetically sealed" approach to these "purely fictional realms" in melodrama where nothing outside the diegesis would have been allowed to intrude.[29] He points out that typically no one turns on a radio or TV to admit nondiegetic music or sounds. Although we do see a clip of Eisenhower one evening as Frank watches TV and we hear music from a jukebox when Cathy and Raymond enter Eagan's Bar, Bernstein's diegetic setting of the two main themes adheres to this approach. The bands perform music that is already an important part of the film's text, recalling similar settings in other classic Hollywood films. The example that comes easiest to mind is David Raksin's score for *Laura* (1944), where the main title theme is heard several times throughout the film in diegetic versions. In *On the Waterfront* (1954) Leonard Bernstein similarly presents themes performed by diegetic bands. Recycling the themes in different presentations allows the composer to maintain the film's closed environment and also blurs the lines between diegetic and nondiegetic, thus drawing the audience further into the drama.

Elmer Bernstein's talent for subtlety is exemplified especially well in the cues that underscore the scenes when Frank's homosexuality is revealed. While a defined melodic shape, with repetition and tonal outlines, characterizes the two previous themes, many of the thematic fragments associated with Frank's homosexuality consist of seconds (usually minor) in combination with more consonant intervals, like the fourth and fifth. Rather than lyrically constructed lines, Frank's music tends to be more disjunct. The audience is musically alerted to problems in Frank's life in two places before we are finally presented with the truth. The first is early in the film, when Cathy receives a phone call from the police department. As Cathy picks up the phone (5:31), we hear warning music consisting of ascending triplets and other melodic fragments in the flute. The ascending minor second connects these bits of music to each other and foreshadows the thematic material that will be associated with Frank later on.

This indeterminate and fragmented music continues throughout the scene as Cathy retrieves Frank from jail. The dissonant melodic motives and dark orchestration, featuring woodwinds, strings, and piano in their lower registers, will recur in other scenes associated with Frank's "problem" and thus provides viewers with extra information about Frank. As Haynes remarks, "Often in melodramas we [the audience] know more than the character knows."[30] In this way the music begins to reveal what is hiding "below the surface of things," an important theme of the narrative.

The second musical indication that something is wrong occurs when Frank enters his office. The music, which begins very upbeat and cheery as he walks through the lobby, changes dramatically as Frank shuts his office door (12:42). Even before he takes the flask out of his desk, the music tells us that his life is not as perfect as we may think. The perky music slows down and halts on a sustained low E in the bass, followed by a short melodic fragment that previews the melody that will be associated with Frank (Example 13.8).

EXAMPLE 13.8 Elmer Bernstein, *Far From Heaven*, Motivic foreshadowing of Frank's Theme. (Transcribed by M. Whitmer.)

As Frank talks to Cathy on the phone, the music reiterates a different fragment, but it similarly includes a leap (a fourth in this instance) followed by an ascending minor second (G–C–D-flat). The orchestration continues its dark tone, featuring a flute and clarinet still in the low registers. The similarities in all these melodic ideas assist the audience in making the aural connection between the mysterious incident at the police station and Frank's unease at the office. As Haynes describes Bernstein's music for Frank, "There is something sad at the root of it that calls you into his struggle."[31]

These melodic hints at problems with Frank's life come together in a new melodic line in the next scene, where we finally begin to understand what lies below the surface. This extended scene can be divided into three sections (as outlined in Table 13.1) with the focal point being Frank's visit to the movie theater, where we see a clip from *The Three Faces of Eve* (1957). The scene not only situates the film chronologically in the 1950s, but also suggests a sub-text through important connections, both narrative and musical, with *Far From Heaven*.[32] The clip we see is the first instance where Eve's other personality "comes out" (using the terminology from the film), paralleling Frank's behavior in *Far From Heaven*, as this is also his initial venture into the world of his other (homosexual) personality. In *The Three Faces of Eve* we experience three different personalities, each accompanied by a different style of music, as provided by Robert Emmett Dolan's varied but unimaginative score. In this instance it is the "bad" Eve (Eve Black) that emerges: hers is a promiscuous and immoral persona characterized throughout the film by a bluesy saxophone riff accompanied by guitar.

TABLE 13.1.
FAR FROM HEAVEN, DVD, CHAPTER 5

Part 1:		
8:44	Frank exits from steakhouse (dialogue).	Sustained chords; G–A-flat–F motive.
14:04	Frank walks away.	Frank's melody in clarinet.
Part 2:		
14:42	Frank approaches the Ritz Theater (shot of marquee).	G–A-flat–F motive.
14:50	Scene fades and changes to Cathy at home.	
15:27	Clip from *The Three Faces of Eve*.	Music from the film.
Part 3:		
15:51	Frank exits the theater and follows the two men.	Frank's melody (oboe/flutes). Incomplete.
16:18	Frank approaches the bar.	Repetitive motive in the piano.
16:52	Frank enters the bar and eventually sits down.	Jazzy flute, then piano.

In *Far From Heaven* Bernstein uses the narrative connection between Eve and Frank to suggest a musical connection as well. Like Eve's theme, Frank's also starts with a consonant ascending interval (a fifth instead of a fourth), followed by an ascending (rather than descending) second. Instead of the tenor saxophone associated with loose sexual mores in film scores, like *Three Faces of Eve*, Bernstein sets Frank's melodic material (Example 13.9) in the similarly timbred upper registers of the clarinet (accompanied by a syncopated string bass).

This melodic line, anticipated earlier (Example 13.8), is introduced in its entirety at the beginning of the scene, as Frank walks out of the steakhouse (13:41). Sustained chords introduce a motive in the high winds that develops as the scene progresses (G–A-flat–F). Despite his assertions and references to a past military career, Frank's manly demeanor falls away as he walks alone. The solo clarinet in the upper registers plays the melody (Example 13.9), one that conveys a sense of loneliness and becomes associated with Frank's homosexuality (14:06). The material retains the bluesy character of Dolan's score for *Eve*, with the frequent slides from one note to the next, in addition to the intervallic similarities (an ascending fourth and descending major second in Eve's melody versus an ascending fifth and ascending minor second in Frank's). The melodic line is connected to "Autumn" harmonically in its modal conception, which is also a minor scale without the raised seventh.

The second part of the scene begins when Frank turns the corner (literally and symbolically) and regards the movie theater. As he looks at the theater, we again hear the opening motive from this scene (G–A-flat–F; Example 13.9, m. 2) but in diminution, as though reproducing his accelerating heartbeat as he nears unchartered waters.

EXAMPLE 13.9 Elmer Bernstein, *Far From Heaven*, "Walking Through Town." (Transcribed by M. Whitmer.)

A cutaway to his home interrupts, reminding us of his "perfect family." Sustained chords and then solo flute accompany Cathy's scolding of their son, a motive that is linked intervallically to Eve Black in the score. It is also similar to that heard earlier during her interaction with the police department. This flute motive has emerged as a signal that all is not well and also anticipates the music that will accompany Cathy's discovery of Frank's homosexuality. The film transitions to the clip from *The Three Faces of Eve* followed by the liaison between the two men that piques Frank's interest.

The third part of the scene begins as Frank leaves the theater. We hear the same melodic line as in the first part, but in the oboe this time and with a different ending. The melody continues in the solo flute, changing as Frank decides to follow the two men. The theme transforms and rather than an ascending fifth followed by a descending minor second, Bernstein develops an ascending minor second and an ascending fifth (or fourth). Without a clear resolution, the music repeats, keeping us suspended. Frank shadows the men to the bar (note the canted camera angle at 16:38, reproduced in Figure 13.1), and the repetitive music, which circles around the minor second (in the piano) at this point, increases the tension.

As Frank enters the different (homosexual) world, moving from the cool blue of the street to the red/green tint of the bar, his hesitation at the door is punctuated by repeated dissonant intervals in the vibraphone that resolve as he walks in. We also experience a further thematic transformation to a syncopated, jazzy melody, featuring a solo flute accompanied by a plucked string bass, with the ascending fifth now followed by a descending minor second.

Once Frank is in the bar, we hear a solo piano as implied source music. The unexpected entrance of a very high clarinet, played dissonantly against the piano/bass

FIGURE 13.1 Frank (Dennis Quaid) shadows the men to the bar.

duet, however, suggests that although Frank is settling in, he is still uncomfortable. All of the musical material in this scene can be connected motivically to Frank's melodic line, specifically the intervals of the minor second and fifth. The instrumental, rhythmic, and melodic contrasts with the two previous themes clearly differentiate Frank (and his homosexual urges) from Cathy and Raymond.

We hear Frank's music in other instances where his emerging homosexuality is at the forefront. The most telling example is when Frank and Cathy are poolside in Miami, a scene where the sexual and racial tensions in the narrative converge. We know a romantic liaison is imminent when we hear the opening intervals of Frank's theme (as in Example 13.8; 1:16:53). Bernstein then culls references from the third part of the theater scene, as well as motives from an earlier scene in which Cathy discovers him in his office with another man (23:56). Bernstein helps the audience aurally make the connection with Frank's "problem" by placing these motives once again in the flute. Finally, there is a complete restatement of the music that accompanied Frank's initial entrance into the office (Example 13.8), heard after the argument about Raymond, as Cathy realizes there is another reason why Frank is home from work (1:07:44). Reusing this cue brings to the forefront Frank's position as a successful sales executive and the impact his sexual urges (ultimately the cause of all the upheaval in their relationship) are having on his job.

While much of Bernstein's score for *Far From Heaven* underscores the emotional aspects of the narrative, some of the cues are action driven, and the music changes considerably when there is physical movement. Specifically, these cues are heard during key climactic points in the narrative. The tension that builds during the course of the film as a result of both the sexual and racial discourse finds its release in two scenes that feature violent aggression. The pressure on Cathy and Frank's sex life finally results in a physical confrontation after the party, culminating with Frank hitting her (46:36). The cue that accompanies this scene refers to "Autumn" as the passionate driving force, specifically the harmonic palette.

The racial antagonism in the film climaxes in the scene when the three boys throw stones at Raymond's daughter (1:19:00). The spotlight on the children, as the future generation and inheritors of racist ideology, is accompanied by a repetitive, percussive motive in the low tessitura of the piano that quickens as it creates anticipation and tension. This cue, which reflects the climax of the racial tension, was foreshadowed earlier in the film by the percussive use of the piano heard when Sarah leaves the art show to go outside and play with the boys (40:34) and also when Raymond grabs Cathy's arm in front of the movie theater (1:11:53). While Bernstein builds tension in other cues throughout the film that accompany emotional scenes, it is these two instances of action-driven music that cause us to become more involved in the aggression inherent in these climaxes.

To conclude, a brief comparison with the score to Sirk's *All That Heaven Allows* is illuminating as it highlights Bernstein's enhanced perception of the film's text and all its subtleties. As with many 1950s melodramas, Frank Skinner's score for Sirk's film is shallow in comparison. Modeled after romantic music in the style of Chopin and Brahms (the former is directly referenced in some of the source music), Skinner's music serves merely as accompaniment and lacks the narrative commentary and depth of Bernstein's score.

Bernstein's statement, quoted at the beginning of this chapter, articulates how a successful score can be part of the film's text: not added as an afterthought, but intrinsic to the narrative realm. Understanding the social complexities and their nuanced presentation in *Far From Heaven*, Bernstein incorporated those aspects into his music, successfully supporting Haynes's re-creation of the Fifties in much the same way as the sets, the colors, and the script. Bernstein's music adds an aural dimension that completes the nostalgic experience. Evoking his earlier score for *Mockingbird*, Bernstein focuses on an orchestral palette created by small groups of instruments in interesting combinations and modernized by the occasional use of vibraphone and marimba. These transparent textures reflect the emotional content of the scenes with romantic or jazzy melodies that transport us into the realm of the narrative.

Todd Haynes has made relatively few films; most are primarily means for exploring individual and social issues or conflicts. *Far From Heaven* was not a box office hit, perhaps because it dealt with uncomfortable topics (homosexuality and racism). That Bernstein's score is often mentioned in popular and scholarly appraisals of this film speaks to its conception as a formidable musical work and its importance as an integral part of the filmic experience. To quote Todd Haynes one final time, "This film would not be what it is without the music of Elmer Bernstein."[33]

NOTES

1. Elmer Bernstein, as quoted in Fintan O'Toole, "Elmer Bernstein Finds Himself in Tune With Movies," *The New York Times*, October 28, 1990.

2. James Morrison, ed., *The Cinema of Todd Haynes: All That Heaven Allows* (London: Wallflower Press, 2007), 3. For additional textual analysis of the film, see Sharon Willis, "The Politics of Disappointment: Todd Haynes Rewrites Douglas Sirk," in *Camera Obscura* 18, no. 3 (2003): 131–175; and Lynne Joyrich, "Written on the Screen: Mediation and Immersion in *Far From Heaven*," in *Camera Obscura* 19, no. 3 (2004): 187–219.

3. Willis, 131.

4. Quoted in "The Making of *Far From Heaven*," Special Feature, *Far From Heaven*, DVD, directed by Todd Haynes (Universal City, CA: Universal Studios, 2003). This short feature includes interviews with Elmer Bernstein and Todd Haynes.

5. Ibid.

6. Cynthia Miller, Elmer Bernstein Interview, *The Guardian*, October 9, 2002, accessed September 2010, http://elmerbernstein.com/bio/interviews/guardian_1.html.

7. Richard C. Phalen, ed., *How We Have Changed: America Since 1950* (Gretna, LA: Pelican, 2003), 31–34.

8. Miller, interview.

9. Biography from the official website for Elmer Bernstein, accessed September 2010, http://elmerbernstein.com/bio/biography.html.

10. While many in Hollywood, including actors, directors, and writers, actually had their names physically placed on a list indicating that they were not to be hired, others (like Bernstein) were simply passed up when jobs became available. Bernstein was not specifically shunned by the studio heads, but he was not considered for the better scoring opportunities due to his leftist leanings. Bernstein was eventually brought before the House Committee on Un-American Activities in 1955, after the Senate had censured McCarthy but before the "scare" had diminished.

11. Phalen, 33.

12. DeMille, characterized by Bernstein as "well connected" and "a very controversial character" (Phalen, 33–34), was famously anti-Communist and actively involved in the formation of the Motion Picture Alliance for the Preservation of American Ideals in 1944. DeMille has been credited with salvaging the careers of blacklisted artists, including Bernstein, although technically Bernstein was only graylisted. Online biography, accessed December 2012, http://www.cecilbdemille.com/bio.html.

13. Phalen, 33–34.

14. Roger Friedman, "Knowing the Score: The Wiseman of Movie Music Composition, Elmer Bernstein, Celebrates 50 Years in Hollywood" (March 2003), accessed April 2010, http://www.elmerbernstein.com/bio/interviews/redcarpet.html.

15. Scott Higgins, "Orange and Blue, Desire and Loss: The Colour Score in *Far from Heaven*" in Morrison, *The Cinema of Todd Haynes*. Willis and Joyrich also make some interesting observations about the color palette.

16. Haynes actually states that he chose "that smoky, cool blue and that sort of puce green to convey something both mysterious and forbidden." It is unclear if he meant that the blue equates mysterious while the green means forbidden or if both colors together can be interpreted either way. Haynes, director's commentary, *Far From Heaven*, DVD.

17. Higgins, 104.

18. Bernstein talked about how he sought to maintain the children's perspective at a special performance of the score for *To Kill a Mockingbird* held in 2003. See Neda Raouf, "Bernstein, Actors from 1962 Film Regale Long Beach Crowd," *Long Beach Press Telegram*, February 27, 2003, accessed December 2012, http://www.elmerbernstein.com/news/mockingbird_lb.html.

19. Haynes, director's commentary, *Far From Heaven*, DVD.

20. All timings refer to *Far From Heaven*, DVD.

21. There are two instances where portions of Bernstein's cues were cut from the film. In this one, Haynes admits that he didn't want the music to detract from the dialogue.

22. All titles in quotes are taken from the cue breakdown sheet for the recording sessions. I am grateful to John Brockman at the USC Cinematic Arts Library for graciously providing me with a copy.

23. All transcriptions are by the author. Bernstein's cue titles are given in quotes; those without are the author's designations.

24. Haynes lists the other titles considered in the director's commentary, *Far From Heaven*, DVD.

25. Willis, 145–146.

26. Willis describes this instance in some detail: "A kind of aural pun, this tone reminds us that Sirk specialized in tingeing his happy endings with sour notes, even as it recalls the abundance of false details that shape Haynes's own film, much as they do Sirk's" (145).

27. The cue was recorded for the original soundtrack. Elmer Bernstein, *Far From Heaven*, Original Motion Picture Soundtrack, CD, Varèse Sarabande, VSD-6421, 2002.

28. Haynes, director's commentary, *Far From Heaven*, DVD.

29. Ibid.

30. Ibid.

31. Ibid.

32. For a thorough discussion of the connection between Frank and Eve, see Joyrich, 193.

33. Haynes, director's commentary, *Far From Heaven*, DVD.

14 The Very Essence of Tragic Reality

Aaron Copland and Thomas Newman's Suburban Scoring

ANTHONY BUSHARD

AARON COPLAND'S INFLUENCE on contemporary film music has been well documented, most notably in Neil Lerner's 2001 *Musical Quarterly* article, "Copland's Music of Wide Open Spaces: Surveying the Pastoral Trope in Hollywood."[1] Here, Lerner suggests that although Copland wrote several film scores, it is the "pastoral" textures in much of his concert music—especially the ballets *Billy the Kid* (1938) and *Appalachian Spring* (1944)—that provided a wellspring of musical material for scores composed by James Horner (*Field of Dreams* [1989]; *Apollo 13* [1995]; *The Perfect Storm* [2000]) and Randy Newman (*The Natural* [1984]), among others.[2] Some filmmakers employed Copland's music exclusively, as Spike Lee did in *He Got Game* (1998), thus removing the middle man altogether.[3] Moreover, Lerner maintains that a feeling of "wide open spaces" evoked in the aforementioned Copland works blends well with advertising campaigns aimed at suburbia because of its association with the Old West, Manifest Destiny, and ultimately the "American Dream."[4]

As Lerner and Sally Bick[5] have pointed out, Copland alluded to this sensibility in his film scoring through his work on *Of Mice and Men* (1939). As George (Burgess Meredith) and Lennie (Lon Chaney Jr.) begin to go to sleep in the woods before heading for the Jackson Ranch, George expresses the carefree life of a free man as Lennie desires a place where rabbits of all colors can get along (Figure 14.1).[6] To accompany the cue, Copland writes an appropriately pastoral texture through light, diatonic passages in the flute and English horn, complemented by an ostinato in the strings and horn outlined by a rising fourth and a falling seventh (Example 14.1).

Following World War II, the destiny of many Americans was made manifest in the flight to the suburbs—that most American realization of middle class aspirations. Far removed from the urban hustle and bustle, young families flocked to single family homes lured by the promise of peace, quiet, and above all else, normalcy. Yet, behind the white picket fences, neatly groomed lawns, and "cookie-cutter" homes, suburbia for many became an island far removed from any real contact with society. Consequently feelings of isolation, anxiety, and paranoia often ensued, creating a life that for many was a distorted remnant of the suburban appeal. These sentiments have been captured in studies by David Riesman,[7] films by William Wyler (*The Best Years of Our Lives* [1946]), Elia Kazan (*On the Waterfront* [1954] and *A Face in the Crowd* [1957]), and more recently Sam Mendes (*American Beauty* [1999] and *Revolutionary Road* [2008]) and Todd Field (*In the Bedroom* [2001] and *Little Children* [2006]).

These latter two directors are particularly pertinent to this chapter as they both employed a composer, who like Horner above, demonstrates an indebtedness to Copland's music on a consistent basis: Randy Newman's cousin Thomas Newman. The son of film scoring pioneer Alfred Newman, Thomas Newman studied with David Raksin at USC and later worked with Jacob Druckman at Yale before befriending Stephen Sondheim upon his graduation from Yale. As Newman recalled, Sondheim exerted perhaps the most important influence on his early development as a film composer:

A lot of it for me was Stephen Sondheim. I remember I had done a showcase of some of my songs and I met Hal Prince through another guy, and Prince

FIGURE 14.1 *Of Mice and Men*. George (Burgess Meredith) and Lennie (Lon Chaney Jr.) dream about a better life together.

EXAMPLE 14.1 Aaron Copland, *Of Mice and Men*, "The Wood at Night," mm. 1–8. © 1939 (Renewed) Robbins Music Corp., Rights Assigned to EMI Catalogue Partnership. All Rights controlled and administered by EMI Robbins Catalog Inc. (Publishing) and Alfred Music Publishing Co., Inc. (Print). All Rights Reserved.

brought Sondheim down to the showcase that I had done. I asked Sondheim if I could just come and talk to him . . . [a]nd I remember he *listened* to me. [Later] I wrote a musical . . . [a]nd it was just awful . . . I remember calling Sondheim, just kind of half in tears, and him saying, "Ah, it's just a knuckle sandwich." He said, "Come on." I remember asking him, "You've done all these great things, you've had this incredible career." He said, "It's not like I charted this career, I just did what came next. I did the opportunity in front of me." And you know, on a certain level I think that's what's defaulted me to being the pragmatist. I don't want to be the effete artist; I don't want to be the guy coming off as a something. I want to get to the good ideas. I want to identify the bad ideas and make it as good as I can and grow honestly.[8]

Newman also performed with an improvisation-centered group called Tokyo 77, the influence of which can be seen in the electronic sounds and pop elements in several scores throughout the 1980s (e.g., *Revenge of the Nerds* [1984], *Real Genius* [1985], and *Desperately Seeking Susan* [1985]).[9] Newman incorporated more symphonic scoring beginning in the 1990s with *The Player* (1992), *Scent of a Woman* (1992), and, most notably at the time, *The Shawshank Redemption* (1994). For instance, in one of the opening scenes of *The Shawshank Redemption* (Figures 14.2a–d), in which we meet Red (Morgan Freeman) for the first time welcoming new prisoners—among them Andy Dufresne (Tim Robbins)—to Shawshank Prison, Newman accompanies the helicopter shot (and our first glimpse) of the prison with what Newman called the "Stoic" theme.[10] Newman presents an ostinato in the low strings that outlines a minor seventh and opens with a perfect fourth (Example 14.2).[11] The upper strings then answer with a descending perfect fourth.

This opening gesture in the "Stoic" theme's bass should call to mind a similar bass progression from Copland's *Quiet City* (Example 14.3).[12] In both instances, the strident arpeggiations suggest urban cityscapes whose facades rise ever upward.

FIGURES 14.2A–D *The Shawshank Redemption.* Andy Dufresne (Tim Robbins) arrives at Shawshank Prison.

EXAMPLE 14.2 Thomas Newman, *The Shawshank Redemption*, "Stoic Theme," mm. 1–6. (Transcribed by A. Bushard.)

EXAMPLE 14.3 Aaron Copland, *Quiet City*, lower strings beginning at Rehearsal 12.

While the music in *Shawshank* and *Quiet City*—one a film score the other a concert piece—both yearn skyward from profound depths, Newman connects with Copland's film music as well. Recalling the clip from *Of Mice and Men* (Example 14.1), notice how Newman in the "Stoic" theme (Example 14.2) utilizes the same intervallic material transposed down an augmented fourth, recast in the lower strings, and on the first beat of the measure, rather than the fourth. Another shared characteristic between the films is the idea of hope. For George and Lennie their dreams lie in the rabbit farm always visible in the distance but never really in reach. Andy continually reminds his fellow prisoners of a world outside Shawshank Prison—Zihuatenejo in Mexico as it turns out—and the way to get there is to hope.[13]

But the outside world isn't always so kind to those who have been "institutionalized" as Red puts it. When Brooks (James Whitmore) is paroled, we learn that he has much trouble dealing with the world outside Shawshank Prison (Figures 14.3a–d).[14] Through what serves as a suicide letter sent to Brooks's inmate friends, we learn that Brooks experiences much loneliness and anxiety. For this montage, Newman comments via a drone in the strings underneath a melancholic melody in the upper range of the piano accompanied by open harmonies in the piano's middle range (Example 14.4).

A drone. A wistful, perhaps nostalgic melody wandering throughout the texture, trying to find its way like Brooks through his new world. He's made it to the outside. He's free! There are no rabbits but there are plenty of pigeons.

FIGURES 14.3A–D *The Shawshank Redemption*. Brooks (James Whitmore) feels isolated in the outside world.

EXAMPLE 14.4 Thomas Newman, *The Shawshank Redemption*, "Brooks Was Here," mm. 1–6 (piano only). (Transcribed by A. Bushard.)

Where is Copland's abounding hopefulness suggested in the opening clips? To begin to answer this question Lerner describes a scene from *He Got Game* in which: "We find out it is Attica through a rapid series of increasingly close shots on the Attica sign, creating a sense of claustrophobia. It is rare to find the Copland pastoral trope used in this way."[15] In an insightful footnote he adds, "The Copland pastoral idiom almost always seems to underscore exterior images, although Thomas Newman makes effective use of pedal tones and disjunct melodies in several interior scenes in his score for *The Shawshank Redemption*."[16] To this idea of "pedal tones and disjunct melodies" I would add, so did Copland. Whereas the precedent for the pastoral trope in Hollywood music depends largely on Copland's ballets, a possible source for Newman's more individualistic style that frequently employs solo piano, or solo piano and a string drone, derives largely from Copland's absolute music for piano. The Concerto for Piano and Orchestra (1926), Piano Variations (1930), Piano Sonata (1939–1941), and Piano Fantasy (1952–1957), to name a few, all contain some of the most challenging textures and rhythms in contemporary American concert music. Yet in each there occur brief respites from the more dissonant, aggressive, and sometimes violent textures.

For example, in Copland's Piano Concerto, when the piano first enters and reiterates the opening orchestral declamation, one notices a descending melody in the right hand (marked "*liberamente*") suspended above perfect fifths in the accompaniment (Example 14.5).[17] Notice also the series of parallel tenths formed between those parallel perfect fifths and the corresponding notes in the piano's melody. Copland employs these fifths again when the orchestra returns at Rehearsal number 3.

EXAMPLE 14.5 Aaron Copland, Concerto for Piano and Orchestra, First Movement, mm. 18–19.

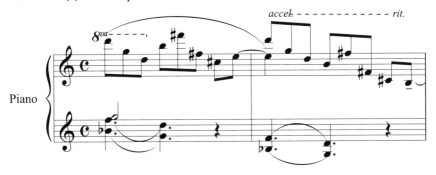

When Copland later composed the difficult and acerbic Piano Variations, the composer's professional colleagues and closest friends were both awestruck and confounded by what Copland biographer Howard Pollack has called:

> a defiant howl of a piece [that] struck a responsive note among America's young composers of the 1930s, not only because of its technical command but because its predominantly stark and tragic tone spoke to a world made bleak by economic collapse and political despair. While such gloom recalled both *Vitebsk* and the [Symphonic] *Ode*, here the tragedy moves beyond the crushing portraitures of shtetl and city life into some more personal terrain, its moments of innocence and humor only heightening the prevailing darkness. "To live on," Copland wrote Lola Ridge in reference to the work, "to develop means, as I see it, to enter always more and more deeply into the very essence of tragic reality."[18]

In the midst of the Variations, the eleventh variation offers some of the most heartrending moments of the work and captures a sense of innocence in a world of darkness to which Pollack refers above (Example 14.6).[19] Here the reader should take note of the vast, empty space between the wandering, ethereal melody and the dissonant drone established in the piano's left hand.

Larry Starr, among others, has noted the special place the challenging Piano Sonata occupies in Copland's output, immediately preceded and followed by considerably more accessible works. Starr argues effectively that the anomalous Sonata was, like the Variations, Copland's attempt to respond to the fractured world around him, in this case a society increasingly wary of war drums in Europe and elsewhere. In addition to highlighting the work's important structural points and salient thematic features, Starr observes the following:

> The Sonata proclaims and declaims with tolling bells in the first movement and gives free rein to the expression of nervous restlessness in the second. To be

EXAMPLE 14.6 Aaron Copland, Piano Variations, Variation 11, mm. 1–6.

sure, there are respites of sentiment and gentle expressivity in the former, and even the hint of a songlike passage in the trio section of the latter. But it is only in the finale that Copland truly allows his music to mourn, and in so doing to silence—if only temporarily—the harsh sound world of war. Copland marks the concluding passages of the Sonata "elegiac," a unique descriptive term, one that captures the essence of the composer's intent.[20]

In Example 14.7, one notices the point at which this "elegiac" aesthetic begins. A dialogue starts at the anacrusis to m. 46 wherein a drone underpins a contrapuntal exchange between registral extremes. At m. 55 three "transparent" chords, the first two built largely on sevenths and the last one a quartal sonority, usher in further contrapuntal layers and rhythmic intensification.[21]

Among related sections in the Piano Fantasy one finds corresponding expressive markings like "crystalline; with simple expression," (mm. 185–188), "bell-like" with an "echo" (mm. 976–981), or "delicate, uncertain" (Example 14.8).[22]

EXAMPLE 14.7 Aaron Copland, Piano Sonata, Third Movement, mm. 46–56.

In each of these examples from the Piano Concerto, Piano Variations, Piano Sonata, and Piano Fantasy one notices (among other characteristic Copland tendencies) a penchant for small, repetitive motives, harmonic drones and/or sustained chords, a predominance of fourths, fifths, and sevenths for intervallic material, and widely spaced chords within and between registers of the piano. Moreover from a dramatic perspective, Copland often incorporates expressive markings that highlight each excerpt's ethereal qualities, and each example represents relief from

EXAMPLE 14.8 Aaron Copland, Piano Fantasy, "Delicate, uncertain," mm. 205–216.

surrounding material that is often highly dissonant, rhythmically intense, or polyphonically dense. How then does Thomas Newman incorporate similar material (1) into his general stylistic idiom (and for decidedly different ends than Copland) and (2) into scores that enhance narratives concerned with suburbia?

Though also indebted to minimalism, Newman's use of repetition, drones, and open harmonies also shares much in common with Aaron Copland. In each of the works mentioned above, Copland initiates musical material first through a small amount of motivic material and often expands that material through contrapuntal means and rhythmic intensification. Newman also views his style similarly, noting:

I think my style is based in repetition. By that I mean I think in short motives—two-measure motives or three one-measure motives. And that if those motives are being repeated, then the way in which you add sound makes you listen dimensionally. You're not challenged by harmonic information, but you're encouraged by color. And then where does color become composition?[23]

Newman clarified this position by describing what was most identifiable about his style.

> I mean is that style? Is that an approach to harmony, or lack of harmony? Or is it color? Often I ask myself, if you hear piano, my kind/style of piano, which I think is pretty scaled down, it's like three notes. I've often thought it's three notes because three notes has enough harmonic implication. I guess you can imply harmony from two notes as it relates to the next two notes, but that if you played triads [then] that's enough harmony.[24]

One finds evidence of this in numerous Newman cues—for instance the main theme from *Revolutionary Road*, first introduced in "Route 12" (Example 14.9), wherein the opening three-note motive is treated sequentially. Following an intensely heated conversation between Frank Wheeler (Leonardo DiCaprio) and his wife, April (Kate Winslet), about the misery of suburbia in the late 1950s, the theme serves both to break the tension and follows Frank to work the next morning while April retreats to her expected duties as homemaker (Figures 14.4a–d).[25]

Perhaps a more famous example lies in "Dead Already," which opens *American Beauty* and in which the marimba supplies the iconic thematic germ (Example 14.10) that permeates the cue. Newman then layers this cell with percussion, synthesizer, and piano, further complementing the opening theme and enhancing the cue's overall groove, which serves as dissonant counterpoint to Lester Burnham's (Kevin Spacey) mundane life (Figure 14.5).[26]

Another integral component and one that pertains more closely to the present study is Newman's equally pervasive use of static harmonies in the form of pedal

FIGURES 14.4A–D *Revolutionary Road*. Life with the Wheelers (Leonardo DiCaprio and Kate Winslet).

EXAMPLE 14.9 Thomas Newman, *Revolutionary Road*, "Route 12," mm. 1–6 (piano only). (Transcribed by A. Bushard.)

FIGURES 14.5A–D *American Beauty*. Opening Sequence.

EXAMPLE 14.10 Thomas Newman, *American Beauty*, "Dead Already," opening thematic material. (Transcribed by A. Bushard.)

tones and drones. Referring again to *American Beauty*, Newman describes the famous "American Beauty" sequence (discussed in more detail later):

> In the case of the end of *American Beauty* ["Any Other Name"] or that plastic bag scene ["American Beauty"], there's something so dreamy about it, you think, "What elements could you add that give it a kind of frozenness" and typically static harmony does that. It ends up being like a zoom on a camera lens. I guess the thing I've always been interested in drones is that it sets the ear someplace and then whatever you're doing in relief of that drone pivots off this sense of stasis. The ear recognizes [the drone] and then puts it in a place and suddenly you're in this dreamy, lifted space, which is kind of stretching out a sense of static, stillness; it replaces stillness. It's almost like amplified silence in a way. Now somehow you're listening to piano and there's a sense of it being heightened. Now you add image to that and it's a whole other thing because image tends to heighten things too but it elevates the importance somehow. If I played that tune from "American Beauty" without the drones underneath it's probably a little more earthbound than if these things were just floating. It's very elemental. It gives the ear a context for how to listen. What is wide? What is epic? What has great scale? I guess I've said it before in the case of *The Shawshank Redemption*: interior/exterior. What do we associate with exterior? *Star Wars* [is] a huge example of exterior, big, boldness and something like *American Beauty* [is] very, very small and intricate, but equally compelling in the right context, dramatically certainly.[27]

Besides incorporating these static elements into his scores, equally interesting is Newman's use of open harmonies not only to achieve these drones, but also as basic building blocks for his overall harmonic palette. While Newman employs the technique in each of the examples that follow, Adam Schoenberg has demonstrated the presence of drones and quintal harmonies going back to at least the early 1990s and his score for *Scent of a Woman*.[28] In "A Tour of Pleasures," Schoenberg notes the drone in the strings and the parallel, open-fifth sonorities in the piano's left hand (Example 14.11).[29] In addition, and recalling the excerpt from Copland's

EXAMPLE 14.11 Thomas Newman, *Scent of a Woman*, "A Tour of Pleasures," mm. 1–3 (piano only). (Transcribed by A. Bushard.)

Piano Concerto earlier (Example 14.5), Newman's right hand melody establishes a series of parallel tenths to complement the parallel fifths. By removing the third scale degree of each successive triad, Newman displaces the "color" note and creates an extremely "open" sonority.[30]

Newman created a similar sequence (Example 14.12) in "Just the Feller" from *Road to Perdition* (2002) to accompany a chilling sequence in which Michael Sullivan (Tom Hanks) assassinates his former boss and father-figure, John Rooney (Paul Newman), and his associates.[31] Conrad Hall's cinematography is a study in stasis and movement (Figures 14.6a–d).[32] As Rooney and his colleagues move cautiously down a dark street amidst pouring rain, all diegetic sound is removed and replaced by the material in Example 14.12.[33] Eventually machine gun fire erupts, but the audience never hears the shots and only sees the fire. As a series of quintal/tenth piano chords cascades downwards, Rooney's bodyguards also fall one by one, with the camera transfixed on Rooney, frozen with anticipation of whether he will be the next to fall.

In addition to evoking an ambiguous harmonic environment, such open textures accomplish two practical functions alluded to in the preceding interview excerpts. In the case of the *Road to Perdition* scene, Newman succeeds in creating "amplified silence" and allows the viewer to enter more fully into the implications of this scene as it relates to the overall narrative. In addition, when Michael confronts his mentor and the diegetic sound returns, the gunfire sounds even louder and Rooney's murder feels more visceral because it brings the audience out of that "lifted space" and invokes a shocking return to the diegetic world. Secondly—and a point that will be clarified in the analysis of Newman's suburban scoring that follows—the open, widely spaced, triadic voicing provides ample space for dialogue and music

FIGURES 14.6A–D *Road to Perdition*. Michael Sullivan (Tom Hanks) murders John Rooney (Paul Newman) and his associates.

EXAMPLE 14.12 Thomas Newman, *Road to Perdition*, "Just the Feller," mm. 8–11. (Transcribed by A. Bushard.)

to occupy an equally prominent position in the film's soundscape. In each case, Newman's scoring invites the audience to enter into more thoughtful contemplation of the dialogue and more focused attention on the *mise en scène* and thus a more nuanced understanding of the film.

Despite the motivic thematic bases and the open harmonic scoring, Newman's fondness for contextualizing these techniques in the piano is perhaps the most notable facet of his compositional style and the one that adheres most closely with the preceding Copland excerpts. For example, when I asked the composer to discuss what about his style was so distinctive, Newman answered the question through the perspective of his piano writing without ever being prompted to do so. When I later asked him if he developed a "collective memory" of his previous scores when he embarked on new projects, the conversation quickly moved toward Newman's explanation of his prominent piano textures:

BUSHARD: When you move from project to project, do you rely on past experience, or a collective memory [of your previous scores]?

NEWMAN: In film music [the film music tradition]? I don't think so. Personally, no. I suppose the pejorative way of saying that is do you have tricks?

BUSHARD: Well when you say "tricks," I mean Charlie Parker wouldn't have been Charlie Parker without tricks.

NEWMAN: Devices. Tricks is a bad word and I know it's my word, but again how do you treat fifteen seconds of something that turns into something else? Well, it's going to have some kind of intro, [perhaps] static feeling to it then fifteen seconds later, takes off and you think, "Well should I have treated it that way?" or "Is that a device I use? If so is it a valid device?" "Am I going to the well of piano too much?" There are constant [considerations]. And I've said this before too, but why piano? I guess . . .

BUSHARD: That was my next [question] . . .

NEWMAN: Oh, why piano? Well I do have an answer to that but I'm scared of it because I don't want to think that I've stopped thinking this through, but the piano has a loveliness and it's a strike instrument so there's no vibrato. And sometimes vibrato is so emotive that it runs the risk of being too emotive and therefore going towards comment as opposed to some kind of implicit characterological place. So if I plunk a piano chord it just rings and I plunk another chord and it just rings and it has, as I say, this icy elegance to it, this utter loveliness that allows the movie to still penetrate through. [Also] it's a harmony and melody instrument, unlike a violin or a flute where you need a number of those to create harmony and melody so it's kind of an all-in-one instrument. But I think it just happens to be dialogue friendly. It's also the instrument I grew up on so you could argue there's a bit of a default.[34]

True, both Copland and Newman were classically trained pianists, but only Copland really mastered the instrument. In addition, Newman's simple, triadic writing for the piano, while perhaps indebted (consciously or not) to Copland does not approach the complex compositional style Copland often utilized for the piano. Despite these contrasts, clearly both Copland and Newman reserved some of their most intimate, personally expressive writing for the piano, and in the latter composer's case, this intimacy—the search for it and in some cases the loss of it—is precisely what informs most directly Newman's suburban scoring. The remainder of this essay concerns excerpts from *American Beauty* and, using the film as a case study, attempts to explain how the aforementioned discussion of Newman's style enhances incisive commentary on suburban discontent.

In arguably the most famous scene from *American Beauty*, Ricky (Wes Bentley) shows Janey (Thora Birch) a prized example of his penchant for videotaping everyday phenomena (Figure 14.7).[35] Framed by their still figures, the audience sees the bag struggling to break free from the television's border, a metaphor for the spirits of the two young people watching the video, yearning for something beyond a lonely existence where parents and friends are seemingly oblivious to their feelings of alienation. Newman echoes this sentiment by allowing the melody in the piano to flutter above the open, organum-like accompaniment in piano and strings in the same way that the bag dances on a static brick background. (Example 14.13).

FIGURE 14.7 *American Beauty.* Ricky (Wes Bentley) shows Janey (Thora Birch) what real beauty is.

EXAMPLE 14.13 Thomas Newman, *American Beauty*, "American Beauty," mm. 8–13 (piano only). (Transcribed by A. Bushard.)

Perhaps most striking about this scene, beyond the "reverential" feeling engendered through the suggestion of organum accompaniment and chant-like melody, and the silent, emotional connection made between the two teenagers, is the degree to which the overall musical texture represents a literal manifestation of the image. Newman prizes the image, observing the following:

The thing about movies is that images allow certain things, you know? So you find tools, useful instruments, colors, or whatever that work really well under dialogue and sometimes you go to those colors because they work and oftentimes you think, "Well, should I be going to different colors?" You know, many times in writing music for movies you want to be more experimental, but it's the image that ultimately tells you what it will allow.[36]

For this particular series of images, Conrad Hall again juxtaposes stasis with movement and Newman follows suit. Referring to Figure 14.7, one notices visual stasis through Ricky and Janey—who as a "dyad" serve as the static foundation (reinforced by the brick background) and divide the frame into three, mostly equal sections. Hall focuses visual attention to the center of the screen, wherein the bag moves freely within the television's frame but is always tethered to it. Thus Hall forms a triad between Ricky, Janey, and the bag. Accordingly, Newman evokes the dyadic visual motif through the cue's pervasive parallel fifths and allows the melody to dance high above the accompaniment. Moreover because Newman often uses the third scale degree from each corresponding parallel fifth, he both recognizes Hall's visual triad *and* binds those notes that supply the triad's modal color to their respective fifths just as the bag is bound to the static frame.

In addition, by displacing those "color" notes from their "framing fifths" Newman also invokes the film's most important visual motif: the color red against white. Throughout the film—Carolyn Burnham's (Annette Bening) red roses and a white picket fence, Angela Hayes (Mena Suvari) in a sea and bathtub (respectively) of red rose petals among the white bedroom and bathroom during Lester's fantasies, and the red door on the white Burnham house—Mendes and Hall consistently use red against white, as a symbol of traditional beauty standing out from everyday plainness. However, Ricky, Janey, and eventually Lester recognize that beauty really exists in simple things and that traditional conceptions of beauty—like the many false promises of the suburban experience—are often only shallow stereotypes. Thus when the filmmakers inverted the motif in this scene by placing white against red, therefore emphasizing the true beauty of life's simple treasures, color comes not from the image, but from Newman's "dancing" melody comprised of those "color" notes that define a triad's modal quality.

Later as Carolyn arrives at home, presumably to prove that she "refuses to be a victim," Mendes and Hall restore the red-against-white motif in an iconic shot of the red door on the Burnham's white house during a driving rain (Figure 14.8).[37] Again the image tells much about the state of things beyond the door as well as Carolyn's despair as she regards her home, now shrouded in darkness. Absent is Carolyn's confidence conveyed musically in earlier cues like "Lunch with the King," replaced here with the "amplified silence" of a static harmonic background replete with a descending theme that completes each triad (Example 14.14).

FIGURE 14.8 *American Beauty*. Carolyn (Annette Bening) returns home.

EXAMPLE 14.14 Thomas Newman, *American Beauty*, "Angela Undress," mm. 1–8 (piano only). (Transcribed by A. Bushard.)

As opposed to the perfect fifths in "American Beauty" (Example 14.13), in "Angela Undress" Newman employs mainly parallel sixths in the left hand, which seems to ground the cue in a more tonal reality, a feeling obscured by the suggestion of Mixolydian (mm. 1–4) and Dorian (mm. 5–8) modes. Moreover the melodic fragments that complete each triad derive from the respective major or minor sixth. Despite these subtle differences between "American Beauty" and "Angela Undress," the visual triad once again serves as a model for the musical triad Newman employs. As displayed in Figure 14.8, the white picket fence posts frame the red door bathed in incandescent light. As it did in "American Beauty" the open harmonies of the piano encourage the listener to *really* look and contemplate the ramifications of the

FIGURES 14.9A–D *American Beauty.* Lester (Kevin Spacey) sees his life and beauty flash before his eyes.

image. Perhaps for the first time Carolyn—like the audience—sees the door not just as a lovely (yet superficial) accessory on her house, but the entrance to her home. As the cue continues, we see Lester and Angela in the midst of a heartfelt conversation following their uncomfortable exchange in the living room, discussing his daughter Janey and "how she was doing." For the first time the two engage one another as human beings rather than use each other as artificial means by which to regain a shallow identity and a false sense of control.

Later Newman returns to the "American Beauty" musical material during a parting montage as Lester describes the beauty inherent in simple things as he floats—like the bag, freely above yet tethered to the diegesis—and witnesses his former life "flash" before his eyes (Figures 14.9a–d).[38] As the images move in and out of color, the listener is once again reminded of Newman's question about his own music: when does color become composition? In answering this puzzle, Newman continues to place melody against stasis, color suspended above neutral, here as the musical essence of Lester's tragic reality.

In the final analysis, cues like "American Beauty" and "Angela Undress" (and other cues in the film with similar thematic material like "Any Other Name" and "Mental Boy," respectively) function largely to expose the tragic reality of the suburban experience. Newman's score for *American Beauty* is also known for pushing the envelope of acceptable orchestrational combinations and incorporation of exotic instrumental timbres that further allows color to become composition in a striking manner. For example, cues like "Arose," "Root Beer," and "Spartanette" all refer to fantasies Lester has for young Angela as he tries to "get back" what's missing in his life through a virtual affair. By incorporating everything from tablas and a mistuned mandolin to striking metal bowls and synthesized chimes, these cues create a truly transcendent listening experience. That said, what each cue also shares—a similarity found in passages from other Newman scores going back to the 1980s—is a rhythmic regularity that doesn't feel quite *human*:

> You know if you take something and it's just going on and on, suddenly the ear stops paying attention to it; takes it for granted, and then starts listening to other things. It's another reason a lot of my sequences are quantized because if you quantize a sequence, the ear accepts this tumbling rhythm but doesn't need to keep listening to it. Unlike if I'm grooving with something and then suddenly I'm loose with my groove or I'm ahead or I'm behind, suddenly the ear recognizes performance. I don't know if you know the end title of *Lemony Snicket*['s *A Series of Unfortunate Events*], which is a groovy piece and the groove is in quantize, but it really allows the ear, in my opinion, to move into depth, to perceive depth and color more so than rhythmic propulsion. People will say [about quantizing], "No that's very dehumanized, we don't want to do that, we want humanity in our performance" and therefore to quantize is to make something more robotic. But I've just found that the more rhythmic precision that you have, if something in fact does have rhythmic propulsion, the more the ear is allowed to listen to other things because the ear takes for granted that which is precise.[39]

Interestingly, those cues that accompany Lester's fantasy scenes sound quantized as well, giving them an artificial sameness that defies reality. Further, the characters embrace suburban "stuff" like Lester's red 1970 Pontiac Firebird, or Carolyn's four thousand-dollar, Italian silk-upholstered sofa, or Angela's bedroom collage of super-model magazine layouts, as fabricated ways to ease suburban suffering. Thus cues like "American Beauty" and "Angela Undress," while they often include synthesized ambient tones, stand out for their freedom from artificiality as characters in those scenes invoke the filmmakers' plea to "look closer," beyond the comfortable com-modities of the middle class, the false promises of the suburban marketplace, and to instead focus on those simple things that embody true beauty.

The preceding Copland excerpts, in addition to sharing several musical charac-teristics with these selected cues from *American Beauty*—and others like them in *Revolutionary Road*, *In the Bedroom*, and *Little Children*—also stand out as oases of contemplation in the midst of Copland's very personal, pianistic expressions about his life and times at different points in his career. In many ways, Copland's use of open sonorities, wide intervallic spacing, and frequent drone harmonies asks the listener of those piano pieces to "listen closer" to a new sound world. Regardless, can a few cues here and there by themselves be enough to say definitively that Newman was "influenced" by them? Until a recent interview, Newman certainly hadn't helped this author, citing influences as diverse as Charles Ives,[40] Igor Stravinsky, and Miles Davis.[41] So, when finally given the opportunity, I asked the question:

BUSHARD: To what degree do you draw upon the composers of the past?

NEWMAN: I don't.

BUSHARD: What about the larger American tradition?

NEWMAN: Do you mean like cowboy music or *Horse Whisperer* [1998] stuff?

BUSHARD: No, well I guess Copland is what I notice a lot. And I'm wondering, I mean everybody [borrows from Copland to some degree] . . .

NEWMAN: No. Well . . . you're right. You're talking iconography now and acceptable idioms and to that end it's like, "See a golden field of wheat and what kind of string chords do you have and how much are you going to resonate *Appalachian Spring* or something like that?" That again may be part of a film's expectations, [or] a way to consider genre without being generic, [or] follow convention without being conventional. And sometimes there is a requirement. Now that's a tough word . . . an obligation. Why do those [obligations] even exist? Why do we see these kinds of shots and think about *Red Pony* or something?

BUSHARD: There's that kind of Copland but there's this more intimate . . .

NEWMAN: You mean the Clarinet Concerto?

BUSHARD: Well not really. [I was thinking of] the Piano Concerto for instance . . .

NEWMAN: I don't know this stuff as well [listens to the Concerto beginning with the material in Example 14.5). Oh you mean the soloistic thing? [Listens more] Oh wow! You mean it's similar in terms of a two-note left hand and a one-note right hand. Oh wow!

BUSHARD: Exactly.

NEWMAN: I remember one of the piano pieces that did have an impression on me was the second movement of the Bartók Third Piano Concerto, which I want to say is triadic and deeply moving.[42] [Also] some of it was Charles Ives, [especially] the 114 songs. I think I always appreciated the range of emotional expression from the simplest little love song for his niece to these incredibly towering pieces of political songs. That's interesting. [Of course] I never pored over this [particular] Copland and thought, "this is it," but that's fascinating. That's *very* interesting.

So while Copland's piano music may not have been a direct influence on Newman's stylistic development, clearly the composer recognized enough of a similarity between his triadic/drone style and similar passages in Copland's piano music to be quite intrigued. Regardless, issues that concern Thomas Newman, arguably more than anything else, are (1) experimenting to create new sounds, (2) the proper sound environment for a given film, and (3) the primacy of the image above all else. In other words, for Thomas Newman, only the "choicest" sounds will accompany the image properly and achieving those ends is a large part of his individual style. For Copland as well, only the right notes—*la note choisie* as he learned from Nadia Boulanger—would do, and Copland's musical output embodies that ideal.

The most well known of Copland's music had been used for years to appeal to the suburban frontier. As Lerner makes clear:

> Copland's music has become closely associated with these images of wide open spaces and, by extension, the limitless possibilities of the so-called American Dream. And hence the appeal of that music to advertisers of suburbs, luxury automobiles, beef, and patriarchy.[43]

American Beauty, for instance, does not appeal to these same sensibilities. Instead it warns of the dangers inherent in clinging too dearly to the status quo, convention, routine, and the corporate ideal. Suburbia was no longer the answer and escaping—often through tragic means—was the only way out. Thus, the very dramatic and personal scenes sampled here demanded an equally intimate yet subdued underscoring. It is fascinating then that surrounded by composers who channeled Copland's greatest hits routinely—including Newman's cousin Randy—Thomas Newman, whether consciously or not, went beyond the pastoral trope and instead latched on to the suburban drone.

NOTES

Earlier versions of this chapter were presented in 2010 at the National Meeting of the Society for American Music (Ottawa, ON) and the National Meeting of the College Music Society (Minneapolis, MN). I would also like to express my deepest gratitude to Thomas Newman for allowing me to interview him at his studio in Pacific Palisades, California, in 2011.

1. Neil Lerner, "Copland's Music of Wide Open Spaces: Surveying the Pastoral Trope in Hollywood," *Musical Quarterly* 85, no. 3 (2001): 477–515.

2. See also Alfred Williams Cochran, "Style, Structure, and Tonal Organization in the Early Film Scores of Aaron Copland" (PhD diss., Catholic University, 1986); Frederick W. Sternfeld, "Music and the Feature Films," *Musical Quarterly* 33, no. 4 (1947): 517–532; and Sternfeld, "Copland as a Film Composer," *Musical Quarterly* 37, no. 2 (1951): 161–175.

3. Krin Gabbard, "Race and Appropriation: Spike Lee Meets Aaron Copland," *American Music* 18, no. 4 (Winter 2000): 370–390.

4. Lerner, 503. See also Beth E. Levy, *Frontier Figures: American Music and the Mythology of the American West* (Berkeley: University of California Press), 2012; Wilfrid Mellers, "Skyscraper and Prairie: Aaron Copland and the American Isolation" in *Music in a New Found Land: Themes and Developments in the History of American Music* (New York: Oxford University Press, 1987), 81–101; Mellers, "American Music (An English Perspective)," *The Kenyon Review* 5, no. 3 (1943): 357–375; Judith Tick and Gail Levin, *Aaron Copland's America: A Cultural Perspective* (New York: Watson-Guptill), 2000; Anthony Tommasini, "Composers for the Common Man: Aaron Copland, Champion of the American Sound," *New York Times* (4/21/99), 58+; and Barbara Zuck, *A History of Musical Americanism* (Ann Arbor, MI: UMI Research Press), 1980.

5. Sally Bick, "*Of Mice and Men*: Copland, Hollywood, and American Musical Modernism," *American Music* 23, no. 4 (2005): 426–472.

6. *Of Mice and Men*, DVD, directed by Lewis Milestone (1939; Chatsworth, CA: Image Entertainment 2001), 14:15.

7. David Riesman, *The Lonely Crowd: A Study of the Changing American Character* (New Haven, CT: Yale University Press), 1950.

8. Adam Schoenberg, "Finding Newman: The Compositional Process and Musical Style of Thomas Newman" (DMA diss., Juilliard School, 2010), 3–4.

9. This group formed the nexus of collaborative personnel with whom Newman still composes and improvises for each of his film scores. For a thorough account of these artists and how they contribute collectively to Newman's scores, see Schoenberg, 13–30.

10. Linda Danly, "An Interview with Thomas Newman," *The Cue Sheet: Journal of the Film Music Society* 12, no. 3 (1996): 9.

11. *The Shawshank Redemption*, DVD, directed by Frank Darabont (Burbank, CA: Warner Home Video, 2004), 8:58–10:23.

12. Aaron Copland, *Quiet City* (New York: Boosey and Hawkes, 1941).

13. Of course, Stephen King's short story on which the film is based is entitled "Rita Hayworth and Shawshank Redemption: Hope Springs Eternal," from the larger collection, *Different Seasons* (New York: Viking Press), 1982.

14. *The Shawshank Redemption*, 1:01:20–1:03:12.

15. Lerner, 505.

16. Lerner, 514, note 92.

17. Aaron Copland, Concerto for Piano and Orchestra (New York: Boosey and Hawkes, 1926, 1956).

18. Howard Pollack, *Aaron Copland: The Life and Work of an Uncommon Man* (Champaign-Urbana: University of Illinois Press, 1999), 152. For Ridge's entire quote see Aaron Copland and Vivian Perlis, *Copland: 1900 through 1942* (New York: St. Martin's/Marek, 1984), 182–183.

19. Aaron Copland, Piano Variations (New York: Boosey and Hawkes, 1930, 1956).

20. Larry Starr, "War Drums, Tolling Bells, and Copland's Piano Sonata," in *Aaron Copland and His World*, ed. Carol J. Oja and Judith Tick (Princeton, NJ: Princeton University Press, 2005), 250.

21. Aaron Copland, Piano Sonata (New York: Boosey and Hawkes, 1942).

22. Aaron Copland, Piano Fantasy (New York: Boosey and Hawkes, 1957). Consider also Copland's *Night Thoughts: An Homage to Charles Ives* (New York: Boosey and Hawkes), 1973; and the first variation in "The Seven Ages" from Bernstein's Symphony No. 2, "Age of Anxiety" (New York: Boosey and Hawkes), 1949, 1965.

23. Schoenberg, 31.

24. Thomas Newman, interviewed by the author, August 12, 2011, Pacific Palisades, CA.

25. *Revolutionary Road*, DVD, directed by Sam Mendes (2008; Hollywood, CA: Paramount Home Entertainment, 2009), 9:30–10:25.

26. *American Beauty*, DVD, directed by Sam Mendes (1999; Universal City, CA: DreamWorks Home Entertainment, 2000), 1:13–4:11.

27. Newman, personal interview, August 12, 2011.

28. Schoenberg, 35–36.

29. Schoenberg, 35.

30. Ibid.

31. Schoenberg, 37–39.

32. *Road to Perdition*, DVD, directed by Sam Mendes (2002; Universal City, CA: DreamWorks Home Entertainment 2003), 1:38:46–1:39:21.

33. Schoenberg, 38.

34. Newman, personal interview, August 12, 2011.

35. *American Beauty*, 1:01:55.

36. Newman, personal interview, August 12, 2011.

37. *American Beauty*, 1:48:57.

38. Ibid., 1:53:21–1:54:25.

39. Newman, Personal Interview, August 12, 2011.

40. Schoenberg, 61–62.

41. See, for instance, Doug Adams, "Finding Newman: An Interview with the Overdubbing Prince Of Hollywood Film Scoring," *Film Score Monthly* 9, no. 1 (2004): 14–17; and Michael Schelle, "Thomas Newman," in *The Score: Interviews with Film Composers* (Beverly Hills, CA: Silman-James Press, 1999), 267–292.

42. The mention of this Bartók piece was particularly interesting. In his treatment of the symphony's development in the United States, Neil Butterworth described the first variation in Bernstein's Second Symphony "Age of Anxiety" (mentioned in note 22) in this way: "The entry of the piano in Variation I closely resembles the chorale [second movement] from Bartók's Third Piano Concerto." See Neil Butterworth, *The American Symphony* (Brookfield, VT: Ashgate, 1998), 168.

43. Lerner, 503.

Index